Rural Transformations and Rural Policies in the US and UK

Routledge Studies in Development and Society

Rural Transformations and Rural Policies in the US and UK

**Edited by Mark Shucksmith,
David L. Brown, Sally Shortall,
Jo Vergunst and Mildred E. Warner**

 Routledge
Taylor & Francis Group
NEW YORK   LONDON

First published 2012
by Routledge
711 Third Avenue, New York, NY 10017

Simultaneously published in the UK
by Routledge
2 Park Square, Milton Park, Abingdon, Oxfordshire OX14 4RN

First issued in paperback 2014

Routledge is an imprint of the Taylor and Francis Group, an informa company

Library of Congress Cataloging-in-Publication Data
   Rural transformations and rural policies in the US and UK / edited by
Mark Shucksmith ... [et al.].
      p. cm. — (Routledge studies in development and society ; 30)
   Includes bibliographical references and index.
   1.   Rural development—United States.   2.   Rural development—Great
Britain.   3.   United States—Rural conditions.   4.   Great Britain—Rural
conditions.   5.   Sociology, Rural.   I.   Shucksmith, Mark.
   HN59.2.R874 2011
   307.1'4120941—dc23
   2011031179

ISBN: 978-0-415-89010-6 (hbk)
ISBN: 978-0-415-75449-1 (pbk)

This book is dedicated to rural people and communities in the UK and US who are successfully meeting challenges posed by past legacies and future transformations.

Contents

Figures

Tables

Foreword

Local rural areas are facing unprecedented changes as the geographies of national and regional economies rapidly evolve under conditions of globalisation, increased personal mobility for many and as information and communication technologies help reshape consumer societies. At the same time, the roles of land-based industries such as agriculture and forestry, which have been so important in producing rural distinctiveness, are shifting as a result of new technologies but also in response to the challenges of climate change in many parts of the world.

Comparative studies have an important role to play in making sense of the changing place of rural areas in developed economies. While there are strong traditions of comparative studies within national contexts, relatively little research has been carried out to understand the processes and patterns of rural change across different national contexts and particularly across the Atlantic.

When I worked as director of the Centre for Rural Economy (CRE) at Newcastle University between 2004 and 2008, I was always struck by the potential value of international comparative research and was keen to support initiatives that sought to foster international collaboration and comparative work. The QUCAN Network was prominent among these efforts. CRE hosted a very successful and productive sabbatical visit by David Brown and Nina Glasgow during 2006 and the idea of developing a network of rural development scholars, involving Cornell University in the US and the Universities of Newcastle, Aberdeen, Highlands and Islands and Queens in Belfast, quickly took shape. Cornell faculty members had previously visited Newcastle and Aberdeen Universities with the idea of developing formal research agreements. As a result, a formal memorandum of agreement was signed in 2006. A series of colloquia and seminars involving scholars from these UK and US institutions was held in Newcastle, Inverness and Ithaca between 2006 and 2009, the result of which has been trans-Atlantic scholarly visits by Mark Shucksmith, Tony Champion, John Bryden and Philip Lowe, among others; a special issue of the journal *Regional Studies* on rural and regional development in 2009; a number of research working groups held at various scholarly meetings; and now this volume that you have in your hands. What follows is the outcome of sustained scholarly exchange and dialogue between members of the QUCAN Network and is a testament to the appetite for learning from other places. Long may it continue.

Neil Ward
Dean of Faculty of Social Sciences,
University of East Anglia,
Norwich, UK

Acknowledgments

This book could not have been completed without the sustained support of our home institutions: Newcastle University, Cornell University, Queens University Belfast and Aberdeen University. In particular, we want to acknowledge the Centre for Rural Economy at Newcastle University and the Polson Institute for Global Development at Cornell University for their continued financial support of the QUCAN collaboration, and of this project in particular. We also received financial support from USDA multi-state research project W-2001 of which David Brown is a cooperating scientist. We would especially like to thank Max Novick, our editor at Routledge, for his patience, guidance and unflagging enthusiasm.

Mark Shucksmith,
David L. Brown,
Sally Shortall,
Jo Vergunst and
Mildred Warner

Part I
Introduction

1 Rural Transformations
Conceptual and Policy Issues

Sally Shortall and Mildred E. Warner

INTRODUCTION

Rural areas have been seen as both idyllic places of peace and backward areas that stunt the lives of rural people. In the nineteenth century when cities began to grow with industrialisation, there was a population shift from rural to urban areas. Around this time, some scholars and commentators in both the UK and the US presented a romantic idyllic view of rural life compared to the uncertainties of this new urban environment (Tönnies 1887; Borsodi 1929). Both the American Hudson River School of Art and the British Pre-Raphaelite Art Movement were cultural expressions of this rural romanticism. Rural areas were seen as places with intimate human relationships, community spirit, shared goals and values and a strong sense of solidarity. In the US, rural values were also presented as a way of differentiating the nation from a more rapidly urbanising Britain, its former coloniser (Danbom 1997). Urban areas, on the other hand, were seen as characterised by impersonal ties, anonymity and self-interest. In other words, rural areas were characterised by a sense of community while urban areas were seen as characterised by individual self-interest. This also represents the genesis of a 'rural versus urban' debate regarding social relations and a way of life; it introduces the idea that social processes and social interaction are different in different spatial areas. As Newby and Buttel (1980) note, early sociology saw very different traditions of analysis toward 'the rural' in Europe and the US. European scholars tended to dismiss the rural as residual and saw economic and social innovation coming from urban areas and cities. American scholars on the other hand focused on the need to uphold the integrity of the distinctive qualities of rural life (Sorokin and Zimmerman 1929). This led to the development of the urban–rural continuum, an important but flawed model, which dominated much of European and American rural scholarship for the first half of the twentieth century.

Until the mid-1900s, the distinctions between urban and rural areas were relatively obvious and easy to study. The rural economy was distinctive because of its reliance on primary industries, especially agriculture, and sociologists and anthropologists researched differing patterns of social interaction and community relations. While the concepts of rural and urban have intrinsic meaning, their analytical power is obtained through comparison with each other, and until the 1950s this was a relatively straightforward task (Brown and Cromartie 2004). However, post-industrialisation and globalisation have made the task of defining rural and identifying its distinctions from urban much more complex and has even prompted some scholars to call for doing away with it as a concept altogether (Hoggart 1990).

The premise of this edited volume recognises the changed understanding of rural and looks toward future rural transformations. In both the UK and the US, there is a general trend away from arguing for specific policies to deal with distinct 'problems' in rural areas. Porter et al. (2004) pioneered this shift by noting that rural-specific policies to address the decline of rural regions simply were not working. Although rural regions may be different from other regions and sometimes require distinct institutions and policies, in general rural regions are governed by the same competitive drivers as other regions and this does not suggest a need for a fundamentally different economic approach. Increasingly, policy is moving away from distinctive rural policies and emphasizing the positive benefits of urban–rural linkages (Lichter and Brown 2011). Linkages between urban and rural areas are now seen as beneficial to both, and it is recognised that the most thriving rural areas are those that are connected with market towns, which in turn are connected with city regions. The policy priority then is to develop an appropriate infrastructure to facilitate these social and economic interactions. Ideally this would enhance employment and education opportunities, improve access to rural leisure activities and increase population growth in rural areas. Rural areas are dynamic and changing, and so is their relationship with urban centres. While the social and cultural infrastructure of rural areas needs to be maintained, and due regard paid to any particularly rural expression of disadvantage, this dynamic and changing relationship with urban areas is one that is very positive for the future of rural communities. One important feature of the comparative analysis in this book is the illumination of very different policy approaches to rurality in advanced capitalist societies. We discuss how the fundamental differences in rural policy approaches of the US and the UK are based on different social ideologies and values that shape policies relating to rural areas. The volume demonstrates how policies develop within a particular conceptual framework.

Our overall rationale is to illustrate the transformations that are occurring in rural areas and policies related to them at the beginning of the twenty-first century. The political, social, economic, cultural and physical landscapes of rural areas have changed. Processes of globalisation and decentralization, population shifts, technological change and industrial change have resulted in important transformations which are the focus of this comparative volume. These transformations not only consist of the visible or tangible changes in rural areas, but also include the narratives and social construction of rural areas. Whether rural is a place of production, consumption and/or conservation has been the basis of a highly contested scholarly debate (Hoggart and Paniagua 2001; Hoggart 1990; Shucksmith 2000a). We consider this change in the representation of rural, and its disputed nature, to be part of a significant transformation in rural society. The multiplicity of transformations and the complexity of causal forces are played out in different ways in different places. Building on the work of Brown and Cromartie (2004), we examine key rural transformations: social, demographic and economic transformations, and rural policies and governance especially as regards agriculture and rural environments. In each case we examine the evidential and philosophical nature of these transformations. In this volume we are concerned with the different approaches to spatial inequalities within policy regimes. Following Newby and Buttel (1980), we argue that rural policies are situated within the ideological and cultural values of the wider society.

A TRANSATLANTIC DIALOGUE

While not a strict comparative analysis, this book examines the transformation of rural society and economy in the UK and US during the last half century, and through a series of dialogues explores the significance of these trends and changes for community sustainability, the quality of life and environmental quality. While both the UK and US are highly urbanised, rural people and communities continue to contribute to economic development and social solidarity in both nations. Moreover, since the vast majority of land is rural in both the UK and US, social and economic activities occurring there strongly affect environmental quality.

The UK–US dialogue is highly illustrative of how seemingly similar situations turn out to be full of complexity and difference. Even though rural society seems quite similar in both nations with respect to high urbanisation, low employment dependence on agriculture, population ageing, lack of public transport, etc., rural people and communities are situated in entirely different institutional frameworks in the respective nations. In particular, the UK and US have differing regulatory regimes, different worlds of welfare capitalism, differing governance and institutions, contrasting geographies of the rural and differing structures and politics of knowledge used to examine the role and status of rural areas in contemporary society.

Hall and Lindholm (2001) present the social welfare states of Europe and the liberal market approach of the US as two ends of the spectrum of varieties of capitalism in modern industrialised states. Although the UK is more heavily market-oriented than most of its European neighbours, it has a more social orientation than the US and this has important implications for rural policy. Esping-Andersen (1990), describes the 'Anglo-Saxon' states (i.e. the US and UK) as 'liberal welfare regimes' with a low level of government-provided benefits for the needy. Although liberal market economies display limited state intervention or coordination of market relationships, there are divergent institutional forms of market economies and the UK represents a more socially oriented approach than the US (Hall and Soskice 2001).

Rural development policies in the UK and the US reflect the socio-historical traditions of each nation. The experience of two world wars has given the UK a greater commitment to the welfare state (Bryden and Warner, this volume) and recently more importance has been given to social cohesion and social inclusion in UK discourse (Shortall and Warner 2010; Shortall 2008). The more general European model of rural development is premised on an idea of community and collaborative collective action. The European dream emphasizes community relationships over individual autonomy, leisure over unrelenting toil, universal human rights (Rifkin 2004, 3) and a preference for the welfare state's guarantees of Social Security over reliance on the market (Habermas and Derrida 2003). Although the EU's internal and external policies are basically standard neo-liberal ones of deregulation and promoting the increased penetration of market relations into more sectors and regions (Storey 2006, 3), it also espouses a rhetoric regarding the need to build social and political unity. For rural areas this is reflected in explicit territorial policy to promote territorial equivalence (in government services and opportunity) and foster social inclusion. Universal service obligations are just one example of how EU policy, despite varieties of capitalism among its member states, tempers the current market turn in government policy.

The American creed by contrast, emphasizes equality of opportunity rather than outcome. Individualism is a basic value, core to American identity. The Protestant work ethic is part of this culture (Lipset 1997). So too is greater respect for private property rights over collective control for the public good. This leads to a much narrower view of the role of the state. Americans work more hours than Europeans, and believe that dignity lies in morally redeeming work rather than in the solidarity of a welfare state (Fukuyama 2006). Opportunity is the focus, not social equality. This leads to acceptance of an uneven landscape of public services, social rights and economic opportunity (Katz 2001) that has important implications for rural policy.

Our central argument is that each country reflects the overall values and assumptions of the society in which it is situated. The greater commitment to rural welfare in the UK is evident in its rural policies. The UK parliamentary report *The Potential of England's Rural Economy* (House of Commons Environment, Food and Rural Affairs Committee 2008) argues that the UK Department of Environment, Food and Rural Affairs (DEFRA) should not only focus on low performing rural areas, but also invest in those already thriving. However, the entire report demonstrates the UK commitment to striving towards spatial equity. It argues that housing availability for those on low incomes in rural areas should be a priority. It states a concern about the marginalisation of rural affairs within DEFRA. It recognises the need to focus on people suffering from social disadvantage and areas suffering from economic under-performance (30). There is an efficiency argument throughout the report, in terms of investing in both thriving and lagging areas, following the general EU commitment to convergence theory. However, more prominent is the equity argument, and the need to protect vulnerable areas and people from disadvantage.

In the US, on the other hand, the welfare state is less developed, and key principles of equality are rooted in equality of opportunity and individualism (Shortall and Warner 2010). Hence in the US, there is no specific rural policy per se, and the government's biggest influence on rural areas comes through policies that affect individuals irrespective of where they live. Lagging regions in the US are viewed as needing more market, not more government (Brown and Warner 1991). Instead of policies that make the reversal of declining rural areas a priority, the US market-focused 'sink or swim' attitude assumes individual relocation is a natural and acceptable response to changed economic opportunities (Brown and Swanson 2003).

The contrast between equity and efficiency in rural policies is the most fundamental difference that emerges between the US and the UK comparison. To understand these differences, they must be situated in the wider ideological and cultural values that shape the development of rural policy.

Despite these differences, several trends are common across the US and the UK. Common themes guiding rural policy in both countries include decentralization, privatization, market competitiveness and partnership and participation. Our book explores how these themes play out in a number of sectors—from social and economic transformations to rural and environmental policy.

Comparative research is critical in order to identify social patterns or social phenomena that are held in some way to be typical. Lowe, in the following chapter, notes significant differences in the structure and politics of knowledge regarding rural studies and tracks the development of discursive formulations of the challenges facing rural areas. The theoretical, methodological and analytical difficulties posed by cross-national research were recognised by early sociologists, notably Durkheim and Weber, and contemporary scholars continue to grapple with developing robust comparative research (Roginsky and Shortall 2009). Several recent books (Brown and Swanson 2003; Flora, Flora and Fey 2003; M. Woods 2005; McAreavey 2009b; Brown and Schafft 2011) examine social and economic change in rural society in one or another nation. However, for the most part these recent books focus on a single nation, are written from a particular disciplinary perspective and/or pay short shrift to public policy. In contrast, this book differs from others by being both international and interdisciplinary, and by allocating approximately equal attention to processes of rural transformation and to policies developed to contend with trends and changes affecting rural people and communities.

Rural people and communities in the UK and US have experienced a number of fundamental transformations during recent decades. Some of these have proceeded in similar ways in both the US and UK while in other ways the processes of change have differed between the two nations. These transformations present both challenges and opportunities for rural people and communities. Specifically, this book traces the determinants and consequences of demographic and socioeconomic transformations with particular focus on population change, ageing and immigration; the restructuring of rural economies; and new forms of governance and institutional restructuring in addressing rural policy, the environment and natural resources. The book balances the discussion of rural trends and changes with thoughtful policy analysis. It provides an empirically grounded and conceptually based perspective that will inform decisions about public interventions to ameliorate rural problems and policies that take advantage of opportunities inherent in rural environments, and aid in identifying and enhancing conditions leading to greater social and economic opportunity in rural areas consistent with principles of environmental sustainability. The book is the culmination of five years of international, interdisciplinary collaboration between rural social scientists in the UK and US.

DEFINING RURAL

One key component to ensure robust international dialogue is to ensure that concepts being employed have an agreed and shared meaning (Roginsky and Shortall 2009), or at least that differences in meaning are recognised and understood. Yet agreeing on a definition of *rural* is an extremely difficult exercise. There are two traditions of defining what we mean by rural. The first is statistical, the second is conceptual, and in neither case is there an agreed or definitive definition.

There is no agreed statistical definition of what is rural in the UK. In England and Wales, settlements of ten thousand or less are defined as rural (see Annex for discussion of statistical conventions used in this book). In Scotland, settlements of three thousand or less are considered rural, and in Northern Ireland, settlements of forty-five hundred or less are rural. In the US, rural is the residual; in other words, urban is defined, and what is not urban is rural. Nonmetropolitan/rural areas are those that are not metropolitan urban areas. There are three primary definitions of rural. The US Bureau of the Census uses population size and density thresholds. Urbanised areas have a population of fifty thousand and a population density generally exceeding one thousand people per square mile. All persons living in urban areas and in cities, towns, villages, etc., with a population of twenty-five hundred outside of urban areas are considered the urban population. All others are considered rural. The US Office of Management and Budget uses demographic and economic criteria to identify metropolitan regions. Metropolitan areas are urban regions comprising a central county plus adjacent counties that are highly integrated with the centre. They have an urbanised area with a population of fifty thousand and an integrated workforce commuting to a metropolitan central county. Nonmetropolitan areas do not have this but they are distinguished into two categories: micropolitan areas are organised around an urbanised core of 10,000 to 49,999 people, while non-core-based areas are counties lacking even one place with ten thousand people. The Economic Research Service of the US Department of Agriculture uses a rural–urban continuum to distinguish metro counties by size and nonmetro counties by their degree of urbanisation or proximity to metro areas.

Statistical definitions are to some degree arbitrary (Brown and Schafft 2011). Academics have long argued that rural–urban is a variable rather than a discrete dichotomy, and this type of statistical definition presumes similarities within each category that do not exist (Brown and Cromartie 2004; Shucksmith, Thomson and Roberts 2005). Similarly, geographical location has a major impact on rural areas: if a rural area is urban-adjacent then it is likely to be a very different place, with different opportunities compared to a remote rural area. These difficulties are part of the basis for Hoggart's (1990) plea to do away with the concept of rural. 'Rural' presumes similarities that do not exist, it suggests that it has causal properties; it is atheoretical and confuses sociological inquiry. However, government statisticians are just as aware of the difficulties of this rural–urban classification. Across the governments in the UK and US, different departments use varying definitions of rural according to policy needs. The Northern Ireland Statistics & Research Agency (NISRA) prepared a statistical classification and delineation of settlements and specifically recommended that government departments and other users should define urban and rural in ways appropriate for different policies, programmes and projects. They give examples of cases where the same place could be legitimately classified as urban or rural. However, they also note that at a policy level, there is value in a commonly agreed default definition of urban–rural (NISRA 2005, 4).

If the statistical definition of rural presents theoretical and policy difficulties, conceptual definitions of rural present even more. Academics have argued that how we define rural is shaped by the social and symbolic construction of rural areas (Halfacree 1993; Shucksmith 2000b; M. Woods 2005). Whether we see rural areas as primarily areas of production (primary industries, particularly agriculture), consumption (a public good, leisure activities, commuter housing, etc.) or conservation (protecting the environment, protecting the existing rural infrastructure against change) will affect how we define rural. In particular, it will have an enormous impact on rural policy. This shift in understanding from rural areas being seen as primarily locations of private property and production to being seen as a public space and a space for consumption represents a significant rural transformation (Marsden 1998b). The consumption of rural landscapes is a complex issue. Public consumption is often based on a desire to experience a mythical rural idyll (Logan 1997). This allows for privatized interests to create and market such a rural place, but it is often divergent from the lived reality and needs of existing rural communities (Ritzer, Stepnisky and Lemich 2005).

Obviously all of these views of rural areas are to some degree true, and the concept of the 'differentiated countryside' (Murdoch et al. 2003) has been used in the UK to argue that different social relations and representations predominate in different rural areas. Different groups favour different symbolic representations of rural and this leads to an important power struggle in policy circles. Which group holds dominance will shape rural policies that will in turn shape the infrastructure and future of rural areas. There are many examples of these struggles: Should farmers have to allow walkers rights of access through their fields? Should it be possible to build interpretative centres beside heritage sites and areas of natural beauty? Shucksmith (1990) very effectively demonstrated the importance of this power struggle for the dominant symbolic understanding of rural when he studied housing in the Lake District of England. The Lake District is an area of outstanding natural beauty, and conservation groups argued that housing development should be limited to ensure preservation of the area's beauty. Local groups argued that it is a living area, and restricted housing development made it very difficult for local people on low incomes to obtain affordable housing. In some respects these power struggles reflect the struggle to determine what rural ought to be.

Despite the difficulties with rural definitions, and mindful that it is impossible and probably not desirable to have an all-embracing definition of the rural (Coladarci 2007; Halfacree 1993), we agree with Halfacree (2007, 126) that it is premature to write off rural as a relatively distinctive spatial category. This volume reflects a multidimensional approach to conceptualizing rurality in post-industrial societies. The various chapters demonstrate how rural has specific implications for policies and governance, economics, social and demographic trends and the environment. Our social constructivist approach necessarily means that different ideas of rural attach to different societies, so the concept of rural is necessarily contingent. Each chapter defines rural in a form that is relevant to its context and subject matter. Similarly, we do not attempt to impose a uniform approach to subnational geographies. The UK is decentralizing in ways that are very important for expression of different definitions and perceptions of rurality. This shows up in many of the chapters where authors often break down the UK into its constituent parts (Scotland, Northern Ireland, Wales, England). By contrast, although the US is more diverse, most authors do not attempt to give particular attention to each unique region. This reflects our comparative framework of dialogue. Our goal is not to impose uniformity in approach or conception, but rather to use these two contexts, the UK and the US, to illustrate and tease out commonalities and differences in the major transformations on which the book focuses. We organise these into two main categories: (a) social, economic and demographic transformations, and (b) policy and governance concerns.

SOCIAL, DEMOGRAPHIC AND ECONOMIC TRANSFORMATIONS

Rural areas have been undergoing profound social, demographic and economic transitions in the last few decades (Ward and Brown 2009). The major issues in rural population change are outlined in Chapter 3 by Champion and Brown, who note challenges due to low rates of natural increase (or in some regions natural decrease), persistent in-migration of pre-retirement and retirement-age persons and increasing international migration together with the changing composition of the remaining population induced by these population dynamics. Young adult out-migration coupled with older in-migrants is skewing the age structure. Rural areas in both countries are also experiencing changing race and ethnicity by age especially as a result of international migration.

Chapter 4 by Philip, Brown and Stockdale describes the impact of population ageing for rural community life with a particular focus on elderly in migration. Elderly in-migration is viewed as positive in the US because it creates a new source of income (Social Security and retirement savings) and civic investment (elderly represent new talent) for rural areas. In the UK elderly in-migration is viewed less positively in part because of the impact on the housing market where housing prices are pushed up, leading to young out-migration, increased commuting and family fragmentation. Immigration is taking on an important rural dimension as new immigrants are coming into rural areas in two very different streams. The first comprises professional workers (e.g. physicians, nurses, etc.), who are allowed to immigrate if they commit to providing basic services to rural communities. The second is of largely unskilled labourers who fill low-wage service and agriculture jobs (Latinos in the US and Eastern Europeans in the UK). Language barriers, cultural and ethnic difference and tenuous legal status make it more difficult for these new immigrants to integrate into the traditional rural community and economy (Parra and Pfeffer 2006; Lichter and Johnson 2006; de Lima 2004). Chapter 5 by de Lima, Parra and Pfeffer notes that immigration is increasing in rural areas in both countries. This raises special concerns for integration between the receiving communities and immigrants. It also raises implications for local services and for citizenship. The authors point out that locality matters as there is a context specificity of immigrant experience. However transformation works both ways, changing receiving communities and immigrants themselves. An important difference between the US and the UK is that government policy (e.g. legal immigration) makes circular migration more possible in the UK and less so in the US.

Chapter 6 by Schafft and Shucksmith notes that poverty can be measured in terms of people, place, culture, social isolation and social structure. This broader view of poverty as social exclusion leads to a review of causes of poverty and structural policy responses. They note that this approach has more salience in UK policy and academic debates than in the US, where poverty is an absolutist rather than a relative concept and the causes are primarily attributed to individual moral failures rather than structural processes.

The demographic transformations in the rural UK and US are dramatic and these chapters not only seek to outline the demographic trends, but also to explore implications for social interaction and social policy. The view of rural areas as more traditional and conservative is one that is likely to be transformed with these profound changes in demographic patterns. Although rural areas have often been viewed as places with intimate human relationships, shared goals and values and a strong sense of solidarity, human interaction in rural areas is just as likely to be conflict-ridden and divided along lines of power, social class, education, gender and race—especially as rural areas diversify (Pahl 1966; Shortall 2004).

One side of the coin is the rural idyll, and in both the UK and the US increasing numbers of commuters live in rural areas precisely because the rural idyll is alive and well and people believe it is a better place to bring up children, grow old and be socially integrated (Shucksmith 2000a; Shortall 2006; Champion, Coombes and Brown 2009). The other side of the coin is that poverty and processes of social, political and civic exclusion are more prominent in rural areas and this may become more pronounced with the new patterns of immigration. Here we see key differences between the UK and US. Historically UK rural areas have been less diverse than those in the US but currently, legal immigration and universal service obligations make integration more possible. In the US by contrast, ethnic diversity has been a feature for a long time but one often characterised by inequality—made worse by the current undocumented (illegal) immigration where newcomers cannot lay claim to social rights.

Intellectually the UK has a long tradition of studying social exclusion, which is not the case in the US (Shortall and Warner 2010). The US approach to studying poverty primarily focuses on distributional issues, such as the lack of resources at the disposal of the individual or household. Social exclusion is understood as focusing primarily on 'relational issues' (Room 1995a)—low social integration, lack of participation and powerlessness, with its roots in the French Republican idea of universal rights (Mofatt and Glasgow 2009; Shortall 2008, 451; Nolan and Whelan 1999). *Social exclusion* refers to the lack of access to, or denial of, a range of citizen rights, such as adequate health care or educational success, and also a lack of societal integration through limited power or the ability to participate in political decision-making. The 'problem' is usually seen as political structures which are insufficiently open to allow for participation. Research in the UK has provided evidence that the processes and system failures lying behind social exclusion in a rural context are different from those in urban areas, and addressing these social problems requires a specifically focused policy response (Shucksmith and Chapman 1998). These chapters give considerable thought to the extent of demographic transformation and what this means for processes of social exclusion and citizenship in rural areas.

These demographic changes are accompanied by important economic changes as well. Rural areas in both the US and UK are marked by poorer technological infrastructure, lower levels of capital and less diversified economies than their urban counterparts (Gale and McGranahan 2001; Bryden 2005b). Chapter 7 by Atterton, Bryden and Johnson shows that in both the US and the EU, there has been a considerable decline in the importance of agriculture and primary industries. While manufacturing remains a key feature of the rural economy, services are the dominant economic sector. The chapter explores the challenges rural economies will face in the twenty-first century—resource shortages make rural areas more important to overall economies, but there are real questions as to how the trade-offs between economic growth and quality of life will be resolved. There are also concerns about the role of rural areas in the knowledge economy—will they be incorporated or left out?

A key driver of rural economic transformation is the global economy. The concern is that regional and rural development policy may have less importance in a world dominated by the logic of global competitiveness. City regions are now heralded as the harbingers of economic fortune, and some scholars argue the city region is the most important scale for renegotiating economic competitiveness in a global world (Le Gales 1998; Brenner 1999; Swyngedouw 1997). As Brown and Cromartie (2004) note, there is little room for sentiment about rural communities in the globalised economy. Capital flows across national borders to production sites with the lowest costs and fewest regulations, and this presents a key challenge, and potential opportunity, for rural economies.

One opportunity for rural areas lies in entrepreneurship, especially among new arrivals—immigrants and the elderly. Chapter 8 by Bosworth and Glasgow presents theories of entrepreneurship and embeddedness. They show how entrepreneurship to address social problems can lead to business entrepreneurship in rural areas. Entrepreneurs recognise spaces where local initiative can be viable even in a globally competitive economy. But the authors also emphasize that entrepreneurship is not simply economic. Rural in-migrants, especially the elderly, take leadership of social and cultural activities, thereby benefitting the community. Moreover, such social engagement can build bridges to acceptance and integration.

Another relatively new opportunity for rural areas is in the area of local food systems. In Chapter 9, Hinrichs and Charles show the growth in a range of types of local food systems, such as farmers markets and community supported agriculture, and how they promote community development and engagement. These initiatives also can contribute to place making and overcoming rural–urban differences through greater consumer engagement with producers. Both of these chapters show how local economic innovation in rural areas carves out a space for local alternatives to global forces. These practices, especially around local food systems, can strengthen connectivity between urban and rural. Local entrepreneurial innovation is not just about economic benefits, but also contributes to place-making and civic and democratic impulses that help reinforce local community.

RURAL POLICIES AND GOVERNANCE

In the post–WW II period, lagging rural regions were viewed as a drag on national economic development and this logic justified public investment to extend infrastructure (roads, telephones, electricity) to the rural hinterland (Edwards 1981; Brown and Warner 1991). Despite the financial crisis of 2008–2011, which led to a new discussion of Keynesian economic prescriptions, economic development policy today remains focused on urban growth centres and exhibits limited concern with lagging regions. Young adult out-migration to urban and suburban areas makes rural regions politically weak. New technologies can quite simply skip over such underdeveloped places. The logic of city resurgence shifts the scale of action from the nation-state to the local level and articulates the local region as the key actor in global competitiveness (Brenner 2004). Urban areas worry about their development patterns and resources for water, housing or recreation, and that sometimes marks the extent of concern for lagging rural regions.

This shift in the scale of action to the city region and its hinterland creates special problems for isolated rural areas outside the urban hinterland fringe. While European policy recognises the rural landscape as a multifunctional landscape that contributes to culture, tourism, environmental protection and agriculture, in US policy, culture and environmental concerns remain secondary. This is the subject of the concluding part of our book.

To understand policy differences we must start with understanding differences in the cultural and historical bases for state intervention. As Bryden and Warner show in Chapter 10, rural policy in the US is differentiated by a stronger focus on market, individualism and private property rights whereas the UK has a stronger emphasis on universal service obligations and collective solidarity. In both countries rural policy is the 'poor relation' compared to agricultural policy, which still dominates national attention even though agricultural production is a small part of the rural economy (especially employment). In Chapter 11 on agricultural policy, Hubbard, Hubbard, Findeis, Brasier and Salcedo Du Bois point to another key US–UK difference. While US policy remains heavily dominated by agricultural interests, the UK policy is moderated by a broader set of concerns. Agricultural policy is differentiated by the UK's greater emphasis on multifunctionality (for environmental as well as production ends) and on food security, public health and consumer well-being. US agricultural policy, by contrast, is only just beginning to address environmental issues and still gives limited attention to consumer well-being.

The next chapters (12 and 13) turn our attention toward environmental policy. Wolf and Potter look at environmental policy in the context of the dominance of agricultural policy and Vergunst, Stedman and Geisler address environmental management in the context of protected areas. In both these chapters, authors note the continued importance of a productivist focus on agro-ecological services, and the heavy reliance on market approaches to policy and management. However Vergunst, Stedman and Geisler also highlight the importance of working landscapes which leverage public goods production from private management. Through discussion of a national park in Scotland and a state park in New York State, they also explore new forms of governance and public involvement. This intersection of policy and governance recognises the multiple demands on our landscape and complex nature of power relations.

The different status of the environment in policy agendas in the UK and the US is related to the growth coalition with which lobby groups are associated. Although agricultural employment is small and most rural income is not agriculturally related, agriculture remains the most powerful political lobby for rural policy on both sides of the Atlantic. Agriculture is the most politicized actor and has the ability to scale up to represent itself nationally or internationally. It is the core player in the political coalition for rural interests. In Europe, environmental and rural development interests benefit from being part of a coalition that includes agriculture. Delinking agricultural and rural development policy could be detrimental for environmental policy because without having exchange value allies, such as agriculture, the policy clout of the rural environmental lobby would be considerably weakened (Warner and Shortall 2008). Environmental and rural development interests are too diffuse and too focused on use value to gain significant attention in the policy arena. Loose coalitions can be easily trumped by the exchange value interests of agricultural commodity groups (Fluharty 2008). The transformation of the rural environment is, in sum, a deeply political process.

The next two chapters focus on regionalism and participation. In Chapter 14 Thompson and Hewitt describe an example of regionalism from the top, the English Regional Development Agencies (RDAs). RDAs have had problems with democratic governance and face local resistance despite their access to funds. They also exhibited less flexibility than found in rest of the EU (and in fact are to be abolished in 2012). By contrast the US is characterised by voluntary regionalism which has more local acceptance and fewer concerns with democratic accountability, but less power and funding. Chapter 15 by Swindal and McAreavey on participation explores the role of the local in a multilevel governance system. In comparing Northern Ireland with Alabama, the chapter captures two rural regions known for histories of deep religious or racial conflict. While participation offers promise, it also offers the potential for capture.

In the final chapter, Brown and Shucksmith conclude by noting the interpenetration of urban and rural society and commenting on diversity and difference between the EU and the US. They also offer an exciting discussion on how to increase the impact of rural research on rural policy, a question of considerable current interest.

All of the chapters in this part recognise the emergence of a multilevel metagovernance system. Common themes guiding rural policy in both countries include decentralization, privatization, market competitiveness, partnership and participation. Globalisation and post-Fordism reposition the nation-state as one component alongside growing international and regional structures of governance (Jessop 2003, 2005; McMichael 2001). However, this view of the decline of the nation-state is disputed (e.g. Paul, Ikenberry and Hall 2003; Hall and Lindholm 2001). Decentralization and the reformation of political structures bring the concepts of markets and participation centre stage. Although the view that decentralization, privatization and participation make for better government is contested for failing to meet efficiency, social redistribution or democratic objectives (Warner 2009a; Shortall 2008), it remains a primary ideological drive behind rural policy.

On the positive side, participation and decentralization increase the availability and quality of information from citizens to government, and enable citizens to more actively participate in structures of governance. *Governance* is an institutional framework broader than government, based on the idea of partnership, devolving power, and including the community, public and private sector (Jessop 1990, 1997; Tendler 1997). *Participation, social inclusion* and *community* are terms essential to current rural development programmes. Rural policies in the UK and the US are an example of the multilevel metagovernance described by Jessop (2005); they are designed centrally and attempt to reconfigure regional structures of governance. In both places policy design is based on the notion of participation and new network governance involving the public sector, private sector and civil society (Shortall and Warner 2010).

Each of the policy chapters describes new collaborative networks which arise due to the more limited power of national governments in a world dominated by global actors, but enacted at a local territorial scale. The old policy world of hierarchical command and control has been replaced with a network governance model of coordination, cooperation and persuasion (Rhodes 1996; Salamon 2002). Partnership is a key theme—especially partnerships between the public and private sectors. This network governance moves beyond a strict privatization model (Savas 2000), recognising the limits of private sector effectiveness alone (Warner 2008). The challenge, however, is one of network management and negotiation. Such networks often privilege the powerful—private sector and state interests—and lead naturally to growth coalition approaches (Warner and Shortall 2008; Logan and Molotch 1987).

LOOKING TO THE FUTURE

This book is about rural transformations and the policy response. Demographic, social, economic and environmental transformations challenge traditional conceptions of rurality and traditional approaches to rural policy. Concern over global climate change has increased attention not only towards the carbon footprint of urban and rural activities, but also the importance of rural areas as carbon sinks and resource sheds for urban needs. In addition to the traditional focus on rural areas as locations for water, green space and food, today they are seen as important sites for the production of renewable energy (biomass, solar, wind), amenity-based sites of residence and the siting or storage of waste (landfills, nuclear power plants, etc.). Urban and international political concerns drive these shifts; rural communities themselves have limited voice.

The economic, social and symbolic import of the rural environment portends a significant transformation in the way in which we view rural. It affects production, consumption, heritage and conservation constructions of the countryside. There are some important differences in how rural areas are viewed in the UK and the US. European and UK policy is moving towards recognition of the rural landscape as a multifunctional landscape that contributes to culture, tourism, environmental protection and agriculture. In this book we have outlined a broader conception of rural that includes attention to rural–urban linkages, social and demographic transformations as well as traditional concerns with agriculture and environment. Running throughout is a narrative about new forms of governance and new approaches to policy. The comparative dialogue framework between the UK and the US helps to illuminate both policy limitations and possibilities. As readers explore the next chapters, we hope it will broaden their view on the challenges facing rural areas in the twenty-first century and their implications for conceptualizing rurality and addressing rural problems.

2 The Agency of Rural Research in Comparative Context

Philip Lowe

> We shall not cease from exploration
> And the end of all our exploring
> Will be to arrive where we started
> And know the place for the first time
>
> T.S. Eliot, *Little Giddings (No 4 of 'Four Quartets')*, 1942
>
> (Eliot was an American-born poet who sought
> eternal truths in the English countryside)

INTRODUCTION

Rural America and rural Britain differ considerably. The first is so much bigger and much more varied in geography, climate and landscapes. Rural America and rural Britain have different fauna and flora and separate, if deeply intertwined, cultural histories. They have overlapping but divergent social structures and economic functions. The fact that we refer to them both as 'rural' suggests that we see more commonalities than differences, but that begs the question of whether we share a common conception of what is 'rural'. And this cannot be taken for granted, certainly if—as surely is the case—an American's understanding of rural is rooted in experience of rural America and a Briton's understanding of rural is rooted in experience of rural Britain. On what basis then can we establish a common understanding?

This is the role of the social sciences—to discern what is general and what is specific in our understanding, in order to judge whether and how knowledge gained in a particular context is applicable elsewhere. In other words, how far should knowledge travel? The social sciences seek to answer that question through comparative analysis (Durkheim 1895). Of course, they too have a provenance, are indelibly a product of context. Comparative analysis is a means to both understand this circumstantiality and transcend its partiality and parochialism. Comparative analysis is thus an essential aid to reflexivity about the potency and limitations of knowledge.

While recognising that the approach of this book is to put British and American research into a dialogue rather than making formal comparisons, we nonetheless have an opportunity to reflect on:

- commonalities and differences in studying and problematising the rural
- the role of comparative analysis in establishing transcendent truths

The chapter explores these two strands through a review of the history and preoccupations of rural studies in the US and the UK, and the development and rationale of different approaches to international comparative research.

UNIVERSALISM AND PARTICULARISM
IN THE SOCIAL SCIENCES

Research is produced in and of its time and place, but globalisation is leading to tremendous pressures to internationalise knowledge systems. This suits the physical and biological sciences—atoms and molecules are everywhere the same—and they aspire to decontextualized, universalistic knowledge. The social sciences too are striving to internationalise, but can they forge concepts and theories that transcend their specific origins? As Holmwood argues, 'one of the significant challenges posed by globalisation is to the social sciences themselves and the universalism attributed to categories developed in the West' (2007, 85).

Claims to universalism are potent but contain their own hubris. Such claims are temporally contingent: they are always made by particular people in particular cultural and geographical circumstances. Scientific truth is no exception. It is itself historical. As it evolves therefore it should be, but is not always, alert to the limits of its rationality. The difficulty is acute for the social sciences, which must characterise an unequal world in which they themselves are rooted, and are thus both a key medium of understanding and a source of social power. Inevitably social scientists open themselves to the charge of dressing up partial perspectives as universalisms, and marginalising alternative perspectives.

A tension between universalism and particularism runs through the history of the social sciences. The second half of the twentieth century was a phase of strongly formalistic universalism, encapsulated in notions of modernisation, but one which through association with the global projection of the dominant values of the Western world evoked counter charges of parochialism (including Eurocentrism and gender bias).

There is a danger then that social scientists travel further than do their ideas. However, the effort to free knowledge from its context by ridding its makeup of what is context-specific may be an elusive goal. Even globalised knowledge comes from somewhere, and its apparent rootlessness, or absence of provenance, may simply reflect the fact that that somewhere is the international conference circuit.

Comparative analysis offers an alternative. It explores the different socio-cultural contexts in which knowledge is produced—where knowledge comes from, what is its currency and how it is used. Instead of denying the parochialism of knowledge, it seeks to appreciate its very groundedness and boundedness. While this is an acknowledgment of the limitation of the social sciences, it may also be the key to what distinctively they have to offer to the globalisation of scientific knowledge generally.

For, such understanding of the provenance and workings of knowledge-in-context is beneficial not only for purposes of self-reflection, but also to grasp the potency of knowledge. To judge the reach of knowledge one must appreciate its limits. All too often scientific knowledge overreaches itself. Knowledge applied out of context may be disruptive or simply inappropriate. This is not only so for social science knowledge. The ecological crisis has revealed that there are critical limits to the universalistic claims of the physical sciences and technology. The social sciences have a crucial role in analysing and guiding human action in context.

THE ROLE OF CONTEXT IN THE PRODUCTION OF RURAL SOCIAL SCIENCE

The major source of the parochialism of the social sciences in general is their rootedness in the experience and structures of the (Western) nation-states (Wallerstein 1996). Rural social science is no exception. In different countries, rural social science was constructed on a state-centric framework in the early and mid-twentieth century, and helped set in place national agricultural and rural policy systems. The Dutch sociologist, Henk de Haan, when editor of the pan-European journal *Sociologia Ruralis*, commented:

> The origin of rural sociology was, in most countries, less an endogenous development in the social sciences, as a response to concrete demands for applied social research in rural areas. The intimate relationship with community development, rural planning and agricultural policy brought about distinctly inward-looking national traditions, focused on solving specific problems. (1993, 128)

The result has been nationally distinctive rural sociologies—'closely connected with national history and the significance of rural society and agriculture'—'each with its own style, empirical frame of reference and political context' (ibid.).

In these respects, rural social science reproduces the parochialism of the social sciences more generally. The classical social sciences emerged in the nineteenth century as an outcome of, and a means of regulating, social and economic change in liberal states. They tended to take the boundaries of the state as demarcating fundamental social wholes. Thus the modern state set the parameters of the sociologist's society, the macro-economist's national economy, the political scientist's polity and the historian's nation. To help liberate them from this mind-set, it is incumbent on comparative analysis to uncover the state-centric framework of the social sciences.

However, ever since the social sciences emerged there have been exchanges of ideas, concepts, methods and information. Different countries have assumed a leading role over time, and others have developed their own national perspectives in response or reaction. Initially, the social sciences were a European import into the United States. However, in the early twentieth century a distinctive empirical style of social science took hold in the US and, largely through the country's ascendancy as the pre-eminent liberal state, this became a dominant influence amongst Western societies in the mid-twentieth century (Odum 1951). Rural sociology was a product of this period—it began in the US early in the century and spread to Europe in the 1940s and 1950s, as part of a dynamic of interacting yet embedded national traditions.

THE FORMATION OF US RURAL SOCIOLOGY

American rural sociology was a product of the Progressive Era (the 1900s and 1910s)—a period in which government assumed an active role in social and economic development, and in which science was promoted as an instrument of progress (Sanderson 1917; Galpin 1918; Nelson 1969). It is not an accident that a formalised rural sociology first emerged in the United States, and was indeed a defining feature of the new American-style sociology, albeit with its own distinct institutionalisation. At the start of the twentieth century the US was still a predominantly rural nation. Over a third of the population lived on farms, making them a key political constituency. An agrarian ideology—of self-sufficient settlers, fiercely committed to the land and their liberty—formed national identity, in conscious contrast to the Old World order. Of the leading liberal societies then, the US had to confront most centrally the task of reconciling rural and agrarian interests to the disruptive processes of rapid modernisation. (For similar reasons and at about the same time, the US was the first country to formalise the study of other disciplines such as ecology and agricultural economics.)

By the early twentieth century there was a strong sense amongst America's leaders that rural America was not keeping up (Bailey 1911). The rural South, largely unreformed, slumbered in its post–Civil War lassitude. The Western frontier had been settled and there was the beginning of concern that the continent's natural resources were finite and were being exploited profligately. Across the nation, the localised nature of rural life was breaking down with the advent of first the railways and then motorised transport, exposing rural communities and farm producers to external pressures and influences. The depression of the 1890s had mobilised farmers' movements demanding government intervention on their behalf. At the same time, the opportunity to make a better living in the booming cities began to stimulate rural out-migration.

Scientists, public officials, political leaders, journalists and clergymen were aroused to record the difficulties facing farm families, document the state of rural life and formulate proposals to revitalise it, as part of the self-styled Country Life Movement (Wunderlich 2003). The US Department of Agriculture (USDA) responded by establishing a Division of Farm Population and Rural Life. To provide rural people with means to improve their own circumstances, Congress passed legislation to establish a nationalized public outreach programme, the Cooperative Extension Service, based on an unprecedented collaboration between the land-grant colleges and the USDA, to offer community instruction and practical demonstrations in agriculture and home economics.

These new structures created a demand for what we would now call rural sociologists, typically drawn from the ranks of farmers' sons educated at land-grant colleges. They were influenced by the philosophy of pragmatism expounded by the likes of John Dewey, who regarded the mutual distrust between intellectuals and other people as a carry-over from the class societies of the Old World that should be discarded. By putting their knowledge to work for the reform of society, intellectuals could promote both scientific and social progress (Kirkendall 1966; Gilbert 2001). These distinctive structures also set rural sociologists on an institutional trajectory separate from academic sociologists, marking them out not only in the substantive focus and practical orientation of their studies (on the efficient organisation of rural living), but also in their intensive interactions with farming and rural interests and with other scientific groups guiding agrarian change, particularly agricultural economists and agronomists.

The institutional nexus of the land-grant colleges, extension services and the USDA was massively mobilised in the 1930s in response to the Great Depression. The collapse of agricultural markets, the Dust Bowl and widespread rural impoverishment brought political demands for relief, but also for government to act to re-establish stability and to chart a course to economic recovery. Social scientists were in great demand: to identify the needs for relief and to advise on how they might be met. They were amongst the key social engineers of Roosevelt's New Deal (Kirkendall 1966). In particular they played a major role in the development of mechanisms for the planning of agriculture, conservation and rural development in a liberal capitalist society. These achievements were not only absorbed ubiquitously into the routines of American society and government, but they also provided the model for the management of agricultural economies in what, in the post-war era, became the Western world (S.T. Phillips 2007; Gilbert and Howe 1991).

After the Second World War and the end of the New Deal vogue for social and economic planning, the USDA's Division of Farm Population and Rural Life was axed, its sociological interventionism no longer in favour (Larson and Zimmerman 2003; Gilbert 2008). Devoid of a wider framework of social reform, rural sociology in 1950s America was left as a set of local research activities within the land-grant colleges. To be accepted fully within this context, it had to be integrated with the agricultural sciences (Friedland 2010). The latter had demonstrated their worth through the technologies they had generated, which were transforming American agriculture. The way for rural sociologists to place themselves central to the land-grants' technological mission was to claim the field of extension as their very own 'social technology' (Lively 1943, 338). As 'specialists in rural social engineering' (Lindstrom 1944, 276) they would be aids to the diffusion of modern farming technologies. How technologies spread amongst farmers became their major and highly successful research preoccupation, establishing the paradigm for thinking about the diffusion of knowledge and innovation more generally in mass society (Rural Sociological Society 1952; Rogers 1962).

While US rural sociologists developed their insights as the scientists of the extension process in their domestic contexts, the scope for the implementation of their expertise expanded hugely. Indeed, their emerging outlook on the social dynamics of technology transfer was incorporated into the liberal internationalism that began to infuse US foreign policy in the late 1940s and which projected American models, know-how and technology overseas, in keeping with the country's post-war self-image of leader of the free world (Brunner, Sanders and Ensminger 1945). Rural sociology was seen as a key means to rehabilitate and modernise farming regions in war-torn countries of Europe and Asia and other countries of strategic importance to the US, notably in Latin America (USDA Extension Service and Office of Foreign Agricultural Relations 1945; Nelson 1969). American technical aid funded the international diffusion of both farming technology and agronomic know-how, including rural sociology. Indeed, the two went hand in hand in a large-scale transfer of American technology and liberal democratic values, through the exercise of soft power (Loomis and Beegle 1957; Lowe 2010).

Agronomists and rural social scientists in post-war Europe became conscious of US rural sociology as a successful scientific enterprise, and they sought to emulate it. Many were funded to travel across the Atlantic to visit the land-grant colleges, to see for themselves. Major fields of research and supporting methodologies had been established in the US, not just in technology diffusion, but also in community studies, rural demography, farming living standards, rural institutions, rural social structure, sociology of agriculture and rural values and attitudes. European visitors were struck by the methodological creativity of US rural sociology. Research methods pioneered in US rural sociology included community surveys, family life cycle analysis, opinion polls and service catchment analysis. Other methods it had helped to develop and standardise included sociometric techniques, participation indices, regional analysis, random and representative sampling techniques, participant observation strategies, census projections and participatory planning techniques (Brunner 1957; Larson and Zimmerman

2003). Such methods were widely adopted by European social scientists in the post-war period (Hofstee 1963). Given rural sociology's provenance in relation to the USDA—a department of state collecting socio-economic data on a scale and regularity unprecedented in human history—it is not surprising that its character was fundamentally empiricist and data-processing driven. US rural sociology indeed pioneered various quantitative methods (such as multivariate analysis) and helped to give American sociology more generally a quantitative stamp.

THE ESTABLISHMENT OF RURAL SOCIAL SCIENCE IN EUROPE

Interest in rural social organisation had been a long-standing feature of European scholarship, but it had not been so rooted, as in the US, in the demands of agrarian democracy. By and large, therefore, it had not focused on the pragmatic requirements of managing rural change. It had tended to be either of a theoretical, speculative nature or descriptive, in-depth local studies, carried out by academic geographers, historians and sociologists, and preoccupied with the continued survival or impending demise of 'organic' rural communities. In taking on the mantle of rural sociology and adopting American research methods, Europeans set aside these earlier national traditions of detached, eschatological scholarship and consciously bought into the ethos of empirical social science at the service of progressive social and economic change (Hofstee 1963; Kötter 1967).

However, those who sought to construct a rural sociology in post-war Europe faced different conditions and demands than those in America. Firstly, they lacked the strong institutional base of the land-grant college system. What little formal training available to agriculturalists and agronomists was in technical schools and institutes. Agricultural faculties existed in a few universities but they paid little attention to social science. Secondly, there was no broad 'extra-mural' demand for rural sociology that could compare with that generated by the American extension services. Those European countries with farm advisory services had restricted them to agronomic advice for scientifically oriented farmers and landowners rather than, as in the US case, support for the general socio-economic advance of the farming community and rural households (Organisation for European Economic Cooperation [OEEC] 1950; Brunner and Yang 1949).

What demand there was for rural sociological expertise in Europe came from governments and official agencies requiring technical assistance and support in programmes of rural reconstruction and agricultural recovery and modernisation (Constandse and Hofstee 1964). Much of rural Europe lay devastated. Rural settlements and infrastructure needed to be rebuilt. With chronic food shortages there was a pressing need for large-scale programmes of agricultural modernisation and land reclamation. In some countries land reform and rural development were also new priorities for post-war governments. Throughout Europe, and in contrast to the US, state planning, including rural planning, was regarded as essential. This called for social and economic expertise and gave to European rural social scientists more of a technocratic and paternalistic role (Taylor 1965).

In this role, they were more inclined to see the improvement of rural conditions as requiring social and economic planning and not just technical change; indeed, they regarded the former as a prerequisite to the latter. This was because many parts of rural society in Europe were considered to be deeply traditional, inward-looking and resistant to being absorbed into the modern world. The susceptibility of the European peasantry to the appeals of authoritarian political leaders was seen to reside in this recalcitrant insularity. To avoid a repeat of the calamitous polarisation of European politics of the 1930s it was vital to turn the peasantry into citizens and give them a stake in modern society. This is what the New Deal was seen to have achieved in America, while avoiding a breakdown of the political order (Lowe 2010).

European rural social scientists therefore defined rural change in social and cultural terms as part of a broader modernisation project. They did not accept the technological determinism and optimism of post-war American rural sociology, arguing that economic and technical behaviour were themselves subject to the cultural outlook and practices of rural communities. Crucially, this was not just for the sake of combating reactionary traditionalism, it was also to promote a pluralistic view of modernity not subject to American hegemony. The cultural differences apparent in rural Europe were not just associated with the traditional peasantry but included rural communities with their own strongly progressive outlook. It was seen as important to retain what was valuable of this diversity and autonomy.

It was the exploration, progressive adaptation and, if necessary, the defence of this diversity that provided the rationale and impetus for European rural sociology to deviate from the American model (Hofstee 1963). That diversity was itself reflected in the distinct outlook and preoccupations of the different national schools of rural social science that emerged in Europe. Rural sociology was most strongly institutionalised in countries with small farm structures and extensive needs for rural reconstruction, including the Netherlands, Belgium and France, as well as in West Germany and Italy where agricultural institutions were also reformed, under the direction of the Allied powers (in Germany, to purge them of Fascist influences; in Italy, also to promote land reform, to counter the rise of Communism; see Mendras 1960; OEEC 1950, 1954; USDA Extension Service and Office of Foreign Agricultural Relations 1951; Nelson 1956). However, in countries with no significant peasant 'problem', a formalised rural sociology found little or no purchase, as was the case in Denmark, Sweden and the United Kingdom (Kötter 1967).

Britain had undergone the transformation to an urban-industrialised nation way back in the nineteenth century. British social science thus tended to be preoccupied with urban social problems. Rural development was not overlooked but was mainly seen in an imperial context. The economic geography of the British Empire had been constructed on the basis of the overseas Empire providing the primary products and much of the food to supply Britain's manufacturers and urban population. Rural development was thus an established concern of the traditional social science disciplines of Empire—political economy, geography and anthropology. Within Britain, farming was large scale and commercially oriented, and its advancement was seen to call for sound business planning, cooperation and technical advice. The discipline of agricultural economics had thus been established in the 1920s to advise both government and farmers on boosting agricultural productivity (Agricultural Economics Research Institute 1938; Whetham 1981). It dominated social science research on agricultural issues, leaving little room for the separate institutional development of a rural sociology. Other potential outlets were likewise occupied by other disciplines. For example, the ubiquity of urbanisation effects in Britain led to concern to protect farmland and the rural landscape ('the countryside') from dispersed urban development—issues taken up professionally by town and country planners and academically by geographers. American rural sociology—its methods and concerns—undoubtedly had an influence in post-war Britain, but this was filtered through existing disciplinary structures particularly agricultural economics and geography. Thus, while British researchers participated strongly in European rural sociology circles, they were (and continue to be) a motley group, including geographers, economists, anthropologists and planners, as well as a few sociologists (Lowe and Ward 2007a; European Society for Rural Sociology 1960; Kötter 1967; Munters 1972).

Although largely an American import, the European response to rural sociology was thus strongly differentiated nationally. European rural sociology, as expressed through the meetings and publications of the European Society for Rural Sociology, was not only then a shifting amalgam of different national approaches and schools, but also a much more polyglot activity than American rural sociology: less tied to a coherent applied agenda but more strongly in touch with diverse currents of academic social science, and not just sociology (Munters 1972; Fairweather and Gilles 1982). When the European Society for Rural Sociology was founded in 1957 it consciously recognised and embodied this plurality in its constitution. The Society's first objective was 'international cooperation and exchange of experience' (European Society for Rural Sociology 1960, 77). The rationale was well expressed by the Society's first president, E.W. Hofstee, Professor of Sociology at the Dutch Agricultural University:

> Rural sociology in Europe will be greatly aided by an international comparison of the problems studied, the research methods used, the scientific findings and the practical results (. . .) Comparative studies

in different countries (. . .) will furnish a broader and deeper understanding. (Hofstee 1960, 4–5)

In this way, the Europeans sought to carve out an identity and purpose different from American rural sociology, to assert their own particularisms and to resist the universalising tendencies of the 'Americanisation of European rural sociology' (Kötter 1967, 260; Lowe 2010). In doing so, they had to work within and eventually contend with a form of international research, subject to American leadership, that was in full flow by the late 1950s.

CONTRASTING APPROACHES TO INTERNATIONAL COMPARATIVE RESEARCH

At this point, it is necessary to characterise different styles of comparative research, ranging from positivist to interpretive traditions. Positivists assume an objective and singular reality whose regularities and laws can be deduced from systematic empirical observation, done on as wide a scale as possible. Interpretivists assume that human insights and understandings are inevitably culturally bound, but seek inductively—through cross-cultural comparison—to build up intersubjective truths. Positivists emphasise quantitative methodologies and often reject qualitative ones, while interpretivists favour qualitative methods and tend to shun quantitative ones. It must be emphasized, though, that the two approaches are not mutually incompatible, but instead occupy opposite ends of a spectrum. Indeed, much comparative research involves a mixture of international data analysis and cross-cultural interpretation.

International comparative research has experienced two major waves of development in the past century: the first, 1950s–1970s, under American leadership, and largely positivist in its orientation; the second, 1980s–the present, more under European leadership, when interpretive approaches have also gained some currency. The earlier surge of positivist activity was fuelled by the data needs of newly created international organisations, including the United Nations and its specialised agencies. The second surge, both positivist and interpretivist, has been fuelled by the gathering pace of globalisation since the 1980s, with a key driver being the deepening and broadening of European integration.

The European dimension of international comparative research was given a major boost when the UN Educational, Scientific and Cultural Organization (UNESCO) set up the European Centre for Coordination of Research and Documentation in the Social Sciences in Vienna in 1963. The centre had to accommodate the very different scientific and political-economic perspectives of Western and Eastern Europe. This led it to reject as 'asymmetrical' or 'colonialist' the model of international research that had been dominant hitherto. That model had been based on a team of researchers from one country, usually the United States, gathering data across participating countries with a view to analysing and interpreting it, without necessarily seeking the cooperation of researchers in the countries concerned. This approach came under criticism for projecting Western concepts and perspectives. Indeed, it is claimed that 'the implicit objective of much of the "Anglo-Saxon" research in the 1960s and 1970s . . . was to use comparisons to demonstrate the superiority of the Western model of economic and political development' (Hantrais 2009, 15). According to the Vienna centre's alternative 'symmetrical model', which subsequently was adopted in the management of research projects and networks funded by the European Commission, all national groups were expected to be equally represented and involved throughout the research process.

One of the earliest studies—covering ten European countries—was jointly commissioned by UNESCO and the UN Food and Agriculture Organization (FAO) and coordinated by the infant European Society for Rural Sociology. It was on the 'Social Implications of Farm Mechanization' and significantly it focused on the ambivalent and diverse consequences of the widespread adoption by small and medium-sized farmers of that icon of US farm technology exports, the tractor (Jansen 1969). It was followed by a comparative project launched in 1970 by the Vienna centre on 'The Future of Rural Communities in Industrialised Societies', involving researchers from fifteen European countries. Through the exploration of the divergent, endogenous tendencies of rural regions, it was hoped to dispel 'the American image which tends to conceal itself behind the poor imagination of the future forecasters' (Galeski and Mendras 1981, vi). These studies established a particular style of comparative sociological research expressing European scepticism or opposition towards US farm technology, from tractors to contemporary concerns over GM crops.

POSITIVIST APPROACHES

From a positivist position, international data and examples provide material on which to test the wider validity (and thus extend the applicability) of propositions—'to shake hypotheses free from their particular cultural entanglements' (Lupri 1969, 103). Empirical relationships among variables are sought and hypotheses tested about the possible causes of observed phenomena. At its most culturally blind, evidence is plucked from anywhere across the globe. For the purposes of more systematic international analysis, the main concern is the availability and comparability of data. In advance of the realisation of efforts to standardise methods of measurement transnationally, researchers must cope with the difficulties in 'reading across' the partialities of different national datasets. It is not just a matter of data 'harmonisation', but also how to ensure that like is being compared with like.

In the face of national variation in social and economic forms and functions, positivists rely on the notion of functional equivalence to identify appropriate comparators (units of analysis that serve similar functions in their respective countries; see Lupri 1969). Much work has thus gone into efforts to standardise and approximate different national datasets and to compile indicators that can be confidently applied across a wide range of situations. The Luxembourg Income Study, a cross-national comparative data file from a large number of countries over time, is a prime example of such work (Smeeding 2004). Even so, it is said, national time series data still remain 'unreliable for international comparisons' on such socio-demographic topics as unemployment, part-time working, the informal economy, migration or family structure, because of the different bases and criteria on which they are collected (Hantrais 2009, 67). Meanwhile, comparative measures of economic development, such as per capita gross domestic product, have a precision that is quite deceptive (Dogan 2004, 328–329), and it has taken many decades to develop indicators of poverty and social exclusion that could be widely applied (Marlier et al. 2007, 46–53).

In rural studies, most of the positivist work on international comparative research has been done by economists studying comparative agricultural policy. They have developed indicators, such as the Producer Subsidy Equivalent (PSE), that are normative in their orientation to a 'free trade' agenda (the PSE quantifies, on a common basis between countries, the nominal proportion of the financial value farmers receive due to all forms of government support). The technical refinement of economic indicators is pursued at the expense of sensitivity towards political difference (for example, the European Union is routinely taken as the functional equivalent of the US in comparative studies of agricultural policy). Understanding the political rationale of agricultural policy demands a different approach that is sensitive to national differences in political discourse and structures (Potter 1998; Vihinen 2001).

Comparative rural policy has attracted less of a normative approach (reflecting its much lower political salience), but has been dogged by debate over the functional equivalence of national systems of rural definition and classification. Countries have quite different ways of statistically characterising rurality reflecting their different geographies, and international bodies such as the Organisation for Economic Co-operation and Development (OECD) have sought to establish a loose common framework. The way Britain and the US formally classify rural areas is discussed in the Annex. These national classifications are done essentially for administrative purposes and tend to be based on notions of spatial hierarchy, with urban areas defined by a combination of size and density of population and rural areas as the spaces beyond or in between. Rural is then formally categorised negatively—as non-urban. For this and other reasons it may not necessarily coincide with the way in which people, places or organisations portray themselves, or are portrayed by others, as rural. For rural is commonly used not just as a spatial category but also as a functional one (related to occupations such as farming, fishing, forestry, mining, crafts, tourism, conservation, etc.) and a cultural one (related to descriptors such as natural, nativist, undeveloped, small-scale, peripheral, unchanging, primitive, environmental, provincial, bucolic, wild, simple, open, etc.). These functional and cultural associations of rural vary considerably between nations (Rowley 1996; Williams 1973; Bunce 1994; Short 2006). Typically, though, *rural* is a relational term—normalised against its opposite (urban) within any particular society, not against rural in other countries, but this is how international organisations standardise classifications. Inevitably, some national cases drop off the measuring rod. 'Rural England' is such a casualty: under the OECD's classification, because of its compactness and population density, England is deemed to be without rural, or even predominantly rural, territory (OECD 2011).

INTERPRETIVE APPROACHES

Whereas the positivist tradition sees social and cultural differences as obstacles to be avoided or overcome in the transnational analysis of common phenomena, the interpretive tradition sees the exploration of these self-same differences as the key to understanding the meaning of common phenomena in different contexts. Thus the objective of transnational social science exchange should not necessarily be a great levelling and homogenising of ideas, but should encompass the explanation of social and cultural differences. The underlying premise is that, because of differences in national context—for example, the relationship between civil society and the state, the history of industrialisation and urbanisation, demographic structure and culture—transnational developments elicit social and institutional responses that are often strongly differentiated, and similar problems have a different genesis, cultural resonance and political implications. To understand and anticipate these divergent reactions, to explore the implications of common trends in separate national contexts, it is more than ever important to achieve mutual understanding of essential differences and similarities.

A symmetrical comparative study of rural studies in Britain and France illustrates the scope of the interpretive approach (Lowe and Bodiguel 1990). It brought together rural social scientists from different disciplines to confront the rural cultures of Britain and France, as a 'multilayered enterprise':

> At one level, as we explore the variety of functions, values and images associated with rural areas, we can appreciate the diversity of rural cultures not just between the two countries but within each. At another level, particularly when contrasting [national] experiences, the separate

rural cultures appear as more cohesive and characteristic. Then again, when considering each in its context, this singularity is seen to reside not in any putative autarky but in the nature of rural culture as a component of the particular national culture. (ibid., ix)

At the core of British concerns was a sense of the national importance of the rural encapsulated in the notion of the countryside as a set of places, landscapes and environmental attributes. In contrast, to the French, the essence of traditional rurality was a distinctive set of occupations, products, ways of life and communities.

The book brought together rural scholars in geography, politics, anthropology, economics and sociology from the two countries and explored the different ways they each analysed the rural world. It was thus not only a confrontation between rural cultures but between academic cultures too. In this 'comparative sociology of the social sciences' the book revealed 'at this level also . . . singularities and pluralities of contexts and meanings':

Each [discipline] has different ways of analysing and conceptualising the rural world, and it is thereby subdivided as a conceptual space, not just by national boundaries, but by disciplinary boundaries too. [Countries] also have different academic traditions and institutional structures for research and learning. Over and above the separate disciplines, these traditions and structures have strongly shaped the way rural areas have been studied in the two countries. (x)

The comparison revealed not only the different intellectual styles (the British tendency towards empiricism; the French towards abstraction) and social functions of academics (the British emphasizing policy relevance; the French, detached commentary), but also differences in the very architecture of knowledge. The counterpart of the UK's neo-classical agricultural economics (oriented towards the econometric analysis of agricultural policy and markets) was the more heterodox French *economie rurale* (which also embraced, for example, the economic geography of the rural economy). Britain had no other institutionalised rural disciplines whereas France had a distinct rural sociology. 'Rural', though, was a major, subdisciplinary focus of British geography (a discipline with deeper roots in Britain than sociology), as well as the common empirical focus of a group of interdisciplinary scholars.

In this way, the study revealed ultimately the specificity of the way the rural was characterised, structured and represented through different national and disciplinary practices. While the major purpose was to build mutual understanding as the basis for further comparative and collaborative research efforts, the most profound outcome was to reveal to each side some of the particularities, peculiarities and taken-for-granted assumptions about the way they classified, categorised, analysed and performed the rural.

THE ROLE OF LANGUAGE

A study such as that reveals the significance of linguistic differences as either obstacle, or grist, to comparative analysis. Apparently similar concepts—such as the (English) middle class and the (French) *bourgeoisie*—in fact define significantly different categories and imply different empirical measurements. While this is the case for such central sociological concepts, it applies also to key rural concepts: for example, the (English) farmer and the (French) *paysan* are different, albeit overlapping categories; so are (English) agricultural economics and (French) *economie rurale*. Linguistic differences are thus not simply technical barriers but go to the heart of cross-cultural (mis)understanding, as Lisle explains:

> [L]anguage is not simply a medium to carry concepts. It is itself the very matter of scientific observation and discourse. When we study a particular country, we are examining it with the only instruments available, namely a conceptual system and set of ideas produced within and by the society we are investigating, reflecting its history, its institutions, its values, its ideology, all of which are expressed in that country's language. By definition, that overall system and those concepts have no exact equivalents in other societies. (1985, 24)

Indeed, de Haan diagnosed language as the major barrier to establishing a common frame of reference that might integrate different 'national perspectives into a comparative body of rural sociological knowledge' (1993, 128).

In this respect, the widespread assumption of English as the language of transnational scholarly communication has been double-edged. While it has improved the scope for international exchange of ideas and information in rural sociology, it has marginalised communication between national schools whose primary language is not English, thus heightening their isolation and rendering their concepts and cases more inaccessible, except in second-hand (i.e. translated) form. At the same time it has meretriciously reinforced the ascendancy in international communications of what de Haan refers to as 'Anglo-Saxon rural sociology': 'The apparent centrality of Anglo-Saxon rural sociology is not the result of its superior intellectual and scientific achievements. It derives its "mainstream" position from the dominance of the English language' (1993, 128). Representative of this tradition would be the *Handbook of Rural Studies* (Cloke, Marsden and Mooney 2006), a prominent compilation of American sociological and British 'Old Commonwealth' geographical perspectives (the institutional affiliations of its thirty-eight contributors are: UK eighteen; US nine; Australia, New Zealand and Canada seven; rest of Europe four). Certain phenomena come to be projected as universal or given disproportionate emphasis even though they may have culturally specific roots. A significant example would be the extensive generalisation from the peculiarly British experience with counterurbanisation and the so-called rural idyll. Despite its global status, Anglo-Saxon rural sociology, far from constituting 'a shared framework' is, in de Haan's words, yet another 'rural sociological island'. Its academic products are 'context-specific' too, which—to be revealed—need 'critical exposure to other traditions' (1993, 127–128).

UK–US comparisons do not suffer the obstacle of a language barrier. On the contrary, the shared use of English and the intertwined political and economic history of the two countries underpin the considerable interaction and exchange between their strongly overlapping cultural, intellectual and scientific traditions. Such is the transatlantic confluence of social science thinking as to constitute in many fields a shared Anglo-American perspective that typically enjoys international prominence thanks in no small measure to the international status of the English language. A handbook of *International Comparative Research* comments on the predominance of, variously, 'Anglo-American research communities' (Hantrais 2009, xii), 'a Western perspective' (44) and 'Anglo-Saxon research cultures' (166).

British and American researchers have the immense advantage over other national research communities of possessing a lingua franca which greatly eases their involvement in the international arena. The consequences can be seen most recently in the development of the European Research Area within the European Union, intended to increase the global impact of European research and thereby prevent Europe from falling behind the United States, scientifically and economically. The coincidental enlargement of the European Union has reinforced the dominance of English as the working language for trans-European activities, and hence the leadership role of British researchers in joint projects and networks. However, it is argued, 'They bring with them their intellectual styles and working practices, potentially creating a new form of imperialism' (Hantrais 2009, 155). This is said to be because 'researchers whose native language is English tend, as in the natural sciences, to believe that the concepts transmitted through their language are universally understood' (89). These charges levelled at British researchers in pan-European research programmes in the 1990s and 2000s (Lallement and Spurk 2003; Barbier 2005; Kuhn and Remøe 2005) echo those levelled largely at American research leadership in international research programmes in the 1970s—of scientific colonialism and imperialism (Armer and Grimshaw 1973; Warwick and Osherson 1973).

A UK–US comparison offers one way to deconstruct Anglo-Saxon research cultures. To do so it is necessary to come to grips with the context-specific nature of knowledge. That implies an alertness to nuances and differences in the use of American English and English English, including a sensitivity towards divergences in meaning of common terms. For example, 'middle class' has a narrower connotation in the UK than in the US (where it is often taken to include blue-collar workers). 'Liberalism' in the US connotes a belief in big government, and in Britain a commitment to political and social freedoms. 'Native' in the UK implies someone born in a place, but in the US describes someone descended from those who inhabited the place prior to European settlement. This is just one of the elements that make rural ethnicity so complexly different between the US and UK.

Rural terms and concepts differ, too. Some are specific to one country or the other. For example, dirt farmer, rancher, homesteader, sodbuster, sharecropper and planter are distinctively American terms, specific to a settler nation and indicative not only of a certain historical relationship with the land, but also the grounding of the institutions of American democracy and property in an agrarian-republican ideology. Thus other US terms too—such as agrarianism, rural populism, Jeffersonianism, realty and native rights—have limited or no resonance in the UK. The UK's contrasting experience as a long settled society with a different historical relationship to the land (including an historic landed class) is expressed in such distinctive terms as stewardship, custodianship, paternalism, gentrification and right to roam. Nothing captures these differences so sharply as the contrast between the American concept of the wilderness and the British concept of the countryside, both of which are celebrated and idealised. Indeed, pre-eminent examples of each are protected as 'National Parks'. However they embody quite different forms of ownership, governance and use, and express quite different national ideals of the relationship between society and nature. An American conservation historian, having visited some of Britain's National Parks, was provoked to remark:

> These are certainly not like national parks in the US where parkland is publicly owned, where development is limited to custodial functions and where administration lies with an agency of the national government. In Britain private ownership dominates, much incompatible development is permitted and administration is through local government. The term 'national park' in Britain appears to be very much a misnomer. (Hays 1984, 20; see also Vergunst, Geisler and Stedman, this volume)

Same term, different meanings: comparative analysis should illuminate and help bridge such gulfs of understanding between 'two nations divided by a common language' (a maxim about the United States and Britain ascribed variously to Winston Churchill, Oscar Wilde and George Bernard Shaw).

CONCLUSIONS

As all knowledge is produced in specific geographical and cultural contexts, a frank recognition and examination of the social bases of knowledge is required. That is not only necessary for the pursuit of objectivity. It is also important to appreciate the limits of knowledge in considering its relevance or applicability. Otherwise we risk building a globalised knowledge (say, an international rural sociology) on the false assumption that we all speak the same language. Yet, even when we do speak the same language, we do not always share the same meanings.

In recognition that there are competing views of what is universal, the Gulbenkian Commission on the Restructuring of the Social Sciences presented the coming challenge for the social sciences as being to 'promote a pluralistic universalism':

> We start from the very strong belief that some kind of universalism is the necessary goal of the community of discourse. At the same time, we recognize that any universalism is historically contingent in that it provides the medium of translation while at the same time setting the terms of the intellectual discussion and is thus a source of intellectual power. We recognize further that every universalism sets off responses to itself, and that these responses are in some sense determined by the nature of the reigning universalism(s). And we believe that it is important to accept the coexistence of different interpretations of an uncertain and complex world. Only a pluralistic universalism will permit us to grasp the richness of the social realities in which we live and have lived. (Wallerstein 1996, 59–60)

The essence of this approach is not only a respect for diversity of worldviews in seeking universal truths, but also the inculcation of a sensitivity towards the contingency of established knowledge. A pluralistic universalism is one that accepts 'the co-existence of different interpretations of an uncertain and complex world' (ibid., 60), and indeed draws upon that diversity to test the wider validity and reach of its concepts. A pluralistic universalism is also one that 'accepts contradictions within its universality' (59). That implies an appreciation of the limits of the rationality of knowledge systems—a 'contextualisation' of universalisms (x).

One obvious approach to study pluralistic universalisms is comparative analysis. Understanding how others have come to see things differently offers a means not only to widen our understanding, but also to expose and explore the taken-for-granted assumptions on which our own concepts and outlooks are based.

Part II
Socio-Economic Change

3 Migration and Urban–Rural Population Redistribution in the UK and US

Tony Champion and David L. Brown

INTRODUCTION

Population size and change are fundamental aspects of community structure that affect and are affected by local economy, institutions and resources. They influence a community's ability to provide essential services, support retail and commercial establishments, and give local government and other public institutions sufficient capacity to manage local affairs and plan for the future. Population change comprises two primary components: natural increase (the balance of births and deaths) and net migration (the sum of international and internal exchanges). In both the UK and the US, as rates of natural increase have fallen, the migration component has grown in its contribution to both national population growth and internal population redistribution. This is an important development because the determinants of spatial variability in birth and death rates are quite different from the factors associated with variability in migration. Hence, if maintaining sufficient population to justify public and private investment is a policy goal,[1] interventions designed to promote fertility or enhance longevity differ considerably from those implemented to retain or attract population via migration.

In this chapter we compare long-term trends in rates of population change between urban and rural areas in the UK and US, and then examine the components of these distributional changes, giving particular attention to the role played by migration. We show that, while urbanisation typically accompanies broader processes of social and economic development, in a highly developed and urbanised society this tendency tends to be weaker and indeed may lead to a reversal in favour of smaller settlements and less densely populated areas in a process widely known as *counterurbanisation*. After this, we focus on three elements of migration with profound effects on the population composition of rural areas, revealing considerable commonality but also some differences between the two countries; namely, older adult and retiree in-migration, young adult out-migration and international labour migration. While the first two are long-established processes affecting rural populations, the scale and geographical impact of international migration have changed dramatically since the 1980s, rising substantially in volume and spreading out well beyond the gateway cities which were the destinations of most international arrivals up to this time, including into more remote and rural contexts.

RURAL–URBAN POPULATION REDISTRIBUTION SINCE 1970

In this section we examine rural–urban population redistribution trends in the US and UK over the last forty years. Definitions of urban and rural for each country are discussed in the Annex at the end of the book. Suffice it to say here that, unless stated otherwise, we use definitions based on socio-economic criteria rather than physical ones based on built-up area or other land-use characteristics. Also, for the US discussion, we use the terms *rural* and *nonmetropolitan* (nonmetro) interchangeably for ease of presentation even though they are technically different concepts.

Continuous Counterurbanisation in the UK

In one sense the UK population continues to urbanise. If one considers all built-up areas of over a certain physical extent (normally 20 hectares or 50 acres) as urban, then the proportion of the population living in urban areas had reached almost 93 per cent by 2001 (T. Champion 2008). This, however, is not a very meaningful statistic, given the high level of urbanisation already reached by 1901 using this definition (78 per cent for England and Wales; see Law 1967) and also bearing in mind that since the 1940s planning policies have placed severe restrictions on new building in very small settlements.

By contrast, if one focuses on broader areas that contain both urban and rural land, the UK has experienced continuous counterurbanisation over the past four decades. Indeed, as A. Champion (2003) has shown, if the focus is restricted to population redistribution between Local Labour Market Areas (LLMAs) classified as urban, then a clear negative relationship between population size and population growth rate—which is the classic definition of counterurbanisation developed by Fielding (1982)—was already in existence in the intercensal period 1931–1951. At this time, however, the rural LLMA population was growing more slowly than average and actually declined in the following decade. Nevertheless, by 1961–1971 rural growth had exceeded the national average and by 1971–1981 the rural category was the fastest growing tier in the settlement hierarchy.

Population estimates data for the 1980s onwards assembled for a district-level classification (Table 3.1) indicate that the rural growth rate has continued to outpace the urban one. On the other hand, the pace of rural

Table 3.1 Population Change 1981–2008 for an Urban–Rural District Classification of Great Britain

	Annualised change rate (%)			% point difference from GB rate		
	1981–1991	1991–2001	2001–2008	1981–1991	1991–2001	2001–2008
Great Britain	0.18	0.26	0.53	0.00	0.00	0.00
Urban	0.10	0.21	0.50	-0.08	-0.05	-0.03
Rural	0.67	0.54	0.73	0.48	0.29	0.19
of which:						
Urban fringe	0.66	0.65	0.81	0.48	0.40	0.28
Agricultural	0.72	0.56	0.71	0.54	0.30	0.18
Rural extremes	0.55	0.28	0.57	0.37	0.02	0.04

Source: Calculated from UK Office for National Statistics data. Crown copyright. Adapted from data from the Office for National Statistics licensed under the Open Government Licence v.1.0.

growth slackened in the 1980s and 1990s, even though it remained above the national average. After that, rural population growth accelerated again, but the urban growth rate moved up even faster in percentage point terms. As a result, the gap between the two is now at its narrowest since before the height of counterurbanisation in the 1970s. Expressed in terms of difference in annual average growth from the national rate (as in the right-hand panel of Table 3.1), the rural districts' growth in 2001–2008 was only 0.19 percentage points above the overall British rate, much below the 0.48 differential of two decades earlier.

This trend reflects both the resurgence of urban areas, driven notably by the new knowledge economy, rising immigration from abroad and policy support for urban regeneration, and by the onset of more challenging circumstances in the countryside, these being associated principally with the farming economy and the declining availability of low-cost housing and local community services. The latter is reflected in the variation in growth rate between different types of rural district, shown in the lower panel of Table 3.1. During the 1980s it was the main agricultural production districts lying between the urban fringe zones and the remoter rural areas that grew the most strongly, but it is these that have seen their growth pegged back most compared to the national rate, down from 0.54 to 0.18 percentage points above the latter. The rate has dropped next fastest for the rural extremes and least for the urban fringes, with the result that across *rural* Britain the overall population growth rate now declines regularly with increasing rurality and remoteness.

The Changeable Nature of Rural Urban Population Redistribution in the US

In contrast to the UK's pattern of continuous counterurbanisation since the 1960s, albeit with a shrinking rural–urban differential more recently, the US experience has been more variable. The biggest change there occurred in the 1970s. Prior to this, as shown in Figure 3.1, the metro areas' population growth rate consistently outpaced that of the nonmetros. Then, in 1975, Calvin L. Beale of the US Department of Agriculture (USDA) showed that, for the first time in the nation's recorded history, rural areas grew faster than their urban counterparts. Moreover, he showed that this rural growth advantage was the result of net in-migration from urban to rural counties (Beale 1975). The immediate response to Beale's report was scepticism and disbelief. Other demographic researchers doubted the accuracy of the population estimates, and some claimed that the rural growth was simply further suburbanization. However, Beale's contention that rural areas were now growing at a faster rate than urban areas has stood the test of time. Within a couple of years even the strongest critics agreed that the 'population turnaround' was real and important (Hansen, Boertlein and Long 1978). Four interrelated factors were being put forward to account for the turnaround: deconcentration of employment (notably with manufacturing searching for lower wage workers, fewer and weaker regulations, less unionization and compliant local governments that were willing to subsidize industrial re-locations), modernisation of rural life (through the spread of electrification, all-weather roads and telephone services), population ageing (with an increasing number of American workers retiring earlier and having the means to move away from the major job centres), and increasing preferences for rural living (Brown et al. 1997; Brown and Glasgow 2008).

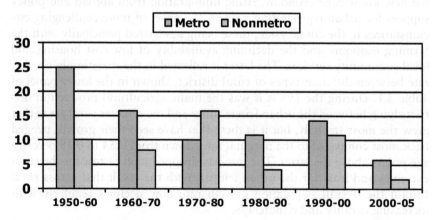

Figure 3.1   Metro–nonmetro population change in the US, 1950–2005, % for period.

Yet, as also shown in Figure 3.1, the 1970s rural turnaround did not usher in a stable pattern of faster rural population growth; instead it was followed by three further shifts in urban–rural population growth differentials (Johnson and Cromartie 2006). First, unlike in the UK, the US urban sector regained its growth advantage during the 1980s, primarily due to a deep agricultural recession at the beginning of the decade as well as to the onset of difficult economic times more generally. The first half of the 1990s then saw the relative rate of nonmetro growth improve once again, such that by mid-decade rural areas were growing as rapidly as urban areas. Again, however, this resurgence proved to be short lived and, by the end of that decade, urban areas had regained a substantial growth advantage which has continued into the new century. Research by the USDA's Economic Research Service shows that 339 counties switched from growth during the early 1990s to decline five years later, with rural decline concentrated in Appalachia, the Northern Great Plains and the Midwestern Corn Belt.

Within nonmetro America, differences in overall growth rate can also be observed between the more urbanised parts labelled 'micropolitan' and the 'non-core-based areas' (NCBAs) that lack even a small urban core (see Brown et al. 2004; Annex, this volume). These two elements experienced similar rates of growth when the entire nonmetro category has been growing relatively briskly (as in the 1970s and early 1990s), but when the nonmetro category has been doing less well (as in the 1980s and since the mid-1990s) the micropolitan areas have outpaced the NCBAs, very possibly because the narrower economic base of the latter make them more vulnerable to the business cycle. Similarly, research by Johnson and Cromartie (2006) has shown that in every decade since 1980 nonmetro counties adjacent to metros have grown more rapidly than their non-adjacent counterparts. Moreover, counties adjacent to larger metro areas have exceeded the growth of those next to smaller metros. Clearly, access to a wider range of urban jobs, services and cultural amenities is a distinct advantage when it comes to differential population growth in rural America, just as has become the case in the UK since the 1980s.

COMPONENTS OF POPULATION CHANGE

In both the UK and US, migration has become the dominant component of rural population change. This is partly because the rate of natural increase in rural areas has declined over the decades, as their traditionally higher fertility rates have moved closer to the lower urban levels and as many young adults have left rural areas before starting families. At the same time, both internal and international migration have grown in importance as drivers of inter-area variability in population change. Though both internal and international migration have slacked off because of the current recession (Johnson 2009), most scholars believe that population mobility will resume afterwards and reassert its impact on inter-area differences in population growth.

Rural Population Dynamics in the UK

The acceleration in rural Britain's population growth since the early 1990s has been driven almost entirely by the migration component. Indeed, the analysis of components data for the same district-based rural definition as in Table 3.1 shows that natural increase has been negative throughout this period, its annual rate dropping from -0.01 per cent in 1991–1995 to -0.13 per cent in 1999–2003 before recovering to -0.05 per cent in 2003–2008. By contrast, migration has been strongly positive and increasing, already at 0.60 per cent a year in 1991–1995 and rising to 0.79 per cent in 2003–2008.

The relative importance of internal and international migration in recent rural growth is shown in Table 3.2 for England, which makes up five-sixths of the UK's total population. This is based on a different classification that groups local government districts into a maximum of six categories based on their degree of urbanness and rurality. Besides confirming natural decrease for the two most rural categories (those with over 80 per cent and over 50 per cent of people living in rural settlements respectively), this shows the clear dominance of within-UK migration for rural England as a whole, adding around 780,000 to its population between 2001 and 2008, more than six times its 123,000 gain from international migration. Net migration gains from the rest of the UK were especially important for the two most rural district types, where conversely the impact of net immigration was the least evident. Indeed, the lower panel of Table 3.2 neatly counterposes a pretty clear 'urbanisation' pattern for net international migration (with the latter's strongest growth rate being for the Major Urban category) with an extremely clear 'counterurbanisation' relationship for internal migration (where the change rate rises regularly with increasing rurality), with the latter prevailing in the all-migration aggregate.

Given the importance of internal migration in driving rural population growth, it is perhaps not surprising to discover that net urban-to-rural migration is a nationwide feature, not something being driven just by events in southern England, where the exodus from London has impacted residents greatly for decades. The level of rural migratory growth is shared almost to the same extent by all four of the broad divisions that represent broad swathes arranged from south to north, being only marginally higher for the two more southerly divisions and not much lower for the less densely populated rural parts of northern England and Scotland. Not only that, but a relatively high degree of consistency is also found when the different types of 'rural' districts are compared. All ten district groups shown in Figure 3.2 (rural Scotland consists only of the 'rural extreme' type) recorded strong net in-migration from the rest of the UK in 2001–2008. In particular,

Table 3.2 Components of Population Change, 2001–2008, England, by DEFRA District Type

DEFRA district type	Number for period (000s)			Rate (% year compound)			
	Natural change	International mig	Within-UK mig	Natural change	Total mig	International mig	Within-UK mig
England	891.1	1229.3	-142.9	0.26	0.32	0.36	-0.04
Urban	863.2	1106.7	-924.4	0.39	0.08	0.50	-0.42
Rural	27.9	122.6	781.5	0.02	0.72	0.10	0.62
Major Urban	623.1	744.6	-832.6	0.51	-0.07	0.61	-0.68
Large Urban	85.5	197.7	-53.6	0.17	0.29	0.39	-0.10
Other Urban	154.6	164.4	-38.1	0.33	0.27	0.35	-0.08
Significant Rural	66.2	75.3	172.6	0.15	0.55	0.17	0.38
Rural-50	-7.9	17.7	265.3	-0.02	0.70	0.04	0.66
Rural-80	-30.5	29.6	343.6	-0.08	0.92	0.07	0.85

Notes: Within-UK migration includes migration between England and the rest of the UK (Northern Ireland, Scotland and Wales). Mig = migration.
Source: Calculated from UK Office for National Statistics data. Crown copyright. Adapted from data from the Office for National Statistics licensed under the Open Government Licence v.1.0.

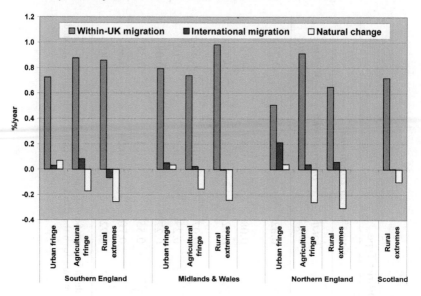

Figure 3.2   Components of population change, 2001–2008, by rural district type, for divisions of Great Britain.

rural remoteness (as represented by the 'rural extremes' type here) does not appear to suffer any significant penalty, for even in northern England the 'rural extremes' district type was gaining more growth through domestic migration than the urban fringes, and further north in Scotland this type appears no less attractive. What Figure 3.2 also shows for natural change is how, by contrast, this falls with increasing rurality within all three parts of Britain that have representation of the three types, this largely being due to the most rural areas experiencing the highest rates of both the youth exodus and older in-migration (see later in the chapter for more details).

Rural Population Dynamics in the US

As shown in Figure 3.3, natural increase was the principal component of rural population growth from the 1930s through the 1960s, with net migration being strongly negative throughout this period. Since then, the contribution of natural increase to rural population growth has declined in each decade, while net migration was positive in the 1970s, negative in the 1980s and positive since 1990 (ERS-USDA 2007). Since the mid-1990s, however, the rate of rural population growth has lagged behind that of urban areas. If migration is such a powerful determinant of population growth in contemporary America, why did rural areas gain more migrants than they lost during this time of slow population growth relative to their urban counterparts? The answer is that urban areas exceeded rural areas in

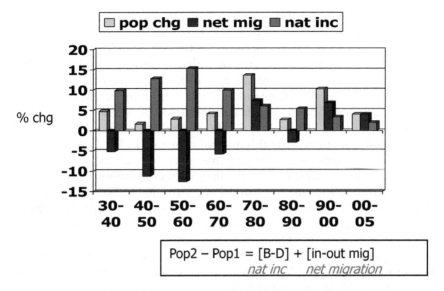

Figure 3.3   Components of nonmetro demographic change in the US, 1930–2005.

overall population growth because, as in the UK, the vast majority of international migration was destined for such areas. In contrast, even though urban areas exceeded rural areas in overall growth, the exchange of *internal* migration still favoured rural areas over urban.

Why has the contribution natural increase makes to rural population growth diminished over time? The short answer is that rural fertility has fallen, while rural mortality tends to be somewhat higher than average.

Rural fertility rates are and have always been higher than urban fertility rates in the United States, traditionally reflecting children's greater economic value on the farm and in other rural industries. However, while the rural fertility excess was still almost 0.5 children per woman as late as 1900, it has diminished dramatically since then (Fuguitt, Brown and Beale 1989). By 1990, completed fertility had declined to 2.1 children in rural areas compared with 1.9 children to urban women, both hovering around the level of generational replacement (Tarmann 2003). Regardless of rural–urban place of residence, women are marrying later and are highly likely to continue their education past high school and have careers. All of these factors postpone the age of first birth and diminish the number of children that women eventually bear.

Mortality rates have declined in both urban and rural areas, but rural rates continue to exceed their urban counterparts, and by an increasing margin. Cosby et al. (2008) have shown that the nonmetro 'mortality penalty' increased from about six deaths per one hundred thousand in 1980 to almost seventy-two deaths per one hundred thousand in 2004.[2] As a result of low rural fertility and higher than average rural mortality, rural natural increase makes a diminished contribution to rural population growth. Hence, in both urban and rural areas, natural increase now has only a modest effect on inter-area differences in population growth, although with geographic mobility temporarily reduced because of the recession, natural increase is currently more important to local population growth than in the recent past (Johnson 2009). In New York State, for example, 233,000 migrants were lost to other states during 2005, but only 95,000 during 2008. Natural increase and immigration more than offset this internal migration loss.

Even so, international migration has steadily been assuming a new importance for the rural US and the migration destinations there are now different from in the past. As Kandel and Parrado (2006) showed, established Hispanic communities in the rural US were mostly in the Southwest. In contrast, since 2000 the fast growth Hispanic areas are mostly in the Midwest and Southeast. This reflects the location of the nation's meat and poultry processing industry. It also tends to turn globalisation on its head. Rather than 'offshoring' low-wage jobs to low-wage countries as was done with non-durable manufacturing, the meat processing industry has actively recruited low-wage workers to the rural US. Johnson and Lichter (2007) reported that 297 nonmetro counties experienced significant immigration for the first time in the 1990s. In fact, a significant number of nonmetropolitan counties would have declined had it not been for immigration.

SELECTED CASE STUDIES OF RURAL MIGRATION IN THE UK AND US

In this section of the chapter we provide a more targeted and grounded examination of three specific migration phenomena that are affecting rural community life in both the UK and the US at the present time: in-migration of retirees and other older people, youth out-migration and international migration. There is considerable overlap between the two countries in the nature and impact of these processes, but also much difference in specifics. Older in-migration can be framed as a care and pensions issue but also presents social and economic opportunities. Net out-migration of youth threatens the sustainability of rural economic and social life in similar ways in both countries. Finally, while international labour migration has a different history in the two countries, with the UK playing catch-up since 2004, again it involves a rather similar set of benefits and challenges in the two countries.

Net In-Migration to Rural Areas at Older Ages

The UK case: Retirement migration to the British countryside dates back at least to the 1950s and was particularly strong in the 1960s and 1970s (Law and Warnes 1973). Its growth at that time owed a great deal to the rise in popularity of rural recreation and holiday-making in the interwar period, just as seaside resorts and spa towns had previously attracted retirees who had enjoyed vacations there during their working lives (Warnes 1992). The countryside still experiences a net migration gain of people about retirement age (Stockdale 2006a), but the rise in overseas holidaying has resulted in more pensioners electing to live outside the UK, especially along the Mediterranean coast and in rural south Europe (Sriskandarajah and Drew 2006). At the same time, the acceleration in counterurbanisation in the 1970s was largely produced by pre-retirement and middle-aged people following the lead of the older pioneers, such that it is people in their thirties and forties that now dominate the rural influx (Commission for Rural Communities [CRC] 2007f; Champion and Shepherd 2006).

This rural influx is selective in socio-economic terms, too. The retiree element has always consisted primarily of better-off owner occupiers who are able to sell their family-size homes in the more dynamic metropolitan areas and downsize to a relatively cheap rural housing market. This phenomenon has become increasingly common among pre-retirement groups, especially those who use the cash released by the change of house to set up a business, notably in the hospitality sector in these holiday-making areas (as in Cornwall; see, for instance, Williams and Champion 1998) but also as freelance workers were prepared to travel to meet clients. Additionally, and even more important numerically as just mentioned, are families with children who are prepared to trade off extra commuting costs for the privilege of accessing what they consider to be the 'rural idyll' (Gorton, White and Chaston 1998). While some of these will be seeking out housing that costs less than the equivalent in the larger towns and cities, the overall effect has been to push up house prices, especially in the more accessible or amenity-rich parts of the countryside. Because of the strict planning controls on new housebuilding in the countryside, this process has had the effect of increasing the social selectivity of subsequent inward movement, which has led to a widespread 'rural gentrification' following on from the earlier 'geriatrification' phase associated with retirement migration (Champion et al. 1998; Phillips 1993).

The US case: Similar to the UK, rural America has been a net recipient of migration at most ages over thirty during recent decades. Even in the midst dramatic rural population losses during the 1950s, the rate of older out-migration was relatively low compared to other age groups. Meanwhile, in the decades of fastest overall nonmetro growth in the 1970s and 1990s, net in-migration rates were high for all ages thirty through sixty-nine. Net migration to rural areas is strongly negative at ages 15–19, but since migration data are displayed for 5 year intervals, this reflects out migration during the late teens not at ages 15–16. Also, similar to the UK situation, older in-migrants to rural areas in the US are positively selected with respect to income, education and other socio-economic indicators.

Moreover, compared with longer-term residents who are age sixty or older, the in-movers are in better health and more likely to be married (Brown and Glasgow 2008). Accordingly, older in-migration typically enhances the human capital stocks of destination communities.

The highest rates of older in-migration are concentrated in particular rural regions, including Florida and the mid-South, the Ozark Mountains, the Upper Midwest, the Southwest and across the inner-mountain West. Research by Brown et al. (2010) has examined why some rural places are more likely than others to have high in-migration rates at retirement ages (sixty to seventy-four). They found that attractive natural amenities are an important factor in older in-migration, but that the majority of high-amenity rural areas do not attract older in-migrants. Rather, only those areas that develop their amenities into recreation and tourism seem to become retirement destinations at a later time. This is because persons who visit in earlier years tend to build social relationships with tourism communities, and with other vacationers, often returning in later life as permanent residents (see Philip, Brown and Stockdale, this volume, for additional examination of the determinants and consequences of older adult in-migration).

Young Adult Out-Migration

The UK case: Rural areas here have seen dramatic net losses of young adults during recent decades. According to the CRC (2007f), the rate of migration loss is highest for fifteen- to nineteen-year-olds, but is nearly as high for twenty- to twenty-four-year-olds and significantly lower only for twenty-five- to twenty-nine-year-olds. Moreover, greater rurality involves the higher rate of loss. In a study of England, Champion and Shepherd (2006) found that rates of loss were highest for the smallest settlements of the more sparsely populated areas, at around 10 per cent a year for both these age groups. Even with these age groups being constantly replenished by the age-ing of local and in-migrant children, these add up to extremely high rates of depletion as individual cohorts move through these age groups.

The reasons behind this major exodus of rural youth are unsurprising, though there has been a heated debate about their relative importance. While the exodus has been used to argue for a greater provision of afford-able housing in the countryside, it is now clear that the majority of depar-tures involve school-leavers moving into further education or seeking work (Bevan et al. 2001; DTZ Pieda 1998; Findlay et al. 1999). This is par-ticularly the case for more remote communities like the Isle of Lewis in the Scottish Western Isles, where Stockdale (2002) found that fully three-quarters of out-migrants had moved in order to continue education. Even in the rather more accessible Scottish Borders, Jones and Jamieson (1997) found that, of those in school at age sixteen, only one-third were still liv-ing in the survey area by age nineteen. This 'brain drain' has become more acute as higher education participation rates have moved up towards the 1997–2010 Labour Government's goal of 50 per cent from less than 10 per cent 50 years ago. Departures for employment reasons dominate among those completing their education at secondary level because of the dearth of secure jobs, even of those requiring few or no qualifications. For these people, however, there are also social reasons for wanting to escape the claustrophobic atmosphere of village life, whom Stockdale (2002) labels 'home community escapees' in her typology of rural out-migrants. Housing reasons also contribute, with some evidence of rural workers having to move to nearby towns to access affordable housing and commute back to their work (Frost 2006; Houston and Lever 2001; Rugg and Jones 1999).

The youth exodus now seems so ingrained in rural Britain that there appears to be a 'culture' of out-migration, where not to do so is seen as a sign of underachievement and indeed where returning after just a few years away is regarded as a sign of career failure (Stockdale 2004). This would seem to pose a huge challenge to the sort of community regeneration advocated by the Taylor Review (M. Taylor 2008) and to the recommendation of Hollywood and McQuaid (2007) that employers in places like Dumfries and Galloway in rural south-west Scotland need to develop strategies for attracting and retaining workers. Given that the departure of much rural youth can be seen as a logical step in their life course, the most promising approach would be to encourage their return after completing education and gaining experience, but the shortage of affordable housing and relative lack of jobs especially for women militates against this (Glendinning et al. 2003; Stockdale 2006a).

The US case: In the rural US, too, there is a massive youth exodus, though here the rates are not as high for the fifteen- to nineteen-year-olds as for the twenty- to twenty-four-year-olds and twenty-five- to twenty-nine-year-olds (see Figure 3.4 and Johnson et al. 2005). In all likelihood, the greater retention of fifteen- to nineteen-year-olds reflects the fact that many institutions of higher education are located in rural areas in the US. Hence, rural youth have the option to attend college or university close to where they completed secondary school, and many urban youth also attend college in rural areas. The challenge, however, is to retain these well-educated young adults in rural areas after college, and the net out-migration data for those in their twenties show that this is not occurring.

Research on rural 'brain drain' in upstate New York, for example, shows that the net loss of well-educated young adults is produced by insufficient in-migration to replace losses, not by higher than average gross out-migration (Dietz 2007). Similar to the situation in the UK, young adults find rural communities unattractive for a number of economic and social reasons. Research shows that young adults, especially those who have completed post-secondary education, perceive rural economies to be poorly matched to their human capital and occupational qualifications (Sanders, Brown and Pfeffer 2010). However, young adults in the US are also put off by poor infrastructure, including a lack of public transportation and broadband Internet service, by poor housing quality and by village main streets that appear shabby and unkempt. In addition, while many young adults find the natural amenities there attractive, they are put off by the perceived lack of access to cultural amenities and recreational infrastructure. Accordingly, rural areas' inability to replace young well-educated out-migrants is not simply a matter of jobs and income.

Similar to the UK, net out-migration at young adult ages is more extreme in the most rural areas. For example, Johnson et al. (2005) showed that during the 1990s twenty- to twenty-four-year-olds in counties with a high dependence on agriculture had a net out-migration rate of nearly 40 per cent. Agricultural counties are the slowest growing of all rural area types, and thus it is unsurprising that they are haemorrhaging young adults. Even counties with developed recreation activities, which are the most rapidly growing type of US rural county, record rates of net out-migration that are still significant: -21 per cent for ages twenty to twenty-four and -10 per cent for ages twenty-five to twenty-nine. It is clear that net out-migration of young adults is a powerful force affecting rural America, a force that seems somewhat insensitive to variability in economic condition and other community attributes.

International Labour Migrants

The UK case: Traditionally, indeed even as late as 2004, international migration had very little impact on rural Britain, but this changed significantly when the UK, Ireland and Sweden were the only European Union (EU) countries not to impose controls on immigration from the eight Central and Eastern European countries ('the A8') that acceded to the EU in that year. As shown in Table 3.3, although even after 2004 international migration still had its largest net impact on the three types of urban districts, England's two most rural district types (Rural-50 and especially the most rural one, Rural-80) switched from a position of no net gain from net immigration to a substantial one. In fact, the transformation was much larger than this table suggests, because its data relate to people moving with the intention of staying at least twelve months whereas many of the new migrants from the A8 considered themselves to be more transient.

The uplift in international labour migration to rural areas at this time is most comprehensively documented through the rise in foreigners registering National Insurance Numbers (NINOs), as all those starting work in the UK are required to do this. Analysis of this dataset by Green et al. (2009) reveals that between 2002–2003 and 2005–2006 the number of foreign registrants rose by 228 per cent (i.e. more than tripled) in England's Rural-80 districts and by 191 per cent in its Rural-50 districts, compared with a less than doubling (87 per cent increase) for the country as a whole. In all, the rural share of England's total registrations increased from 12 per cent to 19 per cent, still well below its 37 per cent share of total population but a big jump nevertheless. That this change was brought about very largely by the new migration from the A8 countries is illustrated by their large share of the total foreign NINO registrants by 2006–2007: 69 per cent for Rural-80 and 64 per cent for Rural-50 (CRC 2008b).

The geographical incidence of the labour migrants from the A8 countries was by no means as even as these figures might suggest (Bauere et al. 2007; Coombes, Champion and Raybould 2007; CRC 2008b). One area has been particularly important, namely, a broad zone around the Wash focused on the Fens but extending through most of Lincolnshire, Cambridgeshire and Norfolk. At the peak of this migration surge in 2005–2006 the Boston area at the centre of this zone recorded seven times more NINO registrants from the A8 countries than the national average level, with the areas centred on Peterborough, Spalding and Wisbech also having a presence at least three times the norm. Herefordshire and some other areas in the south-west Midlands like the Vale of Evesham also had strong representation. These are all areas of intensive farming of the 'market gardening' type with strong seasonal demands for labour. By contrast, areas specializing in highly mechanized grain farming attracted far fewer, while the lowest representation was in upland areas apart from those with a vibrant hospitality sector catering to holiday-makers and tourists.

Table 3.3   Net International Migration, 2001–2004 and 2004–2008, England, by DEFRA District Type

DEFRA district type	Number for period		Rate (% per year)	
	2001–2004	*2004–2008*	*2001–2004*	*2004–2008*
England	475,610	753,711	0.32	0.38
Urban	455,150	651,552	0.48	0.51
Rural	20,460	102,159	0.04	0.14
Major Urban	341,040	403,590	0.65	0.58
Large Urban	60,400	137,280	0.28	0.47
Other Urban	53,710	110,690	0.26	0.40
Significant Rural	21,840	53,490	0.11	0.20
Rural-50	-1,070	18,730	-0.01	0.08
Rural-80	-310	29,940	0.00	0.13

Source: Calculated from UK Office for National Statistics data. Crown copyright. Adapted from data from the Office for National Statistics licensed under the Open Government Licence v.1.0.

What is not so clear at the time of writing (June 2010) is whether this new migration stream will be a permanent fixture and what range of benefits and disadvantages are involved. As regards the latter, it has been seen as a boon for the national economy as it provided a supply of hard-working and relatively well-qualified labour that took up low-paying and generally low-skill jobs which it had been difficult to find others to do, especially while the post-1993 economic boom continued (Gilpin et al. 2006). A particular advantage for the rural economy has been the greater flexibility of availability of this labour compared to the students that had been increasingly relied on for summer work. Yet in the longer term rural employers are likely to be disadvantaged if they have come to rely too much on this new source of workers. By 2009 the onset of economic recession, allied with a fall in the value of the pound, had already produced a national decline in new arrivals from the A8 countries, and this downward trend seems likely to be reinforced when the other twelve pre-2004 EU states are required to lift their controls on this movement. The rural economy is also at a disadvantage in that these migrants have tended to use farmwork as a stepping-stone towards more permanent and better-paid jobs that their previous qualifications make them suitable for and that are much more urban-based (Green et al. 2009).

The US case: As mentioned earlier, immigration to the US has increased dramatically since 1990, and rural areas have received a growing share of this population movement. Moreover, both the origins and destinations of American immigration have been transformed during this period. Whereas immigration prior to 1970 came mostly from Europe, the most recent wave originates in Asia and Latin America, principally Mexico (Kritz and Gurak 2004). Destinations have also changed from large metropolises in a few gateway states to a diverse set of states and regions and, within them, to suburban and rural communities as well as urban ones. As Durand, Massey and Capoferro (2005, 18) have observed, 'In a few short years, Mexican immigration has been transformed from a narrowly focused process affecting just three states into a nationwide movement'.

Although non-Hispanic whites still make up 82 per cent of the US nonmetro population (in 2000), immigration is resulting in increased race-ethnic diversity. Between 2000 and 2005, immigrants accounted for almost 30 per cent of nonmetro population growth. In fact, were it not for immigration, about one in ten growing nonmetro counties would have experienced population loss over this period, and over one thousand declining nonmetro counties would have had even greater losses (Jones, Kandel and Parker 2007). While Hispanic immigration is a major contributor to nonmetro population change, its impact is not evenly spread throughout rural America. Kandel and Parrado (2006) showed that immigration had its strongest impact on overall population growth in new destination communities compared with established Hispanic locations.

Between 1990 and 2000, Hispanic population grew by about 42 per cent in established Hispanic areas located throughout the Southwest, while it grew by over 300 per cent in counties lacking pre-existing Hispanic settlement. These 'rapid Hispanic growth' counties are concentrated in the Southeast, the Ozark Mountains and the upper Midwest. Migration to these locations is 'demand driven', i.e. migrants are attracted to job opportunities paying superior wages to what could be expected in Mexico. As Kandel and Parrado (2006) explain, Mexicans have been attracted to rural labour markets as a result of an industrial restructuring process that has produced a large number of jobs in labour-intensive industries such as food processing, rug making and forestry, which utilize a large supply of low-skill workers. Since domestic labour is not sufficient to fill the labour demand, or willing to work for low wages, many firms actively recruit in Mexico. In addition, meat processing has relocated from urban centres to the rural areas where cows, pigs and chickens are raised. Again, domestic labour supplies are insufficient to satisfy labour demand, and employers look south to fill their needs.

Hispanic immigrants to the rural US tend to be significantly younger than the destination populations they join. On average, nonmetro Hispanics are fourteen years younger than non-Hispanic whites, and only 10 per cent of nonmetro Hispanics are age sixty or older, compared with 20 per cent of their non-Hispanic white counterparts (Jones, Kandel and Parker 2007). These differences in age structure are even greater in rapid Hispanic growth areas compared with areas with pre-existing Hispanic concentrations (Kandel and Parrado 2006). As a result, Hispanics are more likely to form families and have children compared with non-Hispanic populations in nonmetro counties.[3] These stark differences in age structure have dramatic implications for a large number of service, consumption, infrastructure and social issues, with the most obvious being schooling. Kandel and Parrado (2006) reported that enrolment rates for Hispanic children increased by over 500 per cent in rapid growth Hispanic areas compared with 9 per cent for non-Hispanic whites. Hence, immigration is having a dramatic impact on education in these areas.

But it is not simply increased enrolment that is posing a challenge for rural schools where immigration is occurring. Unlike the relatively well-educated A8 labour migrants in the UK, the vast majority of both current and former Mexican farmworkers lack a high school education with over half of current farmworkers having completed less than seven years of formal education. In addition, less than half of current Mexican farmworkers are able to speak, read, write or understand English, although former Mexican farmworkers have much higher levels of English-language ability. Clearly, Mexican immigrant youth who are entering rural schools will require a number of supports, including special language training, if they are to succeed in obtaining an education. In sum, Hispanic population growth in nonmetro America is posing one of the most profound demographic challenges since the post–World War II baby boom. While many longer-term rural residents perceive this demographic transformation in a negative light, many other persons see it for its opportunities rather than as a problem. In a statewide poll conducted in 2004, nearly one-third of New York State residents reported that immigration was an asset while only 16 per cent felt it was a burden (Pfeffer and Parra 2004).[4] Moreover, while Hispanic immigration raises many challenges for intergroup relations (Hernandez-Leon and Zuniga 2005), it is also seen by many longer-term residents as having potential for community revitalisation (Grey and Woodrick 2005).

CONCLUSIONS

Change, not stability, is the typical situation for rural populations in the UK and US. In this chapter we have shown that rural populations are engaged in a process of transformation that is affecting their numbers and their demographic and social compositions. These changes have direct implications for all aspects of community structure and organisation. While demographers and other social scientists are able to project some aspects of future populations, many of the trends and changes described in this chapter are difficult to foresee with a high degree of accuracy. This is because, while some demographic futures are a direct result of past trends, for example, population ageing as it relates to past fertility, other demographic futures are more directly influenced by period-specific occurrences such as unemployment and economic downturns. In the 1970s scholars were pronouncing an 'end of migration' as the per cent of foreign born dropped to historic lows in the US, UK and in many other European countries (Kritz and Gurak 2004; Muenz 2006). Just one generation later, however, immigration had accelerated throughout the world, resulting in what Castles and Miller (1998) call the 'Age of Migration'. Immigration to the rural UK and US is contingent on the availability of jobs that pay superior wages to those available in origin countries. When jobs dry up, immigrants either stop coming or return to their origin countries. This appears to be occurring in both the UK and US during the current recession. Accordingly, while the long-term trend of population redistribution is toward a more decentralized pattern in both the UK and US, the extent of counterurbanisation at any time responds to the relative economic situation in rural and other low-density locations.

The demographic trends and changes discussed in this chapter contribute to a deeper understanding of many of the specific issues examined in other chapters of this book. In particular, the overall demographic picture should be kept in mind when reading the chapters on population ageing, social exclusion and poverty and immigration that make up the remainder of this part of the book. In addition, changes in the demographic context are important to understanding how the rural labour force has been transformed during recent decades and how this contributes to economic restructuring (Chapter 7). Since demographic trends and changes affect and are affected by the natural environment, knowledge of the general demographic situation contributes to understanding the interaction between nature and human activities, discussed in Chapters 12 and 13. Of course, rural policy and governance (Chapters 10, 14 and 15) cannot be fully appreciated without knowing who lives in rural communities, how this has changed over time and how it is likely to change in the future.

Regardless of the specific nature of demographic trends affecting rural communities at a particular time, population changes do not automatically result in social or economic adaptations. More or fewer people, older or younger residents or new residents lacking facility in the native language do not automatically induce more or fewer jobs, school rooms, English as a Second Language teachers or stores and ethnic restaurants. Rather, population changes are mediated by local social structure, and their impact is contingent on the policy environment affecting localities as well as on global–local relationships. Whether population changes are perceived as challenges or opportunities depends on a complex set of internal relationships within communities and their place in a nation's settlement structure. In other words, demography is not necessarily destiny. Understanding how population is changing is important, but understanding the interrelationships between population dynamics and local social and economic organisation requires a more holistic approach to population, society and economy.

4 Demographic Ageing in Rural Areas
Insights from the UK and US

Lorna Philip, David L. Brown
and Aileen Stockdale

INTRODUCTION

Arguably the most important population trend in today's world is demographic ageing. Population ageing is a dynamic bio-social process that fundamentally alters many aspects of society and the economy. Across the Western world in particular, national populations are ageing, primarily as a result of the falling fertility and mortality rates in the final quarter of the nineteenth century and throughout the twentieth century, and also from increasing longevity brought about by medical and other health care advances. At the subnational level, both inflow and outflow migration can also have a notable effect upon the demographic profile especially if the characteristics of in-movers differ from those of out-movers and/or the resident population. Population projections indicate that ageing will continue to be a trend in most national populations for the foreseeable future (UN Population Division 2002).

Evidence of demographic ageing, which may be defined as 'both the increase in the average age of the population as well as the increasing number or proportion of older people in the population' (Blake 2009, 43), is to be found in cities, small towns and remote rural communities. It is useful to consider ageing in a rural context because rural areas are often the first to experience a significant ageing of their population and they can thus be considered to be a 'test-bed' for how ageing may affect national populations as a whole. In the first two sections of this chapter, drawing upon various secondary data sources, patterns and processes of ageing in the UK and US will be illustrated and distinctive rural characteristics of this demographic trend will be highlighted. The implications of rural demographic ageing, both positive and negative, will be the focus of the third section of the chapter, with challenges and opportunities for rural areas associated with demographic ageing being reviewed.

PATTERNS OF DEMOGRAPHIC AGEING

Population Dynamics and Rural Population Ageing

Demographic or *population ageing* refers to changes in a population's age structure that result from the redistribution of persons among age groups.

It does, of course, need to be differentiated from individual ageing, referring to the progression of persons through the life course. When the share of persons in older age groups increases, a population is said to be ageing. When younger persons become relatively more numerous, populations are growing younger. Population ageing results from changes in the three components of population change: fertility; mortality; and migration, although the importance of each varies over time and across spatial regions. Long-term net out-migration of young adults is an important determinant of current rural ageing. Not only are relatively young persons removed from rural populations as a result of net out-migration, but they take their potential fertility with them when they leave. Much has been written about retirement migration to rural communities in both the UK (e.g. Warnes 1992) and US (e.g. Brown and Glasgow 2008), and this also affects age structure and population ageing. However, as will be discussed in this chapter, the immigration of pre-retirement-age adults also plays an important role in rural ageing. Rural ageing is also affected by increased longevity since both in-migrants and longer-term residents are ageing in place.

Who Are the Aged Population in the UK and US?

Before turning to a review of demographic trends, it is useful to define what 'old age' and who 'older people' are. In the UK, the most commonly used definition of 'old age' is the age at which an individual becomes eligible to receive a state pension, currently sixty for women and sixty-five for men.[1] Similarly, in the US, the most common definition of an 'older person' is one aged sixty-five or over, sixty-five being the age at which persons are eligible for Medicare and Social Security.[2] However, those in receipt of a state pension are not a homogenous group and with retirement occurring over a much broader age range than in previous generations, more people living into their eighties and nineties, and increasing numbers of people in their sixties, seventies and beyond living active, healthy lives it is now common to split the older population into sub-groups and refer to, for example, the 'young-old' and 'oldest-old'. Demographic data presented below for the UK and US will normally refer to 'older people' as those aged sixty-five and older and to the 'oldest old' as those aged eighty-five and older.

An Ageing Population in the UK

The median age of the UK's population increased throughout the twentieth century, due principally to increasing life expectancy associated with declining mortality rates and the survival into older age of large cohorts born during the 'baby booms' post–World Wars I and II and during the 1960s. Demographic ageing in the UK is projected to continue in the foreseeable future as the post–World War II and 1960s baby boomers age, as fertility rates continue to sit around replacement rate, as the age at which women have their first child continues to increase and a growing minority of women do not have children. The median age of the UK's population increased from 36.9 in 1997 to 39.2 in 2007 and is projected to increase to 40.0 by 2017. At the beginning of the twentieth century male life expectancy at birth in the UK was forty-five years and female life expectancy was forty-nine years. These figures had increased to seventy-six for men and eighty-one for women in 2002 (Matheson 2009). For the period 2006–2008 life expectancy at age sixty-five showed that the number of additional years men and women could expect to live were 17.4 and 20.0, respectively (Office for National Statistics 2010). Accordingly, the expected years in retirement are far higher now than for earlier generations. In 2007 the number of people over state pension age in the UK exceeded those aged under sixteen for the first time. Approximately 9.8 million people were aged sixty-five or over (16 per cent of the total population) and approximately 1.3 million people (2.1 per cent of the total population), were aged over eighty-five.

Population ageing in the UK can also be considered with reference to the Old Age Support Ratio (OASR). This is a measure of the number of working-age people against the number of people of state pension eligibility age. In the UK in 1972 the OASR stood at 3.5 and remained near this level until the early years of the twenty-first century. Even taking into account the changes to state pension eligibility age that will be phased in over the next three decades (see note 1), the OASR of the UK is predicted to drop to about 2.9 people of working age to each person above state pension eligibility age in 2032 (Dunnell 2008). The UK's workforce will age in the next twenty to forty years, with fewer people aged sixteen to forty-nine and more people aged fifty and older in the population. As these cohorts age there will be fewer people working and contributing to taxation revenue through earned income (although immigrants entering the labour market may substitute for some of the persons ageing out of the workforce and many retired individuals continue to pay income and other taxes). Although the OASR is *not* an indicator of economic support because it does not take into account early retirement, withdrawal from the paid labour market before state pension eligibility age due to ill health or caring responsibilities, or the numbers who chose to remain in paid employment after the age of sixty-five, it is an important indicator of ageing to consider in relation to the costs to the state of an ageing population. These costs will be discussed in the second section of the chapter.

Population Ageing in the US

In 1900, the average age of the US population was 22.9, and 4.1 per cent of the population was sixty-five and older. Since then, the US population has aged dramatically, reaching a median age of 37.4 in 2010 with over 13 per cent of persons being sixty-five or older, and 3.7 per cent of persons aged eighty-five or older. While the long-term trend in the US has been toward an ever-increasing level of average age, it should be noted that this increase was interrupted between the 1950s, 1960s and 1970s, reflecting the high fertility period of the post–World War II baby boom. During these three decades the median age declined by two years and only regained its 1950 level of thirty years in 1980. By the middle of the twenty-first century the US population's average age is projected to reach forty years with one in every twenty Americans being aged sixty-five or older.

As with the OASR, these ageing trends are reflected in the increasing ratio between older persons and persons in the prime working ages. In 1950 this ratio was fifteen and it had increased to twenty by 2010, the year in which the leading edge of the baby boom reached retirement age. According to the Congressional Research Service, there will be almost thirty-five older persons per one hundred persons in the prime working ages by 2030 when all of the baby boom cohorts have reached age sixty-five (Shrestha 2006). This increasing ratio raises questions about the Social Security system's solvency and about the sufficiency of labour supply to maintain the nation's rate of economic growth. However, the old age dependency ratio is only useful for longitudinal comparison if the retirement age is constant over time, and recent research indicates that this is not the case—although the age of eligibility for a Social Security pension may be 'fixed' by government the age at which individuals withdraw from the paid labour market is variable. In fact Gendell (2008) showed that men between the ages of sixty-five and sixty-nine increased their labour force participation rate from 27 per cent in 1994 to 34 per cent in 2007, while the corresponding rates for women aged sixty-five to sixty-nine were 18 per cent and 26 per cent, respectively. Accordingly, the greying of the baby boomers does not necessarily indicate an increase in dependency or a mass withdrawal of persons from active work.

In a low mortality rate country like the US, increases in the level of population ageing are principally associated with declining mortality because the majority of all deaths occur at ages sixty-five and older. Since fertility has been close to the replacement level for both whites and African Americans since 1980, further declines are unlikely. Hence, fertility will have little effect on future increases in ageing. In contrast, life expectancy among whites has increased from seventy-two years in 1970 to over seventy-seven years in 2000, and from sixty-four to almost seventy-two years among blacks (Haines and Steckel 2001). As Weeks (2005, 342) points out, 'At a life expectancy of 65 with replacement level fertility, the average age is 38; the average age rises to 41 as life expectancy increases to 80. The percentage of the population age 65 and older increases from 15 per cent to 24 per cent'.

RURAL AGEING: PATTERNS AND PROCESSES IN THE UK AND US

Across the UK and the US some subnational geographical units have an older population structure than others and population projections suggest that future ageing will be geographically uneven. Population ageing at any geographical scale is a response to locally specific relationships between rates of natural increase and migration. Ageing in the UK and US will now be considered with specific reference to rural patterns. Some reflections on the demographic processes that produce these patterns of rural ageing will then be presented.

Patterns of Rural Ageing in the UK

Variations in median age are evident across the four constituent countries of the UK and are also found at smaller geographical scales. In 2007 the lowest median ages in the UK were to be found in the largest population centres whilst the highest median ages were found in the less densely populated, often coastal and remote parts of the UK. This pattern is expected to continue for the foreseeable future. Official population projections[3] mapped in Blake (2009, 47) suggest that by 2017, for example, the population of eleven of the thirty-two local authority areas in Scotland will have a median age of between 45.9 and 55.6 (compared with a projected median of 42.7 for Scotland as whole) and that all but one of these areas (East Dumbartonshire) is defined as being predominantly remote or very remote rural using the Scottish Government's urban–rural definition (Scottish Government 2008b).

Further evidence that 'rural' ageing is more extreme than urban ageing in the UK is found when the proportion of the population falling into older age groups is considered at the local authority level, and when projections for the geographical distribution of older people in the medium term are considered. In 1997, with the notable exception of Northern Ireland, the local authority areas with the lowest proportion of their population aged sixty-five and older were most commonly found in the most urbanised areas of the UK such as East Central Scotland, Greater London, the M4 corridor (between London and South Wales), Lancashire and the Midlands of England. Many of these areas contain local authority areas that have had high fertility rates and positive rates of natural change in recent years. Many have experienced increased immigration of working-age populations from the European Unions' Accession 8 (A8) countries (Eastern and Central Europe) although, as Matheson (2009) reports, London remains by far the most popular destination for A8 migrants. For example, three of the ten local authorities in the UK with the highest total fertility rates between 1986 and 2006 were in Greater London and another three were in Lancashire (Tromans et al. 2008). The predominantly urban East Central Scotland local authority areas are projected to have positive rates of natural change between 2008 and 2033, higher than the projected national average rate of 1.1, whilst all the rural and remote rural authorities except Perth and Kinross (heavily influenced by the Edinburgh employment market) are expected to have negative rates of natural change (General Register Office for Scotland [GROS] 2010).

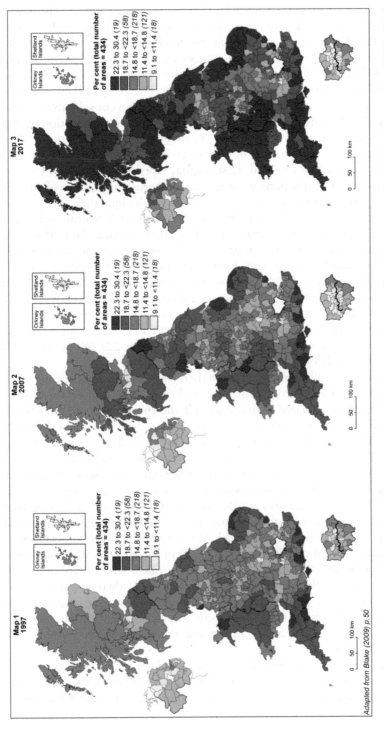

Figure 4.1 Maps showing the change in the proportion of the population aged sixty-five and over, by UK local authority, 1997, 2007 and 2017.

Figure 4.1 displays UK Office for National Statistics data, at the level of local authorities, and shows how the geographic location of the UK's older population has changed and is projected to change by 2017. It is clear that the most remote, peripheral local authority areas in the UK are those projected to have the highest proportions of their population, between 22 per cent and 34 per cent, aged sixty-five and over. For many of these areas this means that, in the next few years, they will witness a considerable increase in both the absolute number of older people and in the proportion of their population in the older age groups. The maps for 1997, 2007 and 2017 all show the highest proportions of over sixty-fives are to be found in coastal areas in the south of England, East Anglia, North Yorkshire and Conwyn in Wales. High proportions were also found across rural areas of the UK, notably peripheral rural areas such as the Scottish Highlands and southern Scotland, most of north-west England, northern and central Wales and, for 2007 and 2017, the eastern coast of Northern Ireland. From the standpoint of a rural perspective on demographic ageing, the pattern shown for 2017 is of considerable interest. Figure 4.1 also shows that only eleven local authority areas (out of 434) are projected to have a decline or no increase in the proportion of their population aged sixty-five and over between 2007 and 2017. These areas are concentrated in Greater London. One hundred and forty-eight local authorities (34 per cent) will likely see an increase of between 15 per cent and 27 per cent, and a further 221 (49 per cent) will see an increase between 27 per cent and 53 per cent.

Champion (2005) observed that there is a net exodus through out-migration of those aged seventy-five and over from remote rural areas, which may be associated with the second and third stages of Ford's (1993) later life migration typology. However, Blake (2009) predicts that rural areas, including many remote peripheral areas, will be strongly affected by the increasing proportion of the population aged eighty-five and over. For example, most of Northern Ireland, the Highlands, Northern Isles and Aberdeenshire in Scotland (remote and very remote rural areas) and the English local authority areas of Berwick-upon-Tweed in Northumberland, Hambleton in North Yorkshire, South Holland in Lincolnshire, Rutland, Daventry in Northamptonshire and East Cambridgeshire in Cambridgeshire (these areas are all classified as 'Rural-80' in the DEFRA Classification of Local Authority District and Unitary Authorities) will see an increase of between 54 and 85 per cent in the proportion of their population aged eighty-five and over. In the context of slow growth in younger age groups, the number of persons aged seventy-five and older ageing in place exceeds net out-migration of that age group and therefore the proportion of the oldest old increases.

Thus, rural areas of the UK are to witness interrelated aspects of demographic ageing: increases in the number and overall proportion of individuals in both the younger and the oldest subgroups of the older population.

The variety of challenges and opportunities to rural areas will be discussed in the final section of this chapter, while the reasons for historical and projected demographic ageing are considered in the following.

Patterns of Rural Ageing in the US

The percentage of the rural population at ages sixty-five and older (15 per cent) exceeds the urban percentage (12 per cent) in the United States.[4] Moreover, population ageing is more extreme in some rural environments than in others. Figure 4.2 maps the percentage of the population aged sixty-five and over, by county and state, in 2006. It shows that almost one in five persons is sixty-five or older in 25 per cent of US rural counties—these 25 per cent include the northern Great Plains, Florida, Appalachia and the upper Midwest. These older than average places can be characterised by their primary economic dependence on agriculture and natural resources and by recent population trends.

In nonmetro counties experiencing population decline in the 1990s, such as those in the northern Great Plains, the Mississippi Delta and Appalachia, almost 19 per cent of the population was sixty-five or older compared with less than 16 per cent for other nonmetro counties (562 of 2,292 nonmetro counties lost population during the 1990s). In the 37 per cent of all nonmetro counties classified as experiencing natural decrease (837 of 2,292 nonmetro counties had more deaths than births), 19 per cent of the population was sixty-five and older and in those classified as dependent on agriculture (420 of 2,292 nonmetro counties) over 18 per cent of the population was sixty-five and older. In rural counties known to be retirement destinations (274 of 2,292 nonmetro counties in 2000, following the ERS-USDA 2004 definition of rural retirement destinations as nonmetropolitan counties having at least 15 per cent net in-migration at ages sixty and older) the proportion was 17 per cent. In contrast, persistently poor nonmetro counties, those with 20 per cent or higher poverty rates consistently since 1970, have lower than average levels of population ageing associated with higher minority percentages, lower educational attainment, and higher fertility rates (Brown and Glasgow 2008; National Advisory Committee on Rural Health 2008).[5]

Aside from their extreme level of ageing, nonmetro counties experiencing natural population decrease and counties attracting older in-migrants contrast in important ways. Natural decrease counties, 37 per cent of all nonmetro counties, had more deaths than births between 2000 and 2005 (Cromartie 2007). The natural decrease counties increased in number from 610 in 1990 to 839 in 1999, i.e. from 27 per cent to 37 per cent of all nonmetro counties. As can be seen in Figure 4.3, natural decrease is concentrated in the Great Plains, the Midwestern Corn Belt and in Appalachia.

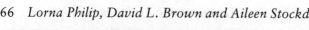

Figure 4.2 Percentage of the population of the United States aged sixty-five and over, by county and state, 2006.
Source: US Bureau of the Census (2006).

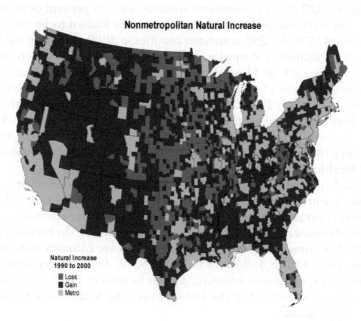

Figure 4.3 Natural population decrease in nonmetropolitan counties.
Source: Johnson (2005).

Natural Decrease and Population Ageing in the UK and US

Natural decrease in any rural area, be it in the UK, the US or any other part of the economically developed world, results from the long-term net out-migration of young adults. Losing young adults distorts the age structure both directly, by withdrawing the migrants themselves from a population, and indirectly since most young adults are of an age where if they do not already have children they could be expected to have them soon. Hence, regardless of the fertility rate of remaining young adults, the distorted age structure results in relatively few births, especially in comparison with deaths experienced at the oldest ages. The population profile of long-term natural decrease areas becomes top-heavy: ageing is thus directly linked to natural decrease as can be illustrated with reference to the Western Isles (Eilean Siar) in Scotland. Mid-2008 estimates put the proportion of the population aged sixty-five and older in the Western Isles at 21.1 per cent, compared to a Scottish figure of 16.6 per cent (GROS 2009a). Between 2008 and 2033 the projected increase in the population of pensionable age and over in the Western Isles is 23.6 per cent (GROS 2010). Over the same period the total population is predicted to drop by 4 per cent. This change will occur over a period when the rate of natural change is predicted to be -12.5 per cent and the net migration gain 8.4 per cent.

Natural population decrease is typically framed as a social problem. Johnson and Rathge (2006) show how age-selective out-migration has drained the Great Plains of the US, where natural decrease is centred, of its entry labour pool. Between 1980 and 2000, their analysis shows that agriculturally dependent parts of the Great Plains lost over one-third of their entry-age workforce via net out-migration, while only about a quarter of entry-age workers were lost in the region's other rural areas lacking such heavy dependence on farming. They comment on the 'downward cycle of population loss' in agriculturally dependent natural decrease areas, and note that 'the prospects for the future viability of many Great Plains communities are not encouraging' (214). In the state of Nebraska, for example, forty-one of ninety-three counties had fewer births than deaths during the 1990s, and twenty-three of these forty-one natural decrease counties also had net out-migration. None of these declining counties had even one place with at least twenty-five hundred people, the US census definition of urban (Diechert 2001). Most of these natural decrease counties had experienced population losses for decades.

Migration and Population Ageing: Pre-Retirement Migration in the UK

Uren and Goldring (2007) noted that geographical variations in population ageing are primarily attributable to three factors: the migration of people of working age, migration in the older age cohorts and regional variations in fertility and mortality rates. These factors, and others, have already and will continue in the future to contribute to rural ageing. Post-retirement migration is known to favour amenity destinations (Warnes 1992), including coastal and rural areas, and the importance of this type of migration is reflected in Lowe and Ward's (2007b) rural typology which includes a *retirement retreat* category (typically coastal areas where retirement-related services such as health, social care and leisure are important components of the local economy). However, for rural England, the Commission for Rural Communities (CRC) noted in the 2008 State of the Countryside report that while 'there are very large gains of people aged 0–14, 30–44 and 45–64 in rural areas (. . .) the picture is reversed for the 15–29 age group. For people over 65, migration to rural areas is also significant, but it is much lower than the middle aged groups, showing that retirement to rural areas is not the major factor in internal migration' (CRC 2008b, 18). This observation concurs with Uren and Goldring's (2007) national assessment that, at the local authority level in the UK, the age distribution of the local population is most affected by the migration flows of adults aged between twenty and fifty-nine. Their analysis of data from the Office for National Statistics Longitudinal Study (1971–2001) for England and Wales concluded that 'differences in the proportion of older people residing in different regions are mainly the result of people migrating earlier in their life course rather than at older ages' (Uren and Goldring 2007, 36). This is one way in which the process of rural ageing in the UK differs from that being experienced in the US.

Of course, there are some rural areas in the UK where retirement migration flows are significant, but for many rural areas the impact of retirement migration inflow is less than the impact of an inflow of middle aged, pre-retirement persons. The expectation of retirement prompts behavioural changes such as a change of residence, identified by Bures (1997) as migration in the *retirement transition* life course period. There is also evidence of retirement transition migration into rural communities (Stockdale 2006b), a phenomenon which has an effect upon rural demographic ageing. Drawing upon illustrative material from the Highlands and Islands of Scotland, one of the most peripheral rural areas of the UK, relationships between pre-retirement-age in-migration and population ageing are now considered.

With limited opportunities for higher education and more numerous and varied employment opportunities available further south, school-leavers and other young adults have left the Highlands and Islands in large numbers for many years. The mainland Highlands as a whole have witnessed overall population growth since the 1951–1961 intercensal period, with the 2001–2006 rate of 3.1 per cent (Highland Council 2008) being the highest rate observed since the reversal of net population decline in the region began. Loss of young adults in the Highlands and Islands today is taking place against a backdrop of net in-migration of people aged forty-four and younger, although these net gains are not enough to stem overall population decline in all localities. For example, Caithness is predicted to have a -8.4 per cent decline in population between 2006 and 2031 whilst Ross and Cromarty's population is expected to increase by 11.4 per cent over the same period (Highland Council 2008.) GROS migration data for 2001 to 2008 report that almost half of all migrants into the Highlands over the period came from outwith Scotland, a sizeable number (15 per cent in 2006–2007) came from overseas and almost a third of the within-Scotland immigrants came from the cities of Aberdeen, Edinburgh and Glasgow. This suggests that counterurbanisation migration is an important component of population growth (GROS 2009b). While the youngest cohort of adults may be smaller than would be expected in a 'normal' population profile, the influx of older-young to early middle aged people, accounting for 74 per cent of in-migrants between 2001 and 2006 (Highland Council 2008), acts as a counterbalance. Despite this, the population has aged since 1981 but, more importantly, is predicted to age at an unprecedented rate in the next couple of decades (see Table 4.1).

Substantial numbers of pre-retirement-age adults have been moving into the Highlands and Islands for a number of decades and it is probable that many of these immigrants will have stayed in the area and will age in place. With negative rates of natural change, continued out-migration of young adults and inflows of younger adults predicted to continue; an assumption that current incomers will age in place as earlier cohorts of migrants have done; and national increases in life expectancy at age sixty-five, it is unsurprising that the population of the Highlands and Islands is predicted to age considerably in the next twenty years. Interestingly, the relatively low numbers of in-migrants of retirement age and over, approximately five hundred people between 2001 and 2006 or 6 per cent of all in-migrants (Highland Council 2008), only make a modest contribution to population ageing. As noted in Table 4.1, the population of pensionable age is predicted to

Table 4.1   Components of Population Change, 2008–2033

Area	Natural change	Net migration	% projected population change	% projected change in children (0–15)	% projected change in working ages	% projected change in pensionable ages
Highland	-1.5	19.1	17.6	7.6	8.8	50.3
Eilean Siar	-12.5	8.4	-4.15	-17.4	-11.7	23.6
Orkney Islands	-6.0	18.1	12.1	-1.2	1.5	50.7
Shetland Islands	-2.0	-5.5	-7.5	-32.5	-18.5	52.2
Scotland	1.1	6.2	7.3	-1.5	2.2	31.4

Source: Compiled from data in GROS (2010, 10, 20).

increase by over 50 per cent in the Highland, Orkney Islands and Shetland Islands local authority areas, rates well above that projected for Scotland as a whole.

Migration and Population Ageing: Retirement Migration in the US.

As shown earlier, population ageing in rural areas of the UK is most commonly associated with the immigration of pre-retirement-age adults who then age in place. In the US, in contrast, retirement-age migration into rural areas is more pronounced. Regardless of the overall direction of urban–rural migration during the last forty years, rural areas of the US have experienced net in-migration of those between the ages of sixty and seventy-four. Rural retirement-age migration[6] seems somewhat insensitive to the period-specific economic swings that influence the direction of rural–urban migration at other ages. Hence, while other rural areas are weathering the storm of economic downturns, retirement destinations continue to benefit from the infusion of financial and human capital older in-migrants bring to destination communities. What processes result in the establishment of rural retirement destinations, or to state the research question more specifically, why are some rural communities more likely than others to have high rates of net in-migration at older ages?

While it is tempting to focus on immediate, short-term explanations, the formation and establishment of rural retirement destinations is an historical process that has unfolded over time. Accordingly, the phenomenon should be examined through an historical lens, such as *path dependency*. Path dependency states that events at any point are shaped in specific and systematic ways by historical trajectories. Path dependency is about probabilities, not predetermination (Gartland 2005). It is about uncovering historical parameters that influence the current situation. In other words, a place's history can either limit future options or enhance them. Path dependency includes the idea of 'branching points', events or circumstances that are capable of altering historical paths (Elster 1978).

When applied to the establishment of nonmetro retirement communities, path dependency suggests that the process is initiated by a set of preconditions that subsequently result in self-sustaining flows of older age migrants. Path dependency is present if actions taken at one point in time affect options available to communities in the future. Since retirement-age migration is typically an amenity-motivated move, the most obvious precondition for becoming a retirement migration destination is that places should have attractive environmental amenities such as mild weather, lakes and shoreline and a diverse landscape (McGranahan 1999). Indeed, research shows that retirement destinations as a group score higher on an additive scale of natural amenities compared with other types of counties (McGranahan 1999; Brown et al. 2010).

However, recent research also shows that most nonmetro counties that score high on the amenities scale do *not* have high rates of net in-migration

Source: ERS-USDA (2004)

Figure 4.4   Retirement destination counties, 2000.
Source: ERS-USDA (2004).

at older ages. Hence, the research question then is why do some high amenity areas attract older migrants while most do not? Using a path dependency framework, Brown et al. (2010) showed that only those high-amenity
counties that commodified their environmental resources by investing in
tourism and recreation infrastructure were likely to develop into retirement
destinations in the future. The logic behind this developmental process is
that retirement migration, similar to other forms of migration, operates via
social networks, and these networks begin to form when families visit rural
communities as tourists. Since some visitors return to resorts year after
year, they build durable relationships with these places. In addition, visitors
build strong connections with other recurrent tourists who they get to know
during summer vacations. Moreover, visitation is often an intergenerational
experience with parents or grandparents buying or renting summer homes
and younger generations joining them for some period of time each year. As
a result of this network-building process, some recurrent visitors establish
permanent residence in their former vacation community around the time
of retirement. Once a community gains visibility as a retirement destination, other persons who are seeking a retirement community, but who have
never visited particular places earlier in life, also move in. Since the process also involves intergenerational ties, it can be expected to continue over
time as parents recruit their own children when they reach retirement age.
Statistical analysis provided strong support for the hypothesized process
discussed earlier. Cromartie and Nelson (2009) observe that this process

is likely to contribute to future population ageing in nonmetro areas. They contend that the migration of baby boom cohorts will favour rural America because of scenic amenities and the low-cost housing. They conclude that if this generation follows similar migration patterns as its predecessors, the rural population aged fifty-five to seventy-five will increase by 30 per cent between 2010 and 2020.

IMPLICATIONS OF AN AGEING RURAL POPULATION

Population ageing in the rural UK and the US is associated with high environmental amenity values and peripheral areas, but quite different patterns and processes drive demographic ageing in diverse locations, and the implications of ageing also vary. We will now review some of the implications of rural ageing in the UK and US, highlighting similarities and differences that could influence rural areas and the older people who live there in decades to come.

In the UK, population ageing is most often cast as a problem with more old people being portrayed in the media as a burden on society, placing demands upon the tax payer through the state pension and more demands being placed upon health and social care services (e.g. BBC News 7.7.10 report about 'unsustainable' pensions in Europe and BBC News 31.3.10 report about population ageing posing a 'huge challenge' to health). The proposal to bring forward the date at which state pension eligibility age will reach sixty-eight in the UK, announced in the June 2010 Budget, reflects these concerns. While it is true that ageing will bring financial costs at a time when the number and percentage of economically active people declines (a reduction in the economic support ratio), older people in rural communities across the UK can, and do already, make a positive contribution to society as, for example, volunteers, tax payers and (unpaid) carers. This point is commonly overlooked by the media and political commentators.

In the US, population ageing in rural areas tends to be cast in a more positive light than in the UK. Rural demographic ageing has been shown to stimulate economic development and the housing market but at the same time it can be a drain on public services and place demands on fragile housing markets (Glasgow and Brown 2008). Drawing upon examples from the UK and the US, we will now consider some of the economic impacts ageing has in rural areas, public sector challenges associated with rural ageing and the positive contribution that older rural people can make to rural society.

Economic Effects of Ageing in Rural Areas

The UK's older population today is more affluent than previous generations were (Lowe and Speakman 2006b). Many older people have occupational and other private pensions, savings and investments, and the impacts of inheriting financial bequests from parents has had a significant effect upon many middle-aged and older people. For example, throughout the 1990s and most of the 2000s the middle classes benefitted from the increases in UK house prices upon the death of elderly relatives. The impact of the current economic downturn on house prices and the increasing costs of, for example, nursing home fees, which are often financed by selling an older person's house, upon intergenerational flows of capital is uncertain. An increasingly affluent older rural population could have notable positive effects upon the rural economy if they spend their 'grey pound' locally. For example, older people may want to make use of local shops and leisure services, to employ local tradesmen, to buy local food at farmers' markets and farm shops, support cultural events and be willing to pay for preventative health care services, all of which could help to support the existing labour market and commercial sector and create a demand for new jobs in rural areas. There is, however, no evidence to date to confirm whether or not older people as a whole buy locally and use local companies or if their local spend is the same as that of the rural population as a whole. However, previous UK research has suggested that retired in-migrants display greater patronage of local rural shops and therefore have the potential to stimulate local markets (Findlay et al. 2001). Considerable economic benefits could therefore accrue to popular migration destinations, especially to those where migrants age in place and retain patterns of consumer behaviour established pre-retirement in later life.

Despite the overall picture of increased affluence amongst the UK's older rural population, a sizeable minority live on very low incomes, with many completely reliant upon the state pension, disability benefits and various means-tested programmes. From an analysis of data from the British Household Panel Survey (BHPS), Gilbert, Philip and Shucksmith (2006) observed that older people in remote rural areas have a higher likelihood of living on a low income than those who live in accessible rural areas. Analysis of the 1999 wave of the BHPS (the most recent date for which BHPS data with urban, accessible rural and remote rural identifiers are available) showed that the proportion of income obtained by those aged sixty-five and over from private pension is highest in accessible rural areas (Philip and Gilbert 2007a, 739). The authors also found that, regardless of geographical area or age, a higher proportion of women than men fall into the low-income category (defined as half-median income) and that women of state pension age and older in accessible and remote rural areas are more likely to have low incomes than their non-rural counterparts. Thus, they are more likely to rely upon the public sector for services such as home care and residential care in later life because they lack the means to pay for these services privately. Low income amongst the older female population is particularly important became women outnumber men two to one in the older age cohorts. Many remote rural areas are low-wage economies: low income during the course of one's working life can make saving for retirement difficult, if not impossible, and leave one reliant upon the state pension and other benefits after retirement. As demographic ageing in many remote rural areas in the UK is associated with ageing in place, including the ageing in place of persons who migrated in middle age and who are thus likely to have been part of the low-wage remote rural economy for at least part of their working life, low incomes amongst the older remote rural population is likely to remain a concern for the foreseeable future. Daily living costs such as the cost of locally purchased groceries, petrol and heating fuel are often higher in remote rural areas than they are in more accessible rural and urban areas. While these costs affect all individuals, community cohesion may be strained if long-term older residents are less well off than incomers of the same age.

In US retirement destinations, older in-migration is sometimes characterised as 'grey gold' (Glasgow and Brown 2008). Older in-migrants are typically better off financially than longer-term residents, and hence bring a cash infusion to the community. In contrast, ageing resulting from generations-long net out-migration of young adults and their children is typically framed as a social problem, an accompaniment to long-term social and economic stagnation and decline. However, the 'sunny' situation in retirement destination communities is not as clear-cut as it might appear. Studies that have examined direct income impacts have examined the induced consumer demand in the retail and service sectors and the expected fiscal costs of an older population. These studies consistently show that retiree in-migration induces about 0.5 jobs per migrant, that public expenditure increases per migrant are in the range of $35–40,000 per year and that older in-migrants pay more taxes than they cost in additional services (cf. Stallman, Deller and Shields 1999; Serow 2003).

However, for every positive impact retirement migration has upon rural communities in the US, be it social, political or economic, it is possible to identify groups in the community who are disadvantaged by the very activities of the older in-migrants that are viewed positively by many other groups. For example, older in-migrants have a positive impact on housing prices and real estate taxes. This is beneficial to real estate brokers, banks and construction companies, but not to low- and moderate-income teachers, nurses or service workers who tend to be displaced from the local housing market and forced to live far from work, or even from relatives in the case of persons born and raised in the community.

Challenges Associated with Rural Ageing

The older population is healthier and more active than ever before, but as the rural population ages, and the numbers of the oldest old increase, there will be increasing demands upon health care providers. In the UK, the National Health Service (NHS) is likely to bear the brunt of increased demands in rural communities as private health care provision is concentrated in urban areas. Although most people who live in rural communities do not expect to have specialist in-patient facilities located on their door-steps, they do expect primary care services (e.g. GP, pharmacies, physio-therapy, podiatry, etc.) to be reasonably accessible. There are real challenges to the NHS as a universal service provider to ensure minimally acceptable levels of health care to dispersed, small rural populations, especially to older rural people who are the most likely demographic group to experi-ence complex long-term conditions that require ongoing, and occasionally acute, medical attention.

Research undertaken in the Highlands of Scotland and reported by Farmer et al. (2010) found conflicting opinions about care home provi-sion amongst older people, health and social care practitioners and ser-vice managers and politicians, which illustrate the difficulties rural areas can face in providing care for older people who are unable to live inde-pendently at home. For example, older people wanted to have access to a small, local care home so that they could stay in their home community. Health and social care practitioners agreed that staying in the home com-munity was important for older people but it might not be possible, espe-cially for dementia sufferers. Service managers and politicians consider small care home to be very expensive to run. They thought that services need to provide the highest gain for the largest number of people and that 'innovative solutions' (ibid., 278) and sheltered housing should be pro-vided. On a more positive note, increasing demands for health care asso-ciated with demographic ageing could have positive impacts upon rural labour markets, safeguarding existing professional jobs (often amongst the best paid jobs in rural areas) and stimulating demands for new posi-tions in the caring professions.

In the UK, local authorities have a statutory obligation to provide non-medical care such as home or residential care to those formally assessed as needing such assistance, but providing these services to rural communities is difficult. The long-standing high rates of out-migration by young adults from rural areas means that, as people age, their adult children are unlikely to live nearby and are therefore unable to provide the assistance with daily living that would allow their ageing parent(s) to remain living indepen-dently in their own home. Mid- and later-life incomers to rural areas in the UK may not have family close by either, although, as noted elsewhere in this chapter, there is evidence that they do in many retirement destination counties in the US. Policy in the UK promotes older people living indepen-dently at home but social care jobs are often low paid and it can be difficult to fill such positions, especially in rural contexts.[7] There can come a time when informal care and support from family, friends and neighbours is not enough. An older rural person's move into supported accommodation very often necessitates leaving their home community and travelling some distance to a care home that can provide them with the support they need. The impact this has on the individual who has to move and the friends they leave behind can be profound.

Few studies in the US have examined the economic costs or benefits to rural communities over a long time horizon as older in-migrants age in place. Many localities are 'betting' that older in-migrants will move away as they grow older and as their social and economic contributions to their home community diminish in relationship to their costs. However, research also shows that many older in-migrants are reuniting with adult children at the same time that they are making an amenity motivated move. Brown and Glasgow (2008) found that one-third of in-migrants had at least one adult child living within a half-hour drive of their new rural residence. Accordingly, it is unlikely that these in-migrants will leave in later life. Since they have already moved to be closer to their children, where would they go later on? Hence, it is important that communities attracting older in-migrants take a longer-term view of economic costs and benefits to ensure that they both capitalise upon what older in-migrants can bring and plan effectively for the challenges these in-migrants may create in the future.

Positive Aspects of Demographic Ageing in Rural Areas

The stereotypical image of older age groups is often one of inactive, unproductive and frail dependents (Butler 1989). However, it is more common than ever before for those in their seventies, eighties and even nineties to live active and productive lives. These individuals can make a very positive contribution to rural communities. In the UK and US many older rural resident are volunteers and are active in local community development.

Using data from the Scottish Household Survey, Philip et al. (2003) found that rural fifty-five- to sixty-four-year-olds were the most likely of all age groups across the country to give up some time for charity and local groups and that the rural over seventy-fives had the highest average weekly hours volunteered of all age groups in Scotland. These older rural volunteers are involved in activities such as transport and escort services (often for the benefit of other older people and particularly important in areas where public transport provision is poor), local gala weeks, staffing local charity shops and providing befriending services. Through local branches of (inter)national organisations such as Probus, Lions and Rotary Clubs older people can use the skills they developed in their working lives in activities such as business mentoring and local fund-raising campaigns. Older rural people are active in endogenous development, engaging in activities that can help their rural community be seen as what M. Woods (2005) refers to as a 'good citizen' community.

UK research (DTI 2000) has suggested that older people's aspirations are believed to be increasingly entrepreneurial compared to previous generations, and self-employment, already much higher in rural and urban areas of the UK, is more prevalent amongst older workers (A. Green 2006). Rural areas with net migration gains of middle-aged adults could capitalise on an influx of economically active 'young old' incomers: middle-aged and older in-migrants have been identified as a group likely to set up new small businesses (Oughton, Wheelock and Baines 2003) and business start-ups by older age groups are more likely to survive than those started by younger people (Loretto and White 2006; see Chapter 8 in this volume for a discussion of social entrepreneurship).

In the US, challenges and opportunities associated with population ageing are closely related. In fact, most opportunities also seem to raise questions and challenges. For example, while it is known that older in-migrants are active volunteers in destination communities, a well-appreciated advantage to the host community, it may also diminish the demand for paid professional workers, thereby reducing a community's ability to attract and retain well-qualified younger people who seek jobs in professions such as accountancy, law, planning and civil engineering that depend upon government contracts for their livelihood. Older in-migrants often take positions of leadership and energize the local arts and cultural scene. However, research indicates that they are sometimes insensitive to local ways of doing things, and can attempt to impose their tastes and preferences on the community. Brown and Glasgow (2008) found that older in-migrants are often politically active in their new communities, and often compete for power with the more established political elite. Again, whether this is judged as being good or bad depends on one's position in the community.

It is ironic that older in-migration is viewed more positively in the US, where older persons are much more likely to be on their own economically than is true in the UK with its more developed welfare and health care systems. In fact, many state governments have explicit policies to attract older migrants to their rural communities (Reeder 1998). However, since pensions and care are so much more limited in the US, communities experiencing demographic ageing have much less exposure to financial risks associated with older residents than do their UK counterparts. They are simply not as obliged to care for the indigent and disabled as is true in nations with well-developed welfare states. Accordingly, the fact that older in-migration is selective of persons who are relatively well off means that many communities view older in-migrants as 'grey gold' and are willing to 'bet' that they will leave before their contributions to community diminish below their costs.

CONCLUSIONS

Whilst demographic ageing is a phenomenon affecting the UK and US as a whole, there are distinct patterns and processes associated with demographic ageing in the *rural* areas of both nations. Our review of official statistics has shown that ageing and projected ageing will be particularly noticeable in the more remote rural parts of the UK. In the US the pattern is less universal: poorer rural areas are ageing at lower rates than those that are more affluent and attractive retirement destinations, and places with chronic long -term population decline have had relatively old populations for decades. We have shown that migration has a clear impact on rural population ageing in both nations. In some regions of the US, rural demographic ageing is closely associated with retirement-age migration. In the UK, migration has an important role to play in shaping the regional and subregional geographies of ageing, but it is pre-retirement-age in-migration and the ageing *in situ* of those who moved to rural areas in the economically active age cohorts rather than post-retirement migration that is likely to be of most importance. In the US the rural population is ageing because of out-migration of younger persons, in-migration of retirement-age persons and ageing in place of both longer-term residents and older in-movers. As the US is large and diverse, not all of these processes contribute to population ageing to the same degree in all regions.

Understanding the impact of demographic ageing on rural communities is important for a number of reasons. In the UK, because remote rural areas are ageing more rapidly than the rest of the country, they may provide a 'test-bed' of how the country as a whole may respond to national demographic ageing in coming decades. The economic impacts of demographic ageing could be profound in both the UK and the US, but there are lessons to be learnt in the UK from the US experience, where a more positive outlook about the impacts of an older population, especially an older population in areas attracting retirement-age migrants, contrasts with the largely negative 'pensions and care costs' view of ageing commonly promulgated in the UK. As we have suggested, rural areas have much to gain from an active older population. Capitalising upon the economic and social potential of older rural persons will help rural communities respond to demographic ageing in the future. However, we have also observed that for every community and individual advantage associated with population ageing, there are challenges. Communities and regions need to take a balanced, long-term view of ageing to maximize the benefits and minimize the costs.

5 Conceptualizing Contemporary Immigrant Integration in the Rural United States and United Kingdom

Philomena de Lima, Pilar A. Parra and Max J. Pfeffer

INTRODUCTION

Immigration is one of the most widely discussed and debated issues globally in the twenty-first century. It represents an important contemporary social transformation, linking nations and diverse peoples across and within national boundaries. Between 1985 and 2005, the Global Commission on International Migration (GCIM) estimated that approximately two hundred million individuals were residing outside their country of birth, of these the largest numbers are hosted by Europe, followed by Asia and then North America (GCIM 2005; United Nations 2009; see also Fix et al. 2009).

Until recently, the United States, Canada and Australia have been described as 'immigration' countries, and contrasted with countries such as the United Kingdom, which have historically been characterised as predominantly 'emigration' countries. These historical experiences, as well as the different immigration policies that have evolved, have undoubtedly shaped policies and discourses on immigration and immigrants in both the US and UK (Pennix, Spencer and Van Hear 2008). Nevertheless, more geographical areas, often beyond the urban or metropolitan areas, are experiencing immigration of diverse groups than at any time in recent history. The dispersal of immigrants across the landscape creates challenges for both rural communities that have little experience with foreigners and immigrants who must navigate their new environs without a support base provided by a large and well-established community of co-ethnics.

The purpose of this chapter is to establish the distinctiveness of contemporary immigrant integration in the rural US and UK and to present a conceptual framework to identify key factors needed to foster integration in communities with relatively few immigrants. The characteristics of immigrants, the rural context and public policy can combine to lead to the exclusion of immigrants from access to the full range of needed public goods and services, often leaving them reliant on informal and contingent sources of employment, housing and social support. The capacity of rural communities and institutions, which have hitherto been unused to immigration, to adapt to increasing cultural diversity suggests the importance of taking into account spatial context in trying to understand the immigrant experience of integration in the rural US and the UK. For this reason the sociology of immigrant integration must emphasize context specificity. The integration of immigrants into the receiving societies is contingent on specific conditions and contexts. In elaborating a framework for understanding 'integration' in rural areas, the chapter will stress the importance of integration as a dynamic and ongoing process between immigrants and members of the host communities.

The chapter begins with an overview of contemporary immigration trends in the rural US and UK. It then elaborates a conceptual framework to help make sense of research on the integration of immigrants into the social and economic life of rural communities, and follows this with a discussion of two cases: northern Scotland in the UK, and upstate New York in the US. The chapter concludes by arguing that migrant experiences and integration are contingent on context.

BACKGROUND: CHANGING IMMIGRATION TRENDS

It is widely acknowledged that immigrants are a pervasive part of the contemporary US and UK. Stories about immigration are regularly found in the media and encounters with immigrants are common, sometimes even in the most unexpected locations. Although accessing accurate data in both national contexts can be problematic, in this section we present the main existing sources of evidence on contemporary immigration.

UK Immigration Trends

Pennix, Spencer and Van Hear (2008, 2) report that Europe experienced a particularly steep rise in immigrants 'from an estimated 23 million in 1985 (United Nations, 1998: 1) to more than 56 million, or 7.7 per cent of the total European population in 2000 (IOM 2003: 29)'. Whilst it is recognised that the history and geography of migration in European countries is diverse and countries such as the UK have been recipients of international migrants over a long period of time, it is only since the 1980s that the UK and a number of other European countries have transformed from being primarily emigrant countries to immigration countries (Pennix, Spencer and Van Hear 2008; Somerville, Sriskandarajah and Latorre 2009). This transformation, it is argued, has been vital in shaping much of the discourse on international migration in Europe generally, as well as in the UK, and is contrasted with the so-called experiences of the long-standing immigration countries, the US, Canada and Australia (Pennix, Spencer and Van Hear 2008).

In the UK, an absence of a consistent system for recording people who enter and leave the country together with the use of a variety of data sources that employ inconsistent concepts in the context of changing policy and legislation are the main barriers in accessing accurate data on stocks and flow of migrants (Dobson et al. 2001; General Register Office for Scotland [GROS] 2009c; Office for National Statistics 2009). The UK has had a long history of immigration with a number of different 'flows' of migrants responding to particular contextual factors which include, *inter alia*, labour shortages, policy and legislation changes in the UK and the European Union, the enlargement of the EU and economic and political upheavals globally. These flows have included migrants from a range of different countries since the beginning of the twentieth century—for example, migrants from Ireland, Central and East Europe in the immediate post-war period in response to labour shortages; West Indies and Caribbean in 1950s and 1960s; India and Pakistan in the late 1960s to early 1970s; and Bangladesh and the African commonwealth in the early 1980s (Stillwell and Duke-Williams 2005, 13–14). In addition, there has also been immigration from the so-called 'old' commonwealth countries such as Canada, Australia and New Zealand and, more recently, asylum and refugee flows from countries such as Somalia, Afghanistan, China and Iraq as well as migration from Eastern Europe, Poland in particular. However, as described earlier, until the mid-1980s the UK was considered to be a net exporter of people. Somerville, Sriskandarajah and Latorre (2009) highlight that it was mainly in the last decade that there has been a marked increase in immigration fuelled in part by economic growth since the mid-1990s, and boosted by mobility from the Accession 8 (A8) Eastern European countries (Czech Republic, Estonia, Latvia, Lithuania, Hungary, Poland, Slovakia and Slovenia), following enlargement of the European Union in 2004 and the guaranteeing of free movement and labour rights (see Champion and Brown, this volume).

Between 1997 and 2007, net immigration contributed 1.8 million to the UK population. It is estimated that since the mid-1990s net immigration exceeded one hundred thousand persons per year with numbers exceeding two hundred thousand in some years since 2000. These figures include workers, asylum seekers, those coming to join their families and students. Overall there were approximately 6.6 million immigrants (11 per cent of the UK population) in 2008 and around 4.2 million (7 per cent) non-British nationals, representing a threefold increase in both categories since the 1980s (Somerville and Sumption 2009). Between 2004 and 2008, non-British nationals were reported to have increased by 41 per cent, nearly half of which (45 per cent) was attributed to the arrival of A8 nationals from Eastern Europe and just over half (52 per cent) to nationals from outside the EU (Office for National Statistics 2009, 44).

Migration of A8 and A2 (Bulgaria and Romania, EU members since January 2008) nationals into the UK is one of the most significant phenomena in contemporary migration into the UK (Pollard, Latorre and Sriskandarajah 2008; Somerville and Sumption 2009). Estimates of the total numbers of A8 and A2 who arrived in the UK from May 2004 to 2008 vary from one million to 1.4 million (Broomby 2009; Fix et al. 2009; Pollard, Latorre and Sriskandarajah 2008). The Polish were the largest foreign nationality group, having moved up from being the thirteenth largest group among nationals from outside the EU.

Increase in immigration has also resulted in a number of distinctive features that characterise the recent waves of migration. One of these is the circular nature of migration especially amongst the East Europeans: several trips may be undertaken between the home country and the immigration country annually or on a seasonal basis. Recent migrants are also more diverse and spatially dispersed across the UK landscape, leading Vertovec (2006) to coin the term 'super-diversity' to describe the diverse countries of origin represented amongst immigrants, not all of whom have colonial links with Britain.

US Immigration Trends

The number of immigrants living in the US is larger now than at any time in its history. During the 1990s, more than thirteen million people moved to the US, an average of one million immigrants per year. About thirty-eight million immigrants (i.e. persons born in foreign countries) lived in the US in 2007, more than 12 per cent of the total population (Grieco 2009). Over the past decade, it is estimated that between seven hundred thousand to nine hundred thousand legal immigrants and at least three hundred thousand to five hundred thousand unauthorized immigrants arrived each year, although this volume has reduced in recent years due to the economic recession and enhanced border enforcement efforts.[1] The decline of the volume of unauthorized arrivals is almost entirely due to reduced Mexican flows from an average of about 500,000 per year during the 2000–2005 period to about 150,000 per year during the 2007–2009 time span (Passel and Cohn 2011). Under this scenario the foreign born will account for 15 per cent of the total US population by the year 2050 (Pfeffer 2008).

Immigration on this scale has not been seen in the US since the early twentieth century. Although the nation has experienced heavy immigration before, today the composition of the migrant streams is very different. As in the UK, the contemporary immigrant population is more diverse in terms of national origin, culture and ethnicity. This diversity is attributable to immigration policy changes in 1965 that allocated immigration quotas more broadly to countries throughout the world (Alba and Nee 2003; Kritz and Gurak 2004). Before 1965 immigration had been heavily European because immigration quotas had permitted larger numbers of immigrants from established sending areas in Europe and specifically excluded immigration from some other world regions. After the implementation of amendments to the Immigration and Nationality Act in 1965, the largest number of immigrants came from Asia and Latin

America. Some observers have dubbed the post-1965 immigration the 'globalisation wave' (Kritz and Gurak 2004).

The dispersal of immigrants across the American landscape became apparent in the 1990s. Although large numbers of immigrants continue to stream into the so-called gateway cities (New York, Los Angeles, Miami, Chicago), substantial numbers of immigrants settle in a wide range of rural and urban destinations that had previously recorded few immigrants. Light (2006) argues that the concentration of immigrants in traditional immigrant gateways reached a tipping point at which wages fell and taxes increased to support public services for a larger (often needy) population, housing prices increased and anti-immigrant sentiments grew. Amnesty for unauthorized immigrants under the Immigration Reform and Control Act of 1986 also made it easier for immigrants to move throughout the country (Massey et al. 2002). All of these factors encouraged immigrants to look for more favourable destinations.

CONCEPTUALIZING IMMIGRANT INTEGRATION

The changing trends and settlement patterns of migrants from abroad has led to a variety of discourses at national and local levels. Some are closely linked to issues of national identity and the type of nation people imagine themselves to be. These discourses have also focused on the ways in which nations might incorporate migrants from overseas, leading to the emergence of terms to describe the process and or their outcome of adjustment in the societies they find themselves in. Terms such as *multiculturalism, integration, social cohesion, assimilation* and so on are used to describe the process of adjustment of immigrants and are all highly contested, with a particular concern about the tendency towards outright incorporation within the majority culture that some concepts are perceived as implying (see Boswell 2003; Castles et al. 2002; Favell 2005; Parekh 2000; Pennix, Spencer and Van Hear 2008; Spencer et al. 2007). Given the changing trends in migration, Castles et al. (2002) argue the need to move away from using a 'race relations' paradigm to understand the relationship between migrants and the receiving society, and towards other concepts (such as 'integration') which can respond to the new immigration context.

The concept of integration is contested by academics and non-governmental organisations on the grounds that it may be vague and normative and has at times come to imply 'assimilation', where the onus on adjustment is placed on the migrants and minority ethnic groups (de Lima 2003). Whilst recognising these dangers, this chapter takes the position advocated by Castles et al. (2002, 196) in their extensive review of integration:

[T]he concept of integration is defined in varying ways by different groups (. . .) However, in the end it is not the label that matters, but the content given to it in social discourse. There is no harm in using the concept of integration as long as efforts are made to establish a comprehensive conceptual framework to define it, and to operationalize it for various areas of research and policy.

While recognising the limitations of the concept, we see 'integration' as an 'umbrella term' (ibid., 126). It involves complex and nested processes, encompassing different dimensions (spatial, economic, social, cultural and political) and levels (individual, community, local, etc.), which are in constant flux and are open ended (see also Pennix 2004). Key building blocks of integration identified across the literature include issues such as rights and citizenship, employment, housing, education, health, social relationships, language and cultural knowledge. It is a reciprocal process involving changes and adjustments among both the receiving communities and migrants, and where initiatives are 'targeted at the whole of society, not just at migrants and minorities' (Rudiger and Spencer 2003, 41). Developing a nuanced understanding of integration also involves addressing at least three other factors.

Firstly, the spatial context needs to be made explicit in order to avoid generalisations based on an urban-centric focus, where the population is bigger and more likely to be spatially concentrated, in contrast to rural areas where the populations tend to be small, diverse and dispersed. Secondly, there is a need to avoid the portrayal of immigrants as invariably 'pawns' or victims of the system, and members of host communities as invariably hostile to migrants. Consideration has to be given to the resources or capital (human, economic, social and cultural) that migrants and members of the host communities utilize within their own networks as well as bring into the process of adjustment to each other, and which in turn affects the outcomes (see Nee and Sanders 2001). And, finally, it should be recognised that both the so-called host or receiving society and the migrants and minority ethnic groups are not homogenous. It is important to avoid privileging any particular ethnic identity (de Lima and Wright 2009; Sen 2001).

Immigrant Integration in Rural Communities

In rural areas, the importance of local context is heightened, especially in relation to immigrant access to resources. Typically this involves building social relationships with members of the receiving community. Such social ties are essential for immigrants in new destination rural areas where they find relatively few co-ethnics. If local social ties are not established, immigrants living in rural areas are at risk of social isolation. On the other hand, although it is important to distinguish between the character of urban and rural locations, this simple dichotomy poses the risk of failing to recognise diversity across rural communities. Regardless of size, some locales may be more open than others to the inclusion of immigrants in the social and economic life of the community (Alba and Nee 2003; Waldinger 1994).

Immigrant agency—their ability to initiate activities and relations themselves—takes on heightened importance in rural settings. The settlement of immigrants in communities with little or no presence of co-ethnics may force them to discover new ways of gaining access to better employment, housing, transportation and other resources. Sociologists and economists have long argued that connections outside the immediate network of family and friends are an important factor in occupational mobility and economic success (Burt 2001; Granovetter 1973; Lin 2001). There is also a growing body of literature affirming that for immigrants to adapt successfully in their new environs, it is not only important for them to have strong bonds as a community, but also to move beyond their close ethnic network ties and pursue opportunities by establishing broader social linkages (Alba and Nee 2003; Furbey et al. 2006; Kasinitz et al. 2008; Pfeffer and Parra 2009; Zetter, Griffith and Nando 2006). But social ties that bridge to other groups may be difficult to cultivate in rural destinations, especially in the contemporary context of historically high immigration levels and increasing diversity (de Lima 2001). For instance, in rural Scotland, challenges arise from a combination of factors: the dispersed nature of individuals and households and lack of spaces (both organised and informal) where people from different ethnic groups may meet; negative attitudes towards migrants and the difficulties (e.g. language issues) experienced in accessing local resident networks; and weak infrastructure (e.g. public sector support) to support a diverse population (Chakraboti and Garland 2004; de Lima et al. 2007; de Lima, Jentsch and Whelton 2005).

Putnam suggests that increasing ethnic diversity associated with immigration results in greater social isolation and the erosion of social capital not only between members of different ethnic groups, but also within ethnic groups (Putnam 2007). For example, unauthorized immigrants who wish to avoid detection may actively seek this isolation. Even immigrants with documents may choose to remain isolated to draw less attention to themselves and their group in the face of strong anti-immigrant sentiments. Under these circumstances, Putnam posits that immigration-driven social diversification results in the erosion of group capacity to facilitate the integration of co-ethnics. This loss of capacity makes it more difficult for immigrants to gain access to work, shelter, education and other necessities, leaving them vulnerable to a variety of abuses and unable to participate fully as members of the community. Putnam's sobering conclusions highlight the need for active efforts on the part of communities to address the needs of immigrants (see also Zetter, Griffith and Nando 2006). If increasing diversity results in greater social isolation in the short run, community organisations have an important role to play in providing a bridge between the receiving communities and immigrants in the process of integration.

CHANGING TRENDS IN RURAL IMMIGRATION

Problems of integrating immigrants into local social and economic life are exacerbated in rural settings. Although contemporary immigration in both the UK and US is a largely urban phenomenon, since the 1990s growing numbers of immigrants began to settle outside urban areas. However, little is known about them as, unsurprisingly, most studies have focused on urban/metropolitan areas (e.g. Bulmer and Solomos 1999; Modood et al. 1997; Waldinger 1996; Foner 2001; Kasinitz et al. 2008). Recent trends towards more spatially dispersed immigration in both countries suggest that a closer look at immigrant integration outside urban areas and metropolises is warranted.

Communities outside urban areas are distinctive in several ways that have practical and sociological significance for immigrant integration. In the UK, a small but growing literature has sought to highlight the distinctive factors that shape the experiences of immigrants in rural areas. These factors include the lack of experience of non-urban areas in responding to migrants and the diversity that their presence might bring; challenges posed by their small size, diversity (culturally and socially) and spatial dispersion; lack of investment in services which are responsive to culturally and/or ethnically diverse groups; and limited social spaces and opportunities which may help to facilitate 'integration' (Eales, Keefe and Keating 2008; Chakraboti and Garland 2004; Magne 2003). Examples of the latter include limited public transport and the closure of some public services such as post offices.

Immigration is perceived as a fairly new phenomenon in much of rural America. Many rural areas have not had a strong immigrant presence for a century or more and earlier immigration to rural areas was mostly by Europeans. Although these earlier immigrants were often displaced peasants in search of employment, much like today's newcomers, residents of the receiving communities have less in common with the contemporary arrivals. Immigrants to rural America often lack valid immigration documents, speak little English, have little formal education and are poor. These characteristics set them apart from established residents and are likely to result in their exclusion from many aspects of community social and economic life. Such exclusion leaves them to rely more heavily on assistance provided by their own ethnic community. This reliance is not unusual, but in rural areas with a small and relatively new immigrant population social and economic resources tend to be more limited. Conditions in the host community are therefore more consequential for immigrant integration. These places typically stand in contrast to urban centres with larger, more diverse populations that offer a more diverse array of opportunities to immigrants. In less ethnically diverse rural places, immigrants may find fewer social resources available to help them become integrated into community life.

Changing Trends and Migration in Rural Areas of the UK

Immigrants continue to settle in urban areas where there are established communities from the same country (Jamieson and Davidson 2007). However, with the increasing diversity of immigrants have also come new patterns of settlements:

> New immigrants with less established networks and patterns of settlement tend to be drawn to locations with a wider range of employment opportunities—principally to London but also to small towns and mid-sized cities (for instance to work in construction), coastal and other leisure-centred localities (where they might engage in hospitality and catering services) and rural areas (usually for short-term jobs in agriculture and food processing). (Vertovec 2006, 22)

In contrast to previous waves of migration from Britain's former colonies (e.g. from the West Indies, the Indian subcontinent and parts of Africa) and the settlement patterns of refugees and asylum seekers that are predominantly urban, rural areas have been recipients of migrant workers from Eastern Europe since May 2004 on a scale not experienced previously. The Commission for Rural Communities (CRC) estimated that 120,000 migrants (representing 23 per cent of migrant workers) had registered in rural England between May 2004 and September 2006 (CRC 2007a, 8). Gilpin et al. (2006, 20) estimated that A8 nationals made up 7 per cent of the workforce in agriculture in the UK, significantly more than in other industrial sectors. Green, Owen and Jones (2007, 32), in their study of south-east England, also acknowledge the rural dimension of the A8 migration: 'Coastal and rural areas both saw an increase in the proportion of migrants from 2004 in a trend indicative of the more general spatial dispersion of A8'. Similar trends were reported in Scotland including the remote rural Highlands and Islands (Aitken 2006; de Lima and Wright 2009; Jentsch, de Lima and MacDonald 2007; Scottish Economic Research [SER] 2006).

Migration, especially in relation to the A8, has made an important contribution to demographic change in Scotland. In rural areas it also coincided with concerns about the consequences of changing demographic trends—a growing elderly population, high levels of youth out-migration, a potential shortage of working-age population and declining birth-rates (see Philip, Brown and Stockdale, this volume). The discussion on what Dobson et al. (2001) describe as 'replacement migration' to address labour shortages is not new. However, these concerns have been very much foregrounded in the recent debates on immigration, and have been most explicitly articulated in rural Scotland where there is much anxiety about the consequences of a declining population. These concerns have led to policy initiatives to attract migrants (internally and from outside the UK) as one mechanism for addressing these demographic trends (de Lima 2005; de Lima and Wright 2009). Against this background, the question of how to attract and retain migrants and ensure their integration into communities that have had little previous experience of living and working with ethnically diverse communities has exercised the minds of policymakers, not just in the UK but also elsewhere (for example, see Frideres 2003 in relation to Canada).

Immigration to the Rural United States

Immigrant dispersal across the landscape has resulted in the establishment of new immigrant settlements and population growth in a variety of new destinations (Fix and Passel 2001; Lichter and Johnson 2009; McConnell 2008; Pena 2009). In fact, some areas of the US would be losing population if it were not for this immigration. This observation is as true for large states like New York and California as it is for many small rural communities across the country (Duchon and Murphy 2001; Kandel and Cromartie 2004).

To be sure, there is less immigration to rural America than to the cities, but the arrival of immigrants is a noticeable and surprising change in more sparsely settled areas. The increasing number of immigrants is not the only change to draw attention; the ethnic composition of the immigrant population is also significant. Aside from the large African-American population in the rural South and Latinos in the Southwest, areas outside the metropolises are not typically associated with racial and ethnic diversity. To the extent there has been ethnic diversity, it often has been among those whose European ancestors immigrated to the US generations ago (Kritz and Gurak 2004). But during the 1990s the Latino (or Hispanic) population living outside metropolitan America surged. In the 1990s this population grew in a variety of nonmetropolitan locations throughout the nation, but especially in the South and Midwest (Donato, Stainback and Bankston 2005; Griffith 2005; Kandel and Cromartie 2004).

Unlike the increasingly diverse origins of immigrants to the metropolitan US, those arriving in the rural America in the 1990s were largely Mexican immigrants (Lichter and Johnson 2009). Prior to the 1990s, a distinctive feature of Mexican migration to the rural US was its circularity. Workers, usually single men, came to the US as young adults to earn money and to send it back to Mexico. Once they accumulated as much money as they needed, they typically returned to their home communities in Mexico. Thus, Mexican immigrants as a group may have had an ongoing presence in the US, but relatively few individuals settled there (Chavez 1988; Massey et al. 1987). More recently, growing numbers of Mexicans in localities throughout the US have settled more permanently, and more Mexican families rather than single men are migrating to the US (Cerrutti and Massey 2004; Parra and Pfeffer 2005).

In these rural communities, the establishment of Mexican grocery stores, restaurants and civic associations are indications of a more permanent Mexican community presence. This raises a number of questions about the relationship between the destination community and the immigrants. In particular, how do immigrants access the resources needed to be full participants in community life? In the following, we address questions of integration and access to resources in our two cases.

INTEGRATION IN RURAL SCOTLAND— THE CASE OF THE NORTH OF SCOTLAND

To illustrate the contingent nature of immigrant integration, this section draws on two research studies undertaken in northern Scotland in rural communities with little or no experience of overseas migration until the expansion of the EU in May 2004 (de Lima 2001; de Lima et al. 2007; de Lima, Jentsch and Whelton 2005[2]) Both studies were based on an analysis of official quantitative data sources on migration to identify trends for each of the two research study areas. Qualitative interviews and focus groups were then conducted in both studies, involving in total 110 employers, 123 migrant works and 61 services providers. The main aims of the studies were to identify the trends in migration since the expansion of the EU in May 2004 and to develop insights into its impact on migrants, employers and service providers. Overall the migrants in the two studies were predominantly from Eastern European countries with Polish people being the largest group. The majority of participants were between the ages of twenty and forty-five and at least half were single. Most possessed qualifications above secondary level, including degrees, but were employed in sectors such as agriculture, food processing and tourism that required low levels of skills, paid low wages and were subject to seasonal variations.

Access to Services

A critical aspect of integration is the extent to which migrants and minority ethnic groups can and do access services to which they are entitled. In the aftermath of May 2004, many rural areas across the UK reported a dramatic rise in demand for services from migrant workers but assessing access and impact on services at a local level has been less well developed (CRC 2007a). Two persistent themes emerge from the Scottish research. On the one hand, A8 migrants lack awareness of entitlements and services on offer, and this is exacerbated by the lack of extensive and accessible co-ethnic networks in rural areas, communication difficulties and different cultural norms of what to expect in a new country. With regard to the latter, for example, car-related offences may indicate a lack of understanding of the legal requirements surrounding driving in the UK. Putting up with domestic abuse may partly be a result of a lack of awareness of relevant services in this area (de Lima et al. 2007; Rolfe and Metcalfe 2009). Evidence also suggested that some migrants from A8 countries were distrustful of public authorities and the police in particular because of previous negative experiences in their home country, and consequently avoided any formal contact with some public agencies (de Lima et al. 2007).

On the other hand, a number of factors also influenced providers of services in rural areas in their capacity to respond to migrants, which were largely based on their own lack of experience of working with immigrant communities. For example, some service providers did not know the entitlements and rights of different categories of migrants in relation to particular services, they had insufficient capacity to make contact with small numbers of migrants dispersed across rural areas (due to a lack of skills as well as limited human and financial resources) and they lacked experience in providing appropriate advice and information on services to diverse cultural groups. Additionally, distance between places, diseconomies of scale and local competition for scarce resources also posed particular challenges for service delivery in rural areas. Following the flow of A8 migrants in rural areas a number of rural local authorities argued strongly for additional government funding to help them address the specific needs of migrants in relation to issues such as language provision, housing and advice. There is little research which focuses in any depth on specific services in rural areas. However, housing and language provision are two of the services that have consistently emerged as particularly problematic in relation to recent migrants in rural areas across the UK. Recurrent findings in research on the former include: limited housing availability; high cost in relation to quality; overcrowding, including 'hot bedding' related to shift working; and the housing of migrants in 'low-demand' areas—i.e. properties that are difficult to let for a variety of reasons. In addition, the prevalence of 'tied' accommodation in sectors such as agriculture and tourism can make migrants particularly vulnerable to homelessness if they lose their job (Bell, Jarman and Lefebvre 2004; Citizen's Advice Bureau 2005; de Lima et al. 2007; McKay and Winkelman-Gleed 2005).

Housing is a useful vehicle for illustrating the perspectives of different actors in relation to integration processes (de Lima and Wright 2009). For example, the lack of affordable housing in rural areas generally has resulted in concerns amongst local communities and service providers that recent migrants have put additional pressures on what is an ongoing problem. This has in turn led to perceptions among local communities that migrants are favoured in housing allocation policies. These perceptions often arise in a context where there are limited spaces and opportunities in rural areas for social interaction between migrants and local community members, reinforcing tensions between groups. Equally important is that migrants may also choose to live in multiple occupancy situations even if it is illegal, because they see this as a short-term measure which enables them to maximize their earned income and send remittances back home.

In rural areas, lack of proficiency in English takes on a particular significance in the absence of access to a community of co-ethnics or where service providers are inadequately equipped to provide language and communication services. The provision of English-language classes and interpretation and translation in rural areas is indeed challenging. The lack of an infrastructure (e.g. trained teachers, financial resources) and diseconomies of scale in responding to small numbers at different levels of English is exacerbated by the ethnic and educational diversity of migrants and their spatial dispersion. Additionally in rural areas, distance and lack of public transport or high cost of transport are barriers to accessing language provision. This not only reinforces migrants' sense of isolation, but also has a detrimental impact on their ability to integrate across other spheres. In relation to employment, this resulted in underemployment and a lack of understanding of employment rights, consequently increasing vulnerability to exploitation. It also impedes migrants overall ability to interact with host communities, reinforcing their sense of social isolation (Green, Owen and Jones 2007; Robinson and Reeve 2006).

Migrant–Host Communities: Spaces for Social Interaction

Beyond a brief acknowledgment in the literature that overseas migration can influence the 'composition of local communities and the lives of existing residents and their attitudes and behaviours can affect the integration of new arrivals' (Rolfe and Metcalf 2009, 43), there is little research which has specifically explored the host communities' views on their relationship with migrants in rural areas. From the little evidence that exists, there appears to be a prevalence of hostile attitudes to migrants particularly in areas where local residents see themselves in competition for scarce resources, such as housing and employment (Green, Owen and Jones 2007; de Lima et al. 2007; de Lima, Jentsch and Whelton 2005; Pillai et al. 2007). However, much of this research is from the perspective of employers, migrant workers and service providers, and the voices and experiences of members of the receiving rural communities continue to be noticeable by their absence in research.

In their review of research on integration of migrants in Scotland, Jamieson and Davidson (2007, 9) argue:

> The positive gloss that reports place on workers' experiences of good relationships with residents is typically based on worker's experiences of polite friendliness or the absence of incidents of hostility, rather than any evidence of social interactions beyond everyday transactions.

This was reflected in the studies undertaken in the north of Scotland, where social interaction beyond the workplace was constrained due to a combination of language barriers, lack of time because of work patterns, the migrants' need to save money, lack of transport and cultural barriers. With regard to the latter, migrants found the role that alcohol played in socializing in some rural communities was not conducive for wider social interaction.

Although there is debate on the extent to which existing networks of migrants can be a positive force or a hindrance in the process of integration, there is also evidence that 'well-established communities' are an important source of advice and information for new arrivals as well as providing psychological and social support as they settle in their new community (Pohjola 2009; Vertovec 2002). Existing networks may help new migrants to ease their way into the new society. However, where immigrants are diverse and dispersed such networks may be difficult to establish and sustain over long distances (de Lima, Jentsch and Whelton 2005; McKay and Winkelman-Gleed 2005). Nevertheless, in some larger migrant communities, such as the Polish, social networks have been an important means not only of accessing employment and services, but also in developing social support. The presence of Polish communities has also been seen as an important factor in the revival of Catholic churches in some rural areas in the north of Scotland. In this context the Catholic Church has played an important role, acting as a bridge between new migrants and local communities in facilitating social interactions between migrants and host communities as well as assisting with learning English and even helping find accommodation. However, this does not address the situation of the migrant groups who are smaller in number, as well as the fact that each group may encompass diverse identities (e.g. those who do not belong to a faith group, different genders and educational levels) with different integration issues.

Despite the constraints and barriers, service providers, third sector organisations (including faith groups) and migrants have developed a number of strategies for addressing some of the challenges of rural life. These have included for example: multi-agency partnerships drawn from the public and community sectors involved in the production of 'welcome packs' to provide basic information about local service provision and support and advice on a wide range of issues (CRC 2007b; de Lima et al. 2007); bridging activities using the arts and media to provide social spaces for dialogue and building relationships between migrants and host communities (CRC 2007c, 2007d; de Lima 2009); and local associations and faith groups where the numbers are sufficient to provide language classes, celebrate festivals and so on.

INTEGRATION IN NEW IMMIGRANT DESTINATIONS—RURAL NEW YORK

A focus on rural New York is a useful way to distil some of the essential ingredients for immigrant integration in rural places in the US. What is most distinctive about rural New York is the relative scarcity of new immigrants. With few co-ethnics to provide a web of support, immigrants need to forge relationships with residents of the destination community to satisfy normal needs. Opportunities to satisfy these needs can vary considerably depending on the local context. Findings from past research highlight some important points about the formation of social ties in new destinations. Research findings presented here were generated in a study in five upstate New York communities. The qualitative data come from two sources: forty-one interviews with key informants and eighteen focus groups each with between four and fifteen male and female participants (149 participants total). The quantitative data were generated from surveys of 2,488 respondents in the five communities, 945 of whom were immigrants (i.e. born outside the US). We also draw on a survey of a representative sample of 820 New Yorkers (Empire State Poll 2004, Immigration Omnibus Survey, Survey Research Institute, Cornell University). More details about the communities and the projects' research methodology can be found in Pfeffer and Parra (2009, 2004).

Immigrants who speak little English, have completed little formal schooling and lack immigration documents have few alternatives but to tap ethnic social ties. But immigrants living in new rural destinations are unlikely to have access to a large ethnic community that can effectively provide informal access to goods and services. The settlement of immigrants in communities with little or no presence of co-ethnics forces them to discover new ways of gaining access to better employment, housing, transportation and other resources.

English Language

Limited English-language ability is an important issue for Mexican immigrants moving to non-traditional destinations, as it is for the Eastern European migrants in Scotland. Ability to speak English enables immigrants to obtain goods and services independently and to explore opportunities to establish themselves in the economic and social life of the community. Because of the relatively recent movement of significant numbers of first-time Mexican immigrants to many of these destinations, a large proportion of the Mexican population has limited English-language ability. With limited English-language ability, Mexican immigrants are less likely to be able to forge linkages with other community members. A consequence of such social isolation is confinement to a narrow range of low-wage employment opportunities. One immigrant straightforwardly noted this limitation and the need to overcome it saying, 'The first thing to do is to learn English, because even if [Americans] open the door for you, what are you going to say?' Language-related social isolation has been observed in existing Mexican immigrant communities, and there is evidence that workers who are Spanish-language dominant have lower earned income (Parra and Pfeffer 2005; Alba and Nee 2003). This outcome is in part the result of limited language ability which confines immigrants to lower paying employment.

For example, in upstate New York English-language ability appears to be an important prerequisite for obtaining year-round employment outside of agriculture. More than 75 per cent of immigrants formerly employed as farmworkers reported understanding and speaking English, but fewer than 50 per cent of foreign-born farmworkers report understanding English and only 33 per cent reported speaking the language (Pfeffer and Parra 2004). The advantages of English-language ability also extend beyond employment. Immigrants who have better command of the English language have more American friends, are more likely to participate in civic organisations, to be homeowners and have higher incomes. Immigrants also do best in communities where there is a larger concentration of immigrants who speak English well (Parra and Pfeffer 2005; Pfeffer and Parra 2004).

IMMIGRATION STATUS

The most significant feature of the Mexican immigrant population is the high proportion without valid visas or residence permits. Mexicans have been estimated to make up a large percentage of all unauthorized immigrants in the US, about 58 per cent (Passel and Cohn 2011). The importance of documents for the life chances of Mexican immigrants cannot be overstated. Immigration and citizenship policies and regulations control access to certain resources. Studies of unauthorized immigrants consistently show that they are excluded from better paying employment, private health insurance, publicly funded health care and quality and affordable housing. These exclusions contribute to lower socio-economic standing and poorer physical well-being (Berk et al. 2000; Chavez et al. 1997; Siddharthan and Ahearn 1996; Hubbell et al. 1991). Debates about unauthorized immigration tend to focus on national policy concerns, but little attention is dedicated to the practical limitations that the lack of documentation places on the practical aspects of immigrants' daily lives, and these difficulties have increased in the past decade (Parra and Pfeffer 2006). The following comments by immigrants highlight the importance of having basic documentation to be able to function effectively:

> After the September 11, it is more difficult to get your driver's license. Before in the offices it was easier to get your driver's license without your Social Security, now for a person without papers it is going to be very difficult to move around.

> The bank asks you for a driver's license. If one has a driver's license, one also can have a bank account. That, the driver's license, would help a lot!

> You can cash your check in the bank, but you can't make deposits, and that is a problem. One would like to deposit at least $25 a week for anything you may need in the future.

One immigrant explained, 'We cannot have credit, which is important. They say, "give us proof of your credit", but if you do not have insurance or you are not a [legal] resident, then you cannot get credit'. Without a credit history, immigrants are forced to rely on close personal ties to make larger purchases. An unauthorized immigrant related that he was able to purchase a vehicle through his brother: 'My brother here, he has papers and good credit. He has received loans to buy three cars. He has no collateral, but he is good at paying on time. He is a man of his word [*cumplidor*]'. But as indicated earlier these close personal social resources are often limited in rural new immigrant destinations.

Education

Mexican immigrants have long been known to have relatively low education levels compared with other immigrant groups, and the most recent waves of immigrants are no exception (Parra and Pfeffer 2005; Pfeffer and Parra 2005a; Kritz and Gurak 2004; Alba and Nee 2003; Portes and Rumbaut 1996). Low levels of education are most common among immigrants from rural origins in Mexico where educational attainment rarely exceeds primary school (Parra and Pfeffer 2006; Tienda and Mitchell 2006). If they lack educational credentials, immigrants are limited to low-wage jobs that have few educational prerequisites. Such employment typically offers few opportunities for advancement, and combined with limited English-language ability, contributes to the creation of conditions conducive to social and economic segregation (Tienda and Mitchell 2006). For example, in upstate New York immigrants employed in agriculture tend to have relatively little formal education (see Figure 5.1). Most farmworkers come from

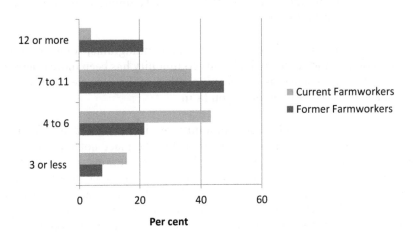

Figure 5.1 Years of schooling of foreign-born farmworkers and former farmworkers in upstate New York.

rural villages in Mexico where school attendance is normally six or fewer years. In contrast, about 70 per cent of immigrants who were formerly farmworkers had more than six years of education, indicating that level of schooling, along with English-language ability, has enabled them to tap employment opportunities outside agriculture.

Host Community Actions

In new destination rural communities, an essential question is how best to integrate immigrants into the social and economic life of the community. The actions that communities take will in part determine whether immigrants become an asset or a burden to the community. However, research in rural New York indicates that most community residents do not have clear notions about the likely impact of immigrants on their communities. A relatively small proportion of community residents have strong opinions about the immigrants, and these are often divided. Negative opinions are somewhat linked to community residents' positions in the labour market, but in most cases even those who might be in competition with immigrants for jobs are ambivalent about whether immigrants are an asset or a liability for the community. This ambivalence is apparent in upstate New York as well as in the state as a whole, as indicated in Figure 5.2. The bottom line is that there is little clarity among community residents about immigrants and their potential role in community development (Pfeffer and Parra 2007c; Parra and Pfeffer 2005). Key informants reported the mixed sentiments about immigrants apparent in upstate New York communities:

> In this area there are persons very supportive of immigrant workers (. . .) and community members that perceive immigrants as the cause of community problems.

> Communities react differently to the new immigrants; some are more welcoming and some are bad. This community has been more tolerant, but the welcomeness is not genuine—they make very clear where the line is in terms of how much you fit in.

Most immigrants and other community residents lack ongoing interactions with one another. Interactions that do take place not only improve other community residents' understanding of immigrants; they also help immigrants become integrated into the social and economic life of the community in material ways such as the purchase of a car or home. However, these interactions tend to be restricted to the work sphere, and they typically take place between immigrants and others in the same economic circumstances (Parra and Pfeffer 2005). Key informants described the limited social interactions between immigrants and community members:

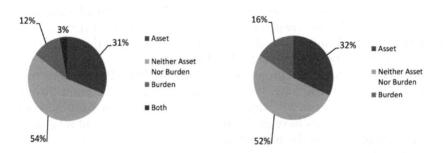

Figure 5.2   Non-immigrant residents in upstate New York and statewide poll: 'immigrants, an asset or a burden?'

> Contacts between the white community and minorities or immigrants are mostly limited to the kind of unavoidable contacts that people have; that would be work or shopping, but there is little socializing.

> Some people acknowledge seeing the immigrants around town; others claim that they hardly see any immigrants. But one thing that everybody has in common is that no one speaks with the immigrants.

CONCLUSION

To be sure, most immigrants move to cities where they are likely to encounter large and fairly well-established communities of co-ethnics and more opportunities to obtain employment, housing, health care and other resources they need. However, the social and economic environment immigrants find outside urban areas and metropolises is substantially different.

Labour market access is particularly constrained in rural areas; not only are opportunities less abundant, but they are also less diverse. Ethnic social networks take on heightened importance when immigrants are excluded from mainstream public and private channels to access resources. But even these informal mechanisms for meeting needs are limited in the rural context. Immigrants to rural areas typically find relatively few ethnic social networks to draw on. Under these circumstances, immigrants are forced to establish social relationships that cross ethnic boundaries if they are to satisfy basic needs like employment, housing, transportation and health care. The formation of such linkages is difficult, but immigrants may be more or less successful depending on the local context.

'Local' is of course situated within other contextual layers that affect the interactions between immigrants and host communities. Certainly the national discourse on immigration, its social and economic impacts and policies to regulate it establish the broad parameters within which encounters with immigrants are framed. The broad rural context also shapes community responses to immigrants in important ways. Smaller and more dispersed populations create both challenges and opportunities for social interactions with immigrants that may vary depending on the specific constellation of factors that define the local context.

In the aftermath of European expansion in May 2004, many rural areas across the UK have become reliant on migrants from Eastern European countries to fill labour shortages. In parts of rural Scotland development agencies have made strategic commitments and invested in strategies to increase the population in their areas. Within that context, there has been a strong emphasis on attracting East European migrants in particular. A combination of factors may mean that rural areas in the UK are likely to face major challenges in attracting and retaining migrants; these include the types of employment available in rural areas and the underemployment of migrants, the impact of the economic recession and the diminution in factors that made the UK an attractive destination for East European migrants. In addition, as argued by Broomby (2009): 'The UK labour market is always just a budget airline ticket or bus fare away (. . .). Modern migration, at least within the EU, is now more like a turnstile than a one way street'.

The increasing diversity and 'circularity' of recent migration, aided by cheap transport, suggests that rural areas in the UK may have to develop more flexible labour strategies and adapt to a high level of turnover of migrants (de Lima and Wright 2009). If rural policymakers wish to attract and retain overseas migrants, they have to address key quality of life issues that are essential to integration such as access to language classes, providing employment commensurate with their qualifications, ensuring equitable access to services and providing opportunities which enable these groups to maintain aspects of their cultural identities.

In the US, the continuing political impasse over immigration policy assures that issues related to immigrant integration will continue to be dealt with in diverse ways at the local level. Regardless of how welcoming communities are, immigrants will likely have a continuing presence for the foreseeable future. If they are to become productive members of the community, immigrants will need more opportunities to develop social ties to other community residents.

Civic engagement is an important element of community development and should also be central to the social and economic integration of immigrants (Putnam 2007; Parra and Pfeffer 2005). Civic organisations offer one avenue for such interactions. Social ties established in such venues offer some opportunities to gain access to needed goods and services. But there are significant challenges in achieving such community development. Involvement in standard civic activities is low for both immigrants and other community members. Nevertheless, greater attention to the encouragement of civic engagement and new forms of it should be a priority goal of communities. It is, therefore, not enough to focus on migrants without also addressing community transformation as a whole. This implies understanding how migration from overseas 'has changed the composition and relationships between members of groups' in rural communities (Bach 1993, cited in Castles et al. 2002, 138). It means moving away from portraying migrants as invariably victims of the system, and receiving communities as inevitably negative towards immigrants, and towards a deeper understanding of what long-term residents in a local community require to help them cope with their changing environment.

6 Rural Poverty and Social Exclusion in the United States and the United Kingdom

Mark Shucksmith and Kai Schafft

INTRODUCTION: UNDERSTANDING POVERTY AND SOCIAL EXCLUSION

This chapter provides an historical-comparative discussion of rural poverty and poverty research in the United States and in the United Kingdom. In particular we look at the ways in which poverty—its causes, consequences and the implications for addressing poverty through policy and practice—are understood across both national contexts. In doing this, we examine the concept of *social exclusion*, a discursive and theoretical frame that has increasingly been used in both disciplinary and policy debates in the UK, and indeed in Europe more broadly, but remains little recognised in the US.

While poverty is statistically assessed by governmental and bureaucratic agencies (as well as by social scientists), it is fundamentally a normative concept reflecting, in different ways in the US and Europe, a socially determined basic level of economic assets. Hence, the concept of poverty is often understood, *de facto*, as a phenomenon that is at its root *economic* in nature: a condition characterised at multiple levels by inadequate economic resources relative to need. Poverty in the US most generally refers, at the micro-level, to conditions in which individuals, families or households lack the basic resources to maintain their sustenance. Poverty associated with places, similarly, is more or less an aggregated assessment of the material well-being of individuals within a particular area. In the UK and in Europe, in contrast, poverty is defined in relative terms, and not in absolute terms. Poverty is understood as the inability to share the standard of living of the majority in society. Although income-based assessments of poverty often serve as a proxy for *broader* disadvantage, including inadequate housing, limited health care access and so on, this is typically understood by many researchers and policymakers to be an outcome of insufficient economic resources rather than a fundamental constituent of poverty itself (Waglé 2008).

In contrast, social exclusion is typically conceptualized as a multidimensional, dynamic process that results in the partial or full exclusion of individuals or households from a variety of social, cultural, political and/

or economic domains (Commins 2004; Walker and Walker 1997). In this respect, social exclusion implies a focus less on individual 'victims' than upon the *processes* that produce (and *reproduce*) poverty and inequality. It also acknowledges the importance of the local context in such processes. Thus, while the notion of poverty is primarily *distributional* and *cross-sectional*, the concept of social exclusion focuses primarily on *relational* and *historically embedded* patterns of labour market detachment, low political and civic participation, social isolation and especially the distribution and exercise of power, and how these phenomena intersect with gendered, ethnic, racial and/or other social identities.

This chapter proceeds with a comparative discussion concerning the ways in which poverty is understood across these two national contexts, indicating the history of poverty debates and how it is that they have evolved differently. We then look at the major features of rural poverty in Britain and the US, examining the ways in which poverty is conceptualized and what this has meant for rural poverty research as well as public policy. Within the course of this discussion we attempt to identify the ways in which social exclusion, as a conceptual and theoretical device, has been used to more fully understand the dynamics of poverty and inequality, and what this, in turn, has meant for both disciplinary and policy debates. We conclude by revisiting the central conceptual and discursive frames that have shaped poverty debates among academics, public policymakers and practitioners, suggesting how these different ways of understanding poverty shape what we see, what we believe we know and how we respond to social disadvantage and inequality.

UNDERSTANDING POVERTY IN THE US AND THE UK

The Framing of Poverty in the US: Structural versus Individual and Cultural Explanations

One of the central poverty debates in the US concerns the extent to which poverty is most coherently understood as a phenomenon caused principally by social-structural factors or by individual behaviours, often understood as 'cultural' in origin. Both academic and policy debates extending back a century or more in various ways have reflected this basic conceptual—and frequently ideological—divide. Some of the earliest social scientific work on poverty and inequality in the early twentieth century was associated with the Progressive Era:[1] Robert Hunter's *Poverty* (1904), for example, established a working poverty line, asserting that as many as ten million Americans lived in poverty (Reef 2007). Hunter's work was largely political-economic in its orientation, noting insufficient wages, job shortages and inadequate social safety nets as major contributing factors associated with poverty. But Hunter was also careful to distinguish between those in poverty as a consequence of social-structural factors and those 'who are poor because of their own folly and vice' (O'Connor 2001, 33).

In the 1920s the Chicago School sociologists shifted the analytic focus slightly to examine the 'social ecology' of neighbourhoods, looking at community disorganisation and 'cultural lag' as causal factors associated with disadvantage, in the process to some extent naturalizing urban poverty as part of a larger process of industrial capitalism's development. Into the 1930s and the New Deal era amidst the Great Depression social scientists and policymakers likewise understood Southern rural poverty principally as an issue of insufficient modernisation, best remedied through increased agricultural diversification, expanded industrial development and a means of effectively addressing the 'cultural backwardness'[2] that many felt hindered the South's social progress (Godden and Crawford 2006; Mertz 1978; Sherman and Henry 1933; Wray 2006).

Poverty as an explicit focus of public policy emerged more clearly in the US in part as a reaction to work that was beginning to enter into public debates concerning the nature of social inequality, such as Gunnar Myrdal's *Challenge to Affluence* (1963) and Michael Harrington's *The Other America* (1962), books that attempted to shed light not only on poverty as a social problem, but at the same time call attention to its structural roots, albeit in ways that also tended to emphasize generational and cultural factors thought to be associated with poverty.

During the Kennedy administration, the president's Council of Economic Advisors (CEA) began to focus in earnest on the issue of poverty and in 1964 released the *Economic Report to the President* with the entire second chapter devoted to the 'Problem of Poverty in America'. The authors argued that one-fifth of the US population could be considered poor, that 60 per cent of poor families had household heads with only a primary school education and that over 40 per cent of farm families were poor. Importantly, it also suggested key structural features associated with poverty, noting: 'When a family and its head have several characteristics frequently associated with poverty, the chances of being poor are particularly high: a family headed by a young woman who is nonwhite and has less than an eighth grade education is poor in 94 out of 100 cases. Even if she is white, the chances are 85 out of 100 that she and her children will be poor' (1964, 57). The CEA report was significant not only because it ultimately served as the template for President Lyndon B. Johnson's 'War on Poverty', legislation that firmly established poverty alleviation as a top domestic political priority, but it also established and institutionalised the federal poverty line as a standard means of measuring poverty through the use of an annually adjusted income threshold-based measure[3] that continues to be widely used (Jensen, McLaughlin and Slack 2003; Rank 2005).[4]

The language contained within the CEA report therefore maintained an often uneasy balance between the *structural* features of society that systematically disadvantage and exclude certain people—such as discrimination, job scarcity, low wages, insufficient social safety nets, weak schools (Bullock, Williams and Limbert 2003; Galster and Killen 1995)—and the *cultural and individual-level* factors associated with persistent poverty that associate particular behaviours and individual attributes with the reproduction of poverty and hold individuals to at least some extent responsible for their own economic status.[5] The policy prescriptions offered by the CEA report were a mix of market-driven solutions—mainly in the form of economic stimulus and job creation through tax cuts—coupled with targeted social programmes such as early and adult education, health programmes, housing assistance and job training to reach those in most immediate need. The underlying logic was economic: poverty as an economic phenomenon would be best addressed through a combined effort to strengthen labour markets through economic acceleration and labour market integration accomplished by enhancing the human capital of those at the lowest social rungs.

The 1965 Moynihan Report followed quickly on the heels of the CEA report and the passage of the 1964 Civil Rights Act, and was written as a means of informing the ongoing debate on poverty and public policy and in particular 'the Negro problem', focusing on the disproportionate rates of African-American poverty, especially in inner cities, and its connections to family instability and the prevalence of female-headed households within the African-American community. In many ways the Moynihan Report ushered in the 'race versus class' debate that would dominate academic and policy discussions in the 1970s, 1980s and beyond, particularly around the issues of affirmative action and hiring preferences, theorization of the 'urban underclass' and the continued (or changing) salience of race in relation to economic disadvantage (Hajnal 2007; Jacoby and Glauberman 1995; Massey and Denton 1993; Swain 1996; W.J. Wilson 1978, 1987).

Massey and Sampson (2009) argue that the Moynihan Report represented a defining moment for the way in which US social scientists would address the issues of race and poverty. Deeply structural in nature, the Moynihan Report attempted to establish the linkages between systemic social, economic and political exclusion and the 'tangle of pathologies' associated with urban African-American ghettos. Liberal critics, however, largely overlooked the structural arguments contained within the report and quickly accused Moynihan of 'blaming the victim'. The ironic result, Massey and Sampson argue, is that conservative thinkers embraced family instability as a causal factor in explaining black poverty and 'for decades, the terms of public debate were skewed away from structural issues such as segregation, discrimination and economic restructuring and toward individual issues such as values, culture and morality' (Massey and Sampson 2009, 13; see also Brady 2003; Furstenberg 2009). These individual-level explanations deeply resonated with conservative arguments about social welfare policies and the creation of welfare dependency through policies that 'inexorably exacerbate the very social ills that they were meant to cure' (Somers and Block 2005, 265).

Despite these currents in thinking about poverty, since the 1960s US social scientists have attempted to integrate structural and cultural understandings of poverty. This includes Stack's work (1974) on family structure in persistently poor environments, Swidler's (1986) arguments concerning culture as a set of skills and habits that functions as a 'tool kit' to negotiate one's social environment and W.J. Wilson's (1987) work on the inner-city 'underclass'. More recently, and following the work of W.J. Wilson (1987) and others (e.g. Jargowski 1997; Massey and Denton 1993), Sampson and colleagues have focused attention on the structural and spatial aspects of poverty, linking them to cultural and behavioural factors that help to reproduce poverty. However, within social science, as Massey and Sampson (2009) point out, there continue to be not simply analytical, but also significant *political* challenges in unpacking the 'black box' of poverty in a way that effectively integrates structural and micro-level or cultural explanations of poverty.

This is reflected in public policy debates that clearly privilege individual-level behaviouralist explanations of poverty, coupled with market-based solutions (Somers and Block 2005). The Personal Responsibility and Work Opportunity Reconciliation Act of 1996 signed by President Bill Clinton, for example, aimed not only at pushing the integration of poor people into the labour market (in part by imposing work mandates coupled with new time limits on eligibility for receiving benefits), but also ending dependency upon social support programmes by promoting 'personal responsibility', two-parent families and discouraging out of wedlock births in what one critic described as 'virtually a national revival movement calling for the restoration of moral compulsion to the lives of the poor' (Piven 2001, 135). In short, for a variety of reasons, many of which reflect ideological currents within political, policy and academic arenas, social science in the US has struggled to develop theoretical and conceptual tools that might meaningfully move policy debates beyond what are for the most part market-based, economically rationalized policy prescriptions based around individual-level understandings of poverty (Hyatt 2001; O'Connor 2004; Somers and Block 2005).

From Poor Law to Social Exclusion: The United Kingdom Context

In the UK debates have similarly reflected structural versus individual explanations of poverty, philanthropy versus (tax-payer-funded) state intervention and universal versus selective policy responses. In general, Labour governments have favoured structural explanations and state provision of universal benefits, while Conservatives favour means-tests to target benefits on the poorest.

State intervention dates back to the introduction of the Elizabethan Poor Laws in 1601 which enabled parishes to offer 'poor relief' through cash donations in a predominantly rural society. By the nineteenth century the traditional patterns of village organisation were no longer adequate to address poverty as the enclosures and industrialisation transformed 'quiet rural poverty to the bitter and more visible squalor of the crowded towns' (Jones 2000, 2). When a Whig government was elected in 1830, legislators drew on the new science of economics, and the ideas of Adam Smith, Malthus, Ricardo and especially Bentham, to devise a radical solution: the New Poor Law of 1834. The New Poor Law established the workhouse and its harsh conditions as the only alternative to self-support. This reflected the belief that poverty was self-inflicted, and reinforced a stigma of poverty and dread of pauperism and the workhouse[6] (Jones 2000).

However, new social statistical analyses began to reveal the role of unsanitary neighbourhood conditions in spreading disease and exacerbating poverty conditions (Chadwick [1842] 1965), leading to a series of Public Health Acts from 1848, which addressed important structural causes of ill health and poverty. Statistics and quantitative analysis were also the foundation for the pioneering reports of Booth (1889–1903) and Rowntree (1901), who documented not only the extent of poverty in London and York respectively, but also asked for the first time 'who are the poor?' and assembled empirical evidence of the causes of poverty. Each concluded that poverty was pronounced, with 27–30 per cent of the population enduring poverty conditions, and that the major cause of poverty was not individual weakness but rather 'the adverse conditions under which so many of the working class live' (Rowntree 1901), including low pay, job insecurity, poor health, lack of services, poor housing and lack of education. State intervention was required, each argued, to ensure a minimum acceptable standard of living.

Rowntree's report is notable for two further conceptual innovations. First, he proposed an *absolute conception of poverty* based on the minimum income necessary to maintain physiological efficiency, defining incomes below this level as primary poverty, and those unable to afford these and other essentials (e.g. fares to work) as secondary poverty. As a nutritional chemist he felt able to calculate this threshold precisely. Second, he developed the concept of the *poverty cycle*, showing that working-class families went through predictable phases of poverty and prosperity: money was scarce while children were young, then rose when children brought in wages, but fell again when children left home to start their own families and once the man was no longer able to work through old age. The Liberal government of 1906 took these insights to heart, legislating for children's rights, a network of labour exchanges, non-contributory old age pensions (1908) and the National Insurance Act (1911) for health insurance and unemployment insurance. These legislative and policy decisions occurred despite the insistence of charities and Conservative politicians that the state should have no role in tackling poverty, but rather that philanthropy should help the (deserving) poor (Royal Commission on the Poor Laws 1909).

After the Second World War and in the wake of mass unemployment in the 1920s and 1930s, a political consensus emerged that poverty and unemployment were not mainly due to individual failings but were structural and systemic, and that governments could manage economies in such a way as to achieve full employment, while also assuming responsibility for looking after its citizens 'from the cradle to the grave' (Spicker 1993, 118). The twin pillars of this approach were Keynesian economic management and the 1942 Beveridge Report's blueprint for a new, egalitarian Britain through provision of universal benefits including free health care, free education, social insurance, social housing and more. The broadly successful implementation of these ideas, despite the UK's bankrupt economy, led Marshall to reflect that social welfare 'once confined to the helpless and hopeless' had been steadily extended to all citizens, with general agreement that 'whoever provides them, the overall responsibility for the welfare of the citizen must remain with the state' (Marshall 1965, 97).

But this consensus around the effectiveness of state provision of universal benefits was challenged in the 1960s from three directions. First, in what became known as 'the rediscovery of poverty', Townsend and Abel-Smith (1966) found that sections of society remained in poverty—particularly large families on low incomes. A Child Poverty Action Group was established, chaired by Townsend, to lobby for increased family allowances and a minimum income level. The second challenge to universal benefits came from the emerging New Right as the supposed failure of the welfare state became a favourite theme of neo-conservative think tanks and academics. Drawing on monetarist theories they argued for a return to selectivity, individual responsibility and choice and a shaking-off of state bureaucracy.

The third challenge came from the deterioration of the UK economy, sterling devaluation and cuts in public spending. The oil crisis of 1973 had even more profound consequences, not only calling into question the Keynesianism underlying the post-war consensus, but necessitating a loan from the (US-dominated) IMF which required severe cuts in UK public expenditure as a condition of the loan. These cuts were multiplied enthusiastically by Conservative governments from 1979 to 1997, proclaiming self-help and frugality in place of a welfare dependency culture. Economic growth was instead prioritized, from which prosperity would 'trickle down' to poorer groups. Accordingly, while unemployment rose to its highest post-war levels, individual responsibility was emphasized with selective, means-tested benefits; a 'rolling back' of the welfare state in education, health, social care and housing; marketisation of what remained of the public sector; and Social Security budget cuts despite rising need and inequality.

In recent years, policy debates about inequality have tended to focus on *social exclusion* rather than on poverty, for a number of reasons. The concept developed out of the EU anti-poverty programme (Room 1995b), when the term 'poverty' was unacceptable to the Conservative governments of the UK and Germany. However, the concept was also attractive to many policymakers and academics because of its focus on the multidimensional, dynamic processes underlying inequality and poverty. The 'New Labour' government made tackling social exclusion an immediate priority, establishing a Social Exclusion Unit in the Cabinet Office in 1997. In the EU, social exclusion is written into the Maastricht Treaty and is seen in terms of an 'active welfare policy' in contrast to a passive, redistributive welfare policy. This UK/EU approach to welfare reform drew on the US model of 'welfare to work' but placed its emphasis on helping people into work, and rather less emphasis on 'individual failings' (such as single parenthood) that might hinder labour market integration (Hirsch and Millar 2004). It targeted young people, unemployed men in areas of industrial restructuring and deprived urban neighbourhoods through a series of 'New Deals', with employment seen as the key integrating force which would bring income, identity, self-worth and networks.[7]

Social exclusion remains a contested term, not only amongst academics, but within the Labour Party. Levitas (1999) contrasts a relational understanding of social exclusion with alternative distributional and underclass perspectives, and shows that all three discourses surfaced in Labour statements at times. Others regarded it as merely a euphemism, diverting attention from necessary redistribution or, worse, code for cultural explanations of poverty and the US 'underclass' discourse. The concept's advocates resist such criticisms, arguing that such a relational understanding of poverty and inequality will enable policy to address the causes rather than merely the symptoms, and that it allows more sophisticated policy design without altering policy objectives (Hills 2002). Even so, substantive criticisms of the concept of social exclusion remain, notably that it unduly emphasizes boundary formation and carries an implicit notion that all but a few are included in a cohesive society undifferentiated by class or social division (Savage 2002). And in UK politics, the 2010 Coalition government no longer refers to social exclusion: both Conservative and Liberal elements of the Coalition emphasize individual–cultural explanations of poverty, once again arguing that selectivity and disincentives to welfare dependency represent the truly 'progressive' approach (Osborne 2010).

DIFFERING US AND UK PERSPECTIVES IN RURAL POVERTY RESEARCH

US Perspectives in Rural Poverty Research

Among US rural researchers the consensus has long been that poverty is at least as much a rural problem as an urban problem (Brown and Hirschl 1995; Fitchen 1981; Jensen and McLaughlin 1993; Lichter and Johnson 2007). Observers have noted that rural economies are typically less diversified than urban economies (Jensen et al. 1999), and jobs tend to be scarcer and have lower pay than urban jobs (Gibbs 2002; Lichter, McLaughlin and Cornwell 1995), making the connection between labour force attachment and escape from poverty considerably less certain. Rural poor also often have less access to transportation infrastructure and live in more physically remote areas which makes access to social services (including education, health and welfare-related services) more difficult, time-consuming and costly (Cushing 1999). Although over past decades the gap between metro and nonmetro poverty rates has narrowed, nonmetropolitan areas have consistently had higher rates of poverty than metropolitan counties (see Figure 6.1).

Even so, poverty research in the US has tended to have a strong urban bias (Duncan and Sweet 1992; Hoppe 1993; Lichter and Jensen 2002; Lichter and Parisi 2008). Even though poverty 'concentrates' in both central city *and* nonmetropolitan areas in the US, only about one-fifth of Americans in poverty live in rural areas, a factor that contributes to the 'invisibility' of rural poverty and the limited attention it receives in research and policy arenas (Weber et al. 2005).

Despite this under-recognition, since the early 1990s there have been several focused efforts to systematically assess the status of rural poverty in the US (e.g. Duncan 1992; Weber, Duncan and Whitener 2002), as well as other efforts examining the incidence and dynamics of rural poverty within particular regions and/or places (Duncan 1999; Pickering et al. 2006). Especially notable was the 1993 publication of *Persistent Poverty in Rural America*, assembled by the Rural Sociological Society Task Force on Persistent Rural Poverty in order to 'provide conceptual clarification regarding the factors and dynamics of society which precipitate and perpetuate rural poverty' (1993, 3). The Task Force argued that three predominant theoretical approaches had been used to explain persistent rural poverty: human capital theories (persistent poverty is a consequence of insufficient skills necessary to obtain adequate employment), economic organisation theories (inadequate employment opportunities explain persistent rural

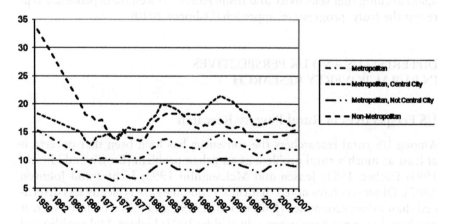

Figure 6.1   Poverty rates across US metro and nonmetro areas, 1959–2009.

poverty) and culture of poverty theories (economically irrational lifestyle preferences explain rural poverty).

The Task Force further argued that these theoretical approaches were insufficient to adequately understand rural poverty and formulate appropriate policy responses. Instead, the authors proposed a number of alternative perspectives emphasizing factors such as the way in which work and gendered relations are embedded within particular social contexts, the effects of historically embedded formal and informal institutions that reproduce inequality across social groups and rational *under*investment in human capital, particularly in environments in which individuals see little economic reward from education, especially within local communities (see also Corbett 2007). At macro-levels the Task Force suggested the utility of dependency theories, particularly for areas dependent on resource extraction, in terms of understanding the effects of global economic restructuring and the failure of national-level policy-making to respond to rural needs or develop effective, comprehensive rural policies extending beyond agricultural policy.

Nearly two decades hence, the record is somewhat mixed on US rural poverty research. To a large extent, rural poverty continues to be largely overshadowed by research on urban poverty. Human capital and economic organisation theories also continue to represent dominant approaches to understanding rural poverty (Jensen, McLaughlin and Slack 2003). On the other hand, rural poverty research in the US has developed and strengthened several theoretical and analytical strands in the past two decades, each of which is at least partially anticipated by the 1993 Task Force report.

These include, first, a more incisive focus on the relationship between spatial inequality and social inequality that goes beyond comparisons of social and economic conditions across different geographies, and instead provides a more nuanced examination of the dynamics by which poverty is distributed and redistributed over space. As Fitchen, writing in the early 1990s, observed about the status of rural poverty research at that time, 'For the most part, attention has been divided between studies of poor people, most commonly households, and studies of poor places, usually counties or regions. The relationship between poor people and poor places, however, often remains unspecified' (Fitchen 1995, 181).

The work of Fitchen (1994, 1995) and others began to examine more seriously the complex relationships between the geographies of poverty and place, often raising new theoretical and policy questions about differential migration patterns of poor movers, 'geographies of exclusion' and the dynamics of rural poverty concentration (Blank 2005; Cotter 2002; Foulkes and Schafft 2010; Lichter and Parisi 2008; Nord 1998; Nord, Luloff and Jensen 1995; Notter, MacTavish and Shamah 2008). Some of this work, directly inspired by Fitchen's research on rural poverty, housing insecurity and residential mobility, has challenged human capital theories of migration and mobility by examining the dynamics of residential mobility of disadvantaged households within and across poor places. This includes macro-level demographic analyses by Nord (1998), Nord, Luloff and Jensen (1995) and Foulkes and Schafft (2010), as well as the community and regionally focused research such as Foulkes and Newbold's (2008) work on residential mobility and rural 'poverty catchments' and the work of Schafft and colleagues on poverty, residential mobility and student transiency in rural areas (Schafft 2006; Schafft, Killeen and Morrissey 2010; Schafft and Prins 2009). Other work has looked at the geography of racial and ethnic exclusion (Lobao and Saenz 2002), such as Lichter and colleagues' (2007) examination of racial and socio-economic segregation and municipal annexation patterns in the nonmetropolitan South, and Lichter and Johnson's (2007) study of poverty concentrations among rural minorities in the context of overall decreasing spatial inequality in nonmetropolitan America.

Secondly, rural researchers have paid increasing attention to the in-migration of foreign-born ethnic and racial minorities into 'non-traditional' rural destinations. This work has not tended to analytically foreground poverty, but nonetheless implicitly focuses on the relationship between demographic change and the shifting economic and social status of rural people, newcomers and longer-term residents alike, and the communities in which they reside. During the 1990s, and particularly with the release of the 2000 US Census data, demographers began to detect marked shifts in the patterns of immigrant settlement, in particular noting movement to 'non-traditional' migration locations, often in rural areas that had not previously attracted many migrants (Barcus 2006; Farmer and Moon 2009; Kandel and Parrado 2006; Kandel and Cromartie 2004). Much of these changing migration patterns were linked to changes in the organisation of the meat processing industry, the siting of new meat processing facilities in economically declining rural areas and the active recruitment of immigrant (and often undocumented) labour (Broadway 2007; Massey 2008; Stull, Broadway and Griffith 1995). Hence, demographic analyses were quickly aligned with political economic examinations of rural disadvantage, industrial organisation and structural changes in North American food processing (especially meat and poultry) all in the context of shifting labour market conditions and international trade and immigration policies.

At the same time, these analyses were coupled with research focused more squarely aimed at the community level, some of which borrowed from the 'boomtown' literature associated analyses of community economic and demographic change in the context of rapid natural resource development (e.g. Broadway 2007; McConnell and Miraftab 2009). Other research in this area examines what these new migration patterns have meant for local culture, community and identity; the social and economic integration of new immigrants within and beyond the ethnic enclave; and community responses and reactions to new immigrant-related diversity in rural America (Crowley and Lichter 2009; Gimpel and Lay 2008; Pfeffer and Parra 2009; Salamon 2003).

Last, there are several notable examples of US rural poverty research that have explicitly examined the relationship between local culture and poverty discourses, and how those discourses, often with specific racial and/or gendered dimensions, are embedded within broader cultural constructions of poverty, race and rurality. This work is largely qualitative in methodological approach and often informed by multiple disciplinary and theoretical orientations. Sherman (2006, 2009), for example, uses an extended case study approach to examine poverty, gendered identity and constructions of morality in the context of logging industry collapse in rural California.

Devine similarly looks at the social construction of poverty 'along markers of difference, such as race, class, gender, and generation' (2006, 953) to examine the ways in which local understandings in the rural Northwest differentially position first-generation 'hard-working' Hispanic immigrants as (deserving) 'working poor', as opposed to those who 'choose' poverty as a way of life. Similar work includes Bonds (2009) and Lawson, Jarosz and Bonds (2008, 2010), who examine how discourses of poverty are embedded within macro-processes of economic restructuring and broader neoliberal ideologies, arguing that 'systems of meaning circulate through economic development practices, institutions and political-economic contexts to produce regimes of truth and practice that actively marginalize the poor' (2008, 738).

Taken together, these three strands of rural poverty research are consistent with the recommendations of the 1993 Task Force report through their multilevel foci and their examinations of how local social, cultural and economic processes are embedded within and reflect (and in some cases resist) macro-structural processes. Additionally, much of this work has seriously attempted to delineate the various relationships and processes that connect the poverty of people to the poverty of place. While social exclusion as a conceptual or discursive device has seldom been used in US contexts (Parent and Lewis 2003), much US rural poverty research, with its emphasis on the relationship between social and spatial inequality (persons left behind in places left behind) contain strong foci on relational and historically embedded patterns of disadvantage at multiple micro- and macro-levels. However, consistent with the broader body of US poverty research, this work has similarly been challenged in its ability to coherently and substantively influence public policy.

UK Perspectives in Rural Poverty Research

In terms of rural poverty, there is nowhere in rural UK resembling the areas of persistent poverty in Appalachia or the Mississippi Delta. Instead rural Britain is characterised by 'poverty amongst affluence', even in areas of poor economic performance such as Cornwall or parts of northern Scotland, which brings quite a different set of challenges for policy as well as for those who experience rural poverty.

Until the mid-twentieth century, rural poverty in the UK was synonymous with agricultural poverty, to the extent that it was recognised by research or policy. Apart from private charity, the Poor Law and the workhouse remained the only support available to farmworkers and bankrupt farmers until 1936, since they were excluded from the National Insurance Act 1911. Rural philanthropy was variable and dependent on local patronage (Newby 1987, 87). From 1873 until 1939 a long agricultural depression, interrupted only by the First World War, 'produced a situation in which thousands of acres of arable land lay unkempt and unfarmed, agricultural bankruptcies had soared and thousands of farm workers were unemployed or suffering from falling wages' (ibid., 180). Waves of rural unrest in 1872 and 1914 encouraged farmworkers, farmers and landowners each to form unions as part of a collective mobilisation of the competing class interests in agriculture, but meanwhile their numbers and economic significance declined. From 1850 to 1925 agriculture's share of GDP declined from 20 per cent to 4 per cent, and its workforce from 21 per cent to 7 per cent (Howkins 1992, 288). Rural workers became socially marginalised as a consequence of nineteenth-century enclosure laws, mechanization of farming practices and increasing suburbanization (Newby 1987). Researchers have tended towards three interrelated explanations for post-1945 rural poverty: the role of the state, the role of class relations and the role of broader economic and social processes.

The post-war reconstruction brought an array of state measures that reached rural and urban areas alike, most notably the National Health Service (NHS), free secondary education and the welfare state. However, these provisions were accompanied by a regulatory framework, proposed by the 1942 Scott Report, which sought to protect the countryside from urban encroachment and to preserve the 'traditional rural way of life', which, in part, meant excluding new housing and employment from rural England. As Newby (1980, 239) observed, 'the rural poor had little to gain from the preservation of their poverty, but they were without a voice on the crucial committees which evolved the planning system from the late 1930s onwards'. The presumption was that the countryside should be reserved for agriculture and that this would ensure rural prosperity. Yet,

> by directing new industrial development away from rural areas, conventional strategic planning policy restricted the economic growth of the countryside and perpetuated a low-wage rural economy (. . .) A parallel sequence of events occurred with respect to new housing developments. New housing was to be restricted—in both the public and private spheres—so that a planned scarcity of housing duly emerged (. . .) By the 1970s not only was public housing in rural areas in short supply, but so too was cheap private housing. In the case of both development control policy and housing policy, attempts to preserve the rural status quo turned out to be redistributive—and in a highly regressive manner. (Newby 1987, 220; see also Hall et al. 1974, 406–409)

Newby (1987, 187) is adamant that these outcomes—a low-wage economy and unaffordable housing—'have not been haphazard nor the result of some immutable natural law, but the result of policy decisions quite consciously pursued'. Further studies of the state's role were prompted by changes to public expenditure targeting in the 1970s, as the Labour government sought to address deprivation in the inner cities. Studies were initiated by rural councils to demonstrate the existence also of 'rural deprivation' in what became known as the 'arithmetic of woe' (McLaughlin 1986), and research continues to assess the impacts of policy on rural disadvantage (e.g. Ellis 2002; Phimister et al. 2005; Commission for Rural Communities [CRC] 2006).

To understand why socially regressive policies have endured in rural areas since 1945, a number of authors have highlighted class relations. In their seminal work on *Property, Paternalism and Power*, Newby et al. (1978) argued that it was in the class interest of farmers and landowners to exclude housing and employment from their areas, and that they leveraged the political power to achieve this by dominating local political bodies. As major employers it is in their interest to exclude rival employers so as to keep wages low and limit the supply of housing, both because this maintains farmworkers' reliance on tied housing (reinforcing social control) and avoids the cost of new housing and related infrastructure. The resulting gentrification of the countryside (Phillips 1993) has introduced new class relations that also militate against development, in that new rural residents can increase their own property values and maintain social exclusivity by opposing further development (Shucksmith 1990, 2000b; Murdoch 1995), even though this maintains a low-wage rural economy and restricts poorer groups' life chances. As Newby argued, 'policies which systematically disadvantage the rural poor can now, therefore, be assured of local democratic support' (1979, 497), suggesting that action to address rural poverty must principally come from national, not local, policy.

A third explanation for UK rural poverty has been found in the economic and social processes of change more generally, including rural restructuring, globalisation, personal mobility and ageing. Shaw (1979) proposed a model of 'the rural deprivation cycle' whereby low incomes were seen to lead not only to poor housing, but also to the inability to afford a car, and so to inaccessibility to jobs, education, health and recreation. This encouraged a simplistic view that rural deprivation equated merely to access to services (Shucksmith et al. 1997). A 1980 study of rural deprivation in England (McLaughlin 1986; Bradley 1986) and a follow-up study of rural lifestyles in 1990 (Cloke and Milbourne 1992; Cloke, Milbourne and Thomas 1994; Cloke et al. 1995) each found around 25 per cent of rural households to be living in or on the margins of poverty,[8] notably elderly people living alone and low-paid, manual workers' households, reflecting the lack of alternatives to low-paid work in agriculture and tourism (see also Shucksmith et al. 1994). Bradley (1986) highlights the social isolation of many elderly people in rural areas as a result of selective migration.

In the 1990s rural studies in the UK, and particularly rural geography, switched its focus from poverty and inequality to cultural identities and differences under the influence of the 'cultural turn' in human geography. Philo's (1992) seminal paper on 'the rural other' showed how people in rural areas may be marginalised through cultural practices in everyday life, and particularly through the social construction of identity and symbolic capital in social and lay discourses (Cloke and Little 1997; Milbourne 1997; Hughes et al. 2005). As in the US, many studies in this style are relational and revealing, but fail to speak to policy and practice (Milbourne 2000). Milbourne (2004, 34) has called for a resurgence of interest in poverty among rural geographers and specifically for a greater interest in the local contexts of rural poverty, investigating 'the linkages between poverty and people in particular places'. He points out that the concept of social exclusion emphasizes the importance of local context, and argues that research should be 'concerned with the productions, representations, materialities and experiences of poverty in particular spaces, as well as the specific mixes of welfare facilities and welfare policy contexts in these spaces' (123). In proposing this place-based approach to rural poverty studies, Milbourne emphasizes its antecedents in the US, specifically Duncan and Lambourghini (1994) and Duncan (1996, 1999).

While rural geographers have emphasized cultural differences and identities, the concept of social exclusion was taken as the basis for multidisciplinary, mixed-method research under the Joseph Rowntree Foundation's Action in Rural Areas programme from 1997 to 2000 (Shucksmith 2000b).[9] The research drew attention to the rural effects of market processes, and the rolling back of state systems, as a neo-liberal hegemony promoted deregulation, privatization, cuts in public spending and global capital's penetration of labour and product markets (Shucksmith 2002). The programme found that labour markets and housing markets were instrumental in generating inequality and exclusion, with many respondents perceiving very restricted opportunities for well-paid, secure employment or affordable housing, while at the same time these markets facilitated in-migration of affluent households. These impediments to inclusion were closely bound up with failings of private and public services, notably transport, social housing and childcare. Moreover, the welfare state was failing to reach potential recipients through selective benefits and the take-up of welfare entitlements was lower than in urban areas (Bramley, Lancaster and Gordon 2000). To mitigate these failings of markets and state, there was a greater reliance on the voluntary sector and on friends and family, although migration and the loss of young people had meanwhile ruptured informal support networks and left elderly people in rural areas socially isolated. The research concluded that the risk of poverty is not confined to a small minority but touches many rural dwellers, especially in old age. The findings pointed strongly towards structural causes of rural poverty, finding no evidence of 'cultures of poverty' nor benefit dependency. On the contrary, while elderly people and lone parents face long-term poverty, for other people it tends to be short spells during which the support of the welfare state is crucial.

Further analysis by CRC (2006) has confirmed these findings, adding detailed analysis of government statistics. These and other studies (Shucksmith, Shucksmith and Watt 2006) suggest that multidimensional conceptualizations of social exclusion and inclusion appear helpful in researching the interconnectedness of the many different dimensions of service provision, transport, childcare, labour market participation and community engagement which characterise the experience of low-income groups in rural areas. Specifically it allows us to consider the complex interactions between bureaucratic, associative, communal and market relations within particular social contexts which give rise to exclusion.

CONCLUSION: RETHINKING RURAL POVERTY

The US and UK are sometimes painted as examples of contrasting welfare regimes, the US operating a residual welfare model in which poverty is treated as self-induced and the UK welfare state regarded as closer to a universal model founded on structural explanations of poverty and social exclusion. As Esping-Anderson (1990) recognised, the picture is far more nuanced and complex. In each country there are ongoing tensions between the left's tendency towards structural, systemic explanations, a strong role for the state and universality and the right's tendency towards individual–cultural explanations, a minimal state role and selectivity. The post-war period of welfare consensus between left and right in the UK may in retrospect be seen as unusual, even though the UK retains a greater public attachment to social solidarity than the US.

A striking feature of US rural poverty research has been the influence of the Task Force on Persistent Rural Poverty, which has no parallel in the UK or Europe. Nevertheless, it appears that UK research has tended to adopt similar theoretical perspectives to those proposed by the Task Force, with research exploring many similar issues such as the effects of global economic restructuring, the impacts of migration, the failure of the state to respond to rural needs and to some extent examinations of the dynamics of poverty prompted by the concept of social exclusion. In common with the US, UK research on rural poverty has similarly been overshadowed by research on urban poverty—partly because rural areas are seen as idyllic and rural poverty is hidden and diffuse—and policy has shown little interest in rural poverty. There are also significant differences between US and UK research, of course. The UK work on migration has focused on middle-class in-migration, not the differential migration patterns of poorer households studied by Fitchen and others in the US. There have also been few studies in the UK of the in-migration of ethnic minorities, largely because so few people from ethnic minorities have lived in rural Britain until recently (see de Lima, Parra and Pfeffer, this volume). Instead UK research has prioritized power relations, especially those of class, along with culture and identity.

Finally, we have seen how the UK (along with the EU more generally) has adopted the concept of social exclusion. The question arises whether this offers any potential added insights from which US research and policy might benefit. Ironically, one of our conclusions is that many US rural poverty researchers have explored similar conceptual avenues to study the dynamics and multidimensional, place-based features of poverty—but without necessarily employing the framework of social exclusion. Milbourne (2004) also has noted these convergences, and indeed the richness of US rural poverty research (to the evident surprise of Tickamyer 2005).

Ultimately this returns us to the question of how social exclusion as a concept should be understood and used. If it is merely about labour market integration then it adds little. But if it can provoke more systematic thinking about how 'history meets biography' (Byrne 1999), and fulfils Room's promise that it offers a stronger theoretical basis for poverty studies, then perhaps, as Donnison (1998, 5) has suggested, 'social exclusion is an idea which poses the right kind of questions'. More importantly, however, we need to pay attention to how conceptual refinements and academic debates are (or are not) translated into wider understandings of the aetiology of poverty as well as the public policy to address it. That is, these are not simply academic debates, but debates and understandings that have real consequences for real people.

7 Rural Economic Transformations in the UK and US

Jane Atterton, John Bryden
and Thomas G. Johnson

INTRODUCTION

Rural economies in the UK and US have undergone major transformations in recent decades, as traditional, primary sector activities have declined in terms of employment and income generation and as new growth sectors have emerged. Homeworking has also become increasingly important as individuals choose to combine their home and work, and new business start-ups have been generated by large numbers of in-migrants moving into many rural areas. Rural economies (particularly those outside urban commuting belts) are also increasingly becoming recognised as providers of important ecosystem services—the processes through which the environment produces resources utilized by humans—including clean water, fresh local food, renewable energy generation and waste management, as well as recreational, habitational and tourism services.

This chapter explores these rural economic transformations in the UK and US over recent decades, starting with a discussion of the theoretical frameworks and differing national policy and institutional contexts in which the data presented later in the chapter must be considered. The second section of the chapter uses empirical data to illustrate the broad shifts in the economies of rural areas in the UK and US in recent years. Beneath these broad generalisations, there are important differences between, and variations within, the UK and US, and these are explored in this section. The final section of the chapter summarises the key points made and discusses the implications for the future development of rural economies in the two countries.

Before continuing it is important to acknowledge the ways in which rural economies and societies differ in the UK and US, and the implications this has for rural economic development. While the two countries share some similarities, for example, a high degree of urbanisation, low employment dependence on agriculture and population ageing, there are important differences in attitudes to private property and public access to land, in social welfare and territorial equivalence policies, in governance and institutional arrangements and in the content of 'rural' policies, all of which have differential economic impacts.

For example, the Land Reform (Scotland) Act 2003 formalised public access rights over private land in this part of the UK, while the limitations on public access to property in some parts of the US mean that opportunities for outdoor activities and recreation can be more restricted outside the national, state and local parks. The different attitudes and legislation surrounding property rights means that it is much easier (and cheaper) to build rural housing in the US than it is in the UK. The welfare and territorial equivalence measures in the UK help to ensure the presence of schools, health care and other public services in rural areas, and that people working in these services are paid an adequate salary (see Bryden and Warner, this volume). On the other hand, the relatively greater powers of subnational levels of government in the US mean that more functions and activities are funded and performed at local levels than in the highly centralized UK. In addition, landownership patterns and associated power relations differ between the UK and the US. The UK still has large landowners and estates which can dominate local—and even national—decision-making about land use and rural development, while the distribution of landownership in the US has tended to be much more even. Finally, there are strong public attitudes in the UK towards the maintenance of rural communities, be that the crofting counties in north-west Scotland with a history of oppression of smallholding tenant farmers (crofters), or the 'idyllic' villages of the English countryside. Such differences and nuances affect settlement patterns, employment opportunities, service provision, incomes and income distribution and quality of life, all of which influence rural migration patterns and the potential for rural economic growth and simultaneously limit the power of general theories to explain the transformations.

Obtaining accurate, up-to-date economic data for the rural UK as a whole is difficult, if not impossible. This is a result of the adoption of different definitions of rurality (see Annex) and different methods of data collection. Thus, the key UK rural economic trends discussed in the chapter are mostly illustrated using data from England and Scotland (using discrete data from Wales and Northern Ireland is beyond the scope of the chapter). Presenting data from the two countries separately also highlights the significant internal variations within the UK and reflects the devolved nature of rural policy there. We turn first to describing the key theoretical and political and institutional frameworks in which the empirical data must be understood.

THEORETICAL FRAMEWORKS

It is not possible to discuss the current status and future prospects of rural economies in the UK or US without considering how jobs, incomes and economic security are affected by globalisation. Definitions of globalisation abound, and M. Woods (2005, 33) argues that the term refers to the advanced interconnection and interdependence of localities around the world, reflecting the compression of time and space. He argues that the term is therefore, in essence, about power—about the lack of power of rural regions to control their own futures, and about the increasing subjection of rural regions to networks and processes of power that are produced, reproduced and executed on a global scale. Transnational corporations are seen as the key units in globalisation processes, stateless entities which attempt to maximize profits by moving their capital to sites with the lowest production costs (a practice known as offshoring). Rural economies may be particularly vulnerable to offshoring and in communities where alternative employment options are limited, the impact of this process can be devastating. However, while globalisation has undoubtedly opened up rural businesses to greater competition, it also presents real opportunities to those rural areas with the capacity to take advantage of them, for example, through developing as sites for niche environmental or cultural tourism or as locations for the production of quality food and drink products which can be sold using the Internet to a global marketplace.

The varying capacities of rural areas to take advantage of the increasingly globalised world in which we live are a critical issue both in research and policy terms. In Europe, a number of multi-country projects have explored this issue from a variety of different perspectives (see, for example, Árnason, Shucksmith and Vergunst 2009; Bryden and Hart 2004; Terluin and Post 2000). Using different approaches, these studies have stressed the importance of 'tangible' factors such as IT infrastructure and the skills of the local population, in combination with 'less tangible' factors such as sense of identity and community, social capital and local and extra-local networking, in explaining the capacity for rural areas to engage with—and thus potentially regain some power over—the rapid economic transformations that have been occurring in recent decades. Theoretical debates in the literature have shifted from a focus on the need for endogenous, locally generated and controlled development in the 1980s and early 1990s, towards a recognition of the need for neo-endogenous development in which development is initiated and controlled locally but engages in a positive way with extra-local processes, actors and resources (Ward et al. 2005; Ray 2001; Lowe, Murdoch and Ward 1995).

It is also important to note the theoretical debates that are occurring in relation to the nature of economic growth and sustainability. This is a huge and complex area with much written about it (see, for example, Bryden et al. 2010; Florida 2010; Hart, Laville and Cattani 2010; Harvey 2010; Newell and Paterson 2010), but it is useful to briefly consider the aspects of the debate that are particularly relevant to rural development. These can be framed mainly in terms of the need for new models of economic organisation and governance as a result of the challenges of climate change and the shift to a 'post-carbon economy'. Drawing on the work of Newell and Paterson (2010), Ward (2010, 8–9) argues that decoupling emissions growth from economic growth will inevitably pose huge challenges for governments and businesses, but the recent financial crisis opens up unusual room for manoeuvre. There are different potential scenarios for how these challenges and opportunities might play out, many of which will have important implications for patterns of settlement structure and our ways of transporting goods and people (see also Rural Coalition 2010, 19–21), and many of which will present important opportunities for rural areas, such as in generating renewable energy at the community and household level.

These debates can be illustrated through the example of the English town and country planning system. The traditional approach to rural development in England has been conservative and preservationist, with the planning system generally in favour of limiting (and sometimes preventing) growth and protecting the countryside and its green space. Power relations are important to this discourse, as wealthy and vocal rural residents have tended to mobilise to prevent developments from occurring (Shucksmith 2010; Newby et al. 1978). More recently, those opposing development in the countryside have taken more of an environmental standpoint, arguing that economic development in the countryside is inherently unsustainable as it encourages more people to travel longer distances by car.

However, the negative impacts of such a conservative approach have increasingly been voiced, including the limitations that it places both on housing development (leading to increasing demand and prices) and the potential for rural economies to diversify from an agricultural base. There have been calls for a more proactive planning system which permits development (albeit at the right level and of an appropriate kind), provides adequate housing for locals and in-migrants, encourages the sympathetic conversion of unused agricultural and other buildings to new uses and the building of new small business workspaces, and offers more people the flexibility to work from home (M. Taylor 2008).

Before moving on to discuss the policy and institutional contexts in the US and UK, it is important to make reference to the recent economic recession and its impacts on rural economies. This started with the collapse of the sub-prime mortgage market in the US, followed by the crisis of the Northern Rock bank in the UK, which only avoided collapse in the summer of 2007 by being brought into public ownership. Crisis followed across the banking system, resulting in expensive tax-payer-funded bank bailouts and large-scale public sector funding cuts (Ward 2010). Hart, Laville and Cattani (2010) discuss the scenarios for a human economy following the financial and economic crisis while Harvey's (2010) work explores the varying international dimensions of the recession, but there has been limited research into the urban and rural impacts of the recession. Work done by Rose Regeneration and the Rural Services Network in England shows that the geographically peripheral areas are likely to be the most vulnerable to the recession. The work uses a 'Rural Vulnerability Index' based on a composite of statistical indicators, including the proportion of jobs in the public sector and average pay (Rose Regeneration 2010). Further work has since been carried out using the Index in Scotland to explore the vulnerability of local authorities and towns (Atterton 2011; Atterton et al. 2011) On the other hand, Ward (2010) argues that there is evidence to suggest that rural businesses may be more resilient to an economic downturn as a result of their loyal customer base and greater reliance on internal rather an external finance due to the intertwining of businesses and households (Atterton and Affleck 2010; Phillipson et al. 2004; Oughton, Wheelock and Baines 2003). Survey research by Atterton and Affleck (2010) found a mixed picture with respect to the impact of the recession on rural businesses in the north-east of England, with some business owners seeing opportunities in the recession and many owners still planning growth and innovating to exploit new markets.

This chapter now turns to describing the different policy and institutional contexts in the US and UK, which are critical in explaining the key economic transformations that have been underway recently in rural areas of the two countries.

THE POLICY AND INSTITUTIONAL CONTEXT IN THE UK AND THE US

The UK Context

Rural areas and rural development issues do not have much influence over national economic and spatial development policies in the UK. This is despite some initial signs from the 1997 Labour government of a new approach to rural policy, including the Performance and Innovation Unit (1999) report and the establishment of the Countryside Agency. In reality, these signs did not materialise into a fundamental shift in how rural areas were viewed in national policy-making and agriculture still retains a national policy profile today (Ward 2006). This is despite evidence from the Organisation for Economic Co-operation and Development ([OECD] 2006), amongst others, that sectoral approaches to agricultural support and development only deliver limited wider benefits for rural people and territories.

Scotland, England, Wales and Northern Ireland all have Departments of Rural Affairs or equivalents, although agriculturally oriented approaches have continued to dominate rural policy and spending in recent years with insufficient prominence and resources given to rural affairs objectives. This is in part due to a strong commitment to a social welfare rationale for agricultural support in Scotland. In England, the treatment of rural areas in spatial policy has developed considerably with Regional Development Agencies (RDAs) required to pay some regard to rural areas (although these have been abolished by the coalition government and ceased to exist in 2011). The rural work of RDAs was also hampered by a number of factors, including a 'fewer-bigger' approach to investment priorities, weak national coordination between RDAs in rural affairs and an increased interest amongst central government departments in the importance of city regions (Ward 2006). This city region focus has also been mirrored in policy documents in Scotland (e.g. Scottish Executive 2002). This raises a number of challenges for rural areas, as it reinforces unhelpful notions of geographical centrality and hierarchies and marginalises rural areas which come to be seen as the passive beneficiaries of the 'trickle down' of urban-focused strategies and investment, rather than as places that can actively contribute to the development of city regions as attractive places for starting businesses (Ward 2006).

More recently, there has been somewhat renewed interest in rural economies in England with the publication of a number of reports outlining their performance and potential economic contribution (Commission for Rural Communities [CRC] 2008a; Environment, Food and Rural Affairs [EFRA] Committee 2008; M. Taylor 2008). The Rural Advocate's report to the Prime Minister in 2008 (CRC 2008a), for example, argued that if rural firms generated turnover levels comparable to the rural share of employment or enterprises in England, the assessed unfulfilled potential growth in output from rural firms may achieve approximately £236 to £347 billion per annum. The report argued that rural businesses should be granted better access to government support and made a number of specific recommendations including the establishment of a Rural Finance Forum, Rural Innovation Initiative and a National Rural Summit. In response, in addition to questioning the figure put forward by the CRC, the government argued in favour of a mainstreaming approach rather than having a separate national framework for differentiated urban and rural policies (EFRA Committee 2009).

In Scotland, rural and agriculture policy are devolved but are highly Europeanised, which brings Whitehall back into the negotiations and acts as a force for convergence of UK policy. Scotland now has its own chapter in the UK Rural Development Strategy and its own Scotland Rural Development Programme. However, devolution has meant that the political and administrative structures and policy communities in Scotland are now more distinct and self-contained, and that a Scottish rural policy agenda is developing. Scotland also has a stronger reliance on professional networks and local government as a result of the relative weakness of policy-making capacity at the centre (Keating and Stevenson 2006). However, despite some evidence of a broadening agenda for rural policy in Scotland, agricultural concerns still dominate. Keating and Stevenson (2006) argue that one reason for this is the operation of the economic development networks in Scotland in parallel to, rather than within, the newer networks for rural policy.

Comparing the 2000 Rural White Paper in England and the equivalent document in Scotland (Scottish Executive 2000) shows that the general approach was quite different, although some proposals appear in both papers, relating to diversification, for example. The English paper was much more concerned with housing pressures and the urban fringe whilst in Scotland the emphasis was more on social inclusion and economic development, and particularly growing rural business. More recently, *Rural Scotland, Better Still, Naturally* (Scottish Government 2007) presented a more comprehensive vision for rural Scotland, but the extent to which the document successfully balanced and integrated the continuing sectoral approach and the regional and national elements of rural policy was questionable (OECD 2008, 11). The recent OECD (2008) review of rural policy in Scotland cites creating opportunities for economic development and diversification beyond agriculture as one of the key priorities for rural policy in the future, through developing niche tourism and creating an environment that is supportive to small and medium-sized enterprises. In 2010, the Rural Development Council (created by the Cabinet Secretary for Rural Affairs Richard Lochhead to be an independent rural voice) released a consultation document entitled *Speak Up for Rural Scotland* (Scottish Government 2010b). The document contains a number of suggested 'step changes', including the need to improve leadership skills and business ambition, the need for businesses to focus on increasing the value-added of their products and services and the need to clarify the business advice and support system. The Scottish Government has since issued its response to the consultation, which sets out its key priorities (Scottish Government 2011a).

The US Context

US rural policy has long existed in the shadow of sectoral and urban policy. For at least the last thirty years, narrow US rural policy has been equated with agricultural sectoral policy. It was assumed that the economies and quality of life of rural regions could best be improved by supporting the income of farmers and by promoting value-added activities. As a result, US rural policy is contained within the farm bill legislation which periodically reauthorizes commodity programmes, food assistance, agricultural research, extension and education and agri-environmental and rural development programmes. Implementation of US rural policy is the responsibility of the United States Department of Agriculture (USDA). USDA Rural Development administers a variety of programmes designed to finance rural businesses, enhance the stock of rural housing and finance rural utilities and some types of infrastructure, notably broadband and certain public facilities.

Responsibility for broad rural development policy is dispersed across several federal agencies, including Health and Human Services, Commerce (which includes the Economic Development Agency), Education, Transportation, Environmental Protection Agency, Bureau of Land Management and others. Despite some attempts to join up these policies through state rural development councils, very little coordination exists. Examples of policies and programmes which contradict and duplicate each other abound, although under the American Recovery and Reinvestment Act (ARRA) in 2009, there has been some coordination and collaboration of programmes.

Urban policy and a handful of regional programmes (the Appalachian Regional Commission, the Tennessee Valley Authority and the Lower Mississippi Delta Development Commission, for example) are among the few place-based development policies in the US. While the regional programmes support rural development objectives within their respective regions, the vast majority of rural America is primarily served by sectoral policies only. Urban policy largely ignores the needs of the rural periphery beyond the commutershed. Only recently have farm advocates come to the realisation that agricultural policy is not necessarily good rural policy and that farm families depend more on their rural communities than rural communities depend on their farms. Given time, this view may lead to changes in priorities in the US Congress, but to date, little attention has been given to rural policy.

In August 2009 the newly installed Obama administration laid out the basic principles of its new economic policy for the US. Referred to as its 'place-based initiative' this policy statement argued that:

> Place-based policies leverage investments by focusing resources in targeted places and drawing on the compounding effect of well-coordinated action. Effective place-based policies can influence how rural and metropolitan areas develop, how well they function as places to live, work, operate a business, preserve heritage, and more. Such policies can also streamline otherwise redundant and disconnected programs. (Orszag et al. 2009)

The policy statement goes on to call for ex ante and ex post evaluations of programmes and projects, bottom-up decision-making and regional approaches.

In February 2010, the Obama administration announced its rural development policy (Vilsack 2010). The new policy has several major components including: (1) the development of renewable energy, (2) local and regional food systems, (3) development of environmental markets (multi-functionality in European terms), (4) a rural innovation initiative and (5) broadband infrastructure development. In April 2010, the White House published *Strengthening the Rural Economy* (Council of Economic Advisors 2010), which directed the Small Business Administration and the Economic Development Administration to support rural innovation systems. While these policies are still a small part of a much larger policy of agricultural supports and still assume that agriculture is key to rural development, there are a number of welcome changes. The proposed changes are much more consistent with the fundamental tenets of the OECD's (2006) *New Rural Paradigm*, for example, since they rely on investments in place of assets. The proposed regional innovation initiative in particular will increase the ability of rural areas to guide their own future. The initiative also has as a goal, the vertical and horizontal coordination of government and governance.

Thus, in both the UK and the US, rural policy has tended to be equated with sectoral agricultural policy, although recently there have been some limited signs of a broadening of the agenda with a recognition of the range of rural businesses and the need to improve support to them in both countries. The chapter now moves on to discuss the broad changes that have occurred in terms of rural employment and the key emerging characteristics of the 'new rural economy' in both countries. The final section of the chapter draws all of the material together and offers some suggestions for the shaping of future rural development policies in the UK and US.

CHANGES IN RURAL EMPLOYMENT

Like elsewhere, in the US and UK there have been dramatic decreases in agricultural employment in the last fifty years or so. Similar declines have taken place in forestry and fishing, hunting, mining and quarrying, all of which were significant employers in many rural areas. As a consequence, agriculture now accounts for a minority of those employed in rural areas of the OECD countries. In the US and UK in 2003, the sector represented less than 2 per cent of total employment (CRC 2008b; OECD 2006, 40). As a proportion of only nonmetropolitan employment in the US, the sector accounted for 5–6 per cent of employment in 2002. However, If 'agriculture-related' employment is taken into account (including upstream and downstream activities) recent data indicates that about 21 per cent of nonmetropolitan employment in the US remains in agriculture and agriculture-related activities (USDA Economic Research Service 2005).

As well as overall decline, there have been considerable changes in the make-up of employment in primary sector activities in recent years. In rural England, for example, the number of full-time farmers fell by 19.6 per cent between 1999 and 2007, while the number of part-time farmers increased by 42.5 per cent. Over the same period there was a 38.9 per cent decrease in the number of full-time farmworkers, with a particularly large decline in male workers (CRC 2008b). In addition, there has been increasing reliance on immigrant seasonal labour, especially from Eastern Europe and the Baltic States, and particularly for the harvesting of fruit and vegetables. In England, 120,000 migrant workers registered[1] in rural areas between May 2004 and September 2006, of whom 33 per cent were in manufacturing; 25 per cent were in Agriculture; and 20 per cent in Distribution, Hotels and Catering (CRC 2007a). In the US, 75–80 per cent of the workforce in labour-intensive agriculture is foreign born (Rogaly, Crook and Simpson 2007).

In the US the number of farms increased by 3.6 per cent between 2002 and 2007, although a large majority of these were part-time farms. At the same time the number of hired workers on farms declined by 13.2 per cent

(USDA 2009). One notable development in the US is growth in the production of fruits, vegetables, nursery and dairy items in, or close to, large cities (Heimlich and Anderson 2001). While the number of jobs involved in these enterprises might be relatively small, 'farming in the city's shadow' is important for social, environmental and health reasons. Despite the well-documented declines in the labour force on farms in both the UK and US, there is little doubt that the primary sector remains vitally important in both countries in terms of its role in food and raw material production, its dominance of land use, the management of natural resources, environment and landscape and its function as a platform for many kinds of economic diversification, such as tourism and renewable energy generation.

The extent to which employment lost from the primary sector has been replaced by new rural occupations has been highly variable in both countries. Between 1998 and 2002 the number of jobs in agriculture and fishing in rural England dropped by 26,000 or almost 16 per cent.[2] However, there was an overall increase in the number of jobs in rural England of 275,000, including substantial increases in jobs in business services and distribution, hotels and restaurants activities. In Scotland, the tertiary sector now accounts for 47 per cent of employment in remote and accessible rural locations, compared to 60 per cent in the rest of Scotland (Scottish Government 2011b). Some rural areas have managed to achieve significant growth in manufacturing activity and employment since the 1970s. In the US, this manufacturing shift was mainly to the regions with low education and skill levels in the 1980s, but since then it has been to a greater extent to those regions with higher education levels, reflecting growing international competition for low-skilled manufacturing activities. In Scotland, 21 per cent of employment in accessible rural areas is in secondary industry activities (Scottish Government 2011b) while manufacturing activities account for 14.7 per cent and 15.4 per cent of employment in Rural-80 and Rural-50[3] districts, respectively (CRC 2006, 85).

At the same time as they are experiencing a shift in the dominant employment sectors, many rural locations have seen an increasing proportion of commuters travelling to nearby urban centres for employment as a result of improved transport infrastructure, increased personal mobility and the pull of rural areas as residential locations. The CRC (2008b, 97) estimates that net commuting to urban areas represents 17 per cent of all employment for rural residents of England. While commuters have tended to be attracted to the more accessible rural locations, some remote rural regions also have a tradition of long-distance, often weekly commuting.

Although rural areas may have lower job densities and a more limited choice of jobs than urban areas, they do tend to offer a rich pattern of different forms of employment, including higher levels of self-, home-based and part-time employment (CRC 2006, 90). In the US, self-employment has been growing rapidly. Goetz (2008) reports that the number of self-employed rural workers has tripled in the last three decades and at present about one in five rural workers are self-employed. High levels of self-employment can indicate a more enterprising population, but can also reflect the existence of fewer alternative employment options and economic disadvantage. Rural self-employment is also significantly less remunerative than employment. In 2005 rural self-employed workers earned just over half the income of other employed rural workers.

Recent data for Scotland indicates a positive message with respect to employment rates in rural areas. A higher proportion of people in rural areas are economically active (i.e. employed or looking for work) than in the rest of Scotland (81 per cent in accessible rural areas, 78 per cent in remote rural areas and 76 per cent in the rest of Scotland), and the employment rate (the number of people employed as a percentage of the total population of working age) is again higher in rural Scotland than in the rest of Scotland (78 per cent, 75 per cent and 75 per cent, respectively) (Scottish Government 2011b).

Unemployment rates in rural areas of both England and Scotland are lower than in urban areas. In rural Scotland, for example, 3 per cent of the working-age population in both remote and accessible rural areas was unemployed in 2007 compared to 5 per cent in the rest of Scotland (Scottish Government 2009). In the US, unemployment rates in nonmetro areas are very similar to rates in metro areas, largely as a result of commuting and migration (i.e. people moving out of rural areas during periods of low job growth). Observations in the US suggest that rates do tend to differ during different phases of business cycles. During periods of rising unemployment, nonmetro unemployment tends to be lower than metro unemployment rates. As the economy recovers, nonmetro employment is slower to respond, leading to higher unemployment.

The phenomenon of 'pluriactivity', working at several kinds of job, typically a mix of self-employed and waged employment, is also more prevalent in most rural areas (Bryden et al. 1993; Atterton and Affleck 2010). In Scotland the percentage of employed people in remote rural areas who have a second job (9 per cent) is more than twice the percentage in accessible rural or the rest of Scotland (4 per cent and 3 per cent, respectively; see Scottish Government 2011b). In the US approximately 90 per cent of farm family income comes from off-farm sources. About 65 per cent of farm family income comes from wages and non-farm businesses (USDA Economic Research Service 2010) and thus from the local economy. The prevalence of pluriactivity in the livelihood mix and income strategies of farm (and indeed non-farm) households strongly links farming income and structure to the performance of the surrounding regional economy. This has led some researchers (e.g. Terluin 2003, 327; Lowe and Ward 2007c; Ward 2006) to argue that, while farmers and their organisations are often keen to propose that farming is that bedrock of rural economies, the truth is actually the reverse as rural economies are the bedrock of farming.

While the data present a relatively positive picture of the employment situation in many rural areas, rural economies also suffer from significant challenges, including underemployment, which is partly linked with season-ality of labour demand, low female participation rates and a lack of certain types of employment meaning a greater likelihood of a mismatch between the skills and qualifications of the labour force and those required by employers. Wages remain low in many rural employment sectors, including agriculture, tourism and retail. In 2006, the CRC (2006, 72–73) reported a clear concentration of low-income households in England's more periph-eral areas and a growing gap in weekly earnings between the most rural and the most urban areas (estimated at approximately £130 per week). In 2006, data on workless households (defined as working-age households where no one aged sixteen or over is in employment) in England showed that in sparse villages, workless households represented 47 per cent of all 95,766 identified households. In the US in 2002, 14.2 per cent of residents of nonmetropolitan counties were poor compared with 11.6 per cent of metropolitan residents. Furthermore, rural residents in the US are much more likely to be persistently poor.

THE CHARACTERISTICS OF THE 'NEW RURAL ECONOMY' IN THE US AND UK

This section of the chapter draws on data from the UK and US to illus-trate the key characteristics of the 'new rural economy'. Again this is a debated term, but it is usually taken to refer to the growth of secondary and tertiary sector employment in rural areas, which has been gaining ascendancy over recent years (Institute of Economic Affairs 2005). This section is not meant to be an exhaustive account of the new rural econ-omy, but rather a descriptive section in which some of the new features of rural economies are highlighted to illustrate the kinds of shifts that are occurring. The section particularly focuses on the growth in new firm formation in rural areas in knowledge-intensive and high-wage, high-value-added sectors, assisted by improvements in IT infrastructure and by recent high levels of in-migration to rural areas amongst groups of well-skilled, creative individuals. It also refers to the potential for rural areas to serve as providers of ecosystem services.

Overall there has been a shift in economic activity away from urban centres as businesses have relocated to rural areas to take advantage of more favourable conditions and as new rural businesses have started up. This has been accompanied by a shift in population as people have been attracted out of urban centres and into rural locations to take advantage of a higher quality of life (a process known as counterurbanisation). Between 1998 and 2006 rural districts in England supported a growth in new firm formation of 2.7 per cent compared to a decline in urban districts of 2.3 per cent (CRC 2008b, 103).[4] Thus, Lowe and Ward (2007c, 307) paint a rela-tively positive picture of rural economies in England, with higher numbers of businesses per head in rural districts than urban districts (CRC 2008b, 104; DEFRA 2005b; Countryside Agency 2003a) and a growth of jobs and businesses in recent decades. However, there is considerable variation in the performance of rural areas with accessible rural areas and rural parts of the south of England showing more positive growth trends than remote rural areas and rural areas in the north of England, respectively. Data from Scotland in 2011 suggests that when the number of businesses is expressed relative to the size of the population, remote rural areas have the highest total number of businesses per ten thousand adults (496, compared to 448 in accessible rural and 321 in urban areas), and accessible rural areas have the highest level of new businesses per ten thousand adults (39, compared to 38 in remote rural and thirty-six in urban areas; see Scottish Government 2011b).

Similar changes are occurring in the US. Around 1990, a shift occurred in rural business growth in the US as for the first time in decades, self-employment growth in rural areas outstripped that of metro areas (Henderson 2002). Most of this growth is occurring in small manufacturing and tourism sectors. A number of rural regions are experiencing business growth in industry clusters. The industrial cluster phenomenon, identified by Porter (1990) twenty years ago, was originally seen as an urban phenomenon dependent on agglomeration economies not easily achieved in rural areas. But Porter et al. (2004) have concluded that the empirical evidence of rural clusters establishes their growing importance (Rosenfeld et al. 2000; Bernat 1999; Barkley and Henry 1997; Gibbs and Bernat 1997; Henry, Barkley and Zhang 1997). Gibbs and Bernat (1997) report that rural industry clusters tend to lead to higher wages.

These relatively positive trends in new business formation help to explain why, although absolute levels of Gross Value Added (GVA, put simply, refers to the value of goods and services produced in an area) are lower in rural than urban areas and are lower per rural worker than urban worker, in terms of average annual GVA growth rural England outperformed urban England between 1995 and 2005 (CRC 2008b, 84–86).[5] No evidence is yet available to explore how the recession has impacted on GVA in both rural and urban areas. In Scotland, GDP data suggests that all predominantly rural regions (with the exception of Orkney and the Shetland Islands) had positive GDP per capita growth between 1998 and 2003. The two highest growing rural regions had comparable rates of growth with the two highest growing (urban) regions in Scotland (OECD 2008).

However, there are important variations between districts with some of the more peripheral rural areas experiencing a loss of business stock, although this is most often due to an increase in the number of business VAT de-registrations in some sectors (including agriculture, financial intermediation and manufacturing) rather than a fall in the number of new businesses being created (CRC 2006, 95). Rural England has a higher proportion of micro-businesses than urban England (85.4 per cent and 82.6

per cent, respectively) and evidence suggests that firms and households are more intricately bound together in rural economies, which can help to make rural businesses more resilient during a crisis (e.g. Bennett and Phillipson 2004).

What is the evidence that rural areas can participate in the expansion in business and other 'knowledge economy' services, identified as being critical to the future growth of national and regional economies? In the 1990s Richards and Bryden (2000) found that high-value-added, high-wage business services (including knowledge- and information-based services) were heavily under-represented in rural areas. More recent data, however, suggest that rural economies are benefitting from increasing numbers of businesses across many growth sectors, including manufacturing and financial intermediation (CRC 2006, 94). In 2005, the real estate, renting and business activities sector (including many types of office-based work such as estate agents, call centres and consultancies) made up just less than one-quarter of total business stock in the Rural-80 districts in England, although this is still a lower proportion than in urban areas (where this sector makes up approximately 30 per cent of business stock). Data from England based on VAT registrations and de-registrations and showing the change in business stock across different sectors (CRC 2006, 93), illustrates that most rural areas have bucked the national trend in some way, for example, in delivering growth in the number of manufacturing businesses. Rural areas have also seen greater than average growth in sectors such as financial intermediation and real estate, renting and business activities.

Growth in these sectors can be explained with reference to a number of different factors, including reductions in real transport costs (for example, as the size of trucks has increased) and the rapidly increasing access to, and significant cost reductions in, information and communications technology (ICT). However, evidence suggests that in general rural businesses adopt ICT significantly more slowly than their urban counterparts. Again this may be due to a variety of reasons, including the higher proportion of business stock in sectors with relatively low adoption rates. Ward (2006) suggests the slower adoption is more the result of weaker drivers promoting ICT rather than inherent barriers to adoption. Although there are certainly cases where investment in ICT has created employment opportunities in rural areas (including, for example, the Western Isles of Scotland), there is also evidence of a widening urban–rural digital divide (particularly in terms of broadband connection speeds) which has serious implications for rural employment and enterprise as well as 'e-governance' in the so-called knowledge society (SQW 2006; Ekos Research Associates 2004; Bryden and Sproull 1997; Sproull, Bryden and Black 1997).

Focusing on the growth of businesses in the sector defined as 'knowledge-intensive business services' (KIBS), including financial services and insurance activities, scientific research and development, advertising and market research and other professional, scientific and technical activities, Figure

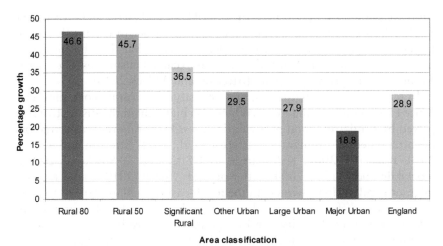

Figure 7.1 Growth in knowledge-intensive business services (KIBS) sectors, 1998–2005. ONS, 2007. Annual Business Inquiry (workplace analysis) (CRC 2008b: 105)

7.1 shows how well rural districts have performed compared to urban areas in England. As reported by the CRC (2008b, 106), these sectors are increasingly monitored by government as illustrative of the move from secondary and tertiary industries to higher value, higher waged economic activity on which our global competitiveness should be founded. Whilst this has been taken by some as illustrative of the innovativeness and growth potential of rural economies, care is required in interpreting this data as overall rural England has much lower proportions of employees in these sectors than urban England (CRC 2008b, 101), and this sector may include some activities (such as call centres) which are low wage, low skill.

In the rural US there is currently little evidence that knowledge-based industries are gaining a significant foothold. Henderson (2002) calculates that while the proportion of rural workers within knowledge occupations increased from roughly 20 per cent in 1980 to 25 per cent in 2000, the proportion in urban America grew even more. Only approximately 9 per cent of rural service sector workers have jobs in well-paying producer service activities (which tend to be concentrated in urban areas) and 40 per cent work in less-well-paid, less-secure personal and consumer services. However, this may be partly due to the different definition of rural in the US, where suburban fringe areas (which are classified as rural in the UK) are classified as urban, thus excluding many of the areas where knowledge-intensive activities are likely to develop.

An increasingly important trend in many rural economies is the growth in the numbers of people who are working from home. Data from 2010 in Scotland showed that 23 per cent of all those people in employment in remote rural areas were homeworkers[6] compared to 17 per cent in accessible rural areas and just 8 per cent in the rest of Scotland (Scottish Government 2011b). In a recent rural business survey carried out in the north-east of England, 38 per cent of business owners reported that their business was part of, or attached to, their home and this excluded businesses where agriculture was the primary activity (Atterton and Affleck 2010).

In terms of the strengthening and diversifying of rural economies, evidence from both England and Scotland has highlighted the distinctive role played by rural areas (and particularly accessible rural areas) as attractors of entrepreneurial in-migrants (Atterton et al., 2011; Atterton and Affleck 2010; Bosworth 2006; Kalantaridis and Bika 2006a; Stockdale 2006a; Stockdale and Findlay 2004). Atterton and Affleck (2010) found that in-migrant rural business owners in the north-east of England tended to start businesses in different sectors than locals; thus they played an important role in helping to diversify rural economies. A more limited role for in-migrants was found by Stockdale (2006a) in two depopulating rural areas of Scotland where few in-migrants were establishing new businesses and those that did were thought to represent 'survival self-employment creating few jobs for others' (see also MacDonald 1996). Nevertheless, although in-migrants may not always create new jobs, they do generate additional local income and often provide vital services that otherwise would not be present locally. They may also have different and complementary characteristics and motivations when compared to local business owners, for example, being motivated to set up a business in order to change their work–life balance or take on a new challenge (Atterton and Affleck 2010) or being more likely to maintain networking relationships that extend beyond the local area and provide access to new information and knowledge that would otherwise not be available to local business owners (Atterton 2007, 2005; Kalantaridis and Bika 2006a). In-migrants have therefore come to be regarded as important facilitators in a neo-endogenous development process whereby actors with both local and extra-local links may be critical (see Ward et al. 2005; Bryden and Hart 2004; Terluin 2003; Terluin and Post 2000; Lowe, Murdoch and Ward 1995). Little research has been conducted on this issue in the US, although Yu and Artz (2009) found that college graduates with rural backgrounds were more likely to start a business if they settled in a rural area than if they settled in an urban area. This suggests that return migrants to rural areas play an important role in creating new businesses. Bosworth and Glasgow (this volume) discuss these issues in further detail.

There is also considerable evidence in the US of 'supply-driven' inward migration to rural regions. Deller et al. (2001) and McGranahan (1999) both show how rural amenities attract new residents in the US, while Salant, Carley and Dillman (1996) provide evidence on the migration of footloose entrepreneurs ('lone eagles') into the rural regions of the US. This and other US research has underscored the importance of amenities (natural and built) and attractiveness to the 'creative class'[7] (McGranahan and Wojan 2007; Kwang-Koo, Marcouiller and Deller 2005; Florida 2002; Deller et al.

2001; McGranahan 1999). It has been clear for some time that nonmetro counties with higher levels of natural amenities were growing in population and prospering more than other rural areas. More recently, following research on metropolitan areas by Florida (2005, 2002), rural researchers have found that while the incidence of creative-class jobs is much lower in rural areas, those rural areas with high levels of creative class jobs have higher rates of innovation and job growth. In fact, creative nonmetro areas had higher rates of job growth than creative metropolitan areas. Interestingly, there are strong complementarities between creative areas and high amenity areas. McGranahan and Wojan (2007) report that creative workers are attracted to high-amenity areas, and that regions that increase their concentration of creative workers increase their level of amenities because of increased artistic and cultural activities. Similar research in England (BOP and Experian 2007; Hepworth 2004) has found evidence that accessible rural areas are also attractive locations for a creative class whose presence can then underpin the economic development of these areas.

The growth potential of many rural areas is thus now linked to the growth in other kinds of service sector activity. As Marsden (1998, 5) noted, these include 'new demands for "quality" food production, public amenity space, positional residential property, areas of environmental protection, for the experience of different types of rural idyll or urban antithesis are now much more entrenched in rural space'. Added to this list could be new functions for rural areas as carbon sinks and as sites for renewable energy generation. As recently discussed by the OECD (2006, 32–33), many successful rural regions have been able to valorise public or quasi-public goods such as a clean environment, attractive landscapes and cultural heritage (including food). Their increasing value is related to several factors, including improved transport links that make recreation as well as residential location in rural areas increasingly feasible, a growing 'consumption' demand on the part of urban dwellers for rural areas, and a local capacity to coordinate several economic actors to supply and promote local collective goods. What is critical is that local rural people and places (including businesses and communities) have at least an equal if not a leading role to play in the development of such activities.

DISCUSSION: THE FUTURE DEVELOPMENT OF RURAL ECONOMIES

This chapter has discussed the ways in which rural economies in the UK (specifically England and Scotland) and the US have transformed over recent decades and the reasons for these changes. It is clear that there are differences between and within the countries in terms of the extent to which a decline in employment in agriculture has been made up for by a growth in employment in 'new' sectors, including knowledge-intensive activities.

However, rural economies in both the UK and the US are showing signs of diversification, which is critical in the current period of economic change. This final section of the chapter discusses some of the key challenges and opportunities facing rural economies in both countries and suggests some ways in which policies may need to respond in order to be able to make the most of these and create stronger rural areas in future.

Firstly, in terms of the theoretical debates, it is important to note that globalisation presents both opportunities and challenges for rural areas, and the capacity of rural areas to take advantage of the opportunities varies considerably. Support may be required for those rural areas which are lacking in capacity. This may be in terms of long-term investment in tangible infrastructure, but also in terms of support for the building of social capital and the generation of bottom-up rural development projects. Building and sustaining local capacity in this way will reduce the potential vulnerability of rural communities to the global challenges they are facing and increase their potential to positively take advantage of them.

Rural areas are at the centre of current debates around the nature of development in the context of questions regarding sustainability, climate change and decarbonisation. These issues raise questions regarding the future shaping of the planning system and the power relations embedded within it, but they also offer potential opportunities for rural areas, in terms of developing novel modes of transport, community renewable energy schemes and new business opportunities in the provision of ecosystem services (see Potter and Wolf, this volume). However, the ability to make strategic decisions regarding these opportunities requires a much more informed and independent evidence base (both top-down and bottom-up) about where development is best placed and why.

However, the continuation of a primarily agricultural policy approach to rural development in both the US and UK may mean that some of these broader rural opportunities remain unrecognised and unfulfilled. Whilst there is no agreement on what exactly constitutes rural development policy in different countries, a more integrated, territorial, place-based approach to rural development is required in all three countries that recognises the growing interdependencies between different sectors in rural areas, and between rural and urban areas. Inevitably, a huge range of factors influence the success or otherwise of rural areas, some of which are local to the area (such as the nature and quality of place-based assets, in- and out-migration rates, levels of human capital, etc.) and some of which are external (such as the global economic situation and flows of international trade; see Bryden and Hart 2004). Some of these are more amenable to policy intervention (such as improving infrastructure) than others (such as the informal and social networks of local and in-migrant business owners).

Key to rural development policy in all countries is diversifying and strengthening rural economies and this can be done by creating fertile conditions for new business creation and growth at the appropriate scale and in appropriate locations. Support should be available for growth-oriented businesses and for businesses that are not seeking to grow but which provide a vital service. Given the particular importance of in-migrants in new enterprise creation in many parts of the rural UK, there is a role for a range of local and regional agencies to encourage such positive migratory trends to continue by exploiting the quality of life in and around small towns and rural areas in a sustainable way. Efforts should also be made to assist newcomers who are likely to have few contacts locally and may find it difficult to link into appropriate support structures, at least initially. This is notwithstanding the challenges this brings in terms of housing and community relations, the varying motivations for individuals to move and the timing of the decision to start up a business. This raises broader implications for the planning system in the UK to be less restrictive and more open to appropriate housing and business infrastructure developments (including premises, office space and hubs) and to home-based businesses (as advocated in England by M. Taylor 2008). Extra efforts are also justified to encourage and welcome return migrants to rural areas. Former residents, especially those who have left their rural homes for further and higher education, entry-level jobs or quality of life reasons, possess place-based knowledge and networks in their former communities, but have new ideas and networks gained while outside their communities and therefore may be crucial actors in positive neo-endogenous development processes (Atterton et al., 2011).

Generating more investment in rural areas is challenging as rural businesses tend to be small, to operate in low-margin sectors with little capital to invest and are often more focused on maintaining rather than growing their position (North and Smallbone 2000). Given these barriers it might be important to create local economic hubs or clusters of related businesses which can pool scarce capital and human resources and encourage innovation and technology and ideas transfer. Such clusters of businesses are based around the idea of agglomeration, which challenges our notion of rurality and has not been widely applied in rural development, certainly in the UK (although see Porter et al. 2004 in the US). There is no reason, however, to suggest that such an approach could not be applied to local rural development. Nevertheless, it is important to recognise that positive growth processes will not simply emerge as a result of businesses locating in close proximity and it is critical that key local business owners with strong networking skills and connections are involved (Agarwal, Rahman and Errington 2009).

Increasing the skills and levels of educational attainment amongst the rural population is critical, for example, by rural proofing[8] current skills, training and education provision. The CRC (2006, 96) reports evidence of some businesses in rural England experiencing recruitment difficulties with a low number of applicants with the necessary skills or insufficient number of people interested in doing the kind of job that is advertised. New skills are also required in emerging growth sectors such as renewables. Rural businesses need to be supported and incentivised to invest in the skills of their workforce and business support and training organisations need to be supported in providing adequate and appropriate training courses locally to upskill the local population and to attract and retain skilled migrants (Agarwal, Rahman and Errington 2009).

Demographic shifts, not least the ageing population and the influx of migrant workers into rural communities in both countries, raise serious challenges for the future of rural labour markets. These include, for example, the potential for older people to remain economically active if they wish or need to and the ways in which overseas workers are integrated into their host rural communities and have adequate access to health, training and other services. The shift towards homeworking will also have important implications for rural economies. A study of rural homeworking by the CRC (2005) found that most regional and local authority economic development agencies and business support organisations were unaware of its scale, diversity and contribution in their areas. Many rural areas face immense challenges as the growth in knowledge- and information-based activities continues and the creative use of residential space and workspace, infrastructure (particularly ICT), and work and leisure time will be very important to the future of rural economies in both countries.

The potential for rural economic growth can be increased by developing the local food economy and connecting this with tourism, culture and landscape quality and by exploiting the commercial opportunities of renewable energy. At present, there is a tendency for these new opportunities to be taken up by large corporations, usually in the form of highly centralized, large-scale development, to whom the benefits generally accrue, rather than to local populations for whom employment and income-generation opportunities are few. However, community ownership and development of renewable energy (usually involving small-scale distributed formats) is increasingly on the agenda in both the UK and US, and may grow in the future, creating new potential for growth. New economic opportunities are also opening up for rural economies in both the US and UK relating to the supply of essential resources such as land, water and local food, or taking on new functions such as carbon sinks and renewable energy generation. These are examples of rural regions valorising public or quasi-public goods, such as clean environments, attractive landscapes and cultural heritage (OECD 2006, 32–33; Bryden et al. 2010). Their increasing value is related to improved transport links that make recreation (and residential location) in rural regions increasingly feasible. But most of all it has to do with both a growing demand on the part of urban dwellers for the many things rural areas have to offer and a local capacity to coordinate several economic actors to supply and promote local collective goods. At the same time, it is important to acknowledge the challenges that such multi-use potential brings for rural land, particularly at a time when the issue of global food security is high on the agenda.

Finally, and more broadly, there are a number of false assumptions that need to be overcome in both the US and the UK if rural economies are to be afforded the recognition they deserve in terms of their contribution and given the support they require. These include the assumptions that cities alone drive growth, that rural areas are dominated by farming and tourism or commuters and the retired, that in-migration is to be discouraged and that the countryside should be protected from development. One important part of challenging these assumptions is improving the evidence base to demonstrate the breadth and importance of economic activity in the countryside. For example, there is a need to move beyond traditional, output-based measures of economic health, such as GVA, which do not adequately recognise or capture the variety of economic activity that takes place in the countryside. A broader view of economic activity is required which encompasses more flexible approaches to work as well as more varied forms of wealth generation and purchasing and is more closely aligned with notions of quality of life. Better quality of life lies at the heart of many household decisions to stay in or migrate to rural areas or of residents' choice to adopt multiple and flexible forms of working including self-employment and part-time work (CRC 2006, 68). Better data will also help to understand the variations within rural economies, and thus will enable more effective targeting of resources in future. For example, peripheral areas may require assistance to take advantage of some of the growth in new rural economy activities, such as improving access to information and developing new knowledge and skills. Making the case for the contribution of rural areas to their regional and national economies depends on the availability of adequate data. Only then will these false assumptions be adequately challenged and scope therefore be given for rural areas to develop successfully.

A number of recent research projects have highlighted the critical need for such developments to be locally grounded and facilitated by cooperative institutional arrangements, strong local and extra-local networks (Lowe, Murdoch and Ward 1995) and a positive sense of identity and self-determination (e.g. Árnason, Shucksmith and Vergunst 2009; Bryden and Hart 2004; Terluin 2003; Terluin and Post 2000). Such factors, aligned with good stocks of social capital, local ownership of land and property, investment in appropriate public goods and a positive 'can-do' approach, can encourage new enterprise formation and thus strengthen and diversify rural economies.

8 Entrepreneurial Behaviour among Rural In-Migrants

Gary Bosworth and Nina Glasgow

INTRODUCTION

Rural areas in developed nations have undergone a significant transition over recent decades. Agriculture is no longer the dominant economic force, leaving space for a new rural population that brings with it new business activities, new demands for goods and services, increased mobility and greater outward connectedness. This mobility has seen counterurbanisation become established as a major trend in rural demography, leading us to focus on the impact of an increased population in rural areas. This new population brings challenges but also opportunities for rural economies and communities, and through analysis of the entrepreneurial activities of rural in-migrants, this chapter seeks to identify how these opportunities are contributing to new processes of rural development.

We begin by considering the meaning of entrepreneurship in a rural context and how different forms of entrepreneurship affect rural economies and communities. There follows a short literature review on the effects of demographic change in rural economies in both the UK and US, which provides the context for analysis of data from both countries to explore patterns of rural economic and social entrepreneurship. The economic impact of in-migrant entrepreneurs can be evaluated in terms of job creation, business growth and trade patterns. Also, through more qualitative investigation, the motivations of these entrepreneurs and their links within and beyond their rural communities are explored. As the rural population is ageing, investigation into older entrepreneurs, both indigenous and in-migrant, enables some comparisons to be drawn on the impact of counterurbanisation and the entrepreneurial capacity that is introduced to rural economies and communities in both the UK and US.

THEORIZING (RURAL) ENTREPRENEURSHIP

The epithet 'entrepreneur' creates certain images, often influenced by media representations of flamboyant business owners or rags-to-riches success stories. Such images, however, are predominated by urban settings so we must step back from these glamorisations to establish the core attributes of entrepreneurship that can then be applied to the rural context.

Derived from French in the 1750s, an 'entrepreneur' was literally a 'go-between', someone who would buy products at a known price to resell at an uncertain price (Cantillon 1931, 51). In this pre-industrial era, the entrepreneur would certainly have been operating in rural markets but as industrialised economies have evolved so too has the conceptualization of the entrepreneur.

The central theme underpinning entrepreneurship since the very first 'brokers' is that of risk-taking. The broker bought products with a degree of uncertainty about whether he could sell them profitably, and today all entrepreneurs take risks of varying form and magnitude, whether investing in a business start-up, moving into new markets or changing methods of production. The concept of risk can be broken down into calculable risks and uncertainty (Knight 1921), with entrepreneurs earning profit for the latter, which is considered an uninsurable risk (Legge and Hindle 2004). Moving away from narrowly defined financial risks, we can also think of social relations, career development, psychological and health risks (Littunen 2000). In rural areas, with a large number of smaller firms and a high value placed on lifestyle and community, non-financial risks become increasingly important.

In order to take risks, there must also be an opportunity, so the entrepreneur, either personally or through the help of friends and advisors, must be alert to opportunities and have the desire and capabilities to act upon them (Chell and Baines 2000). This may come through strategic awareness and knowledge of the business environment, with careful research and planning, or it may come through highly innovative or creative ideas and a willingness to take greater risks in acting upon them.

To understand entrepreneurship requires an understanding of both the entrepreneurs and the environment in which they operate. A farmer diversifying into new business areas is being entrepreneurial, but his or her actions are set within social, economic and natural environments that will influence the development of that new activity. This interface between the external environment and an individual's skills is particularly pertinent in a study of in-migrants as they are able to view the local context in a more objective way, particularly if they are making business plans prior to moving to that locality.

As well as being 'relatively affluent individuals equipped with distinct attributes and networks of contacts' (Kalantaridis and Bika 2006a, 109), in-migrants in the UK are often thought to be more predisposed to entrepreneurial behaviour (Kalantaridis and Bika 2006b; Atterton 2007). In the US, older rural in-migrants have been shown to be more affluent and better educated than the indigenous older rural population, and many have retired from their first career, which frequently was in an executive position in a large, prestigious firm located in a metropolitan area (Brown and Glasgow 2008). Older in-migrants often have numerous skills, talents and forms of expertise. In-migrants have already demonstrated a willingness to take certain risks by moving to a new home, leaving a familiar setting and distancing themselves from networks rich in strong ties, and this is further substantiated by studies of international migrants (Pollard, Latorre and Sriskandarajah 2008; Barnes and Cox 2007). The personal characteristics associated with entrepreneurship have been studied in great detail, and these include a strong internal locus of control (Rotter 1966) and a strong need for achievement (McClelland 1961). Rather than reanalysing these theories, however, we must investigate whether they apply differently in rural areas, particularly among older in-migrant groups.

These personal attributes may be channelled into economic activity, but they may also lead to community engagement and forms of social entrepreneurship. While those in business are investing human and financial capital to generate personal income and profit, social entrepreneurs invest human and social capital to enhance their quality of life and augment collective social capital. In this chapter, both economic and social entrepreneurship are held to offer the potential for the ongoing development of socially and economically sustainable ruralities.

Social entrepreneurship can be associated with ethical behaviour among individual entrepreneurs or entrepreneurial organisations (Harris, Sapienza and Bowie 2009), volunteering and social responsibility (Walsh and O'Shea 2008), not-for-profit and third sector activities (Birch and Whittam 2008). The social aspect of entrepreneurship might concern the rationale for activity, the nature of the activity itself or the use of profits generated by that activity. It might even be 'a means to alleviate social problems and catalyse social transformation' (Mair and Marti 2006, 37). In each case, entrepreneurial skills and motivations will vary and the communities hosting these entrepreneurs will see different benefits. Our focus on rural areas demands that we explore both social and economic development outcomes linked to entrepreneurial behaviour, especially among counterurbanising groups. To ensure that this broad enquiry is maintained, we interpret entrepreneurship as *the investment in forms of capital, whether human, social or financial, through a business or other organisation in the pursuit of planned goals that result in the betterment of an individual business, the local economy or the local community.*

Rural entrepreneurship might traditionally have been associated with land-based activity but the preceding definition can apply across business sectors as well as to non-economic activity. Rather than specific business processes, we are interested in the application of entrepreneurial skills and qualities across this domain. Although the *range* of business activity in UK rural areas now mirrors that in more urban areas (Taylor 2008; CRC 2010b), the rural economy continues to present certain common challenges and opportunities that influence the activities of rural businesses. In rural areas of the US, farming and related industry occupations account for only 4.4 per cent of total employment, but rural workers are less likely (by 9.3 percentage points) to be employed in professional and managerial occupations, while being correspondingly more likely to be employed in lower paying blue-collar occupations (Kusmin 2006). One approach to over-coming challenges and maximizing opportunities is to build and maintain strong local networks.

In rural areas, the overlap between business and social networks tends to be more blurred (Atterton 2007), with business activity influenced by community expectations and a desire to support the local economy. The notion of embeddedness has developed an increasingly spatial meaning within the literature (Amin and Thrift 1994; Jack and Anderson 2002; Kalantaridis and Bika 2006a), raising questions about the extent to which in-migrants become embedded and the ways in which this happens. For rural entrepreneurs, the ability to build and maintain strong links with the local community as well as extensive extra-local networks can become an important feature of their business. This aspect of rural entrepreneurship is placed in particularly sharp focus when in-migrant business owners are studied. Therefore, the next section considers how demographic and economic changes have created opportunities for new forms of entrepreneurship in contemporary rural communities, to provide the context for our US and UK case studies.

PATTERNS OF DEMOGRAPHIC CHANGE

From the 1970s onwards, trends of counterurbanisation were observed in both the US and Europe (Berry 1976; Fielding 1982; Brown and Wardwell 1981). More recently, A. Champion (2003) has reported that England and Wales have experienced continuous counterurbanisation since 1931. In the US, counterurbanisation trends have been more variable over time than in the UK. Following the 'rural renaissance' of the 1970s, most rural counties lost population to urban counties in the 1980s (Reeder 1998), thought to be due to a widespread downturn in the economy. In the 1990s and 2000s, *internal* migration was predominantly from urban to rural areas, but large cities were the primary destinations of immigrants from abroad. Such counteracting trends caused overall rural versus urban population growth rates to bounce around during the time period (Johnson 2006), but *older* in-migration to rural areas has been a continuous, uninterrupted process during the past forty years (Johnson and Cromartie 2006).

To avoid the oft-quoted criticism of counterurbanisation research being chaotic, inconsistent or elusive (Mitchell 2004; Halfacree 2008), we follow Champion's definition where 'counterurbanisation is the inversion of the traditionally positive relationship between migration and settlement size' (A. Champion 1989). A large amount of literature has focused on the implications of counterurbanisation for the social transformation of rural settlements and rural life. In-migration raises property prices, which often disadvantages indigenous residents (Gilligan 1987; Hamnett 1992), and it has been linked with the loss of a sense of community (Bell 1994). Murdoch et al. (2003) and Brown and Glasgow (2008) discuss the new conflicts that arise in rural societies between incomers and traditional residents, and Savage et al. (1992) describe how gentrification is affecting neighbourhoods as wealthier classes are creating and sometimes enforcing their own identities on rural communities.

The main component of counterurbanisation has been the movement of people at or close to retirement age (Champion and Shepherd 2006), although more recently the same authors recognise that a greater number of younger people, including early retirees, people 'downsizing' into self-employment and typical suburbanizing households with school-aged children are migrating to the countryside. Indeed, in the UK in 2004, only around 10 per cent of rural in-migrants were retired (Lowe and Speakman 2006a), and the dominant age group for rural in-migrants is thirty to forty-four (Champion and Shepherd 2006). However, as these people grow older, the bulk of growth in rural population over the 2010s and 2020s is still forecast to be in the over-sixty age group (ibid.). The ageing rural society has been associated with lower levels of employment, low incomes and an increased reliance on personal services (M. Woods 2005), but increased spending potential, a desire for community engagement and more extensive pre-retirement activity are all recognised as potentially beneficial for rural development (M. Woods 2005; Lowe and Speakman 2006a). It is these arguments that influence our research into rural in-migration, especially among older age groups.

PATTERNS OF ECONOMIC CHANGE IN RURAL AREAS

Changes in rural economy and society have resulted in a shift away from a countryside based around primary sector production towards a 'countryside of consumption' (Slee 2005). Slee describes the injections of wealth and income from new residents into rural areas as having helped the traditional rural population 'weather and adapt to a deep crisis in their livelihoods' (ibid., 255). The new rural economy is more than ever shaped by consumption demands, both private and public. No longer is the rural community a relatively self-contained exporter of primary food and fibre products, but villages today are importers of people, both as residents and tourists, who consume products locally.

Research is increasingly identifying links between counterurbanisation and rural economic development. Stockdale (2005) found that, on average, 2.4 new jobs were created for each self-employed in-migrant, and Kalantaridis and Bika recognised their affluence and entrepreneurial tendencies (2006a, 2006b). A. Champion supports these views, as he found that 'higher-status districts . . . are most prone to fuelling metropolitan out-migration' (1998, 26), suggesting that migrants are well educated, have valuable work experience and have significant disposable income to inject into rural economies. Researchers in the US have also found positive economic impacts of older in-migration to rural destinations in the stimulation of both job and income growth (Fagin and Longino 1993; Glasgow and Reeder 1990; Serow 2003; Serow and Haas 1992; Stallman, Deller and Shields 1999), but the US studies have focused on older in-migrants as consumers rather than as entrepreneurs.

This draw of rurality as a place of residence is reflected in the business population. Approximately 80 per cent of businesses report an attractive living environment as being either helpful or very helpful (Keeble, Tyler and Lewis 1992, 37). This demonstrates that while an attractive environment may be seen as a personal or lifestyle factor for choosing to move, it has economic implications. Keeble and Tyler (1995, 984) also reported that 'most migrant entrepreneurs—and especially those settling in accessible rural areas—moved to the countryside prior to setting up their firm; but one-fifth (21 per cent) of all remote rural founders actually moved there in order to establish their enterprise'.

Between 1998 and 2006 rural districts in England saw a 23 per cent increase in the number of businesses (based on statistics for the number of VAT registrations with the Inland Revenue), contrasting with a decline of more than 8 per cent in urban Local Authorities. As a result, in 2006 there were 456,000 firms in rural districts representing 29 per cent of the stock of VAT registered business addresses in England (CRC 2008b). While the rural business population is growing and diversifying, the average firm size remains smaller than in urban areas, with over 90 per cent employing fewer than ten people and thus they are defined as micro-businesses (Performance and Innovation Unit 1999). Self-employment has been increasing in rural areas alongside the ageing of the population, and Green (2006) explains that self-employment is particularly important for older people. Self-employed people tend to work longer into their old age, as they are able to develop a more flexible life–work balance, although they tend be more financially risk-averse and to sometimes own the smallest and most vulnerable businesses.

Approximately a third of micro-businesses are growth-oriented (Raley and Moxey 2000), with older business owners less likely to report growth ambitions (Bosworth 2009). Despite their lack of growth ambition, many micro-businesses provide useful functions in the countryside. As well as the services they provide, these micro-businesses enable others to participate in the workforce, either directly or through the provision of transport or childcare, which can enhance the business environment for others through the local sourcing of inputs (Lowe and Talbot 2000). In rural areas, small firms tend to be much more socially embedded than larger firms (Atterton 2007). Many employ local resources to meet local needs, which can foster both community identification with business performance and business attachment to the local area. Diversity in the small business sector combined with local embeddedness can also make the community less susceptible to economic downturn (Lowe and Talbot 2000).

Having established the link between in-migrant business owners and economic development, we hypothesize that increasing affluence and economic vitality in rural areas will attract further counterurbanisers, reinforcing the relationship between migration and rural development. Given the importance of these interrelated processes, more needs to be understood about the diverse stimuli for entrepreneurial migration to rural areas and its impact in rural economies. The following analysis therefore explores these issues based on separate research undertaken in the UK and US.

METHODOLOGY

This chapter combines findings from a survey of non-agricultural rural micro-businesses in the north-east of England, face-to-face interviews with forty business owners in the same region, a two-wave panel survey of older rural in-migrants and longer-term older residents of fourteen rural retirement destinations scattered across the US and case studies from four rural retirement destinations in the US. This provides us with access to a range of migrants with different levels of economic and social activity, enabling detailed analysis of the characteristics of business owners and social entrepreneurs who are contributing to rural development.

The north-east England survey carried out at the Centre for Rural Economy includes 1,251 usable returns equating to some 20 per cent of the region's population of rural micro-businesses; Raley and Moxey (2000) provide a summary of findings. New analysis was carried out by focusing on the different characteristics associated with local and in-migrant business owners. This was used to inform subsequent interviews with forty rural business owners in 2007–2008. These were largely sampled from the same population although some new businesses and businesses that had grown beyond the 'micro-business' stage were included. The interviews were selected to include a mix of local and in-migrant business owners across the four most populated business sectors: manufacturing, retail, hospitality and professional services. A biographical approach was taken to investigate the motivations of individuals as well as the narrative that described their business development. These motivations were central to understanding both their entrepreneurial aspirations and the extent to which in-migrants engaged with their new local economies.

In the north-east study, an in-migrant was defined as anyone moving into a locality as an adult from at least thirty miles away. For the US, an in-migrant was defined as a person aged sixty or older who had moved across a county boundary five or fewer years ago. Given the geographic scale and the different life courses identified in the UK and US, a singular definition would not be practical, but this need not preclude comparative reflections. The UK definition can include international migrants although evidence suggests that, numerically, these are a very small percentage of the trend. Only internal in-migrants were included in the US study. Where international migration to rural areas occurs, the challenges are likely to be quite different, so any study investigating this would require an alternative approach that would be expected to raise quite different issues around the individual rather than broader rural development questions.

The US study, referred to as the Cornell Retirement Migration Study, used a multi-methods approach to examine micro and macro aspects of rural in-migration. A two-wave panel survey was conducted in 2002 and 2005 primarily for the purpose of investigating the process through which older in-migrants become socially integrated in rural destination communities. A telephone survey was administered in fourteen purposefully selected rural in-migration destinations spread across the US. This was done to ensure representation from all regions in which older in-migration was occurring. Data were collected from matched samples of in-migrants and longer term residents sixty years of age and older.

In 2002, 788 respondents were interviewed, and 638 respondents were interviewed in 2005. Minus the amount of attrition that occurred between wave 1 and wave 2 of the panel survey, the same individuals were interviewed at both points in time. Interviews were conducted with an approximately equal number of in-migrants and longer term residents in the high-growth rural in-migration destinations selected for the study. In the larger study (see Brown and Glasgow 2008), census data were used to develop a profile of the rural migration destination counties compared with other rural counties. Case studies in four of the fourteen survey sites—one in each major region of the country—were conducted in 2006 to examine how older in-migration was affecting destination communities. Approximately one week was spent in each of the four case study sites, and more than sixty public officials, business owners, service providers and organisational leaders were interviewed. Face-to-face interviews were also conducted with six or seven older in-migrants in each case study area who had previously responded to both waves of the panel survey. For this analysis, we rely primarily on findings from the case studies, but we also refer to findings from the panel survey.

Of particular interest in the Cornell study was the voluntary or third sector participation of older in-migrants in their destination communities. It emerged during the case studies that older in-migrants were active social entrepreneurs, and it was primarily through this type of activity that older in-migrants were becoming socially embedded and integrated into their new communities. Our analysis thus focuses on rural in-migrants as micro-business entrepreneurs (north-east England) and social entrepreneurs (US). The UK and US studies have different though complementary emphases and, by including findings from both studies, we can gain a more complete picture of how rural in-migrants and counterurbanisation are affecting rural economic and community development.

ENTREPRENEURIAL IN-MIGRANTS IN
THE NORTH-EAST OF ENGLAND

The link between migration and entrepreneurship in the rural economy has been observed since at least the early 1990s as Keeble, Tyler and Lewis (1992) reported that nearly twice as many entrepreneurs in both remote and accessible rural areas are not born locally compared to those in urban settings. More recent work has shown that up to two-thirds of new rural firms are created by people moving from urban areas, often attracted by the quality of life (Countryside Agency 2003a). This has seen researchers attempting to quantify the job creation of entrepreneurial in-migrants (Stockdale and Findlay 2004; Stockdale 2005; Bosworth 2008) and demonstrating that it is clearly a feature of the rural economy that merits greater attention.

The micro-business survey in the north-east of England found that 50 per cent of firms were owned by in-migrants, and each of these firms creates an average of 1.9 additional jobs. Agglomerating the survey findings with regional statistics, it was possible to estimate that owners of non-agricultural micro-businesses who moved at least thirty miles into the area as adults have created a total of 3,176 full-time and 2,642 part-time jobs, equating to 6 per cent of the region's full-time and 9.5 per cent of the region's part-time employment in rural areas. For comparison, this is almost 70 per cent higher than agriculture (Bosworth 2009).

Some 40 per cent of in-migrants and 37 per cent of locals surveyed employed no staff. Among the remainder, the mean number of jobs created was 3.14 for locally owned and 3.17 for in-migrant owned firms. Local business owners had marginally higher levels of financial turnover (although not statistically significant), but in-migrants reported a significantly greater desire for growth suggesting that this balance will change over time. With 41 per cent of in-migrants and only 31 per cent of locals reporting that they were seeking growth, this group represents real potential for future rural development, over and above indigenous growth potential.

One feature of this group of in-migrant business owners was that they were older, with 76 per cent aged over forty-five compared to 60 per cent of local business owners (Chi-square test: n = 1287, $p < 0.001$). This was linked with starting their businesses later in life as 55 per cent of in-migrants, compared to just over 30 per cent of locals, were aged over forty at the time that they started running their business (Chi-square test: n = 1255, $p < 0.001$). Research suggests that older business owners overall tend to be less entrepreneurial and less growth-oriented (Bosworth 2009) and this is borne out in our study. As Figure 8.1 illustrates, however, in-migration is boosting growth ambitions among older business owners. They inject much needed vitality into the rural economy and are sustaining entrepreneurial behaviour into later life.

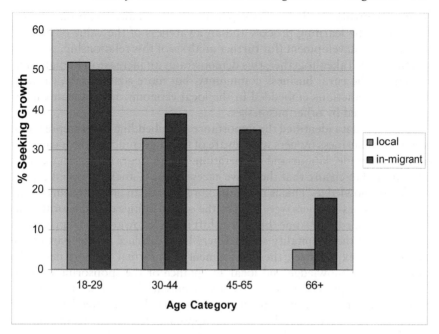

Figure 8.1 The age, origin and growth aspirations of business owners in the northeast of England.

Further evidence of the entrepreneurial characteristics attached to in-migrants can be identified in their views on growth potential. When asked if they thought they could sell more of their current range of products, in-migrants were more likely to have a positive outlook. Forty-one per cent of in-migrants thought they could sell more of their current product range compared to 33 per cent of local business owners. Moreover, of the in-migrants that felt they could not sell more of their products, 37 per cent still reported that they wanted growth, compared to 16 per cent of local business owners in the same situation.[1] This would seem to imply that in-migrants are better able to consider expanding their product range and generating business growth through different methods. Indeed, 13.4 per cent of all in-migrant firms (rising to 20 per cent among in-migrants with a clear intention to run a business upon relocating) compared to just 6 per cent of locals felt that they could not sell more of their current products yet still sought to grow the business. If they are running at full capacity in the marketplace and seeking to expand beyond this, we can deduce that certain types of in-migrants are more highly motivated and innovative entrepreneurs.

As well as the direct economic impact, in-migrants have higher levels of educational attainment, with 34 per cent having a degree compared to 10 per cent of locals. They were also more likely to engage with a range of business networks and business support agencies, indicating both a familiarity with the learning process and an awareness of the value of lifelong learning and development (for further analysis of this relationship, see Bosworth 2009). Taken together, this demonstrates an increase in human capital among the rural business community, but more significantly, through network interactions embedded in the local economy, this human capital can be accessed by other businesses.

Interview data identified the importance of embedding for entrepreneurs. Many local business owners were aware of the importance of the local community for trade, labour and cooperation. For in-migrants, greater efforts are required to ensure that they have access to local stocks of social capital and local knowledge. This is itself an expression of an entrepreneurial outlook, as business owners were alert to the opportunities that the local community provided. For some this saw a shift in trade towards local producers (especially in the hospitality sector where local produce can be part of the overall local experience), the development of informal support networks to build local knowledge and local acceptance or the sponsoring of local events to build positive reputations among potential future staff or clients.

The majority of in-migrant business owners do not intend to start a business when they move but as they approach retirement from salaried employment, this can lead to new opportunities. Two such businesses illustrate the potential value of these individuals for rural economies. One in-migrant working as an IT consultant and web designer saw the opportunity to move into self-employment, having built up a range of contacts in the local community. While the principal motivations were his life–work balance, freedom from long-distance commuting and the flexible nature of his work, he has diversified into other business activities that might not have occurred within the confines of a larger company.

The second example comes from a highly successful, award-winning manufacturer who only set up the business as a hobby after retirement from unassociated employment. Sparked by conversations in the local community, where he had been living for several years, he was able to acquire suitable premises and identify an outlet for his products, and he now employs six members of staff and the business is firmly established in the local community. This particular example highlighted the importance of both extra-local knowledge and work experience combining with a locally based opportunity identified through being locally embedded. Such a combination is most likely to occur among older in-migrants, highlighting their potential capabilities.

Among the older in-migrants interviewed, there was a clear desire to share their knowledge and experience within the local community. In the hospitality sector, this included joining tourism advisory boards and accommodation ratings panels, while retailers and local service providers were supportive of village business groups and other local organisations such as parish councils or village hall committees. In each case, there may have been business advantages to be gained in terms of the business owner's reputation, but a clear sense of altruism was evident as this was an opportunity to give something back to the communities they had joined. Some authors (e.g. Getz and Petersen 2005; Chaston 2008) might question the value of lifestyle businesses but where profit is not the sole driver, these business owners contribute to the local economy and community in a range of other ways, in particular through human and social capital accumulation.

This locally motivated activity is not restricted to visible rural businesses serving tourists or local residents as entrepreneurs recognise that the value of local reputation extends beyond the economic value. The business as the owner of a marketing consultancy explained how they sponsor local events and invite local school pupils to do work experience with them, saying, 'it's supporting the local community, it has to be part and parcel of any rural business because a lot of those people are actually working for us (. . .) and they like to see that their company is helping and supporting people in the local community'. A brewer selling beyond the immediate locality also explained the value of local sponsorship not only to raise the business profile, but also to ensure that the business activity is welcomed by the local population.

In-migrants stimulate competition and raise standards across the rural economy especially in the tourism sector where many small operators focus on high quality to differentiate their business. The clearest example of this came from a farming family who converted several properties into holiday cottages and have expanded this aspect of the business with one of the partners having moved into the area. A second stage of growth was triggered by a local friend and has seen expansion to include a range of other leisure facilities. Summing up the healthy competition, one of the partners explained, 'This friend (. . .) started by asking our advice, and (. . .) his ideas expanded and went beyond anything that had previously existed in Northumberland'.

Whether through new businesses, employment, network-building or competition, in-migrants play a significant role in the rural economy of the northeast. As a new dimension of the counterurbanising pattern, *commercial counterurbanisation* (Bosworth 2010) merits greater research to understand the dynamic impacts of demographic change. In the US, the life stages are more clearly defined and the geography less conducive to the earlier movement and more gradual integration of in-migrants into rural communities. Nevertheless, there remain many entrepreneurial aspects to counterurban trends in the US, and these are explored in the following section.

ENTREPRENEURSHIP AMONG OLDER RURAL IN-MIGRANTS IN THE US

The Cornell survey findings show that in 2002, 37 per cent of older in-migrants versus 35 per cent of non-migrants were employed (Glasgow and Brown 2006); in other words, the majority of both older in-migrants and longer term residents were not working at the time of the first survey. Given that the older in-migrants averaged only three years of residence in the destination community compared to older non-migrants' average of twenty-two years' residence, however, it seems remarkable that the rate of employment among older in-migrants slightly exceeded that of the non-migrants (Glasgow and Brown 2006). Further, fully 91 per cent of the in-migrants versus only 83 per cent of the older non-migrants reported that they had previously been retired. Re-entry into the labour force after retirement from a career job is relatively common in the US, and the in-migrants were more prone to re-enter the workforce following retirement than long-term residents of rural in-migration destinations. Older in-migrants were also shown to be better educated and to have higher incomes than their non-migrant counterparts (Brown and Glasgow 2008), findings which are consistent with many previous studies in the US. While we cannot use the survey data to address the extent to which older rural in-migrants became business entrepreneurs in their destination communities, a positive economic picture is shown for the older in-migrants.

The survey provides greater detail on voluntary social participation, and we can make certain inferences about *social entrepreneurship* from the survey findings. In 2002, 58 per cent of older in-migrants versus 63 per cent of older non-migrants participated in at least one voluntary organisation in their community (Glasgow and Brown 2006). This is a small difference between the two groups, especially when one considers the shorter duration of residence among the in-migrants compared to the non-migrants. As to specific kinds of participation, in 2002 older non-migrants were modestly more likely than older in-migrants to participate in service, political and volunteer organisations (Brown and Glasgow 2008). Remarkably though, by 2005 older in-migrants had become *more likely* than the non-migrants to participate in service (44 versus 42 per cent) and volunteer (47 versus 42 per cent) organisations and activities. The in-migrants continued to be less likely than the non-migrants to participate in political organisations (18 compared to 21 per cent). It appears, however, that voluntary social participation is a strategy older in-migrants use to become socially integrated and embedded in the new community.

Case Study Findings on Business and Social Entrepreneurship

In the course of our face-to-face interviews, we interviewed a few in-migrant business entrepreneurs. For example, one interviewee owned a home repair business, as well as being active in political organisations in his new community. Another older in-migrant was a retired executive from a multinational corporate liquor distributor. In the rural destination community to which he moved, he became the owner and manager of a small inn, a winery making wine from grapes grown in his own vineyard, a creamery and a horse stable—all on the same large parcel of land. This man was also a social entrepreneur who was volunteering his time and expertise on the local economic development committee, among other similar organisations.

In two of our case study sites, older in-migrants had formed artists' cooperatives as a venue for selling their artwork.

The majority of older in-migrants interviewed in the US case studies were not employed, but they excelled in *social entrepreneurship*. They were civically engaged and committed to giving something of themselves to their new communities. Their social entrepreneurship was recognised by the older in-migrants themselves as important to their well-being. Moreover, the public official and other community leader interviewees were unanimous in perceiving older in-migrants as movers and shakers in starting new or expanding the capacity of already existent not-for-profit community organisations.

Examples of their social entrepreneurial activities were numerous and the following are just a few. In two of the case study sites, older in-migrants had led successful fund-raising efforts to expand local hospitals and found new long-term care facilities. This resulted in a strong increase in the demand for nurses, physical therapists, physicians and other allied health professionals, and consequently an increase in available health care for the entire community (Brown and Glasgow 2008). In a community in Maine, older in-migrants had raised funds to build a new YMCA with a state-of-the-art fitness centre, raised money for and volunteered their labour to found a large coastal botanical garden (see Figure 10.2) and started a new theatre company. These are only a few examples of what resulted from the social entrepreneurial spirit in-migrants brought to their new community. In a North Carolina community, in-migrants had raised money for and donated money to the new public library and were active volunteers in a well-established local music school; retired executives were providing free consulting to community residents on how to start their own businesses. In the Michigan site, older in-migrants had started a mutual help service for older people having health problems, and in Gila County, Arizona, where the public social services sector was somewhat underdeveloped, older in-migrants were heavily invested as volunteers in a variety of social service agencies. The specific types of social entrepreneurship varied from one case study community to another, often in response to the communities' needs, and there was ample evidence of social entrepreneurial activity among older in-migrants.

In-migrants who were retired lawyers, architects, accountants, engineers and so on were providing free consulting services to local governments in the case study sites, and one of the public officials interviewed (a mayor) was himself an older in-migrant who had lived in the community fewer than five years. In one of the case studies, a local official said that he actively recruits in-migrants for participation on task forces because of their experience and training. For example, on a local project involving dealing with wastewater runoff, older in-movers provided most of the expertise on the task force, including a PhD geologist, two PhD chemical engineers and two persons who were retired from careers in municipal waste management. The local public officials and community leaders interviewed in the US study were in full agreement that, because of the energy and know-how older in-migrants possessed, economic and community development efforts in their counties had substantially improved.

Some of the key informants, however, also discussed tensions and conflicts between the newcomers and longer term residents of the high growth-communities. Older in-migrants had started a number of new arts and cultural organisations, but not all longer term residents were interested in participating in them. The question arose as to whose cultural interests the new organisations were promoting. In the communities where older in-migrants had achieved electoral office, some old-timers felt their agenda had been displaced in favour of newcomers' agendas. In another town, an elected official expressed the opinion that he welcomed the free consulting older in-migrants were providing to his local government, but that he was opposed to any newcomer ever becoming a public office holder in his jurisdiction. The real estate markets in the case study communities were booming, but this had resulted in younger families of modest income being displaced to less desirable parts of a county or even beyond the county boundary. Nonetheless, community leaders and public officials were unanimous in their perception that older in-migration, on balance, had benefitted their rural communities, even though older in-migration had also produced some strains within these local contexts.

Figure 8.2 Social entrepreneurship in action: Older in-migrants were fund-raisers, financial contributors and volunteer gardeners in the creation and maintenance of the Coastal Maine Botanical Gardens. Photo courtesy of Barbara Freeman, Coastal Maine Botanical Gardens.

DISCUSSION

Older in-migration situations differ somewhat between the UK and the US, with pre-retirement-age migration to rural areas less common in the US. A possible explanation for this is that US residents are not eligible for Social Security benefits prior to the age of sixty-two, and sixty-five is the 'traditional' retirement age in the US. Also, the UK has the National Health Service (NHS), whereas the majority of US residents who currently have health insurance get it through their employers, who subsidize insurance premiums and negotiate lower rates for employees than are available to individual purchasers. US residents are not eligible for Medicare (government-sponsored health benefits) prior to age sixty-five, making pre-retirement-age individuals in the US less likely to leave jobs. As a result, by the time older in-migrants in the US move to retirement destinations, the majority have retired from their primary career.

Despite these differences, counterurbanisation has been found to have some similar positive outcomes relating to rural economies and communities. In-migrants bring new demand for goods and services, the ability and time to engage with the wider local business community and the entrepreneurial capabilities to initiate new businesses as well as social and community activities. In the UK, earlier migration is also linked with the potential for migrants to create jobs and develop bigger businesses that go beyond 'personal interest' activities. Although rural migration tends to occur later in life in the US, in-migrants were found to use employment and forms of social entrepreneurship as means of developing their social and economic engagement.

In assessing the relative levels of entrepreneurship, adhering to our original definition concerning the investment of forms of capital, whether human, social or financial, through a business or other organisation in the pursuit of planned goals that result in the betterment of the local economy and/or community, we can see that entrepreneurial activity is evident. In-migrants are investing personal and communal assets to develop the local economy and the local community. While the investment is often risk-averse in a financial sense, they are expressing their entrepreneurial capabilities through new business creation, the development of new networks and cooperatives and the instigation of innovative community projects. Through these activities, in-migrants are demonstrating an understanding of the local context and employing a range of skills and experiences, often learned outside of the local area, to maximize opportunities within. In doing this, they crystallise the core idea of neo-endogenous development (Ray 2001; Lowe et al. 1998), where forms of development are thought to be most appropriate if they are rooted within the local area but engage with extra-local influences.

Given that entrepreneurship results from 'the interplay of entrepreneurs' social networks and cognitive biases' (DeCarolis, Litzky and Eddleston 2009, 528), a more mobile rural population with a diversity of experiences and networks offers great potential for rural development. Moving away from traditional profit-focused views of entrepreneurship this research demonstrates the value of entrepreneurial skills and traits for wider development objectives. In rural communities with a lower critical mass of businesses and other organisations, the contribution of in-migrants and their accumulated capital stocks has the potential to make a significant impact. Extending DeCarolis's statement, however, the interplay for a rural entrepreneur must also be embedded in the spatial and environmental context of a particular rural area, as this is an integral feature of the community's local identity.

CONCLUSIONS

Entrepreneurial in-migration is playing a significant role in the restructuring of rural communities and economies. Some older in-migrants establish small businesses and, where this takes the form of social entrepreneurship, it can also enhance the wider community. The continuing ageing of rural populations seems inevitable, so policy must be directed towards encouraging greater economic engagement and entrepreneurship among older people. As such, in-migrants and older residents should be viewed as a potential source of rural development rather than a 'problem' for rural communities.

In the rural cases presented in this chapter, the rural place itself provides an important resource for entrepreneurs. For some, the desire to play an active role in the local community motivates both social entrepreneurship and other forms of business activity; for others local identity and local resources provide the opportunity for entrepreneurship. In both the UK and US examples, embeddedness is an important feature for rural entrepreneurs, providing supportive business networks, local trading opportunities or community engagement, especially with social enterprises. Many rural businesses are small and plan to remain that way but this does not mean that they are not adding value to a local economy. Adding to the critical mass of businesses, supporting the local community and creating new business activity are all essential to prevent the spread of dormitory rural settlements and to ensure the sustainability of rural living, especially for older populations who are more reliant on local services and at the same time less mobile.

Future research that systematically investigates business and social entrepreneurship in tandem in the UK and US could lend additional insights into the entrepreneurial processes we have discussed in this chapter. Given the severe economic recession of 2008 in both the UK and US and the extent to which it lingers, we need additional studies that show whether counterurbanisation trends will continue or if individuals will choose not to move.

Either scenario will have implications for the innovativeness of the rural population and economic and community development prospects. In both the UK and US the ageing of the baby boom generation is occurring, and the migration behaviour of baby boomers will need to be monitored for their potential economic and social impacts on rural areas.

9 Local Food Systems and Networks in the US and the UK

Community Development Considerations for Rural Areas

Clare Hinrichs and Liz Charles

INTRODUCTION

This chapter examines growing community and policy interest in local food systems and networks, focusing on the implications for rural places in the UK and the US. In the twenty-first century, food production and consumption have become topics of public debate and private anxiety, prompting increased attention from the media, researchers and policymakers.[1] Intensified patterns of industrialisation, specialization and concentration in agriculture (Lyson 2004) and the mounting pressures of global neo-liberalization (Buttel 2004) have engendered concerns about the environmental impacts, economic inequalities, health risks and cultural homogenisation served up by the modern food system, alongside its featured offerings— efficiency and productivity. As most food in developed countries continues to be produced in rural areas (despite growing interest in the possibilities of urban agriculture), this heightened concern for food and the resultant drive for social and economic change in the food system have implications for rural people, places and policies.

Issues of control and power in the food system have become particularly charged. Globally and nationally, food systems have become increasingly concentrated and centralized, leaving little power in the hands of consumers, despite the rhetoric of consumer sovereignty (Lang 1999; Lang, Barling and Caraher 2009). Accordingly, the concept of food democracy, with 'citizens having the power to determine agro-food policies and practices locally, regionally, nationally, and globally' (Hassanein 2003, 79) exerts growing appeal. Increasing citizen involvement in decisions about issues that have a direct impact on their livelihoods and well-being is central to community development theory and practice. This chapter explores the ways in which local food initiatives in the US and UK offer diverse spaces for community development in rural places.

We begin by establishing the parameters and extent of local food systems and networks in the UK and the US, and why their development is important for rural areas. We focus here on the intersections of local food with community development, as variously understood, practiced and experienced in the UK and the US.[2] Community development may differentially emphasize entrepreneurship, community capacity-building and social equity. These different emphases in turn shape the emergence, form and outcomes of local food systems and networks in the US and the UK. We then examine the role of policy in constraining and enabling the broader community development potential of local food systems and networks. Finally, we conclude with some thoughts about the future prospects of local food systems and networks to improve the well-being of rural people and communities in the US and the UK.

CHARACTERISING LOCAL FOOD SYSTEMS AND NETWORKS IN THE US AND THE UK

The terminology surrounding local food, as used by academics and practitioners, tends to differ across the US and the UK. In the US, the term 'local food systems' has been favoured, while 'local food networks' or 'links' are more typical usage in the UK. In this section, we contrast these understandings and review the parameters and extent of local food systems and networks in the two countries.

In the US, a language of local food systems has prevailed since the 1990s, as interest in sustainable agricultural production and alternative food markets gained force. 'Systems' implies a comprehensive view, and indeed, practitioner-researchers often discuss local food systems in terms of sustainability goals across environmental, economic and social arenas (Feenstra 1997). While the US Department of Agriculture (USDA) now references local food systems, the term as yet has no legal definition (Martinez et al. 2010). It most often signifies geographic proximity between producers and consumers, but may also imply particular social or supply-chain characteristics (Martinez et al. 2010). Direct agricultural markets (including farmers' markets, community supported agriculture operations [CSA], roadside farm stands and U-pick operations) have assumed near-iconic status as the exemplary form of producer–consumer exchange in local food systems (Ostrom 2006, 2007).

Although direct agricultural markets often serve as shorthand for local food systems in the US, conceptually and practically the 'systems' of local food systems entail more involved and potentially complicated overlays of economic activities, institutions and networks. Related food enterprises such as bakeries, breweries, wineries or independent speciality food processors may transform local crops to create other food products that are sold directly to local residents or purveyed through other local outlets. Some local food supply chains make use of intermediary distributors, through whom local farmers supply public institutions, restaurants, groceries or hospitals that ultimately feed local residents (Bloom and Hinrichs 2011). Here direct contact between producer and consumer is subordinated to the goal of moving local food into more diverse markets, both institutional and commercial.

In the UK, local food networks and links are the more prevalent language, stressing social and economic ties between food system actors and allowing for a range of formal and informal interactions. The term 'local food' has become widely used and popular in the UK, but there are as yet no nationally agreed upon criteria that define precisely what a 'local food' product is. There is some consensus around the need for a clearer definition, but also reservations about potential negative effects, should a definition not be flexible and pragmatic (DEFRA 2003a). Accordingly, the National Association of Farmers' Markets specify recommended distances depending on market context, such that thirty, fifty or even one hundred miles might be the allowable distance from which participating vendors might come. An important distinction, one largely absent in the US, has been made between 'local food' and 'locality food'.[3] The former is food that is produced and consumed within a given geographical area, while the latter is food that has a specific geographical provenance (e.g. Welsh Lamb, Cornish Ice Cream), but can be marketed anywhere (Policy Commission on the Future of Farming and Food 2002; Action for Market Towns 2002). DEFRA added the concept of quality—'exceeding the legal minimum requirements in some aspects of production' (DEFRA 2003b, 1)—to the definition of locality food. There is clearly an overlap between 'locality' and 'local' food when locality food is also marketed locally.

The issue of local food becomes more complex when additional non-geographic criteria are introduced. Two distinct features of local food have been identified (DEFRA 2003a). First, a short-chain food system relates to the geographic criteria provided in the preceding. Second, 'a way of delivering a range of social, environmental and economic benefits' (DEFRA 2003a, 85) summarises additional features often associated with the local food sector. Some commentators consider a more useful terminology to be 'sustainable food', defined as 'food associated with high levels of well-being, social justice, stewardship and system resilience' (Sumberg 2009), where proximity of production and consumption is just one element in a more holistic approach. This is the approach taken in the UK by Sustain, the Alliance for Better Food and Farming (http://www.sustainweb.org/).

Despite public and institutional enthusiasm for local food, some academics and even some local food proponents have suggested that the notion of 'local food' can be vague, overly normative, socially exclusive and not necessarily aligned with quality attributes such as ecological or organic (Hinrichs 2003; Winter 2003; Allen 2004; Feagan 2007). Born and Purcell (2006), for example, caution about the 'local trap', where a particular scale is assumed to achieve desired social, environmental or political goals. Partly in response to such critiques, both US and UK academics and practitioners now question whether local food systems and networks centred on direct market exchange can be expected to deliver all necessary food system change. This has engendered interest in how local food systems and networks nest within larger regional food systems, which themselves merit renewed attention and development (Clancy and Ruhf 2010; Kneafsey 2010).

While recognising these caveats, we retain a focus on local food because of its continuing hold on popular imagination in both countries and because directly sold local food offers a useful point of entry to varied understandings of community development. Of particular interest is: (1) food that is grown or reared by the seller and primarily sold directly to consumers living within a distance that they would normally travel to purchase food (e.g. farmers' markets, farm shops, box schemes run by independent growers); (2) processed foods (e.g. bread, cakes, preserves, cheese) sold in this way that use mainly locally sourced ingredients; and (3) food which is grown largely by consumers themselves, at community allotments or city farms. In all these cases, there is some opportunity for direct contact between producer and consumer, and hence for interactions that animate community development.

The actual spread of local food systems and networks across the US and UK has not been uniform. In the US, there has been tremendous growth in the numbers of operating farmers' markets and CSA operations. US farmers' markets increased from 2,746 in 1998 to 5,274 in 2009, a 92 per cent increase (Martinez et al. 2010). CSA operations, which can be single or multiple farm operations, are estimated to number 2,500 in the US as of 2010 (ibid.). Yet despite absolute growth in *numbers* of such local food initiatives, local food markets, as indicated by any direct-to-consumer farm sales, still accounted for less than 1 per cent of total US agricultural sales of edible products in 2007 (ibid.). Thus the symbolic reach of local food in the US is far greater than actual economic impact by conventional measures. Moreover, local food production and marketing are not evenly dispersed either spatially or in terms of scale across the agricultural sector. Small-scale, diversified farms in rural areas near or adjacent to metropolitan counties are most likely to engage in local food production and marketing, with activity particularly concentrated on the US East and West Coasts and in parts of the upper Midwest. Some, although not all of this activity, occurs on farms at the rural–urban interface (Jackson-Smith and Sharp 2008), for the obvious reason that customer populations are more abundant. Most survey research has found that consumer motivations to buy local food are rooted in beliefs about its superior quality and freshness, with support for local farms and the economy being secondary (Martinez et al. 2010).

The UK has experienced a similar explosion of interest in local food. Box schemes selling vegetables and fruit first appeared in the early 1990s and have grown to well in excess of five hundred (http://www.soilassociation. org, accessed 15 January 2010). The first UK farmers' market opened in 1997, with farmers' markets numbering more than five hundred at the time of writing (www.farmersmarkets.net, accessed 15 January 2010). Farm shops, selling directly to the public, are also popular with more than one thousand now across the UK (http://www.farmshopping.net, accessed 29

June 2010). Beyond this, all of the major supermarket chains have begun to offer varying amounts of produce marketed as 'local'. Research conducted in 2005 revealed that 70 per cent of British consumers want to buy local food and 49 per cent want to buy more than they do now (Groves 2005, iii). The availability of local food through supermarkets has the potential to reach more consumers, but the effects of such local food market 'competition' on smaller-scale, direct initiatives have not been assessed.

In contrast to the US, the CSA model in the UK has seen more limited uptake and diffusion. The first example of CSA appeared in the 1990s with Earthshare, near Forres, Morayshire (Scotland) in 1994. This is now the longest running CSA operation in the UK.[4] An accurate figure for CSA operations in the UK does not exist, but as one telling indicator, there were only seventy entries on the Soil Association website list of CSA projects and potential projects in June 2010. The growing availability of local and organic food via alternative outlets, and increasingly through supermarkets, could be one explanation.

As in the US, the geographical spread of local food networks is uneven in the UK. In England, the more affluent and more densely populated south has shown the highest numbers, with the strongest region being the south-west. The northern areas generally score poorly, with the exception of North Yorkshire and Cumbria (Ricketts Hein, Ilbery and Kneafsey 2006). This is similar to the distribution pattern of CSA operations listed on the Soil Association website. Notably, these two northern counties have national parks within easy reach of urban populations, indicating the probable influence of tourism. A related study examined the distribution of local foods within two regions (south-west and West Midlands). They found a flourishing, but unevenly distributed, local food sector. Although speculative, they offered some possible explanations for the distribution patterns, suggesting that influencing factors might include proximity to urban centres, access to trunk roads, landscape designations, the geography of farming types and 'the presence of "alternative" culture and lifestyles' (Ilbery et al. 2006, 5). Research on local food activity in Scotland found farm-based local food enterprises concentrated in the more populated central belt. The distribution of non-farm-based local food enterprises in the Highlands and Islands showed some overlap with the incidence of crofting, but it is unclear whether this indicates persistence of established local food networks or new patterns of food relocalisation (Watts, Leat and Revoredo-Giha 2010).

LOCAL FOOD SYSTEMS AND NETWORKS: COMMUNITY DEVELOPMENT INTERSECTIONS

We argue that a community development lens is useful for examining the social implications of local food systems and networks for rural areas. We first briefly consider general orientations to community development in the two countries, and then examine in turn (1) entrepreneurship and small business development; (2) community capacity-building; and (3) social equity and inclusion, in relation to local food systems and networks.

Community development in the rural US has historically privileged the role and wisdom of outside expert technical assistance to resolve community problems and improve local well-being (Garkovich 2011). Since the mid-1990s, community development professionals and practitioners have come to favour processes facilitated (or at least steered) from within the community that uncover community members' own accounts of their needs and mobilise existing community assets and resources (Green and Haines 2008). In addition to a shift in emphasis from technical expertise to capacity-building, community development practice in the US increasingly recognises the need to move from mere involvement to fuller empowerment and from individual action to meaningful collaboration (Pigg and Bradshaw 2000). While such orientations to community development processes are implicit in some recent US local food systems projects and initiatives, US community development practitioners have not as yet focused a great deal on local food systems (but see Warner et al. 1999 for an exception). Green and Robinson (2011) argue that the intersection of local food systems and community development deserves more attention from community development theorists and practitioners.

Community development in the UK has its roots in both informal community-initiated action and a more paternalistic philanthropy (Popple 1995; Gilchrist 2004). Different approaches have dominated according to prevailing political power, and social and economic conditions. Funding for community workers has derived primarily from the state and in recent years has witnessed a resurgence following a period during which it almost disappeared. The Labour government elected in 1997 was concerned with a perceived democratic deficit and lack of progress on tackling long-term social issues, and in a variety of policy documents restated the importance of public participation and involvement (e.g. Home Office 2004a, 2004b; ODPM 2005; Department of Communities and Local Government [DCLG] 2008). The Conservative–Liberal Democrat coalition that replaced Labour in May 2010 is continuing and extending this theme with David Cameron's promotion of the 'Big Society'. The Community Development Challenge specifically acknowledges that: 'The implementation of policies on community involvement and engagement depends fundamentally on community development' (Community Development Foundation [CDF] 2007, 3).

In practice, in the UK as in the US, the term 'community development' assumes a variety of meanings depending on context. It can refer to community development practice, as in the activity of professional community development workers employed by statutory or voluntary sector agencies, or the effects of such practice; or the development that occurs in a community arising from the actions of independent community activists without external intervention. It can also refer to economic development focused on social enterprises or small businesses in an economically stagnant area. It has been a contested term within the profession itself with debates about what community development is, what represents good practice and how outcomes can be measured. These points of debate present challenges, and yet the very elasticity of the idea of community development under-scores its relevance and potential applicability to local food systems and networks. Charles (2010) outlines five characteristics that should be con-sidered when reviewing the community development aspects of local food initiatives: social justice, sustainable communities, self-determination, working and learning together, participation and reflective practice. We now address three community development themes which resonate across US and UK contexts: entrepreneurship, community capacity-building and social inclusion.

Local Food Intersections: Entrepreneurship and Small Business Development

In the US context especially, local food enterprises and activities have often first gained support and resources through their promise to serve as engines of local economic development. Entrepreneurial initiative and innovation, small-scale value-added processing and the creation of new small and medium enterprises represent alternative approaches for traditional land-based sectors in both the US and the UK. This emphasis on local food accords with the prevailing neo-liberal reliance on market-based solutions to broader problems facing rural areas. In the US, it corresponds to deep-seated American cultural values privileging individualism and business initiative. This entrepreneurial thrust is also found in UK policy, but it is tempered with a concomitant concern with social inclusion—a theme more typically absent in US rural development policy and practice (Shortall and Warner 2010).

Since their renaissance in the 1970s and 1980s, US farmers' markets have been seen as critical venues for community agricultural economic development in large part through the possibilities afforded by the direct market arrangement. While their presumed civic and social benefits for communities constitute part of their great popularity, their potential to serve as small 'engines of rural economic development' (Lyson, Gillespie and Hilchey 1995) has stimulated efforts to establish farmers' markets in diverse communities and ensure their success. Farmers' markets are seen as institutions where new business ideas can be piloted and practiced, and taken further to other farmers' markets or additional market venues. However, research on US farmers' markets and their vendors across three states (New York, Iowa and California) highlights the variability in how entrepreneurial development and business incubation play out across dif-ferent settings (Feenstra et al. 2003). In general, vendors with higher sales at farmers' markets demonstrated the most deliberate and coordinated entrepreneurial and small business practices. Even if based in more remote rural areas, such growers often favoured travelling long distances to sell at busy urban-based farmers' markets, with larger and more diverse customer mixes, where high prices for heirloom tomatoes or mesclun mix raised few eyebrows. Waiting lists to sell at the 'best' urban and suburban farmers' markets are now common. In contrast, in many declining rural areas, farmers' markets struggled to attract both vendors and customers. Participating vendors tended to be older than in urban markets, and more likely to emphasize lifestyle and service dimensions of selling at their rural farmers' markets. Similarly, Gasteyer et al. (2008) found that three of the four rural farmers' markets they studied in Illinois were precarious, having only modest commercial activity. Such situations contrast claims that direct local food markets bring greater entrepreneurship and small business development to rural areas. UK research on farmers' markets has focused less on entrepreneurial development or its absence, but instead on the forms and dynamics of producer–consumer reconnection, through new conventions of regard surrounding local food (Kirwan 2006).

In the US, 'Buy Local Food' campaigns organised within specific communities and regions represent coordinated marketing efforts seeking to foster local food systems entrepreneurship and small business development (Allen and Hinrichs 2007). These campaigns arose in the US in the late 1990s and early 2000s as activists and practitioners recognised that despite the spread of direct market venues like farmers' markets and CSA operations, consumer demand for local food products often remained undirected to local producers. The campaigns sought to create a more explicit 'local food' brand, with farms, shops and restaurants enrolling as providers and/ or purveyors of local foods. 'Buy Local' signage, local food logos and directories (paper and electronic) of local food producers all strive to increase commercial exchange and develop a local food economy. 'Buy Local Food' campaigns offer media messages that include mention of potential environmental and community benefits arising from local food systems development, but stress the ability of and need for local food systems to invigorate local economies (Allen and Hinrichs 2007). Such prioritization corresponds to Winter's (2003) findings regarding the 'defensive localism' in UK rural consumers' motivations for supporting local foods and local farming.

Growing interest in the potential of public food procurement to support local food and farming is now evident in both the UK and the US. Darlington Hospital in north-east England was the first hospital to award a contract to a local dairy when they switched their milk contract to Acorn Dairy, an organic producer two miles from the hospital (DEFRA 2005a). The Cornwall Food Programme, which started in 2001 with the aim of addressing the food supply needs of the National Health Service (NHS) in Cornwall, is now seen as a model for sustainable food procurement (Kirwan and Foster 2007). Working in partnership with local producers, suppliers, and distributors to encourage tendering for NHS and other public sector contracts, the programme serves multiple roles including local business development and support.

Local Food Intersections: Community Capacity-Building

When citizen involvement is high, local food initiatives can also build social capital, empower groups and individuals, strengthen networks and encourage community action. These spaces may be small and they may not appear economically robust, but they may still engender 'resistance and creativity in which people themselves attempt to govern and shape their relationship with food and agriculture' (Hassanein 2003, 79).

Charles (2010) profiles a strong example of community capacity-building as part of CSA development occurring in two communities in County Durham in the north-east of England from 2006 to 2009. The north-east region displays poor economic performance in comparison to the other English regions and has the lowest GDP out of all nine English regions (One North East 2006) and the lowest gross household income and proportion of adults qualified to degree level in the UK (Worthy and Gouldson 2010). It has also been subject to deindustrialisation due to the closing of the mines and quarries. The CSA efforts in County Durham sought to promote local entrepreneurship and citizen involvement using a participatory action research model. 'Growing Together' evolved from a gardening group at a day centre for people with learning disabilities and used seven allotment plots at a site owned by the local authority. Weardale CSA, meanwhile, set up a community interest company and acquired two plots of land to lease. Aside from the actual production of local food, both CSA operations demonstrate outcomes that combine social capital, empowerment and community action—concepts which are foundational to community development. Both groups have built strong partnerships with other local organisations and local authorities to enhance access to resources and markets

In the US, local food systems development is often seen as an opportunity to develop community capacity and problem-solving with Thomas Lyson's (2004) notion of 'civic agriculture' significant here. While Lyson's framework stresses the economic potential of community-based agriculture enterprises to 'create jobs and encourage entrepreneurship', it places such outcomes alongside more social aims of 'strengthened community identities' and better problem-solving capacities. Collective engagement with local food systems development entails collaborative work across often diverse groups of food system 'stakeholders'. This can involve identifying and prioritizing locally important food and agriculture issues. The resulting process of 'problem-solving' necessitates deliberation, discussion and compromise within communities and under the best circumstances prepares communities for engagement with other pressing issues beyond food and agriculture.

Figure 9.1   Planting the raised beds at Weardale CSA, north-east England. Image ©
Louise Taylor, www.louisetaylorphotography.co.uk.

However, community capacity-building outcomes can also dovetail with
entrepreneurship and small business development, as suggested by Holley's
(2007) account of the development of a specialty food cluster in impoverished Appalachian Ohio. In a region that had seen the loss of both traditional agriculture and manufacturing, concern arose to develop enterprises
'where the jobs and wealth were less susceptible to [these] large international forces'. A kitchen incubator provided low-cost access to equipment
for prospective local food entrepreneurs, but technical infrastructure,
while necessary, was not sufficient for developing a cluster of entrepreneurs
centred on local specialty food products. Facilitating networks of starting
entrepreneurs and fostering collaboration with related non-profits and supportive agencies added an important civic dimension to this effort to build
local community capacity for small business success. Brasier et al. (2007)
found similar evidence of enterprise and community capacity-building
through local food cluster development in the north-east US.

In many ways, public food procurement, especially through the rise in
farm-to-school food initiatives in both the US and UK, represents a key
arena where local food intersects with civic interactions and community
capacity-building. Morgan and Sonnino (2008) detail cases of rural counties in England, Scotland and Wales that have developed innovative partnerships and collaborations to reform their school food services in ways
that prioritize healthy, locally sourced food. In the US, fresh public concern about childhood obesity paired with long-standing qualms about the

viability and sustainability of local agriculture has also led to efforts to reform school food services to incorporate more healthy, locally raised fresh foods. However, efforts to increase local food supplies in school food services can be hampered by distribution bottlenecks, lack of local processing facilities and changes in how school kitchens are now organised, staffed and equipped. As a result, nutrition education and food literacy activities also serve as important components of farm-to-school programmes in some parts of the US, as they do in many parts of the UK. Because of the multiple constituencies interested in farm-to-school (i.e. farmers, parents, producers, food services, educators and students), collaborative problem-solving processes have been important for identifying and prioritizing the focus of farm-to-school programmes (i.e., child nutrition and health, local agricultural connections, small business development), which necessarily vary across contexts (Bagdonis, Hinrichs and Schafft 2009).

The collaborative, community-building aspects of local food initiatives have been explored in several US studies. Hultine et al. (2007) described a successful local food systems project in a small rural Illinois community, involving the creation of a small-scale in-house farmers' market within an independently owned grocery store. In discussing the responsiveness of this project to local circumstances and interests, Gasteyer et al. (2008) noted how multiple networks (producer, consumer, political and financial) in this small town came into conversation to determine local food needs, community capacities and workable models for organising some portion of a local food supply that improves food access for rural residents.

A food democracy framework corresponds to this community development perspective emphasizing community capacity-building. Hassanein (2008) examined the orientations of diverse participants in a collaborative community food initiative in Missoula, Montana, involving a university's sustainable farm, a non-profit community agriculture group, a local food bank and local government. The initiative distributes fresh produce to CSA members and also to food-insecure local residents through the food bank. The initiative was held to stimulate participants' food system knowledge, foster deliberation and discussion, promote individual efficacy in the food system and develop shared orientations to the community good, corresponding in sum to the wider community capacity-building aims of local food systems development. Yet Hassanein's case study analysis also reveals important differences across her indicators of 'food democracy in practice' for the university students associated with the farm, the paying CSA members from the community and food bank clients receiving produce from the initiative. These differences point to important issues of equity and inclusion.

Local Food Intersections: Social Equity and Inclusion

Other approaches to community development have begun to recognise the limits of processes that attempt to minimize internal tensions and differences in interest, capacity and power within communities (Stoecker 2005). Through problematizing the formation and practice of community and bringing out the competing interests of food system stakeholders, it becomes evident that a purely economic development orientation to local food systems and networks may exclude or disempower more disadvantaged and vulnerable populations in rural areas. And to the extent that community capacity-building may paper over internal differences, leave prevailing power relations unquestioned or omit certain voices, local food systems initiatives may not adequately acknowledge or address the most pressing concerns of some residents. Hassanein's (2008) assessment of food democracy in the Montana community food initiative found that although university students reported strong, practical experiences of food democracy in social and collaborative terms, CSA members offered more individually focused accounts and food bank members reported few experiences suggesting the presence of food democracy. Her findings parallel research (in another rural university town) noting challenges for social inclusion in local food systems projects in Iowa in the late 1990s (Hinrichs and Kremer 2002).

By contrast, the work by Charles (2010) in the UK profiles an explicit effort by two CSA operations in northern England to address social inclusion concerns. For some, joining a CSA is a political act in response to concerns about the food system and its sometimes negative environmental and social consequences (Cox et al. 2008). The initiators of Weardale CSA alluded to this element of social justice, saying their CSA aspires to be 'an ethically thoughtful CSA which fosters citizenship that relates to others, sees citizens in the round, and adds what they have in common to what they are entitled to have for themselves'. They also included in their aims a desire 'to promote the involvement of people who could benefit therapeutically'. The central vision for the Growing Together Project was similar—to reach beyond their core base of people with learning difficulties to work alongside others in their community on a more equal footing.

Equity and social inclusion concerns related to local food in both the US and the UK now encompass a broader set of issues affecting producers and consumers. In the US context, this has included attention to how the development of local food systems may require consideration of *domestic* fair trade, as applied both to farmers (Jaffee, Kloppenburg and Monroy 2004) and farmworkers (Brown and Getz 2008). While many local food systems initiatives emphasize the economic and environmental benefits of local foods and pay scant attention to the social equity impacts of local foods (Allen and Hinrichs 2007), new certification and labelling initiatives have begun (initially in California) that attempt to prioritize labour conditions, practices and fair wages in local food systems. The labour intensity of fresh fruit and vegetable production is at the heart of local food systems and raises issues about the treatment of farmworkers, both documented and undocumented, which are important for fuller consideration of the community development outcomes of local food systems. Such issues are clearly important and salient in the rural farming communities where farmworkers themselves reside and work, yet are often overlooked by urban consumers of local food (Jarosz 2008). Assumptions about the superiority of local food supply chains for farmworker well-being may be poorly founded. In a study of the health and welfare of UK farmworkers in local food supply chains, their levels of self-reported health were actually lower than for farmworkers in Spain, Uganda and Kenya producing the same products for UK markets (Cross et al. 2009). Such outcomes suggest that local markets in themselves provide no automatic guarantee that vulnerable workers will experience enhanced welfare. The specific conditions and context of local food production and exchange require examination.

Equity and social inclusion considerations also arise in accessing and consuming local food. Local food initiatives, particularly farmers' markets and CSA operations, have long faced charges of elitism and exclusivity. The most colourful and abundant farmers' markets (and generally the most desirable markets for producers from the standpoint of profitability) are frequently priced outside the range of modest or low-income consumers. Ironically, the very markers of successful local food development can prove to be at odds with some interests of long-time residents. Writing of Hardwick in rural Vermont, Hewitt (2010) describes the town's celebrated transformation from an economy based on granite and dairy to a successful local foods 'district' comprised of interconnected local food producers, processors, distributors and retailers. Long-time residents of Hardwick see the intense media attention and welcome the new entrepreneurial vigour in their town, but also find the idea of paying $20 (or more) per pound for a local specialty cheese incompatible with their own material circumstances and thrifty Yankee values. New challenges of inclusion and access can emerge with the success of local foods.

THE POLICY CONTEXT FOR LOCAL FOOD SYSTEMS AND NETWORKS

The productivist cast of both US and UK agricultural policy, especially since World War II, has encouraged industrialisation and specialization in both national systems of agriculture. In emphasizing efficient production of low-cost food, agricultural policies ensured a bimodal distribution of farms—one with smaller numbers of large-scale, commercial farms and larger numbers of small-scale, sometimes part-time enterprises (Findeis et al., this volume). Such productivist priorities have long eclipsed broader rural development concerns (Bryden and Warner, this volume). As average farm sizes increased, previously diversified local and regional agricultural systems became more standardised and concentrated. Agricultural restructuring in turn made small- and medium-scale food processing, distribution and retailing infrastructures less viable. Thus productivist policies for agriculture have had ripple effects throughout the food system.

In the UK, a broad shift in EU rural policy from sectoral to more territorial approaches (Ward and Brown 2009) has helped focus attention on the place of local food networks and enterprises in rural regions. Interest in food policy at the national level in the UK has also grown markedly in the 2000s, driven by concerns about the impacts of global climate change on food production, agriculture's contribution to greenhouse gas emissions, food safety issues, diet-related health problems and uncertainties about longer term food security. The observation that 'the food system is a stage on which some of the major societal challenges of our time are being played out' (Cabinet Office 2008, 18) illustrates the recognition that food impinges on many areas of current concerns.

Prompted by the widespread foot-and-mouth disease outbreak in 2001, with its significant impacts on British agriculture and rural tourism, the government appointed a Policy Commission on the Future of Farming and Food (chaired by Sir Donald Curry) with the remit to 'advise the Government on how we can create a sustainable, competitive and diverse farming and food sector' (Policy Commission on the Future of Farming and Food 2002, 5).[5] The resulting report stressed the need for farming to 'reconnect' with the rest of the economy and the environment and it strongly supported growth of the local food sector as an economic opportunity for farmers, whilst recognising that many local food sector businesses are driven by environmental concerns as much as profit (ibid., 43). The Sustainable Farming and Food Strategy (SFFS; see DEFRA 2002) built upon recommendations of the commission's report. The SFFS acknowledged the link between more sustainable agriculture and wider social, environmental and cultural benefits for rural communities and set out several key principles for sustainable farming and food that emphasize social, environmental and animal welfare concerns. Both the strategy and its successor (DEFRA 2006) include measures to promote local and regional food and farmers' markets. Regional Development Agencies (RDAs) were tasked with producing delivery plans and have supported regional food production and marketing. The Public Sector Food Procurement Initiative, launched in support of the SFFS in 2003, had as a priority objective to 'increase tenders from small and local producers and their ability to do business with the public sector' (DEFRA 2010a) whilst remaining in line with EU procurement regulations. These rules prohibit specifying goods by geographical region (e.g. 'local') but do allow criteria based upon quality and environmental sustainability. Public sector bodies are encouraged to break up contracts into smaller lots that can be met by smaller producers.

In the UK, millions of pounds of grant money from the Big Lottery are now providing resources to support new and emerging local food networks and initiatives. A £10 million five-year lottery programme, Making Local Food Work, was launched in 2007, and a £50 million grants programme (the Local Food Grant) opened in 2008. The Food for Life Partnership is another £16.9 million lottery-funded programme directed at enabling schools to provide healthier school meals and to use school grounds for pupils to grow some of their own food. Landshare, a web-based scheme to connect people with underused land to people who want access to land to produce food was launched in 2009 and had attracted over forty-four thousand participants by January 2010.

The continuing and growing debate around the future direction of UK food policy is illustrated by a plethora of publications from think tanks and government departments (e.g. Lucas, Jones and Hines 2006; Midgley 2008, 2009; DEFRA 2008b; Cabinet Office 2008; Ambler-Edwards et al. 2009; Steedman and Schultz 2009; Bridge and Johnson 2009). These documents represent a search for new policies and practice to respond to the multiple environmental, social and economic forces currently threatening the stability and sustainability of the food system. Interest in local food enterprises and shorter supply chains forms part of such discussions. The recommendation of the Policy Commission on the Future of Farming and Food that 'reconnection' should be the key objective of public policy included reconnecting 'consumers with what they eat and how it is produced' (2002, 6). However, most emerging policy has continued to focus on the ability of the market to produce food security and fairness (Cabinet Office 2008). Nevertheless, the efforts of social enterprises and local groups working on food issues have not gone unnoticed. The Cabinet Office report (ibid.) acknowledges that 'community engagement on food is a success story' (66) and is contributing to tackling some 'big problems' through projects such as food co-ops and community allotments. In the prevailing policy environment, local food networks and organisations might expect to receive public sector support, although financial backing could be restricted in the current economic climate.

Recognition of broader public and stakeholder interest in UK food policy is also evident in the appointment by the government of a new Council of Food Policy Advisors, which held its first meeting in January 2009 and produced its first report in September 2009 (DEFRA 2009). In January 2010, the government launched a national food strategy for England—'Food 2030'—arguably the most important national (as opposed to European) food policy document to appear since the Agriculture Act of 1947. The strategy addresses the question of how more food can be produced with a lower environmental impact and moves closer towards a policy for food that is also low carbon, healthy, ethical and affordable (Lang 2010). Within the document, there is recognition that 'community food growing initiatives' can improve access to 'affordable, nutritious food' (HM Government 2010, 13). The wider benefits of practical involvement in growing food at home or in an allotment or community garden such as 'better mental and physical health, bringing people together, and improved skills'—benefits that might accrue to any community development project—are also acknowledged (15). Local food partnerships between landowners and community groups are to be encouraged to enable access to land for community food production (19). The direction of the policy presents 'windows of opportunity' for a pragmatic approach to community action (M. Taylor 2003) on local food although at the time of writing, it is uncertain how the new Coalition government will respond to the strategy.

In some UK localities, partners are now coming together to produce food strategies for smaller geographical entities. One of the first was the Brighton and Hove strategy published in 2006, which was developed 'to strengthen the growth and development of a localised food system which promotes social equity, economic prosperity, environmental sustainability, global fair-trade and the health and well-being of all residents' (Brighton and Hove Food Partnership 2006, 3). In 2007, a food strategy was produced as part of a wider sustainability strategy for a planned new urban development proposed by the Duchy of Cornwall in Newquay, with similar goals around health, affordability, sustainable production and to develop reliable markets for local food businesses (Sustain 2007). Other examples of developing strategies and food initiative case studies in the UK can be found on the Food Vision website: http://www.foodvision.gov.uk.

Despite evidence of interest and activity in local food networks in the UK, uncertainty surrounding future public sector funding due to the impacts of the 2008 recession and likely shifts in programmatic and funding priorities following the 2010 General Election mean that longer term trajectories remain difficult to predict. Initiatives in regions with stable population bases, knowledge resources and stronger economies may be best positioned to develop and survive independently of government support. In many rural areas, government support and funding sources remain essential for a local food sector to grow and thrive. It remains to be seen whether grassroots enthusiasm and support in the UK will be sufficient to survive cuts in public funding that may reduce the availability of community development resources and grants.

As in the UK, the policy context in the US has shaped the form, vigour, distribution and impacts of local food systems development. Federal policy, in its emphases and omissions, has set the stage, both constraining possibilities and directing the development that occurs. In the 2000s, state and local policies have also played growing roles in leveraging resources and legitimizing particular approaches. National agricultural policy is most fully set through the so-called Farm Bill, the large, increasingly unwieldy and contentious piece of legislation that is renegotiated and authorized approximately every five years. As omnibus legislation, Farm Bills now include multiple titles on diverse topics under the purview of the USDA, from commodity crops, forestry and energy to nutrition, trade and food aid, conservation and rural development. Before the most recent Farm Bill in 2008, few Farm Bills offered provisions directly supporting the development of local food systems.

Passage of the federal Farmer-to-Consumer Direct Marketing Act of 1976 sowed the first significant seeds of current local food systems activity in the US. Passed as the farm crisis was gaining steam in the US, this legislation sought to find alternative markets for family farmers then struggling in commodity export markets. The renaissance of US farmers' markets and the strong emphasis on direct marketing for US local food systems can be directly traced to this policy, which brought the USDA's Agricultural Marketing Service and state Departments of Agriculture into partnerships to rediversify agricultural markets within the states. Addressing farmers' economic needs more than consumers' food interests, this act and the USDA's more recent Farmers' Market Promotion Program have provided some statutory basis for developing local agricultural markets (Hardesty 2010), even as the dominant productivist and export-oriented focus of US agricultural policy has arguably worked against local food systems.

Perhaps because the 2008 Farm Bill ultimately retained the increasingly contested production subsidies for major commodities, several provisions to support local food systems also found political pathways into the final legislation. These provisions attempt to address the gap in the US between growing consumer demand for local foods and the capacity of farmers to produce such food and then also get it processed and distributed. For example, expansion of the long-standing Farmers' Market Promotion Program and the newer Value-Added Producer Grants Program (which provides funds for business planning and working capital for projects involving processing agricultural products), as well as the addition of a new Local and Regional Food Enterprise Guaranteed Loan programme (aimed at rebuilding local and regional food system infrastructures), all aim to improve enterprise performance and amplify the economic development potential of local food systems. It remains unclear, however, how the benefits of these new programmes will be distributed across rural, suburban and urban communities. Rural farmers' markets, for example, face special challenges in terms of vendors' economic performance and satisfaction which can weaken farmers' markets' viability (Schmit and Gómez 2011).

Other US national policy initiatives have mobilised nutrition and food access rationales alongside interest in agricultural enterprise development to widen consumer access to direct agricultural markets and build local food systems. The Women, Infants and Children (WIC) Farmers' Market Nutrition Program (FMNP) was established in 1992 to help low-income women and their children increase access to the fresh produce available at farmers' markets. While the federal government pays direct programme costs, partnering states must provide 30 per cent of programme administrative costs. Coupons for twenty to twenty-five dollars are provided to eligible families to use at FMNP-authorized markets or roadside stands. The success of this programme in supporting both low-income access and farmers' direct market revenue led to authorization through the 2002 Farm Bill of a companion Senior FMNP, using the same model to support purchase of local produce in direct market venues by low-income elders. Together coupons through the two FMNPs can support forty million dollars annually in local food purchases. Beyond meeting direct goals of improving consumer access and producer revenues, implementing the FMNPs has also required planning and collaboration between local agencies and educators in rural communities, with evidence of wider gains for community capacity-building (Dollahite et al. 2005).

Policy attention to social inclusion in US local food systems development was first and most strongly evident in the USDA's Community Food Projects Grant Program, launched in 1996 in part as a result of lobbying by community food security activists. Generally targeting non-profit community groups, these grants aim to increase the supply of fresh foods for low-income populations through community-based entrepreneurial agricultural initiatives. In a formal evaluation of the programme, Maretzki and Tuckermanty (2007) observed that the most successful projects gave focused attention to collaborative processes that fostered leadership development and meaningful participation by low-income participants. While many of the projects they evaluated were urban-based, community food projects on Indian reservations, for example, involved restoration of traditional rural food systems centred on indigenous crop farming and native foodways. These projects addressed and integrated local community-identified concerns about food knowledge, youth education and tribal health.

The USDA's introduction of its Know Your Farmer, Know Your Food (KYF2) Initiative in 2009 under the new Obama administration indicates heightened focus on local food systems at the US federal policy level. Although most of the USDA programmes bundled under the new KYF2 banner actually predate the initiative, the umbrella framework (and catchy branding) suggest the most coordinated attention to date within the USDA on local and regional food systems. Identifying programmes in rural development, risk management and elsewhere that can be harnessed to promote and support local food systems development, KYF2 signals a new level of integration and legitimacy of federal programmes in this area (Hardesty 2010). Although local food systems development is most directly shaped by agriculture and nutrition programmes and policies under the aegis of the USDA, there is increased recognition that policies and regulations of other federal agencies, such as the Departments of Commerce and Transportation, also shape options for developing local food systems and need better coordination (Gosselin 2010).

While federal policy sets the stage in the US context, its fundamental and continuing commitment to productivist, export-oriented agriculture constrains its potential to support development of local food systems. Such 'lock-in' of federal policy has created both the need and space for smaller, targeted, but important subnational policies and initiatives. Examples include state- and local-level policies to protect farmland (of particular importance to states with significant peri-urban agricultures that constitute the base for local food systems; see Jackson-Smith and Sharp 2008), state-level policies to support public procurement of local foods for school food services (thirty-three of the fifty states have now passed legislation either supporting farm-to-school pilot projects, allowing local food preference or increasing reimbursement for purchase of local food or implementing grant programmes; see www.farmtoschool.org) and to conduct comprehensive strategic planning for the regional food and farming sector (such as Vermont's Farm-to-Plate initiative, approved in 2009 to develop a ten-year strategic plan that will enhance the place of local and sustainable foods within this small rural dairy state). The complementary rise of state and local food policy councils across the US, particularly since the 1990s, has also been important in 'putting food topics on politicians' radar, elevating discussions about food, making connections and getting useful projects implemented' (Clancy, Hammer and Lippoldt 2007, 140). Although membership structure, organisational viability and power of food policy councils vary widely across the US, they nonetheless represent new models of food governance with potential to address rural needs and interests through more comprehensive and democratic dialogue with urban and suburban concerns.

CONCLUSION

In this chapter, we have examined the development of local food systems and networks in the US and UK, focusing on the importance of direct connection between producer and consumer. We have applied a broad community development lens to consider the motivations for and outcomes of local food relations in the two countries. While many patterns for local food systems and networks in the US and UK are similar, differences are also evident. Community development, as linked to entrepreneurial and small business development, provides a stronger frame and justification for local food initiatives in the US than in the UK. A community capacity-building orientation has been more explicitly framed in state discourse in the UK than in the US, although civil society groups in both countries strongly stress such social and civic rationales for attention to local food. Community development, encompassing social equity and inclusion, represents a more recent consideration for many local food initiatives. Here the UK policy's focus on social inclusion in other areas (see Shucksmith and Schafft, this volume) may spill over to UK food policies and strategies, while in the US, civil society groups and activists are beginning to press for social equity agendas in the food and agricultural system.

Evidence of so-called food deserts in many rural areas, in both the US (Morton and Blanchard 2007) and the UK (Furey, Strugnell and McIlveen 2001), underscores the importance of developing local food systems and networks that begin to feed rural as well as suburban and urban populations. The decline of traditional small markets and groceries in rural areas and resulting longer commutes to large supermarkets present challenges of healthy food access, particularly for more vulnerable rural residents who lack reliable private transportation or live in areas with little or no public transportation. However, the diversity of rural areas in both the UK and US makes it difficult to offer sweeping assessments about either the need for local food systems and networks or their prospects. We have highlighted the community capacity-building aspect of local food systems and networks, yet the broader conditions of rural regions range from resource dependence to abundance of natural amenities, from chronic poverty to recent economic decline and from population growth to dispersion. The diverse conditions of rural regions surely influence the community resources from which capacity might be built. Such differences across (and sometimes within) rural regions affect the needs and interests behind more localised food systems and networks. Food democracy begins with the politics of planning and designing the form, scope and scale of local food efforts.

Peri-urban and more affluent rural areas in both countries are most likely to experience the development of comprehensive local food systems and networks in the absence of strong governmental support, such as that provided through the UK Big Lottery–funded programmes. There, consumer density and demand could stimulate and perhaps sustain individual and interconnected local food initiatives. More distressed or depopulated rural areas may fare less well in developing local food systems and networks, unless such areas retain remnants of diversified regional agricultures and food businesses on which local knowledge and energy can build.

Aside from the diverse contexts of rural areas in the US and UK and present economic uncertainties in both countries regarding government support, several emerging trends could shape the prospects for local food systems and networks. Intensifying debates on national and international food security, concern about climate change and growing public health imperatives are particularly important and interrelated. Though framed as a needed alternative to fossil fuels, increasing production and trade of agricultural biofuels are widely seen as contributing to volatility in global food commodity prices and rising levels of food insecurity (Lang, Barling and Caraher 2009). In the absence of other alternative transport fuels, it is unlikely that public opposition to biofuels will completely prevail. Declining, less populated rural areas could be the most feasible and favoured sites for extensive biofuel crop production to address national energy needs. More research is needed to determine if and how rural places can produce both biofuels and local foods and with what implications for local communities and the environment. While the push to dedicate land resources to biofuel crops will increase, the renewed salience of food security may work to balance attention to developing local (and regional) food systems that can reduce dependence on globally sourced foods. Although 'food miles' provide a poor measure of environmental impact, climate emission impacts of the broader food and agricultural system are a growing concern (Edwards-Jones et al. 2008). More diversified and less concentrated food systems and networks can be framed as solutions to the energy and food security challenges of the future, which will increase the popular appeal of and policy attention to local food. To the extent that local food systems and networks can also deliver healthy food, particularly fresh fruits and vegetables, to diverse populations, they converge with national concern in both countries to address diet-related health problems. Although complex and evolving, the 'health-environment-society interface' (Lang, Barling and Caraher 2009, 8) represents a promising arena for local food systems and networks both within and beyond rural areas in the US and the UK.

Part III
Governance

Governance

10 Policy Affecting Rural People, Economies and Communities

John Bryden and Mildred E. Warner

INTRODUCTION

In this chapter we compare key general policies in the US and the UK that have an impact on rural areas as well as those which have explicitly stated rural objectives. By rural policy, therefore, we mean both 'narrow' policies specifically directed at rural problems, regions, communities and sectors and 'broad' policies that have a major influence on rural regions and people. We explore the history and ideas lying behind policies for rural areas in the UK (and Europe) and the US. Our understanding of broad rural policy is territorial and cross-sectoral, and is framed by the Organisation for Economic Co-operation and Development's (OECD) 'new rural paradigm' published in 2006, but with antecedents going back to the 1990s. We contrast the way in which rural policy has emerged in the UK (conditioned largely by the European Union) and in the US. We give special attention to efficiency versus equity debates. We examine the notion of territorial equivalence, which refers to policies that specifically address rural–urban economic and social disparities. We further look at the rural impacts of general processes of decentralization, centralization, privatization and the growth of partnerships as 'new governance' mechanisms. We assess the shifts in policy thinking since the 1980s and into the economic crisis of 2008–2011. Finally, we conclude with some ideas about future issues likely to change the nature and content of broad and narrow rural policies, drawing some contrasts between the UK and US throughout.

THE CONTEXT OF RURAL POLICY IN THE UK AND US

Rural policy has evolved in different ways and within very different overall contexts in the US, UK and Europe, even though a common element has been the fact that 'agricultural' policy has tended to determine 'rural' policy. However, there are still significant differences in the driving forces for rural policy and the logic and politics underpinning it.

By 'rural' we mean all that is not predominately urban, or within the main commuting belt of the urban regions with their large and diverse labour markets and easy access to services. In the US, it broadly means 'nonmetropolitan' areas. However, the precise definitions used differ between Europe and the US. Because of the differences, we organise the chapter first with a discussion of the evolution of 'rural policy' in Europe and the US before undertaking a comparison to identify similarities and differences, and finally discussing contemporary issues that rural policy must address.

European states, the EU itself and the UK in particulars were formed out of centuries of internal and external conflict, the development and demise of feudalism, the development of mercantilism and capitalism, the expansion and subsequent contraction of empires, the technological changes and related growth and territorial concentration of industry and related economic and social crises. In the twentieth century, the two world wars and related food shortages were important factors underlying the development of a protectionist set of agricultural policies (Tracy 1982). Rural settlements were the most ancient settlements, and associated not only with the important business of food production, but also with cultural images and identities, history, nature and industrial development. However, because of conflicts, internal and external colonialism and the business of nation-building, governments in Europe became almost uniformly centralized and powerful. Especially in the aftermath of the economic crisis between the wars and following World War II, this allowed them to implement strong 'welfare states'.

Whereas Europe has been characterised historically by out-migration (largely to the US), the US is a nation of immigrants. The notion of a frontier territory available to homesteaders and developers laid the basis for the American Dream as a land of individual opportunity, unfettered by historical constraints. In the North east and Midwest a pattern of smallholder farming developed and with it a structure of local government that was democratic and locally controlled. In the South, a large plantation agriculture system developed which was heavily dependent on slave labour and international trade. In the West, mining and ranching dominated. As a result both the South and the West developed a more limited system of local government and of social rights. Private property and individual liberty are hallmarks of US philosophy and practice. Attention to community obligations and social rights is weak. This is an important and distinguishing difference between the US and Europe that gets reflected in both broad and narrow rural policy.

Current rates of immigration to the US exceed those of the earlier peak period of 1880–1920 (Kritz and Gurak 2005). While much of the earlier peak in immigration was to urban centres, the current influx is heavily rural and this is changing the character of many rural communities as immigrant workers, often undocumented, fill positions in agricultural production and processing (Crowley and Lichter 2009). In contrast to the earlier period of legal immigration, the current wave largely lacks rights or claims to government services and tends to receive low wages. This creates special challenges for rural communities and rural policy. Immigration is also increasing within Europe, but EU protocols make these flows more likely to be legal and carry some (if variable) social rights.

The structure of agricultural landholding and production had important historical impacts on US rural policy. The US Constitution respected the power of the constituent states as a compromise to build a nation based on two very different systems of economic organisation. The more limited power of the central government led to lesser efforts in relation to social welfare than in Europe and significant variation in social welfare rights based on location and on race. Finally private property rights were considered paramount—leading to a relatively weak view of collective responsibilities and a heavy reliance on the market and private means for securing public goods.

These axes, notably constitutional provisions and the 'social contract' as developed in social welfare systems, property rights, the political position of rural people at critical historical periods and the role of 'rural' in culture and identity, lie beneath rural policies and still partly explain their comparative content and efficacy in different jurisdictions. Thus, for example, the notion and practice of collective rights over property in some parts of Europe is enshrined in public access rights as well as in strong planning regulations, and it allows people ready access to nature and recreation, a partial *quid pro quo* for political support for rural causes and, especially, for agri-environmental subsidies. Similarly, the stronger welfare state in the UK and elsewhere in Europe underpins the provision of public services, the securing of minimum incomes and some territorial evenness in salaries of public servants and professionals such as teachers and nurses. Such policies underpin a quality of life in the rural regions of the UK and Europe and enable people to live there in ways and numbers which reliance on the private sector would allow only at lower levels of welfare and employment. In the UK such services as infrastructure provision, telephones and electricity, nurseries, schools, Internet access, medical services and income support are covered by national policies and include universal service obligations which are not particularly 'rural' in their conception or ideological underpinnings. By contrast, in the US some of these areas are regarded as part of a rural policy because universal service obligations are not national policy (except in the case of primary and secondary education).

THE RECENT EVOLUTION OF RURAL POLICIES IN THE UK AND EUROPE

Rural policy addresses major rural sectors, like agriculture, forestry and fishing, protected areas and national parks, and also includes policies *impacting* rural places and people, including policies for social welfare, fiscal matters, local government, environment, physical planning, education, health, transport, infrastructure, trade, competition and so on. Specific territorial rural policy aimed at promoting development in rural places was more rare, at least until the late 1980s.[1]

In some countries, especially the Nordics, strong ideas of citizen equivalence and rights to live anywhere and be treated in an equivalent way in terms of access to public and private services, livelihood opportunities and political life ('territorial equivalence') were backed up with fiscal equalization schemes and powerful local governments. In the UK, the post-war welfare state heralded by the Beveridge Report (Beveridge 1942) had the effect of equalizing provision of many public services, including schools, nurseries, health care and social welfare across the country. These equivalence policies constituted a territorial rural policy without being named as such. Only when the welfare state began to be dismantled in the 1980s did territorial rural policy begin to take shape at the European level.

In the US there has been little policy support for territorial equivalence. In the 1950s and 1960s Keynesian logics were used to justify investments in lagging regions to build infrastructure and promote market penetration as exemplified by the Tennessee Valley Authority and Appalachian Regional Commission, but since the 1970s, the focus has been on promoting growth centres and individual mobility (Brown and Warner 1991). Incomes and social rights differ by place of residence and this creates an uneven landscape of rights and opportunity across the US (Katz 2001). In fact, in the US context of highly autonomous and self-financed local government, the term 'fiscal equivalence' means local areas only receive services for which they are willing and able to pay. This creates economic pressure to ensure efficiency and prevent over supply of public goods. However, it also justifies inequality as preference and leads to a highly uneven landscape of social rights. Warner and Pratt (2005) have shown how such decentralization has led to vicious cycles of underinvestment leading to underdevelopment in poor rural areas.

Our analysis faces the key problem that the nature of the governance context in the US and UK is quite different. The US has a federal constitution, while the UK is a unitary state with devolved parliaments since 1999, which is at the same time part of the European Union. The European Union is a collection of member states that have ceded, through treaties, certain government functions and decisions to the European Commission, controlled mainly by the European Council (a body of national government representatives, typically ministers), and to a lesser extent the European Parliament (containing directly elected representatives from all the member states). It can be regarded as a *quasi*-federation or supranational government. This multilevel governmental structure has implications for our analysis since central government policies and spending are not merely related to national political issues, but also to the balance of powers between the federal and quasi-federal levels, the states/provinces and the local governments (typically regions, counties or municipalities). Thus, within the EU, it is important to recognise that a complete analysis would consider *common* (EU), *national, regional* and even *local* policies, there being a division of competencies and some overlap between these. Two important common policies from an expenditure viewpoint that impact on rural areas are agricultural policy (Common Agricultural Policy [CAP]) and regional policy (social and cohesion policy). Others with regulatory and/or expenditure impacts include transport infrastructure, environmental policy, competition policy, monetary policy, trade policy, research and technology policy, energy policy and telecommunications policy. In addition, since 1999, some relevant powers have been devolved to the national parliaments of Scotland, Wales and Northern Ireland in the UK. These powers include the development of rural development plans and programmes under the overarching EU scheme.

In the US, federal, state and local policies are all important, because localities and local governments have more autonomy and responsibility than they do in the UK and most other European countries. The position of local government is determined by the states, rather than the US federal government, and it varies from state to state. Federal policy is the most likely to articulate a rural component. Whether states give special attention to rural differences depends on the political and geographic make-up of each state. Diversity and competition characterise policy differences between states and localities, leading some to argue that a destructive competition or 'race to the bottom' is occurring between states as they limit local taxation and social investments (Donahue 1997). Devolution also has been an ongoing process in the US and reflects the tensions between the nation and the states in a federated context (Conlan 1998). Three waves have been seen in the last thirty years: devolution with increased federal dollars under Nixon in the 1970s, devolution with a reduction in federal financial support under Reagan in the 1980s and devolution of authority (e.g. mandate relief) under Clinton in the 1990s. The last two waves reduced federal responsibility, funding and authority for infrastructure and social welfare investment and transferred those responsibilities to the states. The most recent census data show that federal aid to localities averages less than 3 per cent of local government expenditure (less than $100 per capita on average). Local governments fund 57 per cent of their services with locally raised revenue, and states are the most important source of intergovernmental aid—accounting for nearly 40 per cent on average (Warner 2001; Cimbaluk and Warner 2008). This contrasts markedly with the UK. In England, for example, some 74 per cent of budgeted local government revenue expenditure and 40 per cent of capital expenditure in 2009–2010 was funded by central government (Communities and Local Government 2009).

The period since 1980 has been a challenging time for rural policy in most OECD countries. Traditional agricultural and regional policies came under increasing pressure due to changing priorities, politics and circumstances. People engaged in agriculture and primary production form an increasingly small minority of the rural population in most OECD countries (Bollman and Bryden 1997). Many rural economies have successfully diversified into tertiary sector activities, whilst others have declined and even died (Bryden and Hart 2004; Egan 2002; Atterton, Bryden and Johnson, this volume). These social and economic changes, the enlargements of the EU, the pressures of international trade agreements and changing ideas about the role of government and the means of public management after 1980 led to a significant transition in rural policies in many OECD countries including the UK and the US (Bryden 1999). The specific changes concerned:

- a *shift from sectoral to territorial policy* involving specific rural policies aimed at stimulating integrated *local* rural development;
- *decentralization* of policy administration and, within limits, policy design to regional or county levels;
- an increased use of *partnerships* between public, private and voluntary sectors in the development and implementation of local and regional policies;
- increasing *privatization* of public services, and the application of private sector norms to public management;
- the introduction of mechanisms to try to ensure better *coordination* of different policies affecting rural areas and people at central government levels;
- the evolution of new, *more flexible mechanisms* for supporting regional and local policies;
- the encouragement of a *'bottom-up' approach* to rural development;
- greater *emphasis on diversification of rural economies*, including local initiatives that build on existing resources and skills and stimulate networking between small and medium enterprises;
- a *focus on specific local assets*, which may provide new competitive advantages, such as environmental, archaeological or cultural amenities; niche food and craft products; or information technology;
- a shift from an approach based on *subsidizing* declining sectors including agriculture, fishing and mining, to one based on strategic *investments* to develop new activities.

Examples of new policies or programmes which reflect several of these tendencies include the LEADER programme in the EU, introduced in 1990, and the Regional Development Councils and Rural Empowerment Zone and Enterprise Community Program (EZEC) established in 1993 in the US. LEADER and EZEC both aimed at stimulating local partnerships to plan and implement their own local development programmes, and represent a new approach to 'community economic development' in rural regions (Douglas 2010; Shortall and Warner 2010; Reid 1999). We return to these later.

The changes overall concern issues of governance and institutional frameworks, including the definition of 'development' in a context of neo-liberalism, globalisation and localisation, and the goals and content of policy. Taken together they constitute elements of what the OECD calls the 'new rural paradigm' (2006). However, shifts in the language or rhetoric of rural policy have not always been matched by reality, as both the US and Europe maintain large agricultural policy programmes directed almost exclusively to farmer clients. While rural people and their civic organisations support the kind of policy shifts we have outlined, these groups are weak compared with the large and well-organised farming, environmental and corporate lobbies (Warner and Shortall 2008). In the mid-2000s, the US Farm Bill increased the budget for agricultural support, and the EU reforms for the period 2007–2013 proposed an increase in environmental payments to farmers as the keystone of what it *now* calls its rural development policy. The WTO talks remain unresolved. The 2001 foot-and-mouth disease epidemic in Britain demonstrated clearly that agricultural and related policies had simply not evolved to reflect the changed realities of rural economy and society.[2]

Meanwhile, other elements of the policy reform also appear problematic. Privatization has failed to reduce public expenditure and improve services as shown in meta-analyses of studies across the US and Europe (Bel, Fageda and Warner 2010; Boyne 1998). In fact, rural areas are the least likely to be able to take advantage of privatization because the high costs of serving sparse settlements makes rural areas less attractive to potential private suppliers than their suburban and city counterparts (Warner 2009a, 2006). This has led to a process of reverse privatization in both the US and the UK (Hefetz and Warner 2007; Entwistle 2005), and a search for alternative forms of public sector reform focused more on inter-municipal cooperation (Warner and Hefetz 2002, 2003). New Public Management has confused the citizen with a consumer, and more attention is now given to serving citizens and regulating monopoly to ensure best value and promote public participation (Entwistle and Martin 2005; DeLeon and Denhardt 2000; Warner 2008). Decentralization has led to increased spatial inequality (Warner and Pratt 2005; Rodríguez-Pose and Bwire 2004). Ironically, it also has been accompanied by significant recentralization processes—especially as regards intergovernmental funding and national mandates, as witnessed in the various local government campaigns in the UK (from competitive tendering, to best value, to contestability) and by welfare and education reform in the US (Hart and Munro 2000; Warner and Pratt 2005; Mackinnon 2009).

Partnership approaches to network governance are another key element in these policy reforms. While they are celebrated for their flexibility and ability to engage multiple sectors in collaboration (L. Salamon 2002), coordination and accountability have been recognised as problems (Shortall and Warner 2010; Bryden 2005a; Rhodes 1996). In addition, the partnership project has been critiqued, especially in rural areas, for by-passing traditional units of regional and local government (Ray 2000). The economic crisis since 2008 has brought the whole neo-liberal project into serious question (Ramesh, Araral and Wu 2010), but policy has yet to make a major shift back toward regulation and state provision. Thus, the significant transformations left by privatization, decentralization and partnership remain with us.

AGRICULTURAL POLICY, REGIONAL POLICY AND RURAL POLICY IN THE UK AND THE EU

Prior to its accession to the European Community in 1973, the UK had an agricultural policy that was protectionist, but gave preference to Commonwealth countries in matters of trade. The UK's regional policy had its roots in the problems of old industrial regions, and was mainly an urban regional policy using both incentives and regulatory measures to steer economic activity to deprived regions. The establishment of the Development Commission in 1909, the Highlands and Islands Development Board in 1965, with wide powers for the remote and sparsely populated north of Scotland, and the later establishment of the Development Board for Rural Wales were exceptions that addressed rural problems and issues different from those of agriculture.

In the European Union, experimental 'integrated rural development' projects were introduced in the early 1980s with the prospect of 'southern enlargement' to Spain, Portugal and Greece. This enlargement, together with the creation of the Single Market through the Single European Act of 1986, led to the first major reform of the Structural Funds in 1987 that identified priority regions for EU regional development actions. This period also coincided with the start of reforms of the CAP following overproduction, the complaints of food-exporting countries, budgetary constraints and a growing awareness of modern farming's environmental impacts. External pressure also came from the ongoing 'GATT' Uruguay Round of Trade Talks, where agricultural policies were being negotiated for the first time. These pressures and opportunities opened the door for new thinking on policies for rural regions of the enlarged EU.

In this context, *The Future of Rural Society* (Commission of the European Communities [CEC] 1988) was an important document setting a new framework for rural policy, and influencing subsequent policy shifts. In it, the Commission laid down the three 'logics' of rural policy as follows:

(1) economic and social cohesion, in an enlarged Community of very pronounced regional diversity;
(2) the unavoidable adjustment of farming in Europe to actual circumstances on the markets and the implications of this adjustment not only for farmers and farmworkers but also for the rural economy in general;

(3) the protection of the environment and conservation of the Community's natural assets. (CEC 1988, 5)

Regarding the newly reformed regional policy, the document noted:

If rural development is to be assigned the importance it merits in regional policy, two considerations must be borne in mind:
(i)   it is a mistake to concentrate development effort on a few major central poles of economic activity, and a larger number of intermediate centres (subpoles) should be assisted in their development, scattered over a wide area;
(ii) local initiative must be given the fullest support, in particular as regards the SMEs, and the development of indigenous potential must enjoy privileged status (although outside contributions will always be of value); in this connection, a much greater emphasis must be laid on economic and social initiative and leadership, and the supply of services to firms must be diversified. (CEC 1988, 10)

This was the high point of European Commission thinking on rural policy. From being conceived as a sectoral issue bound up with agriculture and the CAP, it was now seen as a cross-sectoral issue cutting across the policy domains of agriculture, regional and cohesion policy; environmental policy; social policy; and community development. Placing rural policy within the frame of cohesion policy was confirmed in Article 120 of the Treaty of Union (Maastricht Treaty) of 1994. The innovative and bottom-up LEADER programme, jointly funded by the three main structural funds, Agricultural Guidance, Regional Fund and Social Fund, was implemented in 1991, and gave immediate and concrete expression to the new approach. LEADER bordered on being a community development policy for rural regions and was implemented through local action groups, involving a partnership of local interests. It aimed at both collective and individual action to stimulate integrated rural development.[3] In addition to LEADER, there were rural elements in the Regional Development Plans and Programmes for Objective 1 regions (those with less than 75 per cent average GDP per head), and rural development programmes for Objective 5b regions ('rural areas in decline'). These programmes were also jointly funded by agricultural, regional and social funds.

In 1996, the EU organised a large rural development conference in Cork, Ireland, as part of the preparation for the programming period after 2000, and anticipating EU expansion to the former Soviet Bloc countries in Central and Eastern Europe and the Baltics. The central points in the declaration produced at Cork concerned the promotion of sustainable rural development, the establishment of a new rural development fund and the importance of the role of LEADER. These proposals were only partly implemented in the 'Agenda 2000' reforms, which essentially took rural development policy back into agricultural policy. Rural development now became known as the 'second pillar' of the CAP, but it remained the 'poor relation' in the CAP, accounting for less than one-tenth of the budget.

In the UK, the rural development programmes dealing with the implementation of the second pillar of the CAP were prepared at a subnational level for England, Northern Ireland, Scotland and Wales from 2000 to 2006 and 2007–2013. The UK rural development programmes gave priority to agri-environmental measures and axes, indicating the powerful influence of the environmental lobbies and agencies. Rural community interests were only weakly present in the emerging policy frameworks and this was generally reflected in the weakness of the 'third axis' of Pillar 2 dealing with rural quality of life, economic diversification and services in the UK as a whole. Nevertheless, there were variations within the UK, as Table 10.1 shows.

Axis 1 is devoted to agricultural competitiveness, and is generally the favourite element for the Farmer Unions, relatively strong in Scotland. Axis 2 is devoted to agri-environmental measures, and is the favourite of environmental organisations and interests which are very strong in England and Wales. Axes 3 and 4 are generally favoured by community, social and rural development interests which are relatively strong in Northern Ireland. Broadly speaking, the allocations reflect the relative power of the different lobbies and interests in the constituent devolved parliaments of the UK and in England.

At least for the more rural parts of the UK, the 1990s were the 'golden age' when many areas had EU cohesion policy priority Objective 1, Objective 5b or transition status, benefitting from integrated regional development programmes as well as LEADER programmes. The loss of priority status for regions after the EU eastern enlargement meant that the UK lost

Table 10.1 UK RDPs as Approved, 2007–2008—Total Budgets by Axis, Percentage and Showing the Minimal Percentages Laid Down by EC Funding

	Axis 1	Axis 2	Axis 3	Axis 4	Tech Assist	Total
England	9%	81%	6%	4%	0%	100%
N. Ireland	8%	68%	0%[2]	24%	0%	100%
Scotland	14%	69%	12%	5%	0%	100%
Wales	11%	75%	9%	4%	1%	100%
EAFRD Minima	10%	25%	10%	10%	0%	50%

Source: Calculated from data in the English, Northern Ireland, Scottish and Welsh Rural Development Programmes for 2007–2013.
Notes: Includes EU, European Agricultural Fund for Rural Development Contribution, National Contribution and Voluntary Modulation from Pillar 1. In Northern Ireland, a decision was made to join Axes 3 and 4 and distribute the funding via LEADER.

regional and social funding from the EU under cohesion policy, and remaining regional funding focused on city regions in England and Scotland at the cost of regional spending in rural areas. In any case, by the 2000s rural development policies and programmes, with the main exception of Northern Ireland, reverted largely to agri-environmental programmes, with agricultural competitiveness as a second string. The regional prioritization or 'equity' component has been watered down by rural development programmes becoming available everywhere, whether poor or rich.

AGRICULTURAL, REGIONAL AND RURAL POLICIES IN THE US

In the US, narrow rural policy, and a significant portion of broad rural policy, is contained in federal legislation known as the Farm Bill. Although the Farm Bill has long contained provisions for rural infrastructure and housing, it was not until the 1990s that attempts to insert the kind of rural development policies that we observe in the EU and UK were included. For example, President George H.W. Bush created a President's Initiative on Rural America in 1990 which conceived of a National Rural Development Council with representatives from most federal agencies to coordinate federal programmes of importance to rural areas. This was an effort at broad rural policy. The partnership was formally created in 1994. It included a national coordinating council and also encouraged the development of state rural development councils. By 2000, thirty-seven state councils had been formed. The programme enjoyed mixed success, with some state councils developing into successful organisations while others languished (Radin et al. 1996; Shortall and Warner 2010). The programme's main contribution was greater attention to inter-agency coordination at the state and federal levels (Radin 1997).

A related effort at broad integrative approaches was focused at the local level. The EZECs were created in 1993. Similar to the LEADER programme, the EZEC encouraged collaboration across the public, non-profit and for-profit sectors in rural regions to promote economic development. There were both rural and urban components to the programme and communities and regions were chosen in three rounds of competition in 1994, 1998 and 2002. While the number of EZs and ECs is quite modest (less than sixty), several hundred communities which competed in the programme were designated Champion Communities. Since the 2008 Farm Bill, no new EZs or ECs have been created. Although the programme has some similarities to the LEADER initiative, it is much smaller in scope and funding. For a critical analysis of this programme, see Shortall and Warner (2010).

The 2002 Farm Bill provides a recent example (before the economic crisis of 2008) of how rural development policies fare in the broader agricultural policy arena. Although almost one-fifth of its four-hundred-plus pages are devoted to the Rural Development Title and significant levels of funding were authorized, little of this is mandatory spending as are the provisions in the Commodity and Nutrition Title. In the end less than half of 1 percent of mandatory spending in the Farm Bill was for Rural Development Title programmes (Johnson and Bryden 2006).

Many of the programmes in the 2002 Farm Bill provided funding for infrastructure in rural areas, and they descend from earlier programmes such as the Rural Electrification Act of 1936. Traditional categories of rural infrastructure include water, wastewater, electrical distribution, community facilities such as medical clinics and housing. Newer infrastructure programmes include childcare facilities, tribal college facilities, broadcasting systems, broadband and telemedicine. In the UK, some of these programmes would be dealt with by education, health and welfare policies, regional development and infrastructure policies or water and sewage authorities.

A second general category of rural development programmes focus directly on rural economic development. This category includes such programmes as the EZEC programme described earlier, the Rural Business Opportunity programme, the Renewable Energy Systems programme, the Rural Business Enterprise Grants programme, the Rural Cooperative Development Grants programme, the Business and Industry Loan programme, Rural Business Investment programme and the Value-Added Agricultural Grants programme.

A third category might be described as community development or governance programmes. This category overlaps to some extent with the rural development category but includes the National Rural Development Partnership (described earlier), Multi-Jurisdictional Regional Planning Organisations, Rural Cooperative Development, Rural Community Advancement Program, Delta Regional Authority, Northern Great Plains Regional Authority and Rural Strategic Investment programmes.

The 2008 Farm Bill, which became the Food, Conservation and Energy Act of 2008, has a similar set of chapters as the 2002 bill. The Rural Development Title provisions have many of the same programmes as before but give greater emphasis to less advantaged farmers and rural areas. The Rural Development Title funds 'planning, coordination, and implementation of rural community and economic development programs'. There is some emphasis on value-added agricultural activities, including renewable energy (which has wider provisions than previously), and locally and regionally produced agricultural products. Funds for rural water and waste disposal are included and the bill also prioritizes broadband expansion to underserved areas and establishes a new regional collaborative investment programme.

Many of these programmes, while authorized, are not mandatory and thus require appropriations to be funded. The programmes are more important for their rhetoric in illustrating shifts in rural policy thinking than for their impact. For example the 2002 Farm Bill authorized the Fund for Rural America, intended to provide dedicated funding for rural development research, but after one year all funding was shifted to agricultural research programmes. Similarly, a rural strategic investment programme was designed to create incentives for public–private partnerships to pursue innovative economic development strategies, but funds were never appropriated. Another example of the logic of partnership across public, private and non-profit sectors for infrastructure and economic investment was the National Board on Rural America, which was authorized to award planning grants and promote regional partnerships. These initiatives reflect the community development/public–private partnership theme found in rural policy on both sides of the Atlantic, but lack investment to follow the rhetoric. The lead parts of the 1990 Initiative on Rural America, the NRDP and ECEZ, never received much funding and in the late 1990s attention shifted from community development partnerships to direct support for private investment to promote economic development. The New Markets Tax Credit made approximately twenty billion dollars in tax credits available from 2000 to 2009 to private entities willing to invest in lagging regions— with minimal involvement of the broader set of community actors reflected in the earlier NRDP and ECEZ programmes (Shortall and Warner 2010). This privileging of private investors over broader community development interests continued in the bailouts after the financial crisis where the Toxic Asset Repair Program bailout for banks sailed through Congress quickly in 2008, but the American Resource and Recovery Act, which included broader support for state and local government infrastructure and public services, had a more difficult time getting passed in 2009.

Rural development concerns have always taken backstage to agricultural and commodity interests in the Farm Bill (Gardner 1996; Fluharty 2009). Now, financial sector interests are being privileged over broader community development and public service concerns (Fine 2010). Charles Fluharty, long-time champion of 'place-based' rural development policy in the US and president of the Rural Policy Research Institute, argues 'this current fiscal crisis may well overwhelm the ability of sub-national governments to lead and/or support such efforts. If subsidiary considerations are to drive this framework, there must be sufficient local capacity, investment and engagement. Even if additional, stimulus-based national funding is targeted to budget relief for sub-national governments, this will remain a regional policy challenge'. He continues: 'The rural dimension of this question remains the most problematic. Given very difficult fiscal decisions at both the national and sub-national levels, will place-based policy solutions become largely metropolitan policy constructs?' (Fluharty 2009, 10).

OTHER CHALLENGES FOR RURAL PEOPLE AND PLACES: WELFARE REFORM, FISCAL CRISIS AND CLIMATE CHANGE

Welfare Policy

Many policies other than those related to agriculture and rural development matter to rural areas in both the UK and the US. Among these are welfare policies that address the worst aspects of material poverty, education and childcare policies, health policies, housing policies, fiscal support for local authorities, transportation and other infrastructure policies and regional policies. Unfortunately, the period since the 1980s has seen a weakening rather than a strengthening of such policies, largely due to the continuation of privatization and decentralization policies first promoted by the Thatcher and Reagan governments in the 1980s and largely continued by subsequent administrations. For example, the efforts in the past decade to 'target' welfare policies in the UK (to make them more 'efficient') have not taken adequate account of rural needs (Shucksmith 2005, 2009). In addition, regional development efforts in rural regions have been watered down in most of the constituent parts of the UK with the greater emphasis on city regions, the reorganisation of development agencies and the reduced presence of European cohesion policies.

In the US the welfare reform of 1996 put emphasis on work supports over welfare payments. For rural areas, where job opportunities are more limited, childcare and transportation were recognised as key work supports that needed strengthening (Weber, Duncan and Whitener 2002). One concern of decentralization economists is that the new welfare policy is procyclical and that in bad economic times, states and localities that have capped levels of federal support would not be able to meet increased demand (Powers 1999). This is happening at the time of writing. While the federal government can issue debt, states and localities are required to balance their budgets. Heavy reliance on the property tax at the local level is made even more problematic by the home foreclosure crisis that is the basis of the current financial crisis in the US.

Fiscal Crisis

During the financial crisis of 2008–2011 both the US and the UK have given attention first to shoring up the financial sector. In the US, state and local governments received some stimulus support in 2009, but the effects of the recession are more severe at the state and local government levels and will worsen in the coming years as tax revenues are slower to rebound. To the extent that states can focus on territorial policy, it will likely be focused on the urban regional growth poles that drive the economy. Rural development, always second to agricultural support at the national level, is also second to broader state needs (health, education, criminal justice). The outlook for rural development policy in the coming decade is weak.

The fiscal crisis reflects a broader structural crisis in how US state and local government services are financed. The federal government has refused to allow state and local governments to tax the growing parts of the economy—Internet-based businesses and services (Warner 2010). This comes on top of a crisis in infrastructure. For example, most of the municipal water systems across the country are fully depreciated and need replacement.

While in the past there was significant federal investment to enable communities to build infrastructure, today there is not (Warner 2009b). Some argue that public–private partnerships will solve the problem, but private credit is more expensive and concerns have been raised about the financial viability of many of the partnership schemes and the lack of accountability in their management (Sclar 2009). Finally, there is no tradition of 'rural proofing' in national or state US policy as there is in the UK. So the differential needs of rural areas are more likely to go unnoticed.

Climate Change

New issues are appearing on the rural development agendas of governments and civil society organisations in the UK, EU and US related to environment and sustainability. First among these are climate change and its potential impacts on agriculture, food supplies, forests and water. A second is energy, both to reduce and mitigate greenhouse gas emissions and to increase security of future supplies. A new emphasis on renewable energy has emerged, much of which will be produced in rural areas. Third is the need for recycling of water and nutrient management to ensure sustainability.

New models of rural development that more explicitly link landownership, agricultural production and environmental protection are emerging. Within the UK, Scotland implemented a modest but unusual programme of land reform in the early 2000s that privileged communities by giving them a right to buy land coming on the market (Bryden and Geisler 2007) and encouraged community energy activities by ensuring that a higher proportion of the GDP created by renewable energy was retained by rural residents. The growth in the Land Trust movement in the US also reflects increasing public concern about the need to preserve environmental resources and community control—in ways which parallel such concerns in the UK (Davis 2010).

In both the US and the EU the organic and local foods movement (such as the Slow Food Movement founded in Italy) highlights environmental issues (transportation, carbon footprint, organic production), social issues (farm size, labour conditions, local food culture) and economic concerns (as an economic development strategy; see Hinrichs and Charles, this volume).

But the tension between rural development and production agriculture remains. For example, renewable biofuel energy was supported by the US Farm Bill and energy legislation at the cost of food production. Indeed there is wide agreement that the subsidy-led switch to use of corn as energy feedstock rather than feeding stuffs precipitated the dramatic global food price rises of 2008. Water issues have also been important on both sides of the Atlantic, with predictions from climate scientists of drastic effects on the future location of agricultural production. Rural areas are being recognised on both sides of the Atlantic as critical resource sheds for the broader population. But does this extend to a concern for the type of development that occurs within rural communities?

CONCLUSIONS

In this chapter we have shown how history has shaped different approaches to rural policy in the US and the UK. Table 10.2 outlines some of the key historical, cultural and policy differences between the US and the UK as they affect rural policy. Although the problems facing rural areas in both countries have strong similarities, we can expect the policy responses to be different. The US individual, market-oriented approach will likely allow more variety of innovation and experimentation, while the more collective and directed approach of the UK may be more likely to yield rural policy that balances economic development concerns with environmental management and social cohesion.

Since the 1980s deregulation and pressures to privatize public services in both the US and the UK have led to a more market-oriented approach to public sector provision, and new public management and new governance regimes that emphasized efficiency over equity. However, after two decades of market dominance, the pendulum between efficiency, which the market was supposed to provide, and the 'old Europe' policy of equity may be swinging back to some kind of balance. There is certainly recognition that the efficiency claims of the market paradigm were overstated and more attention needs to be given once again to the importance of regulation, government service delivery and citizen participation (Warner 2009a). Paradoxically, however, the Coalition government elected in 2010 in the UK has used this failure of markets as justification for radical neo-liberal policies, cutting public expenditure (especially on welfare), dismantling regulation, abolishing all regional government structures and seeking to marketise education, health and other core aspects of the welfare state. This is being achieved by recasting the banking crisis as a sovereign debt crisis.

The financial and economic crisis of 2008–2011 has therefore raised critical questions about the efficacy of the neo-liberal market-based approach to rural development. Heightened concerns about the social, economic and environmental impacts of globalisation, free trade, privatization and

Table 10.2   Key Differences in Rural Policy

United Kingdom	United States
More national control, greater emphasis on regional management	More state and local autonomy, regionalism voluntary
Concern with social cohesion	Concern with individual opportunity
Preserving culture and environment	Promoting free market
Longer history of environmental/landscape management	Frontier mentality, less concern with landscape management
More attention to collective rights	Privileging private individual rights

market dominance in allocating resources and regulating human and corporate behaviour have been challenged. In addition, global warming and the impacts of reliance on non-renewable energy resources have led to calls for carbon markets or taxes to reduce greenhouse gas emissions and energy consumption and help develop renewable energy sources. Food and water availability and price have again become key issues as a consequence of growing demand and limitations imposed by climate change and resource constraints (nitrates and phosphates), as well as undesirable impacts of modern intensive agriculture. All of these new issues—markets, trade, climate change, food, renewable energy, water, nitrates, phosphates—have large implications for the future of rural areas, and new institutional and governance questions are posed by all of them for rural policy on both sides of the Atlantic.

Rural policy has begun to shift out of agriculture and into such issues as environment, resource management, territorial development and dealing with an increasingly urbanised landscape. These concerns will intensify and be augmented by the new roles of rural areas as reserves of energy and water, as carbon sinks and as places for urban waste recycling or landfilling. Future rural policy research will need to address the role of new technologies and new interest groups while at the same time attempting to reclaim a space in policy dialogue for broader rural development concerns.

11 The Evolution of Agriculture and Agricultural Policy in the UK and US

Kathryn Brasier, Jill L. Findeis, Carmen Hubbard, Lionel Hubbard and Rodrigo Salcedo Du Bois[1]

INTRODUCTION

A new paradigm has emerged in the UK and US in which agriculture and its place in the rural landscape is being reframed. The discourse has transitioned from agriculture viewed almost solely as a provider of food for domestic consumption and international trade, to agriculture as part of the rural landscape with broader roles and responsibilities than previously ascribed. These may range from maintaining environmental integrity in a managed ecosystem, to ensuring open space in a countryside threatened by development, to contributing to human health and to the richness of heritage and culture. Agricultural policy is beginning to reflect this perspective in the UK and US, although funding to support conventional farm programmes continues to dominate. This chapter explores the reframing of agriculture's place in the rural landscape, and how policy is adapting to meet new perceptions of its roles and responsibilities. The chapter explores recent transformations in the structure of agriculture, drivers of change and the responsiveness of rural and agricultural policy in the UK and US.

Agriculture in the UK and US has evolved markedly over the last century (UK: Harvey 1995; Hubbard and Ritson 1997; Swinnen 2009; US: Tweeten 1970; Gardner 1992; Organisation for Economic Co-operation and Development [OECD] 2001a; Hallberg et al. 2001). In the US, the massive shift of population out of farming, the diffusion of yield-enhancing agricultural technologies, the economics-driven push toward larger farm operations and the widespread adoption of genetically engineered (GE) varieties since the early 1990s (Fernandez-Cornejo and Caswell 2006) represent examples of outcomes of this evolution. In the early twentieth century, agriculture was *the* major employer in rural areas of the United States (OECD 2001a), although the 1920 Census of Agriculture pointed out that 'It is evident that the [US rural] population (. . .) includes much more than the farming population' (1920 Census of Agriculture, 23). Today, fewer than 2 per cent of the population in the US and UK is engaged in farming.

A bimodal or dualistic structure of agriculture is evident on both sides of the Atlantic, with the majority of farms classified as either large farm operations or small businesses. Census counts show that of the 325,000 active farms in the UK, it is only the relatively few farms above one hundred hectares in size that account for most farmed land (71 per cent). In contrast, 60 per cent of UK farms have less than ten hectares but account for only 5 per cent of farmed land. In the US, the largest 10 per cent of farms now produce 75 per cent of farm output (Hoppe et al. 2007), with 90 per cent of farms classified as 'small' (United States Department of Agriculture [USDA] 2004).

Agricultural policy in the UK is dictated largely by the Common Agricultural Policy (CAP) of the European Union (EU) whereas in the US, federal Farm Bill legislation defines farm policy. During the 1970s and 1980s, UK and US agricultural policy shared a common emphasis: the provision of affordable food through high levels of productivity and subsidy. In the 1990s, EU decision-makers reconsidered the role of agriculture beyond the provision of food by stressing its 'multifunctionality'. By producing a range of non-commodity goods and services, shaping the environment and affecting social and cultural systems, agriculture, it was argued, was essential in contributing to the sustainability and vitality of rural areas. During this same period in the US, greater public awareness and concern about the environmental issues and food safety led to more emphasis in Farm Bill legislation on environmental provisions, although US farm policy (and particularly money flows to it) still remained largely focused on farm income support. More recently, the establishment of rural development within the 'second pillar' of the CAP is shifting the focus of EU agriculture further from its traditional role; while, in the US, the emergence of rural development remains by and large nascent, although grassroots rural development activism shares some similar characteristics in the UK and US (Dwyer and Findeis 2009). In the UK, policymakers place agriculture at the heart of two global challenges—food security and climate change (Benn 2009). Similarly, the USDA recently began refocusing its integrated research and education programmes on five global challenges—sustainable bioenergy, climate change, childhood obesity prevention, food safety and global food security.

PERSPECTIVE: THE UK EXPERIENCE

Agriculture's contribution to the UK economy has declined from around 3 per cent of national output in 1973, when the UK joined the EU, to 0.6 per cent today (DEFRA). However, farming remains an essential link in the UK food supply chain. As the single largest manufacturing industry, the food and drink sector accounts for a Gross Value Added (GVA) of around £73.4 billion, 9 per cent of national full-time employment and 19 per cent of part-time employment. In 2007, food, feed and drink exports were valued at

£11.4 billion and their principal non-EU destination was the US (DEFRA). Marsh (2001, 23) points out that 'supply and (. . .) processing industries—feed, fertilisers, pesticide producers and distributors, abattoirs and packing factories—can only exist if farming continues'. Moreover, although self-sufficiency[2] has fallen from around 80 per cent in the early 1980s to around 60 per cent today, the sector still meets a large share of UK domestic food demand (DEFRA 2010b).

In 2009, almost nineteen million hectares of land in the UK (77 per cent of total area) was in agriculture. Over the last twenty years, land use has changed little (Table 11.1). Geography, particularly climate and topography, has a marked effect on the two main types of farming: pastoral farming is predominant in areas of higher rainfall and the hills in the north and west, and arable farming is concentrated in areas where climate is drier and soils deeper in the south and east. UK farms average fifty-five hectares in size (DEFRA, various dates), but their distribution by land area shows a clear dualistic farm structure (Table 11.2). Further, despite the generally larger size of UK farms compared to most in Western Europe, UK farmers still find themselves under pressure to maintain economic viability, and hence the continual search for economies of size.

There is a long tradition of livestock farming in the UK. Three-quarters of farms specialize in livestock; over a third specialize in sheep, goats and other grazing livestock; 17 per cent in rearing and fattening; and 16 per cent in cereals, oil seed and protein (Martins 2009). Although some changes in structure by farm type have occurred over time, livestock (mainly beef and sheep) and cereal farms remain dominant. A large part of beef production is a by-product of dairy farming, with calves being either reared or sold to be fattened elsewhere; about two-thirds of national beef production is supplied in this way. Also, a significant

Table 11.1   Agricultural Land Use in the UK

	Average 1986–1988		2009	
	'000 ha	%	'000 ha	%
Crops	5,254	28	4,695	25
wheat	1,959	10	1,814	10
barley	1,877	10	1,160	6
Total arable land	6,985	37	6,212	33
Total grazing land	11,616	63	11,521	61
Other	-	-	1,019	6
Total agricultural area	18,678	100	18,752	100

Source: DEFRA.

Table 11.2   UK Farm Distribution by Size, 2008

Size (ha)	Number of farms ('000)	Per cent	Total hectares ('000)	Per cent
< 20	198	61	926	5
20–50	49	15	1,620	9
50–100	36	11	2,567	15
≥ 100	42	13	12,345	71
Total	325	100	17,458	100
Average (ha)	-	-	54	-

Source: DEFRA.

amount of beef is farmed in the Less Favoured Areas, which account for about 42 per cent of total UK agricultural land area (DEFRA). Production systems tend to be less intensive than in many other European countries, with most beef cattle grazed outdoors during summer and fed on silage or arable by-products in-house in winter.

The recent past has seen two major crises in farm animal health that have had significant impacts on the livestock sector and the political economy of farm support (L. Hubbard 2003). Bovine spongiform encephalopathy (BSE) or 'mad cow' disease in the mid-1990s, followed by the 2001 foot-and-mouth disease outbreak, led to the slaughter of millions of animals[3] and cost British tax payers around £3 billion in compensation payments to farmers.[4] The BSE outbreak also prompted the EU to impose a three-year worldwide ban on all UK exports of live cattle, beef and beef products. The ban, which had an annual cost to the British farming industry estimated at £675 million (National Farmers Union 2006), was not lifted until 2006.[5] The crises heightened consumers' concerns regarding food safety and animal welfare, and these issues have featured prominently in subsequent policy measures.

The impact of foot-and-mouth disease extended beyond farming to the wider rural economy, with the nature and scale of the outbreak being unprecedented (National Audit Office 2002). It also highlighted the role of farming in the countryside and the vulnerability of local rural economies to a farm crisis (Donaldson et al. 2006). Rural tourism and other small businesses were badly affected, particularly in England. Over a period of seven months, English tourism and supporting industries lost revenues of £4.5–£5.4 billion, equivalent to around 0.2 per cent of GDP (National Audit Office 2002). Donaldson et al. (2006, 7) argue, however, that 'the measures aimed to assist businesses in the wider rural economy were relatively small-scale, piecemeal and complex', with only £39 million allocated for compensation to rural businesses, as opposed to £1.4 billion paid to farmers for loss of livestock.

The animal health crises, *inter alia*, led to significant structural changes in UK livestock production. Over the ten years to 2007, dairy farms declined by 21 per cent to 28,100 (Table 11.3), with the decline most pronounced for medium-sized farms. Simultaneously, the number of farms with herd sizes of one hundred or more (with almost 70 per cent of the total number of dairy cows) increased. Average herd size increased over the period from sixty-eight to seventy-one cows (DEFRA, various dates). While a similar long-term trend is evident for beef farms, with numbers of farms declining from 71,500 in 1998 to 66,400 in 2007, recent official figures suggest a possible 'de-concentration' of production. For example, between 2007 and 2008 the number of small beef farms (one to nine cattle) *increased* slightly, and the overall average herd size *fell* from twenty-six to twenty-five (DEFRA). Indeed, the total number of small farms in the UK has been increasing from the early 1990s, and accelerating after the foot-and-mouth disease outbreak in 2001. The number of farms with less than five hectares almost doubled between 2000 and 2003, from 54,000 to 104,000 (C. Hubbard 2009). This increase is also evident using the Economic Size Unit (ESU),[6] a measure of output employed by Eurostat to ensure comparability across EU member states. In 2007, farms with less than one ESU accounted for 40 per cent of the total number of UK farms (C. Hubbard 2009). Although there is no clear explanation for this reversal, it may be due to the imposition of various measures on farms following the foot-and-mouth disease crisis, such as the precautionary movement restriction of animals which led to land fragmentation for animal tracing purposes, and more recently to the implementation of the Single Farm Payment, a form of support supposedly 'decoupled' from a farm's level of production (Martins 2009). An increase in 'hobby' farming is another possible explanation (DEFRA).

In 2009, employment in UK agriculture was 535,000, or 1.6 per cent of the national labour force, almost a third fewer than in 1996 (DEFRA, various dates). Although farm households remain at the core of farming activity, there is a clear downward trend of those involved full-time, an increase of part-time farming and a resultant increase in the number of

Table 11.3   Distribution of Dairy Farms by Herd Size Group in the UK, 2007

Size group	Number of farms ('000)	% change 1998–2007	Number of livestock ('000)	% change 1998–2007
1–49	14.0	-7.9	163	-59.0
50–99	6.3	-50.0	460	-49.4
≥ 100	7.8	4.0	1,331	19.3
Total	28.1	-20.6	1,954	-19.3

Source: DEFRA.

small farms. The decline in agricultural employment is inevitable, as the sector 'makes use of resources that are open to competition from other sectors' and as increasing real wages encourage the substitution of capital for labour (Marsh 2001, 8). Employment in agriculture is linked to the evolution of farm income and the economy as a whole; as rural economies grow and farming itself becomes less attractive, more and more farm operators and farm family members look for opportunities outside agriculture to improve their livelihood. Fifty per cent of farms in the UK have diversified activities, and for around one-fifth of these the income from such activities is more than that from farming (DEFRA 2010c).

THE US EXPERIENCE

Today, the number of US farms totals 2.1 million (Table 11.4). Mirroring the UK, US farms are considered by policymakers and the public as critical contributors to domestic and export food supply and value chains. Recent transitions in the size distribution of farms in the US and UK are similar, with the possible exception that US farm size structure is very strongly tied to region, reflecting subsidy distribution patterns as well as proximity to consumers (Findeis et al. 2009; Womach 2004). The US Midwest, the region with the highest federal farm programme participation rates and receiving the highest levels of farm subsidy (see Figure 11.1), has the highest concentration of large operations. Regions of the US with lower percentages of farms receiving farm subsidies are those where small farms are more prevalent (on a percentage basis of total farms in the region); US regions with higher population densities are also those with higher concentrations of small farms (percentage of total farms in the region). Compared to the UK, the overall structure of US agriculture is relatively diverse, but also reflects a bimodal size distribution.

Large farms have increased in numbers over time, even when comparisons are made in constant dollars[7] (Hoppe et al. 2007; Hoppe 2010). Of the 120,000 largest farm operations that in 2004 produced 60 per cent of all agricultural output, about seventy thousand constituted very large family farms (annual farm sales of $500,000 or more), with the remainder being non-family operated farms. In 1982, about twenty-seven thousand large family farms, measured in 2002 constant dollars, were in operation (Hoppe et al. 2007). The nation's small farms—at the other end of the size spectrum—have increased in numbers,[8] although very recent statistics show that numbers could be declining (Hoppe 2010). The rise of multiple job-holding among farm families (farm operators and farm spouses alike) has had major implications for farm survival (Hallberg, Findeis and Lass 1991; Gardner 2002). Small family farm operations, which constitute the vast majority of farms in the US, now control 61 per cent of farmland and 68 per cent of farm assets

Table 11.4 Numbers of Different Types of Farms in US, 2004

Characteristic	Small family farms					Large-scale family farms		Non-family farms	All farms
				Farming-occupation					
	Limited-resource	Retirement	Residential/ lifestyle	Low sales	Medium-sales	Large	Very large		
Total farms (number)	197,734	338,671	837,542	395,781	133,299	86,087	71,708	47,103	2,107,925
Distribution of (%):-									
Farms (%)	9.4	16.1	39.7	18.8	6.3	4.1	3.4	2.2	100.0
Production value (%)	1.0	2.0	5.3	5.5	10.8	14.8	45.4	15.2	100.0
Sales class (%):									
Less than $10,000	76.2	72.6	71.6	47.1	—	—	—	39.5	57.0
$10,000–49,999	19.2	18.6	20.9	29.4	—	—	—	18.1	19.0
$50,000–99,999	4.0	6.3	5.2	23.5	—	—	—	9.6 (s)	8.1
$100,000–174,999	na	1.9 (s)	1.8	—	59.4	—	—	6.8 (s)	5.0
$175,000–249,999	—	0.6 (s)	0.6	—	40.6	—	—	4.1 (s)	3.0
$250,000–499,999	—	—	—	—	—	100.0	—	5.9	4.2
$500,000–999,999	—	—	—	—	—	—	57.8	7.0	2.1
$1,000,000 +	—	—	—	—	—	—	42.2	8.9	1.6
Acres operated per farm:									
Mean	167	212	163	413	1,170 (s)	1,700	3,138 (s)	1,232	470
Median	60	80	67	145	530	834	1,055	173	100

Source: Based on Hoppe et al. (2007), which used data from USDA, Economic Research Service, 2004 Agricultural Resource Management Survey, Phase III.
na = insufficient observations.
(s) = Standard error is between 25 and 50 per cent of estimate.

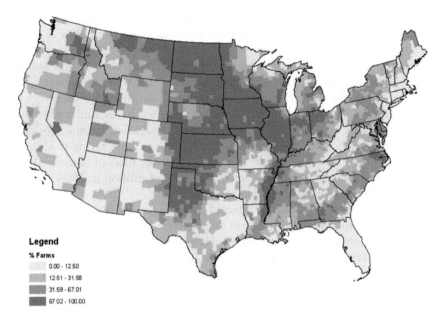

Figure 11.1 Distribution of US federal farm payments, 2007 (per cent of county total farms receiving payments).

(Hoppe et al. 2007). Small farms in the US have been resilient, adapting to fill niche markets, and capitalising on organics, other specialty crops, value-added production, community-supported agriculture (CSA; see Hinrichs and Charles, this volume), direct retail, farm-to-institutions (e.g. schools, restaurants), 'agritainment' or agri-tourism (e.g. hayrides, corn mazes, u-pick, etc.) and other opportunities. The rise of multiple job-holding among farm families—in part a result of great mobility (including higher rates of commuting; Goetz et al. 2010)—has had major implications for farm household incomes (Mishra et al. 2002) and farm survival, especially among small and mid-sized farms (Hallberg, Findeis and Lass 1991; Gardner 2002). Some also view small farms as contributing to local civic structure (Lyson 2004) and social cohesion (Dwyer and Findeis 2008), although the explicit nature of 'social cohesion' is not conceptualized in US policy as it is under the CAP. The bottom line is that the US population living on farms is an extremely diverse population, with strong regional differences in what constitutes agriculture and how the matrix of land, people and policy coincide to influence agricultural production systems.

Subsidies paid to agriculture are a sensitive political issue, in part because of the regional concentration in the Midwest, but also because of larger national discourses related to government spending. Large farms generally produce a very narrow band of programme commodities (corn,

wheat, soybeans, etc.), receive a disproportionate share of federal farm payments and attract the bulk of attention when federal farm policy is legis-
lated (Hallberg 2001). Farm subsidies have resulted in maintaining more
resources, including human resources, in agriculture than is efficient or
optimal, although they have kept land in agriculture that might have gone
to other uses. The distortionary effects of farm subsidies have been widely
criticized (see, for example, OECD 2001a; Gardner 2002), and many have
questioned why large-scale US family farms now receive income subsidies
since the wealth position of households living on large farms is already
high (Mishra et al. 2002). Table 11.4 shows that the median household net
worth of large family farms in the US was US$1.4 million in 2004, and of
very large farms over $2.2 million.

Farm structure is also being affected by the drive for alternative energy
options, resulting in land conversion to biofuels, and the long-term implications of urbanisation, the latter particularly in states that have traditionally
been major farm states. Over the last two decades, 'hotspots' of population
growth, urbanisation and economic growth have developed along the rural-
exurban-urban transition zone. Comparing land use in the US in 1945 to
1997, Hellerstein et al. (2002, 3) report that urban land share increased in
all US regions and that 'the heaviest urbanization between 1982 and 1992
occurred in the Northeast and the Lake States, with California, Florida,
Texas, and Appalachian States also undergoing extensive urbanization'.
These states historically have been important agricultural states. Further,
the loss is occurring disproportionately in highly productive ('prime') soils
(American Farmland Trust 2009). The urbanisation trend is influencing
regional food production and local food access, land cover and natural
resources and ecosystem function and services (Batie 2003; Rindfuss et al.
2004; Brown et al. 2004; Barnard 2005).

Unlike the UK, the US has not (yet) suffered the same level of major
crises in agriculture that shocked the UK farm system during the BSE and
foot-and-mouth disease outbreaks. The US has nonetheless experienced
a number of food-borne illness outbreaks that have heightened public
awareness and concern about the safety of the domestic food supply, e.g.
the spinach *E. coli* outbreak of 1996 (Arnade, Calvin and Kuchler 2010),
and August 2010 shell egg 'recall'. But while US consumers changed food
consumption behaviours in the 1996 case of spinach, substituting other
leafy vegetables for spinach in their diets (Arnade, Calvin and Kuchler
2010), the overall impact on US farms has been comparatively small
across all outbreaks to date. Perhaps it is best said that while the US
public expresses concern about food safety, many US consumers are comparatively unaware of the full range of potential health issues challenging
the US food supply. At the same time, the 'double digit' growth of organic
agriculture—and its mainstreaming in the US over the last decade—cannot be ignored.

AGRICULTURAL POLICY IN THE UK
AND US: SHIFTING LANDSCAPES

The EU Common Agricultural Policy (CAP) and Reform

Farming in Western Europe is primarily a family business (Gasson and Errington 1993) and medium-sized family farms are perceived as integral to the 'European model of agriculture' (Cardwell 2004). The nature of agricultural—and more recently rural—policy in the UK is closely linked to the evolution of the CAP. This policy continues to account for approximately half of the EU budget, making agricultural and rural affairs an important and politically sensitive policy domain, particularly after the recent enlargements of the EU (Rizov 2006). Created in the early 1960s during a period when food scarcity was considered a major threat in the aftermath of World War II, the CAP has been blamed, *inter alia*, for high food costs (burdening consumers) and, until recently, food surpluses (burdening tax payers). Agricultural production expanded rapidly under the CAP, leading to high levels of self-sufficiency for most major commodities. The infamous 'mountains' of cereals, butter and beef, and 'lakes' of milk, wine and olive oil became common phenomena in the 1970s and 1980s.

Although it was clear early on that the CAP had to be reformed, no significant decisions were made in this respect until the introduction of the milk quota in 1984. More radical measures followed with the adoption of the MacSharry reforms in 1992. These reduced price support for major agricultural commodities and introduced compensatory payments for farmers for loss of income. However, Fennell (1997, 172) noted that the introduction of these 'direct payments' was an 'opportunity lost' and 'did little—if anything—to shift support in the direction of disadvantaged farmers'. Although budgetary constraints were initially regarded as the major reason behind this reform, Tangermann (1998, 33) argued that 'the real motivation behind the MacSharry reform was the need to make the CAP consistent with international obligations on agricultural policy which the EU could not have avoided unless it was prepared to let the Uruguay Round of overall GATT negotiations go down the drain'. He noted that although it resulted in an agricultural expenditure increase, in 'economic terms this reform made a step in the right direction' (ibid., 13).

The next milestone in agricultural policy reform was the EU's adoption of Agenda 2000. This heralded a new dimension for the CAP, which was divided into two major components: Pillar 1, which addressed support for agricultural products and producers, and Pillar 2, which was to focus on the 'multifunctionality' of the farming sector and rural development. Agenda 2000 also allowed for measures (modulation) which could transfer funds between the pillars, and also introduced as a novelty the 'cross-compliance' concept, meaning that direct payments should be paid conditional on farmers' compliance with environmental targets (similar to the US concept). Although it has not brought radical change, Agenda 2000 represented a continuation of the MacSharry reforms with a further cut in intervention prices for cereals and beef and the use of compensatory payments in the form of direct aid (income). Reform was mainly motivated by the desire to prepare the EU for its most ambitious enlargement—involving eight central and Eastern Europe countries—in 2004 (Gorton, Hubbard and Hubbard 2009). Further, only a year before this EU expansion, the Mid-Term Review measures were adopted, which sought to provide a framework for CAP post-enlargement (ibid.). Most direct support was 'decoupled' from production and, from 2005, EU farmers started to receive a 'single payment'. In addition, some funds were transferred from Pillar 1 to Pillar 2 through modulation of direct payments, cross-compliance was made compulsory and new measures were introduced such as promotion of food quality and animal welfare (Commission of the European Communities [CEC] 2006). How did UK agriculture respond to these changes?

The UK had joined the EU (then the European Economic Community) at a time when more than 80 per cent of the total EU budget was allocated to agriculture, mainly as price and market support. Prior to accession, UK farming was supported by tax payers, who funded deficiency payments for the most important agricultural products. As the cost of these subsidies rose, the government switched to policy measures which encouraged farmers to be more selective, to produce less and to farm more efficiently (Marsh 2001). Accession to the EU and adoption of the CAP shifted a large part of the cost of UK farm support from tax payers to consumers and, as a net agricultural importer, the country also had to remit import levies back to those EU members who exported agricultural products (Harvey 2008). Marsh (2001, 28) notes that although 'the immediate effects were diluted because of the world price boom (. . .) the implications for farm policy in the UK were clear'; hence 'this was a wholly unsatisfactory policy. It meant that consumers would pay higher prices for food, politically unattractive and socially regressive'. Unsurprisingly, therefore, UK governments have been long-term critics of the CAP.

The adoption of the MacSharry reform package in 1992 was welcomed by the UK, which argued much earlier for agricultural price cuts. Nevertheless, the government was keen to ensure that larger farms were protected from any unfair effects of 'set-aside' (idling of land), which was part of the package. Importantly, compensation payments (later to become direct payments) introduced to offset price cuts continue to play a crucial role in British farming (see Mordaunt 2009).

Although criticized for its inability to promote further and more serious reform (e.g. Lowe and Brouwer 2000), Agenda 2000 had the merit of 'transforming the CAP from a sectoral policy of farm commodity support into an integrated policy for rural development and environmental enhancement' and allowed for more 'decentralisation of policy implementation' at the national level (Lowe, Buller and Ward 2002, 4). The rural development dimension under Pillar 2 was well received by the UK government, but also by NGOs and other agencies interested in environmental conservation and sustainable land management, and the political commitment was clearly reflected in the application of modulation (Ward 2002). Indeed, only the UK and France took up voluntary modulation (Lowe, Buller and Ward 2002). However, Pillar 1 policy measures (direct payments and market support) still account for over three-quarters of the agricultural budget. Further, integrated development of rural areas is hampered by the financial imbalance within the CAP, and many so-called rural development measures remain 'farm-centric', being seen as yet another way of subsidizing farmers (Bryden and Warner, this volume; Dwyer et al. 2002; Darnhofer and Schneeberger 2007; Gorton, Hubbard and Hubbard 2009; Dwyer and Findeis 2009).

Changing Priorities in the UK

In 2000, the Food Standards Agency (FSA) was established by government as an independent food safety watchdog to protect public health and consumer interests related to food. It was established in the aftermath of the BSE fiasco to provide advice and information to the public and government on food safety 'from farm to fork', nutrition and diet. In the following year, the Ministry of Agriculture, Fisheries and Food—heavily criticized for its handling of both the BSE and foot-and-mouth disease crises—was replaced by DEFRA This signalled a change of emphasis in responsibilities within a wider remit of sustainable development, and with consumers' interests elevated to counter the former ministry's preoccupation with agriculture and farming. Indeed, in the name of the new department, the word 'agriculture' is conspicuous by its absence. DEFRA's objectives include explicit reference to food safety, the countryside, animal welfare, the environment and the prudent use of international resources. Shortly after the establishment of DEFRA, the Policy Commission on the Future of Farming and Food underlined the need for sweeping change, calling for further radical reform of the CAP, retargeting of public funds towards environmental and rural development goals and a new national champion for 'local' food.

Although the focus of consumers' interests relating to agriculture and food has traditionally been weak, it is now stronger: witness the broader remit of DEFRA and its equivalent bodies in the devolved nations of the UK, the inception of the FSA and official efforts at both the national and EU level to promote quality assurance and labelling schemes. However, in a recent survey of EU citizens' views on the CAP (CEC 2010), 57 per cent reported never having heard of it, although 90 per cent thought agriculture was important. Food safety and environmental protection were top priorities among those surveyed and over 80 per cent were in favour of the EU continuing to support farmers' incomes.

On the other side, UK farmers' unions, once staunch advocates of production subsidies and market intervention, now accept that the rules of the game have changed. They support further reform of the CAP, recognising the internal pressures of EU enlargement and budgetary limitations, and the external pressures of further trade liberalization and WTO commitments. They now realise the need for the UK (and Europe) to lessen reliance on production and export subsidies. Farmers' unions in the UK have always argued that their members are among the most efficient in Europe because they employ modern technology and high levels of investment. They believe that UK farmers are well placed to compete in world markets, given a 'level playing field'.

Agri-Environment, Food Quality, Animal Welfare, Organic Food

Agri-environmental schemes have been evident in the UK since the 1980s and many farmers participate in them. These schemes are usually long-term voluntary agreements with DEFRA or other agencies to manage and enhance the countryside. Payments to farmers for these types of agreement have grown, and many farmers feel they have an obligation to maintain the appearance of the countryside and to preserve wildlife and habitats; almost all report some form of environmental practice as part of their farm management (McInerney et al. 2000). However, whilst environmental protection continues to be an important consideration within agricultural policy in the UK and EU, a number of other concerns have come to the fore in recent times.

As evidence of heightened consumer concerns over food safety, in a 2001 survey across fifteen EU member states only 36 per cent of respondents thought agricultural policy ensured that the food they bought was safe to eat. The UK (and EU) government and food industry have responded with a number of measures to allay concern. For example, since 2002 all retailers are obliged to label fresh and frozen beef with its origin, including birth, rearing and slaughtering. Together with the identification and registration of all live animals via cattle passports and ear tags, this enables beef to be traced from farm to fork. Compulsory country-of-origin labelling also applies to imported beef from third countries.[9] The EU also operates a system of quality labels that relate to foods produced in a particular region or by a traditional method—the Protected Designation of Origin (PDO) and the Protected Geographical Indication (PGI) labels—linking at least one of the stages of production, processing or preparation to a specific place or region. More generally, the increasing popularity of 'local foods' presents farmers with a new market to explore (Hinrichs and Charles, this volume).

In the UK, farm assurance has been a key element in livestock production since the mid-1990s. Schemes have been set up to provide a mechanism for farmers to demonstrate to consumers and retailers that standards of husbandry, welfare and environmental protection on the farm meet nationally agreed levels of best practice. An independent organisation, Assured British Meat, sets standards covering all elements of the meat supply chain from feed suppliers through to retailers. Consumers can identify farm-assured food by a 'Red Tractor' stamp of approval and products bearing this logo can be found in most supermarkets. The logo itself is managed by another independent organisation, Assured Food Standards, that licenses producers, processors and packers. Its wider remit is to provide a forum for liaison between various schemes and to promote assurance throughout the food chain.

Since livestock production in the UK is predominantly pasture-based and extensive in nature, it can be considered relatively 'animal-welfare friendly'. The farm assurance schemes include the Farm Animal Welfare Council's codes of practice and five basic freedoms—freedom from hunger and thirst; freedom from discomfort; freedom from pain, injury or disease; freedom to express normal behaviour; and freedom from fear and distress. Consumers now have the reassurance, when buying livestock products displaying an appropriate logo, that animals have been reared in an acceptable, welfare-friendly way.

Consumers' fears about unsafe food and technological developments such as genetic modification and a growing public awareness of the damage to the environment caused by agriculture have led to a general and widespread reappraisal of farming and production methods. Organic farming, once seen as serving a niche market, is regarded by some as both safer and more environmentally friendly. The EU market for organically produced food has been growing rapidly and in 2000 the EU launched its own organic farming logo. The UK has been the fastest growing market for organically produced food in Europe and in 2003 DEFRA launched an Organic Action Plan to increase domestic production.

US Farm Policy and Policy Reform

Many consider that US farm policy lags behind where it should be; for example, the marked evolution of US agriculture led Dimitri, Effland and Conklin (2005) to observe: 'A common point in the debate over U.S. farm programmes has been that current policies were tailored for a time in American agriculture that no longer exists'. But will US farm policy evolve to meet the new reality? Some will answer that farm policy, given the continued (regionally derived) strength of the US farm lobby, is unlikely to be 'reformed' anytime soon. The continued close alignment of US farm policy and farm payments with traditional farm interests is well known, and unlike EU programmes under CAP, US farm payments remain 'coupled' to levels of agricultural production. US farm subsidies still depend on the farm's prior years' production levels (OECD 2006). US programmes continue to favour a small number of programme crops, including corn, soybeans, wheat and other food grains that tend to have high regional specificity in terms of production and orientation to export markets; important exceptions include specialty crops added in the 2008 Farm Bill (Rawson 2008). In this arena, family farms with less than $250,000 in annual farm sales—the clear majority of farms in the US as shown in Table 11.4—can effectively get lost despite their numbers, their control of farmland and farm assets, and their regional importance. Structural changes within US agriculture, coupled with a rising environmental consciousness among the public, are resulting in new attention to regional and local considerations.

However, even amid the pessimism, a new paradigm is thus emerging in which U.S. agriculture and its place in the rural landscape has been reframed. The reframing has at least three interrelated dimensions:

1. environmental concern regarding agriculture's negative impacts on ecosystem health and also how agriculture could contribute to provision of ecosystem services to enhance farm household incomes
2. public awareness and concern over food safety but also nutrition and obesity
3. regional and local concerns, ranging from regional and local food provision to the broader multifunctionality of farms

For some time, there has been general agreement that there will be increased 'environmentalization' of agriculture, or increased regulation of agriculture's environmental impacts (Buttel 1995). Voluntary agri-environmental programmes are a key component of environmentalization, and provide incentives for farmers to adopt practices that decrease the environmental costs of production (Lenihan and Brasier 2010). However, von Haaren and Bills (2009, 67) are right when they contend that 'the range of environmental issues addressed by the United States has been too narrow'. Growing interest in farmland protection and preservation, particularly in places proximate to expanding population centres, also points to the role that farms across the size spectrum can play in a shifting urbanising landscape, and how the public perceives their amenity value (Adelaja et al. 2009). Finally, issues around multifunctionality, long a topic of debate in the EU, are becoming more important in the US, but to date have largely been confined to federal policy discussions and carried out only in specific regions (Lenihan and Brasier 2010; Lenihan, Brasier and Stedman 2009).

Two federal agencies govern US agri-environmental policies, the USDA and to a more limited extent, the US Environmental Protection Agency (USEPA). Environmental impacts attributable to agriculture are broad and well documented; for example, US agriculture has been the leading cause of water-quality degradation to the nation's streams, rivers and lakes, and one of the leading causes of impairment of estuaries (USEPA 2002).

USDA Soil Conservation Service programmes to stem erosion began in the Great Depression, but it was not until 1985 that US farm legislation directly addressed environmental impacts stemming from agriculture. The Conservation Reserve Program (CRP) was initiated and cross-compliance with environmental programmes was required for income support under other provisions of the Farm Bill. Since then, additional programmes have been created, falling into two general categories: farmland retirement and conservation on 'working lands'. These include the Conservation Reserve Enhancement Program (CREP), Environmental Quality Incentives Program (EQIP), Wetlands Reserve Program (WRP), Wildlife Habitat Incentives Program (WHIP), Farm and Ranchland Protection Program (FRPP), Grassland Reserve Program (GRP) and Conservation Security Program (CSP), now the CStP (Conservation Stewardship Program). The regional distribution of selected programmes is shown in Figure 11.2.

The CRP is a voluntary programme where farmland is put under long-term contract, removed from production and planted with cover crops that reduce soil erosion and promote wildlife habitat. The CRP was initially conceived in response to the 1980s farm financial crisis as a means to limit production surplus and remove highly erodible and environmentally sensitive land from the production base. In 2007, 36.8 million acres were under CRP contract ($1.82 billion; see ERS 2009). In 2007, 1.88 million acres were also under WRP contracts ($139 million; see ERS 2009). The goal of the WRP is to restore and protect wetlands. Farmers are offered permanent or thirty-year easements to retire land from production and technical assistance to restore wetland areas.

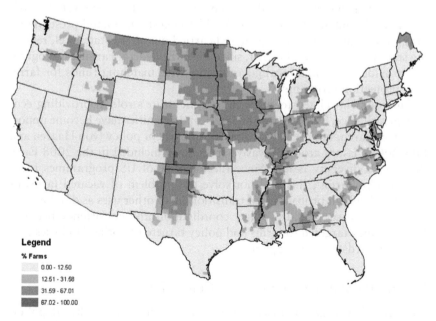

Legend
% Farms
0.00 - 12.50
12.51 - 31.58
31.59 - 67.01
67.02 - 100.00

Figure 11.2   Distribution of CRP, EQIP and CREP payments in the US, 2007.

The Food, Conservation, and Energy Act of 2008 (2008 Farm Bill) provided a 17 per cent increase in conservation programme funding, largely to 'working lands' programmes. There are currently two main working lands programmes: EQIP and CStP. EQIP provides financial and technical assistance to farmers implementing conservation practices or structures on their land. The majority of funds (60 per cent) are targeted for livestock producers, and a proportion of all funds are set aside for new, beginning and socially disadvantaged farmers. To be eligible for the CStP, farmers need to have previously implemented at least one type of conservation practice. Farmers are then paid for incorporating additional practices that address one or more media (air, water, soil quality). The intent is to compensate and reward farmers for the foregone income and ecosystem benefits resulting from conservation practices already under way. This programme comes the closet to fulfilling multifunctional policy goals (Lenihan and Brasier 2010).

Farmland preservation constitutes a final arena of active engagement for policy but at multiple levels—federal, state and county. The need for farmland protection is predicated by land market failure, i.e. the failure of markets to accurately reflect amenity values associated with farmland. Public interest in protecting farmland reflects preferences related to reducing sprawl, ensuring food security and choice, preserving the rural agrarian heritage, protecting natural resources and supporting local businesses (Heimlich and Anderson 2001; Hellerstein et al. 2002). By the early 2000s, all US states had enacted farmland protection programmes (e.g. right-to-farm and use value assessment) with the goal of protecting farmland and its associated amenities from development pressure (Hellerstein et al. 2002; American Farmland Trust 2009). As this suggests, farmland preservation programmes are largely designed and carried out at the state level, reflecting state-level priorities. Further, since 1996 the Federal Farmland Program has provided state and local governments with matching funds for farmland protection programmes.

Environment-related topics such as agriculture's role in providing ecosystem resilience, biodiversity and landscape amenities have become important in research, but are not yet important parts of policy (von Haaren and Bills 2009). Issues around invasive species are included in the 2008 Farm Bill but biodiversity is not. Since the majority of US programmes focus on 'working farms', this will not solve the problem of vacated farms or farms with a high probability of transitioning to other uses as development pressure increases. Finally, policy coordination and consistency between federal policy targeted to farms and policy targeted to other land uses (e.g. forest stewardship) is not apparent.

Impetus for Shifting Priorities and Constraints

Now is a key time for discourse on the future of agricultural policy, including the integration of farm and non-farm perspectives. There are several reasons why discourse is important now. First, US farm operators are becoming on average older, and lack of a farm heir is a problem for many US farms (Findeis, Brasier and Salcedo Du Bois 2009). In 2007, the average age of US principal farm operators was over fifty-seven, compared to 55.3 five years earlier (USDA 2007). Also, between 2002 and 2007, the number of principal operators under twenty-five years old declined by 30 per cent (ibid.). In short, intergenerational transfer is not assured for many farm operations (Errington 2001). The ageing farm population, smaller family sizes and better economic prospects in non-farm labour markets that create an unwillingness among the next generation to farm could strongly influence farm structure in the US, and the spatial configuration of farmland and open space across the country. Second, continuation of negative environmental spillovers stemming from reliance on voluntary compliance coupled with voluntary coordination across state lines and agencies has recently resulted in a more hard-line regulatory stance to restore one of the nation's most environmentally fragile landmarks, the Chesapeake Bay. President Obama's 2009 executive order to restore the Chesapeake Bay signals what may become a more restrictive regulatory environment. This will make compliance among small and mid-size farms more difficult, creating challenges for maintaining farmland and open space in environmentally vulnerable environments. Being able to efficiently access well-coordinated programme information and understanding what viable options exist for small and mid-size farms will be critical. And third, opportunities for agriculture as a producer of biofuels has created the potential for new opportunities for US agriculture, but also potential for greater environmental costs. Market-based credit trading schemes to provide additional revenues to farmers also may positively influence the sustainability of agriculture but could well create distortion effects; to date, experience in the US has been mixed.

Closer integration of farm and non-farm perspectives also is warranted from a regional quality of life perspective. In regions across the US characterised by small farms and in rural-exurban-urban transition zones, alignment of policies and farm programmes with public preferences will become increasingly critical (Adelaja et al. 2009). The reframing of agriculture from farm production to agriculture as a provider of multiple services to the public requires that public preferences be known as public preferences may diverge from perceptions and goals held by government agencies and the agriculture industry. Regional understanding of the impacts of current trends and potential scenarios for the future is a critical path for action (Nelson et al. 2009).

Further, given current agriculture-related policies and programmes, a key question begs asking: to what extent are farms below the $250,000 annual farm sales threshold now able to meet the strict eligibility requirements of current multilayered agri-environmental, farmland protection and county-level agricultural land assessment programmes (see Lambert et al. 2006)?

Having a clear understanding of the barriers that small and mid-size farm owners face in terms of gaining knowledge of and access to the range of federal, state and local programmes—and overcoming these barriers where they exist—should be a major goal in regions where small farms are characteristic, including in rural-exurban-urban transition zones. Limitations in programme compliance at the individual household level imposed by farm size, farmland fragmentation (non-adjacent parcels) and the restriction to 'working farms' in places where vacant farmland is common may influence landscape outcomes and the ability at local, state and regional levels to meet policy goals from environmental and non-farm public quality of life perspectives. Our understanding of these barriers is not complete.

Finally, land fragmentation across multiple uses, creating a mixed-use landscape, is characteristic of many transition zones proximate to urban corridors (Jobin et al. 2003; Lubowski et al. 2006a, 2006b). This characteristic underscores the need for close collaboration among government stewards of the landscape in relation to farms, forests and water resources alike. The close integration of ecosystem, socio-economic system and food system that characterises transition zones such as the US Northeast region challenge cooperation among agents at multiple levels. The realities of small-farm landscapes call for a vision and coherent plan for action that goes well beyond conceptualizing and realising the contributions of agriculture.

CONCLUDING OBSERVATIONS

The US and UK share common trajectories of change; however, events have pushed the UK and EU faster toward a perspective on agriculture that more explicitly considers the implications of agriculture on the environment, food safety and human/animal health, and the condition of the countryside—in other words, the integration of farm and non-farm perspectives. In the US, reframing of agriculture is occurring in public discourse and research, but policy has not adapted to nearly the extent as is observed in the UK and EU.

UK agriculture has changed dramatically over the last century, most recently as a consequence of implementation of the CAP, although in the absence of a counterfactual it is not possible to know exactly what the sector would have looked like had the UK not joined the EU. Under this EU-wide policy, farming has been massively supported by food consumers (through higher prices) and tax payers (through budgetary expenditure); for most farmers, the CAP has been a godsend. Recent reforms have resulted in a slightly more rational approach, driven as much by new concerns as by avoidance of the economic waste associated with the original policy goals. Attitudes of the main stakeholder groups have changed markedly over the years. Farmers and farmers' unions now recognise that historic levels of protection to agriculture are unsustainable. Budgetary costs, WTO negotiations and the reality of a greatly enlarged EU have cemented this change of attitude. Consumers may not understand the CAP, but increasingly they are aware of its shortcomings. In response, government has rethought policy, giving due regard to the 'multifunctional' role of agriculture in which environmental protection, rural development and issues related to food safety, food quality and farm animal welfare all feature prominently. Future policy reform in the UK and EU is likely to centre on these or similar concerns, underpinned by the notion of the family farm, which persists despite the apparent dichotomy and coexistence of large and small farms.

US agriculture has moved in a similar though not exactly the same direction and certainly not as far. This has occurred through a broader suite of agri-environmental policies in recent years, through continued development of a multilayered (federal, state, local) approach to protect and preserve farmland and through increased awareness and consideration of the non-farm public's preferences for attributes associated with agriculture beyond staple food production. The persistence of small farms and their greater integration into the US non-farm public's consciousness has helped to build this new vision of what agriculture can contribute.

Nevertheless, there is still an in-built conservatism in agricultural policy in both countries. Decades of subsidized production in the UK and US have left an agricultural sector needing to be gently weaned off support. The extent to which direct payments are considered decoupled from production and therefore not trade-distorting will be a crucial issue for both the EU and US in WTO negotiations. Less trade-distorting support implies more international trade, but for many products there is an in-built consumer preference for the domestically-produced good—a 'home bias'—and perhaps for locally produced foods. UK and US agriculture should look to capitalise on this, rather than on continuing dependence on farm subsidies.

Arguments relating to economic welfare losses stemming from agricultural policy have held little weight with the general public or policymakers in the past. Interestingly, in the future on both sides of the Atlantic the more successful pressure groups are likely to be those aligned with the indirect issues: environmental degradation, food safety, animal welfare, etc. But as long as the UK remains within the EU, its agricultural policy will continue to be governed principally by what happens in Brussels. US farm policy reform and a major redirection of farm payments is unlikely to happen anytime soon, but the reframing of agriculture is just as unlikely to end.

12 Agri-Environmental Policy, Rural Environments and Forks in the Road

A Comparative Analysis of the US and the UK

Clive Potter and Steven Wolf

INTRODUCTION

State support for agriculture in the United States and the European Union (and thus, by implication, in the UK) has for decades been accompanied by overlapping, and not always consistent, policy narratives. These narratives variously assert the role of the state in promoting agricultural modernisation, the support of farming incomes, the social and economic integrity of rural communities and the sustainable management of rural environments. Historically, the dominant impulse has been to place the enhancement of agricultural productivity and the support of farming incomes at the centre of this bureaucratic project. Although expressing optimism about technological advance and exhibiting a largely economistic imperative, accountability has been weak in relation both to social dimensions (e.g. farm structure, public health, animal rights and landscape aesthetics) and to the ecological consequences of production and landscapes (e.g. soil conservation, water quality and biodiversity). By the 1980s this state project for industrialised agriculture was coming under attack from two directions. Critics of the domestic budgetary implications of farm support argued that agricultural subsidies were too costly, exceptionalist in their treatment of a diminishing occupation, lacked transparency and were ineffective in supporting farming incomes (W. Cochrane 2003; Potter 1998). Later they were joined by agro-food interests, neo-liberal commentators and development advocates who emphasized the heavily trade-distorting nature of subsidies offered to farmers through commodity support and production aids (Peine and McMichael 2005). In an era of market governance and the incorporation of agriculture into the Global Agreement on Tariffs and Trade (GATT) for the first time, it seemed the moment to dismantle state support for agriculture and to liberalize production and markets.

Significantly, in terms of the subsequent evolution of policy, these pressures towards budgetary retrenchment and market liberalization coincided with the emergence of an environmentalist and social critique of modern agriculture (e.g. Jackson, Berry and Colman 1984; Lowrance, Stinner and House 1984). This critique not only identified the role of the state-dominated productivist complex of subsidies, extension and technological change in degrading rural environments, but also questioned the assumed economic centrality of agriculture within rural economies. While explicitly critical of the state's role in agriculture, sustainability advocates conceded that state support to agriculture would need to continue, albeit more directly linked to rural development and agri-environmental policy objectives. Far from fracturing the agricultural and rural policy community, these tensions—on the one hand, pressure to unleash the productive potential of agriculture through market integration and liberalization, and on the other, pressure to address the social and ecological contradictions of industrialised agriculture—made possible a new and, in retrospect, durable consensus between farming, conservation and state bureaucracies. While protectionism, income transfer and the preservation of historical policy entitlements were part of the dynamic, a 'public money for public goods' justification for continued agricultural support began to emerge during this period. Conservationists and farming representatives came together in both the US, UK and in other EU member states to develop new funding streams for agriculture ostensibly designed to publically fund agri-environmental stewardship.

To advance these policy beliefs, farmers accepted the notion of socially responsible agriculture delivering public environmental goods alongside the production of food and fibre. Conservationists used the growing evidence in the 1990s of the deleterious consequences of farming practices not to mount a critique of agriculture per se, but rather to press for further extensions to agri-environment funding (Potter and Tilzey 2005). Indeed, beginning in the mid-1990s, the shorthand term 'multifunctionality' emerged to describe a vision of agriculture that layers a range of policy objectives onto highly productive agricultural landscapes at various spatial scales (Hollander 2004; McCarthy 2005; G. Wilson 2007). The differences between multifunctionality and previously articulated visions of sustainable agriculture reflect the resilience of productivism and the pragmatic orientation adopted by its critics in recent decades (see, for example, Andrew Jamison [2001] on pragmatism, its origins and its discontents, applied to the environmental movement and environmental policy processes). Without suggesting that the two narratives of productivism and multifunctionality are equally reflected in laws, allocation of financial investment or the adoption of technical practices in the farmed landscape, we can say that the tension between productivism and multifunctionality continues to structure agri-environmental policy-making in the US, the UK and throughout other EU member states. That is to say, debate and decisions on issues such as land-use controls and subsidies, as well as research and development priorities, are framed with reference to these discourses. The relevant policy networks and research communities also conform to these frames. Since 1985, policy has situated agri-environmental management within a moving band between these poles (within a portion of the spectrum that is not centred).

Recognising that the political settlement and policy coalitions that emerged in the 1980s have produced substantial continuity in agri-environmental policy in recent decades, we identify the contemporary moment as a potential tipping point. Climate change, the threat of global food insecurity and the need for an energy transition in an era of peak oil are contemporary policy concerns that have already reframed the policy agenda for agriculture (Potter 2009). Additionally, there is a growing unease among a growing range of centrist organisations regarding the capacity of the industrialised model of agro-food production to enhance the security of the world's poor in terms of nutrition, economic development and climate change adaptation (International Assessment of Agricultural Science and Technology for Development [IAASTD] 2008). This set of global, interwoven risks may destabilize this political settlement and the paradigm of state assistance that it has so effectively held in place. Each of these imperatives, we would argue, has the potential to crowd out established forms of bureaucratic control in relation to agriculture, favour particular knowledge claims, reconfigure the privileged position of state actors in the provision of public goods and destabilize the policy coalitions that stand behind them. Industrialised country agriculture has been brought relatively late into the climate change debate but its potential contribution to mitigation is likely to be significant (Intergovernmental Panel on Climate Change [IPCC] 2007). At the same time, the re-emergence of food security and a push to expand markets for biofuels, each closely interconnected as policy objectives, implies a reassertation of the productivist thinking that has been dormant (in agricultural policy circles at least) since the early 1990s. The intersection of a new productivist impulse with imperatives emerging from climate change suggests a fork in the road.

The central argument of this chapter is that these intersecting productivist and 'new environmentalist' agendas will not only bring new actors and insert different rationales and bureaucratic routines into the agri-environmental policy domain (and the larger rural policy context in which these sit), but will also likely usher in different accountability regimes and a more market-orientated approach to the provision of what will become a vastly expanded category of global public goods linked to farming and rural land. The potential for departure from the long-standing state-centred bureaucratic mode of coordination in agri-environmental policy and management, and movement toward market-based accountability, constitutes a second fork in the road we explore here. We see in this potential institutional transition a significant new incursion of neo-liberal thinking into rural governance and subjectivities and connect this to the largely neoclassical way in which climate change policy discourse is framed. This discourse (and indeed the broader debate about the economics of sustainability to which it is linked) is dominated by ideas from environmental and

Coasean economics. A key assumption is a need for market institutions premised on establishment of alienable property rights that will enable transactions in environmental commodities at a distance and across time. This abstract economistic logic focuses on economic efficiency concerns while neglecting distributional issues and, for critics, justifies Ricardian thinking that supports the logic of the Clean Development Mechanism (CDM) and the broader project of sustaining profligate lifestyles at the expense of marginalised people and territories (Lohmann 2006). In combining a look back historically and a look ahead as to what climate change means in the context of the institutional relations of agri-environmental governance, we identify an important set of questions.

We offer for comparison the cases of the US and the UK, jurisdictions that are in many ways very different in terms of history, constitution and politics but which for our purposes are comparable because of well-established agri-environmental programmes built on broadly similar socio-political foundations. In seeking to reconcile the international imperatives of climate change with these long-standing traditions of agri-environmental intervention, policymakers appear to be resorting to a similar set of policy ideas centred on market processes. We compare the nature of the discourse and developments surrounding marketisation in each region, the different patterns of actor enrolment in these discussions and in policy formulation and implementation and the implied evolution in relations between state bureaucracies and market discipline.

ADAPTING THE STATE PROJECT FOR AGRICULTURE IN THE US AND EU

The longevity and persistence of an essentially Fordist state project for agriculture in industrialised countries—those state-directed market supports, infrastructure elements, production aids, investments in research and development and extension services that have underwritten the post–World War II expansion, intensification and globalisation of agricultural production—have long intrigued policy commentators. Various explanations have been offered for the continuation of heavy state support in these neo-liberal times, ranging from the susceptibility of public policy to special interest group capture and incorporation (in this case from a well-organised, adaptable and politically agile farm lobby), through to the way in which certain ideas and arguments have been used to frame, fix and limit debates about the possibility and desirability of reform (Bonnen, Browne and Schweikhardt 1996). In this latter sense, the socio-environmentalist critiques of agriculture which emerged in both the US and in selected EU member states like the UK, Denmark and the Netherlands in the early 1980s seemed fundamental. Together with criticisms of the limited social contribution of a highly farm-centred conception of rural development and how best to promote it, they appeared to question the justification for, and effectiveness of, farm support in public good terms (Browne et al. 1992). In practice, implicit agreement between conservationists, rural development advocates and the farm lobby that the focus of any green reforms should be on reallocating some part of the agricultural budget to conservation and rural development rather than cutting production subsidies per se, meant that a deal could be struck which altered only marginally the overall balance of spending. In the US this gave rise to a Conservation Title under the 1985 Farm Bill; in the EU to an encompassing 1985 Agri-Environment Regulation.

Eventually, mounting domestic budgetary tensions coincided with increasingly insistent international pressure from neo-liberal agro-food interests to reform commodity programmes and production subsidies. This debate produced a further consolidation of agri-environmental policy in both regions, with more ambitious green payment programmes on offer from governments. These agri-environmental programmes were required to do triple duty as environmental incentive payments, supply controls and income supports at a time when large numbers of farmers were adapting to the decoupling of commodity supports or in the case of 'cross-compliance', a policy innovation that appeared first in the US and later adopted in the EU, actually enabling farmers to retain eligibility for farm programme payments in return for meeting minimal environmental conditions. The explicit linkage between compliance with environmental conservation standards and eligibility for production subsidies highlights deep entanglement between these agendas further represented in the concept of 'decoupling' that emerged in the late 1990s (i.e. breaking of the bond between production supports and conservation payments).

Environmental economists appear only recently to have discovered agri-environmental payments as an unexceptionable form of 'payment for an ecosystem service' (PES), in which government is the contractor and farmers the suppliers of first resort for these public goods.[1] For instance, a recent UK Department of Environment, Food and Rural Affairs (DEFRA) Evidence and Analysis paper commends agri-environmental payments under the CAP as market-based instruments, alongside measures such as the EU's Emissions Trading Scheme and the UK Landfill Tax. To some extent this is an accurate interpretation. Agri-environmental management in both the US and in the UK (as well as other EU member states) takes the form of state contracts, in which farmers receive payments ostensibly in exchange for producing a stream of conservation benefits, for example, reducing pollution to water bodies or enhancing wildlife habitat quality. In the vast majority of cases what farmers are paid for on the extensive margin is to continue farming (chiefly important in the UK) or to take land out of production (most significant in the US under the Conservation Reserve Program [CRP]). On the intensive margin, farmers are paid to apply or abandon specific technical practices on working farmland. Note, however, that none of these land-use changes or practices for which payment is made could be construed as ecosystem services. Importantly for the argument we seek to make in this chapter, the existing model of agri-environmental policy is not predicated on market exchange. Under the current model, payments are generally awarded for inputs, not outputs or outcomes, the government is the only buyer of conservation, and with some limited exceptions prices have been fixed and are non-negotiable. Thus, exchange has not been governed by market principles and the actors have not been subject to market discipline. We take up this point again later.

Furthermore, historical analysis suggests that agri-environmental programmes are much more complex constructions than a market-based instrument interpretation would suggest. Far from being simple contracts between purchasers and suppliers, they are best understood as politically negotiated extensions of the state project for agriculture (which promotes a rather dirigiste model of environmental governance embedded in a complex network of relationships between state bureaucracies, conservationists and professional bodies representing farmers). Indeed, agri-environmental policies and payments to the farm sector have from the beginning implicitly and explicitly served purposes other than conservation, and their wide scope and the trade-offs implied is an important explanation of their durability. In the US, the way programmes are designed and implemented and the distribution of funding reflects the United States Department of Agriculture's (USDA) position in a complex, historically structured political negotiation. In the UK, the origins and subsequent evolution of agri-environmental policy design reflects the equally complex politics of the broader processes of European integration in which it is embedded. Here, the desire for a quasi-federal policy for rural environmental management directed from Brussels is in tension with the administrative imperative of 'subsidiarity' (the policy injunction that EU policy matters should be handled by the smallest, lowest or least centralized competent authority). This has resulted in a highly variable geometry, with the UK's approach to agri-environmental policy design reflecting its distinctive national policy style, biophysical reality and agri-environmental priorities. Tensions between bureaucrats, tax payers, farmers and conservationists are embodied in the very way programmes are designed and implemented. In short, the approach is politically structured rather than rational by design.

The centrality of the state in the resulting provision of agri-environmental goods and services can scarcely be overemphasized, particularly when set beside the steady privatization of other agricultural policy responsibilities, including those with a strong public good overtone. In the US, private sector investment in R&D now exceeds the pace of public sector investment (Fuglie and Schimmelpfennig 2000). Agricultural extension has been substantially outsourced to commercial agronomists and entomologists (Wolf 1996). Responsibility for food safety inspection has been shifted to the food-processing industry. Supermarkets and agribusiness firms in the highly consolidated and integrated input supply and food-processing sector are now seen as regulating production in commodity chains (Busch 2000). By comparison, US government agencies such as the Natural Resources Conservation Service and the Farm Services Administration, supported by durable, if sometimes contentious, political alliances with farmers and conservation NGOs, have long been the central players in agri-environmental policy. Under direction from Congress, USDA and its network of state- and county-level offices articulate demand for conservation on farms and in rural landscapes. These state bureaucracies design programmes, set technical standards, pay farmers for specific actions and have responsibility for monitoring implementation. While there has been a tendency toward decentralization, state- and watershed-level planning and implementation of policy remains a thoroughly government-centred affair.

UK policy is similarly bureaucratised, nested as it is within an overall EU policy structure that is framed by the Agriculture Directorate-General of the European Commission in Brussels but operationalised through the significant discretion given to member state agriculture departments in terms of scheme design and implementation. In the UK the relevant authorities are DEFRA in England, the Northern Ireland Executive's Department of Agriculture and Rural Development, the Welsh Assembly Government's Department for Rural Affairs and the Scottish Government's Rural and Environment Directorate. These are responsible for matters such as levels of expenditure, schemes design and geographic coverage and the extent of resources committed to monitoring and evaluation. The basic model common to all four UK jurisdictions is one centred on contracts offered on a discretionary basis by agriculture departments and their agencies to individual farmers. The underlying premise is that since farmers hold the property rights to alter the environment, they should be given payments to change practices: hence the application of the so-called 'Provider Gets Principle' (PGP) to agri-environmental policy.

While the resulting mode of governance is consistently characterised as voluntary, meaning farmers choose whether they want to enter into contracts to practice conservation in exchange for payments, other non-market institutions are present. In the US, laws restrict how pesticides are used. The Clean Water Act governs manure management in concentrated animal feeding operations. The Endangered Species Act and prohibitions on draining wetlands apply to privately owned farmland. These are examples of regulation that put some kind of floor under the environmental performance of agriculture. Additionally, farmers have long been subject to 'cross-compliance', a *quid pro quo* mentioned earlier under which farmers are held to minimum environmental management standards for erosion control and wetland conservation in return for access to a range of benefits and subsidies including price supports and crop insurance. Farmers have the right to choose to forgo federal subsidies, and thus cross-compliance is technically voluntary, but few go this route. Regulations are equally important in a European context in setting the context within which governance of land takes place. The Birds Directive, Habitats Directive, Nitrates Directive and the Water Framework Directive are all associated with rules that can constrain private land-use decisions.

State agencies have meanwhile used science to engineer the political compromises on which agri-environmental policy has been founded, and science in the service of bureaucracy has proven to be a powerful response to critics of environmental payments to farmers. Faced with the challenge of developing a cost-effective means of estimating soil erosion rates on tens of millions of individual fields in order to determine eligibility for support payments under cross-compliance in the landmark 1985 Farm Bill, USDA was able to forge consensus around the aptly named Universal Soil Loss Equation. Despite well-recognised differences in the accuracy and validity of the algorithm and the data used to calculate T—the rate of soil formation in a given location—and soil loss rates, farmers, conservation interests, scientists and bureaucracies forged a settlement.[2] It has long been recognised that, in order to control the periphery from the centre, bureaucratic control requires universal and justifiable procedural routines (Scott 1999). In the case of agri-environmental policy, field-based science has legitimated the procedures of oversight and bureaucratic management. In a related way, the evolution of the largest and most expensive agri-environmental programme ever initiated in the US, the 1985 CRP, demonstrates a complex interplay between science and politics. CRP came under heavy attack as being poorly targeted, and thus cost ineffective. Contracts were awarded, *de facto*, to farmers largely on a first-come, first-served basis, and thus there was no effort to remove from production those portions of the landscape that imposed greatest social cost or that offered the highest return on public investment. Out of this controversy emerged a wide range of alternatives, including the design of auctions to engage farmers in competitive bidding and the Environmental Benefits Index scoring scheme to integrate a wide range of ecological criteria so programme managers could compare the benefits of retiring varying pieces of farmland. These administrative procedures were refined iteratively over two decades, ostensibly targeting conservation contracts so as to produce greater value for money.

THE CONTEMPORARY MOMENT IN AGRI-ENVIRONMENTAL POLICY

The rapid emergence of climate change, global food insecurity and energy transitions as dominant policy concerns of the early twenty-first century raises many questions about the durability and larger policy framing of these agri-environmental policy trends. While we focus in this analysis on the implications of carbon governance for agriculture and agricultural policy, we recognise the power and interrelatedness of these additional contemporary 'crises' within policy processes—and we also recognise the public health critiques of contemporary agro-food as significant (Winson 2010). Scarcity of both food and mobile fuels have emerged as important interconnected risks that exacerbate and compete with the stewardship imperative implied by climate governance. We observe pressure on the extensive margin, the bringing in of new land to production and on the intensive margin; for example, in the US, in 2008 corn production—the most input intensive field crop—rose 17 per cent relative to the previous year. This increase stems from more intensive use of inputs, including fertilizers, pesticides and water and from devoting more land to corn production (this includes land previously uncultivated and land previously used to grow other crops). Expanding populations, meatification of diets of growing middle classes abroad, declining returns on investment in the Green Revolution technology suite, constraints on land availability and growing demand for biofuels have driven a resurgence of productivism in agriculture.

In the US, the shift toward 'working lands'—directing resources toward lands being actively farmed as opposed to land removed from production—is the most significant development in the past twenty-five years within agri-environmental policy and can be interpreted as part of a productivist (re)turn. Claassen (2007) reports that spending on working land programmes between 1986 and 2002 accounted for 9 per cent of conservation-related spending while land retirement programmes accounted for 69 per cent. Between 2002 and 2006, working lands accounted for 25 per cent of spending, and land retirement programmes accounted for 54 per cent of spending. While these statistics suggest some loss of support for idling land, and additional sign of productivist impulses, it must be noted that the CRP—payments on 10 per cent of the US crop base held out of production—remains the largest agri-environmental programme. Further, despite pressure to bring some portion of this 36 million acres into production, the 2008 Farm Bill retained strong support for CRP.

At first glance, the gaining recognition that industrialised country agricultures have an important role to play in climate change mitigation suggests an opening for further incremental extension to the forms of agricultural stewardship described above. The IPCC (2007) has identified the restoration of degraded lands, the maintenance of extensive grassland system, improved livestock manure management and more controlled fertilizer applications as key climate mitigation activities. Commentators are beginning to talk about the levels of carbon that land managers should have a duty to maintain and of the potential for paying farmers to sequester carbon above reference levels (Hodge 2001). These arguments parallel earlier debates in the EU and within the UK that lead to the establishment of the baselines against which the concept of 'Good Agricultural and Environmental Conditions' was defined (and hence the basis on which farmers' eligibility for a conventional agri-environmental payment would be judged). Current political and technical discussions seek to clarify how reference levels should be set and how best to ensure that farmers are penalized for land-use changes that release carbon (for example sodbusting, i.e. ploughing grassland) while being rewarded for activities that take it up (for example, cover cropping and diversified crop rotations). More ambitious suggestions have been made to refocus agri-environmental payments to farmers and public sector science and technology in order to create a 'sustainable bioeconomy' (Jordan 2007). In this vision of multifunctionality, rural landscapes yield food, cellulosic biofuel feedstocks, carbon sequestration, water quality and biodiversity largely by substituting perennial plants including grasses and trees for annuals (corn, soybeans, cotton, wheat) in targeted portions of watersheds. There is clear potential for the dominant institutional order to prove itself resilient by integrating climate change, and other contemporary pressures, into existing bureaucratic structures, policy networks and landscapes.

In other respects, however, climate change discourse—globally focused, largely abstracted from place and structured around an assessment of long-range risk—looks likely to introduce new and not easily resolved tensions into agri-environmental policy discourse and practice in the US and the UK. Climate governance is fundamentally different to the politically messy, and often country and regionally specific approach to governing the trade-offs between conservation, agrarian and productivist objectives that have defined agri-environmental policy until now. Agriculture's climate mitigation role has largely been assembled as a policy project by the IPCC from outside the agri-environmental policy community. Domestic environmentalists, agriculturalists and policy analysts are consequently struggling to interpret what an agricultural contribution to meeting emission reduction targets will mean for agricultural practices, land use and livelihoods. At the same time, climate change discourse imports a powerful neoclassical economic logic into a policy area that (as we have seen in the preceding) has been heavily bureaucratic and even statist in its assumptions and governance approaches. The environmental policy project of reducing GHG emissions has been dominated from the outset by policy concepts such as emissions trading, offsetting and PES, all of which have been incubating within the environmental economic literature over the last thirty years; indeed, the concept of tradable pollution permits was first outlined by Dales (1968). The introduction of carbon trading, for instance, was easily the most significant extension to earlier, much more piecemeal experiments with pollution permits such as that in relation to SO2 regulation in the US. The concept of PES, construed by some as another way to describe agri-environmental payment schemes, is actually very different in conception and execution. PES is fundamentally predicated on a commodification of environmental goods and services and assumes that these can be commissioned and supplied by individuals or groups of individuals with minimal transaction cost (Ruhl, Kraft and Lant 2007). Agri-environmental policy, by contrast, has been little informed by market logic, despite wide criticism by UK and other European commentators of environmental contracts, and the case for adopting other approaches to environmental provision, including direct land purchase under a hypothecated fund model. Hodge (2001), for instance, points to the difficulties of determining target outputs, the incentives to evade contract requirements and the lack of incentives for entrepreneurship embodied in current policy practice. In the US, there has long been a tradition of policy design rooted in the academic discipline of agricultural economics that takes adverse selection, fraud, geographic targeting and value for money seriously, and these ideas are represented in policy debates and policy, in some measure. There has also, however, been long-standing resistance to this kind of rationalization of agri-environmental policy.[3]

MARKET DISCIPLINE AND MARKET ROLL-OUT IN THE US

It is nevertheless in the US that a roll-out of market discipline in agri-environmental governance is most clearly already under way, to the extent that we expect in the near future to see PES schemes introduced under the heading of agri-environmental policy. The most highly anticipated scheme currently, and potentially the most transformative, would stem from a national (or international) cap-and-trade policy directed at carbon emissions. Under such a programme, polluters could fulfil their obligations by buying GHG emission reductions from farmers or brokers representing groups of farmers. Momentum for this development comes, in part, from studies suggesting that 'for the US, it is estimated that agricultural sequestration of carbon could provide 40 per cent of the carbon reduction required to reduce forecast 2010 GHG emissions to 1990 levels' (see Young et al. 2007, p. 32). Expectations are for policy learning from carbon market governance to support similar applications in water quality (nitrogen and phosphorous) and biodiversity conservation. The USDA established the Office of Ecosystem Services and Markets on 15 December 2008 as required under the 2008 Farm Bill and the Food, Conservation and Energy Act. This newly created office is charged with supporting the Secretary of Agriculture in his responsibility 'to establish technical guidelines that outline science-based methods to measure the environmental services benefits from conservation and land management activities in order to facilitate the participation of farmers, ranchers, and forest landowners in emerging environmental services markets' (Schafer 2008).

Several elements of this announcement warrant attention in the context of the arguments we are developing here. The title of the Farm Bill points directly to the immediacy and interrelated status of food, ecology and energy politics and policy. The elevation of energy considerations within agricultural policy is a particularly novel development, and raises clear tensions with an ecosystem service agenda. Specifically, carbon debt associated with biofuel production (Fargione et al. 2008) in combination with indirect land-use effects (Gallagher 2008) of expanded demand for biofuels and competition for land between fuel and food are major concerns. Second, casting the USDA's role in terms of facilitating private landowners' participation in ecosystem service markets rather than, say, using this policy tool to advance sustainability or maximize productivity of conservation investments is telling. Third, the USDA's emphasis on science-based methods of measurement has a long history in US agri-environmental policy, as we discussed earlier in the context of the Universal Soil Loss Equation and the Environmental Benefits Index. Problems in estimating the quantity and quality of ecosystem service production across heterogeneous biophysical settings, subject to varied management, over time have been seen as a major constraint to the introduction of payment for ecosystem service schemes. Clearly, USDA perceives an imperative to address this constraint head on (before the terms of trade are dictated to them and their farmer clients by market actors). Lastly, it is quite clear that USDA is determined to get out in front of the process of ecosystem service market creation and thereby secure its place and the security for its clients and partners under climate governance.

These developments have implications both for policy practice and design and for actor enrolment within bureaucratic politics. In some respects, market governance seems likely to undermine the historical relationship between state bureaucracies and professional bodies representing farmers. Farmers have long enjoyed support from USDA, and the relationship has been more characterised by protection and boosterism than policing or monitoring. While ecosystems and citizens are normally identified as the beneficiaries of agri-environmental policy, farmers and USDA have been important co-beneficiaries. Perhaps we can go further and include mainstream conservation advocacy organisations (NGOs) as part of the existing agri-environmental policy networks that could find their autonomy and influence diminished. The USDA, farmers' organisations and a subset of interest groups have enjoyed a cosy monopoly, of sorts, for decades. This 'market enclosure' is now potentially at risk. In suggesting that the USDA or farmers or conservation organisations could lose their privileged position as a function of institutional changes that make market transactions more central features of policy, it is important to note that costs and benefits will be distributed unevenly. Within the USDA, it is likely that a unit such as the Economic Research Service would see its status rise in such an environment. Other units in the organisation would ostensibly lose status. Similarly, the geography of investment in conservation under market discipline is likely to be quite different to that under the current political economic order.

Environmental NGOs are central players in agri-environmental policymaking. These NGOs constitute a large and heterogeneous collection of interest groups, some of which would fare better than others if policy were subjected to market discipline. For example, it is possible that wildlife interests or farmland preservation interests will be less central than they are currently relative to biodiversity or sustainable development interests. The types and volumes of benefit streams produced under 'green neo-liberal' agri-environmental policy and the realignment of influence within policy networks would depend on how the markets were designed. Similarly, the expertise and perspectives of the various interest groups will be differentially valued in the construction and administration of market rules. In the contemporary process of exploring, pushing and defending against imposition of market discipline in agri-environmental policy, NGOs occupy an interesting and contradictory position. In the classical formulation of Polanyi, communities and citizens' associations were the vehicle through which state power was enrolled to check destabilizing and degrading aspects of monetization and liberalization. Applied to efforts to mobilise 'fictitious commodities' of carbon or biodiversity, we might expect NGOs to seek interventions that reign in the market. In fact we do observe some reticence (e.g. Carbon Justice; see Lohmann 2006), though the opposite tendency is arguably more dominant.

We find that NGOs in the US are in the vanguard of promoting, designing and implementing market-based instruments in agri-environmental policy and have been notably uncritical of the institutionalisation of market instruments in this context. It is instructive given what we know now about biofuels, that conservation NGOs were silent or supportive of biofuels and pro-biofuels policies, including subsidies that mandated ramping up production (renewable fuel standards) at the early stages of the debate when investments were being made and legislation was being developed. We believe that it is important to understand how it is that some NGOs are acting as primary vectors of markets.

MARKET DISCOURSE AND PUBLIC GOODS IN THE UK

In the UK, and more widely throughout the EU, the reassignment of agriculture's role from mass commodity production to the state-incentivised production of public goods has arguably gone further (and has been more extensively elaborated in public debate) than in the US. While there has been a long-running debate about the need to improve the incentives for more innovative and lasting agri-environmental management on farms this has so far not translated into market governance as such. The first instinct of policymakers, indeed, has been to respond to the emerging climate change agenda for agriculture by following the traditional procedures of bureaucratic politics. In 2007 the European Commission published a working document on the role of agriculture in climate change and in 2009 agriculture ministers agreed to commit additional money under rural development programmes to climate change mitigation. A Draft Communication on the EU Budget in 2009 suggested the creation of a third pillar under the CAP targeted at climate change mitigation activities (though this is resisted by both DGAgiculture and DGEnvironment; see Bryden and Warner, this volume). UK farming groups and environmentalists, meanwhile, are beginning to explore how climate change imperatives could be exploited to extend agricultural stewardship for which a government payment could be made. This comes at a critical juncture in the evolution of agri-environmental policy in the UK, where there has been a long and unresolved debate about how to make agri-environmental schemes more fit for purpose in biodiversity protection terms. Recent years have seen mounting criticism of the effectiveness of agri-environmental measures following a hostile report from the European Court of Auditors, which questioned the measurability and value for money of many programmes and a scientific study, which concluded that there was insufficient evidence on which to assess the effectiveness of programmes. Subsequent UK evaluations have been more encouraging, and in the UK there is now robust evidence to suggest that agri-environmental policy here has made a significant contribution towards meeting biodiversity objectives, particularly following improved incentives under Environmental Stewardship for arable habitats (Boatman et al. 2008).

Critics recognise that the pattern of stewardship likely to optimize climate change mitigation may differ from that required to deliver more traditional conservation goals. For example, while more extensively managed livestock is a central component of traditional conservation strategies for high–nature-value farming and could be seen as an energy-efficient source of protein, indoor systems may be better overall in terms of the regulation of GHG emissions like methane. There might even be a case for reducing livestock numbers on climate change grounds. The 'new stewardship' may also need to operate at a systematically different spatial scale. Traditionally, agri-environmental policy has incentivised management at a field or farm level, largely ignoring landscape level interactions. Ecosystems services thinking, the standard point of conceptual reference in recent debate (see further discussion in the following), emphasizes interactions between ecological structures, processes, services and benefits (Rollet et al. 2008).

The increasing dominance of ecosystems thinking within the UK policy community, exemplified in the contribution from A. Woods (2009), reflects a desire on the part of policymakers to rationalize the public good contribution of agriculture in the context of broader debates about climate change and conflicting demands on the use of land (see also Cooper et al. 2010). Indeed, there is evidence that rural policymakers in the UK at least are coming to regard ecosystem service thinking as a more scientifically refined and politically serviceable justification for future funding than the textbook version of public goods. Despite having its origins in the economic theory of public goods, the ecosystem services and payments for ecosystem services literature is more explicit in its emphasis on the need to assign a value to a service output. The dominance of this set of concepts is testimony to an increasingly integrated (and thus hard to disentangle) climate science and environmental economic research agenda.

In climate change terms it brings referents such as ecosystem resilience into the heart of the policy process. According to DEFRA, for instance, ecosystem function thinking and the valuations associated with it need in future to be embedded within measures such as rural development programmes and the revised strategies for upland areas and nutrient management (DEFRA 2008a). The scale of this ambition will have a number of implications for the future conduct of policy. In an obvious sense, the emphasis on the demand as well as the supply side of service provision means that it will be easier to justify the application of market based instruments in an area of policy where 'the public good' has often been largely defined through political process, NGO lobbying and stakeholder representation. Under this model, large scale peat restoration could be financed as Certified Emission Reductions on the carbon offset market. The voluntary carbon offset market could be enrolled in paying land managers for the services they provide through carbon sequestration. This could signal a more general marketisation of the environmental services farmers provide, though what this will mean for landscape and biodiversity outputs that are specific to place is unclear.

CONCLUSIONS

In this chapter, we have argued that climate change governance, in combination with other pressures on agriculture, will have a profound impact on the way rural environments are managed in coming years. Tensions between productivist and multifunctional visions of agriculture and landscapes will continue to structure debate, investments and practices on the land. At the same time, however, we anticipate an expanded role for market logic and market discipline. This is a macro-historical tendency linked to neo-liberal discourse and governance and reflects the growing influence of neoclassical environmental economic ideas and prescriptions in climate change policy debates. Market rule has the potential to crowd out established forms of bureaucratic control in relation to agriculture, reconfigure the privileged position of state actors in the provision of public goods and destabilize the policy coalitions that stand behind them. Historically, the political alliance among farmers, a collection of conservation interests representing rural and environmental concerns and state bureaucracies that made the agri-environmental policy project feasible, has produced relative stability. In part this has been achieved through the creation of a kind of 'market enclosure'—a field of economic action not subject to open competition, free entry or external monitoring.

If non-state actors begin to contract for environmental services from farmers and rural landscapes, for example, private firms seeking to offset carbon emissions as required under a cap-and-trade scheme, we expect that a very different calculus will begin to guide the allocation of contracts to farmers and rural landscapes. Similarly, even if public agencies remain the primary buyer of conservation from agriculture, climate change politics and the much wider range of interests this entails may trump the dominant agri-environmental policy coalition. Under market rule, the practices structuring agri-environmental management could change at the level of fields and farms, the bureaucratic arrangements could be notably altered and there could be a significant reshuffling of policy networks, for example, NGOs interested in sustainability and global ecology could marginalise interest groups representing the family farm and wildlife.

This latent tendency toward marketisation would appear to be more pronounced in the US than in the UK, and reciprocally the UK appears to have initiated a deeper political debate about the role of the state in securing public goods from agricultural landscapes. We do not want to emphasize comparative differences without also highlighting how much is shared across the two settings. Payment for ecosystem services in agriculture is being actively explored in both the US and the UK. Similarly, we observe parallel efforts to muster evidence-based approaches to establishing equivalencies to undergird carbon accounting and thereby support market-based policies. Finally, resurgence of productivist impulses fuelled by the food and energy insecurity concerns is serving to buffer radical and immediate expansion of a conservation agenda in agriculture in both settings.

In summary then, our analysis points to two forks in the road. The first is a juncture representing climate change and other forms of ecological disorganisation. One path leads to massive expansion of biofuels and an attendant productivist push in farming in the wake of food insecurity implied by competition for land between food and fuel. The other path treats agriculture and rural landscapes as a source of ecological services. Here, multifunctionality and a form of deintensification, for example perennialization of landscapes, is held out as a possibility. The second fork in the road we envision relates to institutional forms that structure agri-environmental policy. One path continues along with bureaucratic controls in service to a political coalition. Down this road, payments for conservation perform additional political economic functions. As a result, social and economic problems in agriculture will perhaps be contained, but not pursued any more aggressively than they have been in the past twenty-five years. The alternative pathway represents marketisation and imposition of market discipline. This would represent a potentially radical departure, and the implications are not clear. The science lying behind construction of markets for ecosystem services and more rationalized targeting of conservation contracts would be politicized, as in the past. But the heightened inclusion of neoclassical economic approaches to mechanism design and global ecology interests would likely marginalise sets of actors that have traditionally been quite central in design and implementation of conservation schemes in agriculture.

In closing we note that the metaphor of a fork in the road implies a linearity and determinism that is objectionable. Much is unclear, the future is open and there are more potential pathways that we can identify. Yet, by looking back, down the shaft of the fork, we can get some perspective on path dependency and process of institutional change.

13 Nature Conservation and Environmental Management

Working Landscapes in Adirondack Park, US, and Cairngorms National Park, UK

Jo Vergunst, Charles Geisler and Richard Stedman

INTRODUCTION

The conceptual separation of nature from society has been a feature of Western thought since at least the Renaissance (Ingold 2000). It also reinforces the long-standing tendency to differentiate 'urban' and 'rural'. As cultural historian Raymond Williams has detailed, cities and towns are seen as centres of industry and of progress. Rural areas, all too often, tend either to be portrayed as rustic, backward and in need of 'development', or as pristine wilderness untouched by humans, and in need of preservation for aesthetic and recreational interests (Williams 1973). For many generations, parks for the conservation of nature have represented the wilderness side of this antipodal separation.

Underpinning this landscape division lie many sociological issues, not least of which is the asymmetrical power relationship between urban and rural interests. A moment's reflection bears out the urban hegemony. Urban intellectuals have led in the celebration of nature in their art and literature; urban visionaries have been the architects of park thinking and creation; urban scientists have made the case for refuges and the protection of biodiversity; and pundits from the metropole, mindful of the profits and prestige that come with tourism and commodified nature, have been the frequent engines of parks legislation. Yet, this urban dominance may be in transition if not in full-scale retreat. Though the change has not been sudden, it has been steady and in some ways momentous. Parks as citadel enclaves, set aside to protect nature against human interference, are becoming relics of the past along with, perhaps, the power asymmetry just noted.

A new conservation paradigm, 'working landscapes', is well known in Europe and making a gradual ascendance in the United States. It is not replacing parks per se but transforming them. Urban dominion over rural landscapes is, for a range of reasons, giving way to a new social space marked by conservation partnerships and governance that break old moulds. Working landscape conservation, however, is neither uniform nor predetermined, but a family of society–nature experiments noticeably more contingent and diverse than the classical park paradigm administered by central states. In fact, if one imagines diversity in terms of organisational pluralism and adaptive governance options, working landscapes offer an evolving structure highly relevant to the world of human–nature relations and conservation needs.

In this chapter we examine the working landscapes that encase two prestigious parks, one in Scotland and the other in the United States. Our intentions are several. One is to demonstrate that conservation governance hinges significantly on the era in which a park is formalised in law. The older of our park examples reflects a century-old governance structure struggling to make way for contemporary working landscape experimentation; the newer park takes working landscape principles as its birthright. Another intention of this chapter is to suggest that, in *de facto* terms, working landscapes have been with us for generations and even centuries. In their early renditions, as we shall see, the conservation content as we now understand it was marginal.

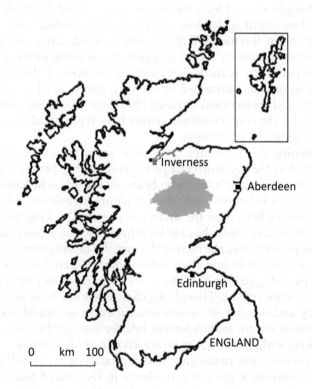

Figure 13.1   Map of Scotland showing the Cairngorms National Park (shaded).

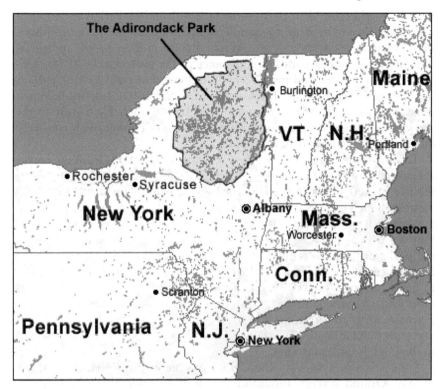

Figure 13.2   Map of the north-east US showing Adirondack Park.

This may have legacy effects upon newer working landscape experiments, for instance. Then and now, there is the abiding question 'for whom do the working landscapes work?' Our final intent is to underscore the dramatically different governance directions working landscape parks may take, which we can show by reconstructing something of the 'biography' of each park in-the-making as well as through cross-park comparisons.

TWO LANDSCAPES AT WORK

In what follows, we situate the parks of interest in their larger social histories and geographies. In strictly legal terms, one park is 'old', the Adirondack Park (AP) of New York State being over a century old, whereas the Cairngorms National Park of Scotland (CNP) is relatively newly minted. Both parks are vast relative to the land masses of their respective countries and dotted with high peaks. The AP contains over 2.4 million hectares (the largest park in the United States outside of Alaska); the CNP extends over 376,000 hectares and is the largest park in British Isles. Permanent residents within the AP in 1970—when the Adirondack Park Agency (APA) was established to manage it—numbered 112,000, along with ninety thousand seasonal residents and an estimated sixty million people (potential tourists) within a day's travelling distance of the park (Flacke 1976), generating a tourist demand more recently estimated at eight to nine million people annually (Hubacek, Erickson and Duchin 2002). Importantly, just under half the park (45 per cent) is owned by the state. The nature of the working landscape on the private lands in the park boundaries hinges very much on APA management decisions.

Turning to our Scottish case, the Cairngorm Mountains form the north-eastern part of the Highlands of Scotland. The area contains four out of the five highest peaks in the UK, the highest being Ben Macdui at 1,309 metres. Shaped by retreating ice at the end of the last glaciation, the granite mountains have a characteristic broad-shouldered and rounded appearance that is very recognisable to the outdoor recreation community. Many of the peaks are linked by the Cairngorm plateau, the UK's largest area of northern montane habitat and highly valued for the support it provides to birds such as Dotterel *Charadrius morinellus* and Ptarmigan *Lagopus muta* and a variety of alpine plants. In the lower reaches there are relatively extensive areas of forest, notable for the native Scots Pine *Pinus sylvestris* and plants including the Twinflower *Linnaea borealis*, although much land in the CNP is under farming.

Population pressures for the CNP are somewhat different from those of AP. Around sixteen thousand people live inside the current park, largely along two river valleys—Speyside to the north-west, which is fifty kilometres from the city of Inverness (population fifty thousand), and Deeside, which runs eastwards to Aberdeen (population 220,000) again about fifty kilometres from the edge of the park. Visitor numbers are hard to estimate but around 1.4 million people are thought to have visited the park in 2007 (Cairngorms National Park Authority [CNPA] n.d.). The presence of people in these different categories and their diverse employment and service needs produces a range of interactions with the working landscape.

For us, a working landscape means livelihood opportunities for humans mindful, in a culturally relevant lexicon, of conservation obligations. Often, but not always, conservation values become obligations in park environments. For example, in 1990 a special commission appointed by the governor of New York to consider future directions for the AP opened its final report with these words: 'The Commission is offering a plan that combines the greatest wilderness system in the East with working forests and farms that will continue to provide needed employment to the Park's 130,000 permanent residents' (Berle 1990, 7), thus attempting to combine conservation and socio-economic aims. Conservation pre-dates formal parks, of course. Even as human communities procure their subsistence over generations, they are apt to express some degree of cultural stewardship behaviours. Failure to harmonise consumption with the conservation of soil fertility, water sources and biodiversity over time can only result in ecological collapse (Diamond 2005).

A working landscape is therefore a place where change and stability coexist and where democratic and ecological principles co-evolve (Cannavò 2007). Unlike many conceptualizations of 'park', working landscapes embody more than semi-frozen land uses, amenities and species fenced off for protection and preservation. They are rather, as Cannavò insists, locations of human practice involving both physical and conceptual organisation and experimentation. Working landscapes in the contexts we discuss here can be thought of as trial governance sites in which local citizens have input, choice and agency. Whether a park evolves in the direction of a working landscape over time or is a working landscape retrofitted with park status, the classic conservation paradigm is shifting away from fixed land uses and authority hierarchies towards lived-in, adaptive, experimental relationships where 'nature' is socially constructed. Cannavò sees the working landscape as an interplay between founding (in the sense of forming or setting up) and preservation as two separate processes of place (2007, 43). Differing slightly, we contend that landscapes are constantly remade and reshaped, and never actually reach a state of being finished that can be preserved. It is the dichotomy of founding and preservation that can be transcended by a notion of a working landscape.

Although the AP and CNP have significant differences when thought of as parks (time of establishment, size, dominant land cover, management budget, visitor numbers, etc.), they converge in interesting ways as working landscapes in which people relate to the environment in modes other than that of purely exploiting its physical resources. Seeking 'drivers' or the impetus for these shifts is complex because of the historical depth as well as the flows of contemporary politics that constitute life in the parks today. However, through coalescing trends in regional development, conservation management and environmental ethics, we can identify a significant transformation in the idea of what a 'protected area' can be. Where the history of land use and land tenure has driven the working landscapes in the past, new land uses and possibilities in economic and social development also contribute now—and are likely to continue doing so into the future. The remainder of this chapter considers both experiments and their evolution into parks in social-historical context. We will revisit the pre-park working landscapes, then the alterations in this frontier era that accompanied industrialisation and produced both public and private park visions, and finally arrive at the roughly corresponding nature parks of the present with their respective stories and lessons for conservation governance.

Figure 13.3   The landscape at Glen Tanar, Cairngorms National Park.

Figure 13.4   A waterfall in Keene Valley on the eastern side of the High Peaks area of Adirondack Park. Photo—Adirondack Park Agency website http://www.apa.state.ny.us/.

WORKING LANDSCAPES ON THE FRONTIER

The first working landscape era in relation to our cases spans several centuries, beginning with the Enlightenment, and ending in the early nineteenth century. It is meditated entirely by British culture, law and entitlement on both continents. It is less an attempt to balance consumption and conservation than an aggressive time of claims-making on seemingly renewable resources (furs in North America and salmon, red deer, kelp and peat in the Highlands). During these years, British colonial thinking prevailed in much of North America and (after 1707) in Scotland as a new member of the Realm. Pacification of the clans and Indians through force of treaty was a governance priority, after which a cornucopia of natural resources were channelled to powerful British citizens. British efforts to control its New World colonies continued on after the American Revolution for another four decades, ending with the War of 1812.

In the now-liberated America, the park formulation of 'working landscape' was delayed for a century and came as a reaction to the plundering effects of the frontier juggernaut (see the following). In Scotland, despite its restricted size as a frontier and its embedded feudal land tenure (or perhaps because of it), ecosystems remained very much at the mercy of mercantilism (Adam Smith's *Wealth of Nations* appears the same year as the American Revolution) and the market—for grain, wool and meat. At the same time American transcendentalists (Emerson, Thoreau, Agassiz, Stillman, Remington and others) were camping in the Adirondacks and sowing in the American mind the seeds of conservation.[1] English lords and Scottish lairds were summoning their feudal prerogatives to create private parks in the Highlands. In the background, sources of wealth were shifting to industry and overseas dominion via the British Empire.

WORKING LANDSCAPES AND INDUSTRIALISM

Oliver Goldmith's poem-requiem 'Ill Fares the Land' aptly describes what happened to landscapes on both sides of the Atlantic as waves of enclosures ran their course. The English enclosures, already under way under Elizabeth I, erased huge repositories of indigenous knowledge as hundreds of thousands of commoners were evicted and drifted to the poorhouses or factories of the UK (Tate 1976). American enclosures swallowed vast swaths of public domain and Indian Territory (Watson 2009) and reset the terms of reference for working landscape in profound (and perhaps perverse) ways.[2] The Adirondack region was no exception. Indeed, its extreme conformity to the norms of unregulated rural industrialisation led, by the late nineteenth century, to agitation by urban elites (especially the New York Board of Trade and Transportation and the *New York Times*) to create a park sanctuary in and around its mountains (Flacke 1976).

Parks in the United States have long had the look and feel of fortifications intended to exclude certain uses. The earliest models of National Parks (Yellowstone and Yosemite) were originally military annexations overseen by military personnel (Runte [1979] 1997; Spence 1999). Once these denizens were expelled, American parks bore a resemblance to military bases with a high degree of 'no trespass', dictation of activities allowed and prohibited, screening of those who might sojourn therein and the manner in which they might 'correctly' encounter the landscape. This legacy and the influence of Scotsman John Muir to protect natural wonders advanced the construction of parks as preserving 'vignettes of primitive America, where man is a visitor and does not remain' (National Academy of Sciences [NAS] 1963). In the Adirondacks, however, it is the interplay between industrial development and conservation that is most significant.

In the eighty years between the War of 1812 and the establishment of the AP in 1892, the Adirondack mountains, rivers and forests became an industrial staging site for the iron, timber and tanning needs of the Eastern Seaboard. The amount of timber needed to make charcoal for iron production, to build cities and railroads and to tan leather (hemlock bark) was almost incalculable and certainly not renewable at the scale of demand in question (McMartin 1992). As Jenkins and Keal (2004, 100) state:

> In 1873 a peak year, the Adirondacks were the third largest lumber-producing region in the country. Over a million logs were floated down the Hudson alone, and the mills at Glens Falls made nearly two-hundred million board feet of lumber from them. About the same time thirty forges (. . .) were producing between thirty thousand and forty thousand tons of iron a year. To do this they used about four million bushels of charcoal a year and clear-cut perhaps five thousand acres of hardwoods a year to produce it.

As the mountains were stripped of timber, three stage-setting events occurred for the future AP. The state (and particularly New York City on the lower Hudson) grew concerned that its water supplies depended on forest cover (APA 1980); timber companies, interested only in board feet and not in land title, opted not to pay taxes, thus putting the land back in the hands of the state (Jenkins and Keal 2004; Erickson 2009); and industrial gentry (the Morgans, Vanderbilts, Rockefellers, Lowes, McCormicks, etc.) seized high-amenity lands and lakes for 'great camps': lavish but rustic second-home woodland estates (Rezelman 1998). Presidents such as Theodore Roosevelt and Calvin Coolidge retreated to the Adirondacks to hunt and fish in much the same way that Queen Victoria repaired to Balmoral in what would become the CNP.

The magnificence of the Adirondacks was extolled by many in the nineteenth century. Verplanck Colvin, a surveyor of the era, wrote upon his ascent of Mount Seward: 'Wilderness everywhere: lake on lake, river on river, mountain on mountain, numberless' (Department of Environmental Conservation [DEC] 1977, 3). Colvin would later write of the wholesale plundering and mismanagement of the forests with little or no thought of conservation for the future (Flacke 1976). The voice of conservation had coalesced into a highly urban-based 'constituency for the Adirondacks' that pushed for wilderness protection. Further, a growing elite culture of conservation among wealthy industrialists coalesced into a natural pres-ervationist constituency; these actors purchased often from the same pool of tax-delinquent lands. By 1893, forty-five private preserves in the area included almost 950,000 acres (McMartin 1994; see also Gilborn 2009). Although these private efforts resulted in the preservation of many impor-tant resources, growing concerns about exclusivity resulted in the state blocking the sale of tax-delinquent lands[3] to private ownership in the final decades of the century (Graham 1978).

Haphazard though it was, the unregulated working landscape of the nineteenth century spawned a regulated counterpart late in the century. Protests over the audacious 'pillage and plunder' of the Adirondacks led New York State to create a Forest Preserve with its tax-delinquent lands in 1885 and, seven years later, to draw a 'blue line' on the map of northern New York designating a new AP (Van Valkenburgh 1985, 15). Two years later (1894), voters in the state amended the State Constitution to insure that the Preserve within the AP would be 'forever kept as wild forestlands'.

From 1892 on, then, state-centric conservation in the classical style played out in new AP legislation.[4] If citizens were offended by this rigid, top-down approach to conservation, they—by and large—kept it under wraps. Indeed, since 1895 to the founding of the APA in 1973, citizens of the state have defeated over one hundred attempts to amend or nullify that part of the State Constitution (Article XIV) that declares the Forest Preserve forever wild (Flacke 1976). This should not be construed to mean that people living within the park or depending on it for livelihood were sanguine about the new regime, nor to signify that the working landscape that arose in reaction to the industrial assault on the region was democratic by local standards. Urban constituents created their share of the problems and genteel urban conservationists largely 'solved' them by imposing their 'Eden'. Importantly, over half the lands in the AP were privately held when the APA was established, making further discussions about public goods, private prerogatives and the potential for working landscapes (under vari-ous names) inevitable.

Industrial landscapes were also significant in the Cairngorms prior to the CNP, although various kinds of recreational and symbolic use of the land also have a long history and have arguably been at least as impor-tant. Some landowning estates, particularly in the well-wooded Spey-side, engaged in commercial forestry as early as the eighteenth century, but cheaper imports from the Baltic Sea region later undercut domestic timber production (Miller 2009). State forestry began in 1919 although the largest expanses of forests were planted outside the main Cairngorms area. Instead, and similarly to elsewhere in Scotland and northern England, estates concentrated on combinations of farming in the valleys with field sports on the high ground and river banks. Angling and deer and grouse shooting provided recreational diversions for lairds, who were also able to sell access for hunting to tourists.

As in the Adirondacks, it was not uncommon for English intellectuals to travel to the mountains of Scotland to commune with nature. Yet, not all Englishmen came away inspired. Smout (2000) tells of English gentlemen visiting rural Scotland and being dismayed by its 'wilderness' and forbidding terrain, begging to be civilized. The landed elite of Scotland, whose feudal authority often stretched from 'horizon to horizon' (Wightman 1999), had a solution: game parks. Many among the aristocracy, wealthy from industrial exploits and colonial spoils, converted their land estates to deer parks, salmon fisheries and hunting aviaries. The mountains were particularly valued for their deer populations and the economic importance of that species. As Lorimer (2000, 439) has recently written: 'Matching the social standing of their human foe, Highland red deer were granted an antiquarian heritage and regal genealogy in the animal kingdom. A distinctive image first coloured from Edwin Landseer's palette, embedded the stag within the romance and wildness of a wilderness environment'. Landseer painted iconic Highland landscape and animal images in keeping with the 'imagined tradition' of Highland life (Trevor-Roper 1983). Park images thus circulated with powerful social class underpinnings that had their own 'conservation' narratives. Scotland's feudal land law notwithstanding, there are parallels with the vast estates ('great camps') in the AP, not the least being the shared sense of private park entitlement among elites. This preceded public park initiatives in the CNP and accompanied them in the AP.

Given the close association between the British monarchy (symbols of the nation *par excellence*) and the Cairngorms through Queen Victoria's rental and 1852 purchase of the Balmoral estate, one might expect the Cairngorms to have been designated as a national park at an early opportunity. Yet the first parks in England and Wales came into existence in 1951 and the royal connection with the Cairngorms remained similar to that of other lairds to their Highland estates: the consumption of leisure landscapes which, while not precluding paternalistic contact with local 'folk', certainly did not involve powers from without (such as regulatory bodies) having a significant say in how the estates were run. In the lead-up to the 1949 National Parks and Access to the Countryside Act, there had been a government committee to investigate the possibilities for national parks in Scotland, but there was then the perception that visitor pressure on the Scottish countryside was minor compared to the Lake District or Peak District in England (Crabtree 1991). Underlying this argument, however, was strong opposition from landowners and other interest groups such as the National Farmers Union, especially when sporting interests were deemed to be incompatible with national parks and full land nationalization was proposed instead (Shucksmith and Lloyd 1983). In 1974 the Countryside Commission for Scotland put forward further proposals for Scottish national parks, but again without success.

The changes that allowed national parks eventually to be introduced in Scotland were politically far-reaching. The Labour government elected in the UK in 1997 had promised constitutional reform, one aspect of which was devolution of political power to the nations and regions of the UK. In 1999 a Scottish Parliament convened for the first time since 1707 and among its earliest actions was legislation to enable national parks north of the border. The new Parliament unanimously passed the National Parks (Scotland) Act 2000, leading to the designation of the Loch Lomond and the Trossachs National Park in 2002 and the CNP in 2003. The national parks legislation was significant for the young Scottish Parliament (Rennie 2006) and showed how images and realities of rural Scotland continue to surface in broader discourses of restored nationhood. It was soon to be followed by a broader land reform agenda that has ended feudal land tenure and established new community rights to buy land and a general right of public access to the land. At the same time, for the Labour administration at UK and Scottish levels, national parks symbolized that nationhood can be attained without needing full political independence. Rennie argues that this was a subtle undercutting of the nationalist argument, although the continued progress of nationalist politics in Scotland leaves open the possibility that the parks may yet be adding to that momentum.

At face value, then, the two working landscapes featured in this chapter have little in common. The Adirondack Forest Preserve grew from 676,000 acres in 1894 to about 2.3 million acres today and spawned a larger park covering six million acres. The CNP then was not yet a glint in the eye of UK conservationists. Scottish conservation, when it came, was to become tangled up in the politics of Scottish sovereignty, land reform, nationalism and rural land laws over access and trespass. Yet British industrialisation and its rural spillovers bring to mind points of convergence in the two landscapes. Extractive economies were integral to rural Scotland (kelp, cattle, peat, wool) and provided jobs and livelihoods for significant local populations (MacGaskill 2005). Like the land-seeking elites of the Adirondacks, landowners in the Highlands removed much of the local population and restructured the economy for their agro-recreational needs (Shaw and Thompson 2006). Further, the working landscape of Scotland in the nineteenth and twentieth centuries thrived on private feudal land in which the owners of vast tracts were the virtual land-use planners and senior decision-makers of what was best for the land and ecosystems (Wightman 1999; Shaw and Thompson 2006; Bryden and Geisler 2010).

WORKING LANDSCAPE TIPPING POINT?

What, then, of the working landscapes of each site today, both cap-stoned with significant public park lands and formal governance bodies? Is there correspondence in their recent stories and in their lessons for conservation? What adaptations and experiments mark each effort, however different or similar they may be? How far do the management plans of each site speak to working landscapes? We end the section by considering what the main sources of impetus have been in both our cases, and other places like them.

The Adirondack Park

The AP was founded in 1892, but it was some eighty years later that the APA was created in response to second-home and highway growth in northern New York. The APA was created and has regulatory authority over all private lands within the AP using the AP Land Use and Development Plan, and advises the state's DEC on compliance with the AP State Land Master Plan. The DEC manages the public Forest Preserve under the 1972 State

Figure 13.5   Adirondack Park entrance sign.

Land Master Plan (Malmsheimer 2009). The AP Land Use and Development Plan serves twin purposes. It protects the natural and open space character of the AP while, at the same time, insures 'ample opportunities for growth and development in the Park' (APA 1980, 3). Specifically, the plan purports, according to the Laws of New York, 1885, Chapter 283, to 'insure optimum overall conservation, protection, preservation, development and use of the unique scenic, aesthetic, wildlife, recreational, open space, historic ecological and natural resources of the Adirondack Park'. Despite this language, elsewhere the purpose of the plan was to accommodate 'the complementary needs of all the people of the state for the preservation of the park's resource and open space character and of the park's permanent, seasonal, and transient populations for growth and service areas, employment, and a strong economic base' (Executive Law of New York, Article 27, S 801).

The plan divides private lands into six land-use classifications: industrial, hamlet, moderate intensity, low intensity, rural use and resource management. The first four refer to roughly 10 per cent of the private lands, the last two to the remainder. The plan assigns mandatory density guidelines and required permits for any building project thought by APA to have 'regional significance'. Importantly, 180 units of government (twelve counties, ninety-two towns, thirteen unincorporated villages and sixty-one school districts) have jurisdiction over portions of the park and receive grants and tax returns for projects and infrastructure from New York State (Jenkins and Keal 2004). The federal government, seemingly invisible in the park, is indirectly present: air-quality standards, regulating hydroelectric plant and transmission line regulation, wetland and biodiversity protection. More directly, its funds enable highways, schools and colleges, municipal facilities, environmental research and an important military base (Jenkins and Keal 2004). Though democracy is a hallmark of the United States in general, much day-to-day management of the park is undertaken by the APA and DEC, neither of which are elected branches of government.

As a practical matter central to the working landscape, if a local government adopts a land-use plan approved by the APA, discretion over regional building projects (i.e. granting or withholding development or reclassification permits) transfers from APA to the local government.[5] The vast majority of such projects have been approved by the APA. However, local governments have often been reluctant to prepare and adopt land-use plans on principle—and due to costs of administration—preferring instead to put the onus of permitting and regulation on the APA while retaining a 'local opposition' stance against central government planning (Terrie 1997). It would therefore be somewhat disingenuous to assume that the AP working landscape operates smoothly as an intergovernmental relationship, despite the structural presence of local government, incentives for partnership and an explicit commitment by locals to multiple-use principles.

In fact, several large and lively local government associations have appeared over the years to supplement, and sometimes counterbalance, the APA and DEC policies. The oldest is the AP Local Government Review Board, mandated in the APA Act (Executive Law Sections 801–810) 'for the purpose of advising and assisting the Adirondack park agency in carrying out its functions, powers and duties' (Section 803–a [1]) and dedicated to a multiple-use park model. More recently (2003), the Adirondack Citizens' Council emerged as a voice for recreational and business interests within the AP who derive pleasure and livelihood from both private and public lands therein. Thirdly, there is the Adirondack Association of Towns and Villages, formed in the early 1990s to amplify the leverage of local elected bodies in decisions central to the working landscape. It has a distinctly pro-economic development slant, as does the Adirondack North Country Association, which seeks to 'unite the communities within the blue line [boundary] of the park . . . to foster, protect, and to publicize in every way, the recreational, commercial, industrial, and civic interests beneficial to the territory defined'. Adding to the complexity, there are powerful environmental organisations that buy and sell land and increasingly engage in conservation while allowing some degree of job creation and sustainable development within the AP.

The Cairngorms National Park

In Scotland, national parks were not intended to identify and preserve wilderness, which was at the heart of the American national park ideal of Yosemite, Yellowstone and elsewhere. Section 1 of the National Parks (Scotland) Act 2000 lists the aims of the parks:

1. Conserve and enhance the natural and cultural heritage of the area.
2. Promote sustainable use of the natural resources of the area.
3. Promote understanding and enjoyment (including enjoyment in the form of recreation) of the special qualities of the area by the public.
4. Promote sustainable economic and social development of the area's communities.

Rather than following the American model, these aims relate to the International Union for the Conservation of Nature's Category V land, i.e. that which is significant because of the interaction of people and nature rather than despite it (Barker and Stockdale 2008, 183). In characterising the CNP, McCarthy, Lloyd and Illsley (2002, 670) echo Cannavò's refutation of both uncontrolled development and wilderness preservationist approaches to landscape planning: 'The Park areas will be working landscapes, needing economic and community stability as well as protection of the natural environment'. Although in Scotland's parks, some nature conservation organisations were concerned in the consultation process prior to the part's founding that not enough protection was being afforded to the environment, if there is conflict between two or more of the aims preference has to be given to conservation.

Both of Scotland's national parks are run by National Park Authorities. The Authorities have formal powers over planning and outdoor access but they are also tasked with a strategic role in promoting the aims of the park—the very idea of the park—amongst businesses, residents, visitors and public bodies. The Authorities do not own land and do not run visitor centres or other facilities themselves, which is a contrast to the AP. Currently, 75 per cent of land in the CNP is under private (mainly estate) ownership, and the rest is split roughly equally between non-governmental organisations, especially the National Trust for Scotland, who after a lengthy struggle eventually bought the Mar Lodge estate around Braemar in 1995 (itself 8 per cent of the park), and public organisations such as Scottish Natural Heritage and the Forestry Commission.

Current staffing in the CNPA is only around fifty but, along with the Loch Lomond and the Trossachs National Park, it is an interesting experiment in the governance of protected areas. Each park executive board has a directly elected component, which in the Cairngorms is five out of a total twenty-five members. Although this is a small proportion, the inclusion of elected members is rare if not unique internationally in national park management and largely absent in the AP. The Authority itself tends to work by incentives rather than regulations, encouraging farmers in the park to engage in pro-environment behaviour through positive management schemes and by attempting to develop a sense of shared responsibility for the park amongst businesses and the public. The CNPA informally hold to a metaphor of Wikipedia—a non-linear, non-hierarchical, shared community (as described by Murray Ferguson, head of Visitor Services at the CNPA, 10 February 2010), suggesting a concern with participative knowledge and openness rather than a centralized bureaucracy.

The presence of the national park is symbolic as well as material. Along its main roads, large granite slabs are carved with the new park logo—a stylised swooping osprey clutching a fish, likely a salmon—marking the entrances to the park. This logo is repeated on visitor signs and on some local products and services. It gives the park an identity beyond that of the bureaucratic or discursive, at once emphasizing the boundary with the outside and encouraging a common bond with nature within. Symbols legitimizing a sense of the working landscape, such as the farming, forestry or community life, on the other hand, are not closely associated with the national park, and this has been noted as a common pattern in regional rural branding logos in Europe (Vergunst et al. 2009). Indeed the Adirondacks have a rather similar virtual logo of a bird and mountain too (http://visitadirondacks.com/), if not actualised on the ground in the same way.

Figure 13.6   Entrance marker to the Cairngorms National Park, Deeside, Aberdeenshire.

A full evaluation of the successes or otherwise of the CNP is beyond the scope of this chapter, but some broad indications can be sketched. On one level the Authority has clearly been successful in raising awareness of the park and its aims, partly through a range of publications (e.g. maps, transport guides, visitor guides and newsletters for locals) and through maintaining a profile in other ways. This might seem insubstantial but plays into the creation of a distinctive place that simply did not exist on a social and political level before. Municipal boundaries converge in the Cairngorms, which produced a fragmented effect that limited planning capabilities in the mountains themselves. The Councils of Aberdeenshire, Angus, Highland and Moray, together with many other public bodies, now have a focus for those parts of their jurisdictions that are within the Cairngorms. However, the Strategic Review found that the Scottish National Park Authorities had fared less well in gaining a national voice for the parks (Scottish Government 2008a, 18), reflecting perhaps the overriding concern to engage with local communities in their early years. Ironically, it may be that the Scottish National Parks provide a model of *local* governance for the future.

Stockdale and Barker have assessed sustainable development in both national parks in Scotland in regard to the IUCN's Category V land described earlier, and examined sustainability in the Cairngorms park specifically

(Barker and Stockdale 2008; Stockdale and Barker 2009). They are positive in recognising that the structures and processes involved in managing the parks reflect multiple environment, social and economic criteria that are novel in national parks. The Authority is beginning to be involved in environmental work through co-management partnerships with landowners, in which the latter need to demonstrate how their land management is contributing to the conservation aims of the park.

Of continuing concern on a landscape level is deer management, as they can be a severe hindrance to regeneration of woodland in the Cairngorms. Efforts are under way to encourage estates to work together in monitoring deer location and produce effective management schemes. The Authority is also supporting specific programmes such as the Cairngorms Water Vole Conservation project, whereby volunteers help monitor and trap American mink, ultimately to remove the species from the Cairngorms (Evely et al. 2008). Support for the Capercaillie bird also reflects concern with native rather than 'alien' species. Community involvement in many of these activities encourages a sense of local ownership and engagement that counters the association of nature conservation with urban outsiders (Mackenzie 2006b). Visitor access is another important management issue. Visitors are encouraged to come to the park but to voluntarily stay to the paths to avoid damage to sensitive habitats (see Blackstock et al. 2008). Car-park charging has also been a contentious issue in recent years (Phillip and Macmillan 2006). In these policy areas, the national parks may be forerunners of public practices to be rolled out elsewhere in Scotland in future years.

Specific social and economic data that evaluate management success in CNP are hard to come by. The Scottish Government's Strategic Review (2008a, 13) noted the possibility that through partnerships the Authority may be gaining benefits for the region that are hard to attribute to the Authority itself. The Authority's planning prerogatives will no doubt become an important function, and although the timescale of twenty-five years in the National Parks Plan suggests that quick results should not be expected, the scale of ambition is considerable. The plan's social and economic objectives address working landscape themes that will be recognised by anyone familiar with similar rural areas. It aims, for example, to maintain population and especially younger people while providing services to the ageing population, to secure higher quality and more year-round jobs, and (more in the context of CNP) to cluster housing development in existing settlements. Although it eschews zoning land for development, it is beginning to produce and use maps of 'wildness' that factor various human and physical criteria into colour-graded maps that can be used in planning decisions. The Authority's own interim reports are positive, but if the park achieves its goals by 2030—by no means the distant future—it will be a model of working landscape success. This is especially so given its current (2009–2010) budget of £4.5 million p.a., relatively small for national parks. With this in mind, Stockdale and Barker (2009, 488) sound a note of caution: 'The Cairngorms National Park Plan is stronger in intent than in the means to deliver'. To maintain their working landscape objectives, the CNPA will need to contend with serious challenges to its rural economy, society and environment.

THE IMPETUS FOR CHANGE: WHAT'S DRIVING WORKING LANDSCAPES?

The historical contexts we have described in this chapter are very significant for what we identify as 'working landscapes'. Power relations around extractive industries, landownership and political control on national and international levels have not only shaped the regions in the past, but are at the forefront of people's awareness as they act in the present too. As a result, the ethic of environmentalism as wilderness conservation—as if the land was or should be empty of human influence—has been increasingly discredited, and contemporary actors instead connect with the histories of land use in their regions.

However, a key impetus for action amongst many people in the parks is a desire to reshape the social relations underpinning that land use. Rather than drawing on and supplying global circuits of labour and capital, an alternative dynamic asserts the importance of development on a regional scale that involves a more localised model of environmental sustainability and democratic control. It has in part been the regional development sphere—and a parallel, if partial, withdrawal from the discourse of globalisation—that has contributed to the parks reflecting the notion of working landscape. In Europe, regional identities and forms of governance are becoming well attested as an alternative rural development strategy (see Hewitt and Thompson, this volume; Árnason, Shucksmith and Vergunst 2009), and parks are in a strong position to formalise and join up these activities.

MacLellan (2007) offers several insights with respect to Scotland in general and the CNP in particular. Noting that national parks in the UK are known for being 'lived in' and fall more appropriately in IUCN Category V protected areas than Category II, MacLellan accounts for this in two ways. One has to do with the truism that older parks dedicated to conserving nature were founded before population settlement became a counterforce, which had seemed to be the case in the US (though histories of Yosemite Park, for example, now describe how the landscape had been extensively managed by the pre-colonial indigenous population; see Olwig 1995). Conversely, Britain passed its first national park law in 1949 and Scotland only in 2000. This posed a costly expropriation dilemma for any park model that excluded people. Beyond this pragmatism, MacLellan argues that integrating conservation with sustainable development and well-managed tourism means much-needed income streams:

Today, everybody wants a piece of the park, in particular local communities that recognised the potential development value the designation brings. The regional development imperative has been acute in Western European peripheral areas resulting from declining values in traditional agricultural produce. Tourism has been promoted as one means of economic diversification and protected areas often form a key part of the destination visitor attraction mix. (2007, 181)

A third motivation posed by MacLellan is more stick than carrot. In the recent past, he claims, Scotland was condemned by the World Conservation Union for its weak conservation efforts. National parks, even those that in practice were to be working landscapes, were a significant strengthening of the conservation position. Though this has not been a driver for working landscapes in the AP, his first two arguments—pragmatism and sustainable regional development—are highly plausible forces for 'lived-in landscapes' in North America as well as Scotland.

CONCLUSION

In this chapter, we have subscribed to the notion of working landscapes as places where change and stability coexist with evolving democratic and ecological principles. We suggested that whether a park evolves toward a working landscape, as in the AP case, or the working landscape is retrofit with park status, as in the CNP, conservation is shifting away from fixed land uses and authority hierarchies towards lived-in, adaptive, experimental relationships where 'nature' is socially constructed and symbolized. Our parks are thus based on a rejection of both industrialisation and wilderness conservation ethics, and instead draw on regional development models that include, to variable degrees, local identity, democratic involvement and participation. The impetus towards working landscapes has been provided by this combination of shifting economic and ecological rationalities and a political drive towards inclusivity in the management of protected areas. Cannavò (2007, 219–258) emphasizes regional democracy and public participation as a key principle underlying successful 'governance of places', and this aspect will be significant to both our cases, and others like them, in the future.

Indeed, a working landscape is an interplay between founding forces and preservation as processes rather end-points. As attested by their ambitious future-oriented management plans, the parks are distinctly unfinished and incomplete compared to the more traditional notion of monumental national parks—a case of working landscape in the sense of a work-in-progress. In the AP, founding was contentious, elongated and prone to by-pass local public involvement: preservation rooted in the American wilderness ideal emerged in reaction to wanton exploitation of the region's timber and mineral reserves and out of concern that metropolitan water supplies were at risk. The CNP park founding was relatively sudden, laden with nationalism and attentive to local understandings of nature and access to it. Local identity and voice against 'outside, urban environmental interests' have been operative in the AP and the CNP. While in the latter, there was concern over the control exercised by a small number of powerful and entrenched landowners, symbolic connections were made between them and urban environmentalists as unwelcome voices (Mackenzie 2006b). Nature conservation plans that are couched in local initiative and ownership seem much more likely to succeed. Identity conflicts continue in AP, and remain acrimonious as traditional productivist (e.g. forestry and mining) activities continue to decline. By contrast, the CNP committed early on to providing inclusive local governance, especially in relation to the environment. This may follow from the prominence of agriculture in rural Scotland and governance traditions that have built on it. Agriculture was and is rare in the AP; its more contentious urban-extractive working landscape lacks an obvious local governance counterpart. Both parks are veering away from 'pristine wilderness' discourse and towards a stronger embrace of tourism as an industry in which insiders and outsiders may yet find common ground.

14 Regionalism and Rural Policy

Sally Hewitt and Nicola Thompson

INTRODUCTION

Undertaking a transatlantic dialogue on regionalism and its implications for rural policy is challenging. First, our research highlights important differences in understandings of what is meant by *regionalism*. What is described as regionalism in the US and what is meant in the UK are very different in terms of scale and process. Second, distinctions within the devolved UK means that regionalism can only be meaningfully talked about in the English context rather than in the UK overall. However, while its importance is largely confined to England, regionalism has had major implications for the development and delivery of rural policy over the last decade, which makes it an important dimension of rural transformation in the UK more generally.

While English regionalism has had a profound effect on rural affairs, this has not always been the case in the US. The common thread in understandings of the term is an emphasis on improving coordination to enhance economic performance (Jonas and Ward 2002). Regionalism in the US is essentially bottom-up, driven by private and voluntary interests and occurring where these interests are able to mobilise through partnership structures. In contrast regionalism in England was a deliberate programme of national government imposed across the country, dominated by public agencies, which has now been altered due to a change in national policy. While in America regionalism was understood as fundamentally centralizing, involving the pooling of 'local' competencies for the sake of effective coordination, in England regionalism is conceived as a form of devolution or decentralization (Pearce, Ayres and Tricker 2005).

Across the globe decentralizing power from the nation-state to 'lower' tiers of government is widely regarded as enabling decisions to be made 'closer to the people' and enhancing coordination (Brenner 2004). Our primary concern in this chapter is to highlight the implications of the transfer of powers and competencies from the national to the regional level for rural territories in the English context. The absence of directly comparative changes in the US means that our analysis necessarily focuses on England. In tracing these implications we demonstrate how state-sponsored regionalism has had far-reaching consequences for rural affairs, impacting on policies and programmes for rural communities in subtle but often significant ways. The experience of the last decade raises questions on the future of regionalism England and, more broadly, on appropriate governance arrangements for the facilitation of rural development.

The chapter is organised around three sections. In the first we compare and contrast regionalism and rural policy in the US and England. The subsequent subsections draw on empirical work. The second section sets out the implications of regionalism for the administration of rural affairs. This is founded on a number of research projects conducted over the last eight years which have involved both interviews with rural development practitioners and participant observation of various meetings and forums. The third section focuses in more detail on perceptions of regionalism amongst those involved in rural affairs at the regional and local levels in two case study regions—the north-west and the east of England. In conclusion we highlight the implications of the regionalisation of rural affairs for the practice of rural development in England and why, following a change of government in the UK in 2010, the regional institutions are being dismantled.

As noted, this chapter focuses on England rather than the UK, but as this book compares the UK and US an explanation of the absence of Scotland, Wales and Northern Ireland is needed. Classically political scientists differentiate between nation-states using the classification federal, con-federal and unitary. The UK is often misleadingly classified as 'unitary' rather than the more appropriate understanding of a 'union' state (Bogdanor 2009). Infamously uncodified, the UK Constitution operates so that the institutional structures in the four nations of the UK are distinctive from each other and have always related to the UK government and Parliament in different ways (Bogdanor 1999). Hence while Scotland, Wales and Northern Ireland have Parliaments and Assemblies with various (asymmetrical) powers, England is governed through the UK Parliament with no directly democratic institutions between the central state and local government. Instead, between 1997 and 2010 (when a new government began to abolish most of the regional tier) England had a series of unelected regional institutions whose powers derived directly from the UK state.

REGIONALISM IN THE US AND ENGLAND

A range of academic literature highlights how regionalism in the US is driven by economic and regeneration concerns. American regionalism is focused on how to achieve higher levels of economic growth and ensure fiscal efficiency (Jonas and Pincetl 2006). In England, while tax policy is not determined at the regional level, economic growth and development has been the predominant concern of proponents of regionalism (Pike and Tomaney 2009). However, additional rationales based on political and administrative efficiency, cultural identity and Europeanisation have also been employed. In England, then, a fuller range of regionalisation imperatives are evident than in the US.

Regionalism in the US has, however, also been used as a means of tackling urban decline (Elcock 2003) with regions constructed as the basis of economic life and hence the most appropriate scale of regeneration intervention (Amin and Thrift 1994). It is most frequently seen as a reaction to the deep-seated problems of metropolitan areas, especially those localities experiencing negative growth and depopulation. These problems cannot be tackled by any one district or county. Hence regionalism is used as an instrument to effect coordination and collaborative working at a scale above the local but below the state (Elcock 2003; Jonas and Pincetl 2006). While predominantly focused on metropolitan areas there are some examples of rural regionalism (see Hamin and Marcucci 2008), but these are the exception rather than the norm.

Regionalism in the US is depicted as a grassroots phenomenon. It is typically driven by private and voluntary sector organisations working in partnership to tackle development issues (Jonas and Pincetl 2006; Hamin and Marcucci 2008). These partnerships often involve public bodies, especially local government, but the extent of government involvement varies across the country. In California the private sector has been the catalyst for growth in regional initiatives (Jonas and Pincetl 2006) whereas empirical work in Columbus, Ohio, highlights the role of local government in attempts to address the fragmentation of metropolitan governance (Cox 2010). In terms of institutional structures, regionalism in the US is closely associated with the formation of cooperative, voluntary partnerships which draw together private, not-for-profit and public bodies. The voluntary and bottom-up nature of regionalism in America results in an 'ad hoc' or asymmetrical pattern of governance arrangements. This has been described by Christopherson (2010, 232) as a 'sea of competitive regional islands'. It also results in fragmentation and a huge diversity in what regionalism means in practice.

The English regions of the 1997–2011 period comprised both urban centres and areas defined as rural. The entire country was divided into regions so that nowhere was left out. Regional institutions were public sector organisations created and funded by central government but supporting a series of partnerships which drew in private sector and voluntary organisations. Policy discourse at the national and regional levels tended to depict the cities as the engines of economic growth with the rural perceived as peripheral 'hinterland' (Caffyn and Dahlström 2005; Ward and Lowe 2001). Coordination across urban centres within regions was a key element of the legitimizing rhetoric used by English regionalists. English regionalism was a project of central government with mixed support from local authorities and various regionalist political movements. It was highly politicized with the major political parties taking radically different stances. This is explained further in the second section of the chapter.

English regional institutions were mainly funded by, and derived their powers from, national government. They focused on economic development, planning, transport and some aspects of environmental policy. In addition, regional institutions had a role in coordinating and monitoring the public programmes delivered by local government and the third sector. By contrast, in the US the non-statutory status of regionalist initiatives means that there is no common set of competencies and responsibilities, although the areas of transport, planning, environment and regeneration are recurrent themes (Elcock 2003). While rural policy figures in the remit of English regional institutions there is little evidence that regionalism in the US is formally linked with state-sponsored programmes of rural development, although the differentiated nature of arrangements across the country will inevitably mean that there have been geographically specific implications for rural areas.

Rural policy in both the US and England has historically been strongly associated with agriculture to the extent that rural and agricultural policies have often been seen as one and the same (Bryden and Warner, this volume). In the US the United States Department of Agriculture (USDA) has traditionally had lead responsibility for rural policy with the result that it is primarily formulated at the national level and is dominated by major agricultural support programmes (Freshwater 1999; Radin 1996). In England, agriculture policy has also been dominant, with the result that wider socio-economic policy has tended to be fragmented and comparatively poorly resourced. In the last decade agriculture and rural affairs have been brought together at the national level in the Department for Environment, Food and Rural Affairs (DEFRA). DEFRA remains dominated by policies and programmes to support the land-based sector. Crucially DEFRA, and the other central government departments and agencies with rural affairs responsibilities, have been subject to almost continual changes in the way in which they are structured. Up to 2010 this involved increasingly working through the regional organisations, including regional economic regeneration agencies (Goodwin 2008; Ward, Lowe and Bridges 2003).

In the US, programmes such as the National Rural Development Partnership and Empowerment Zone and Enterprise Community (EZEC) have targeted localities to incentivise territorial rural development (Bryden and Warner, this volume). These national programmes have been delivered through the formation of local partnerships. The participation of a range of local organisations and individuals is central to the rhetoric of the rural partnership model. Hence the national programmes involve substantial organisational development at the community level as partnerships organised to achieve developmental goals. Rural policy on this model is characterised by the operation of a national framework orientated around community empowerment and collaboration, although in practice over recent years there has also been an emphasis on tax credits to support private rather than community investment.

This basic analysis of how rural policy is delivered in the two countries helps us to understand the fundamental differences in the way in which regionalism and rural policy relate to each other. In the US there is generally no formal interrelationship between the two, whereas in England, critical elements of rural policy have been devolved from the national to the regional level during the 1997–2010 period. The effect is an element of regional distinctiveness in rural policy, albeit within a broader European and national framework.

REGIONALISATION AND RURAL POLICY IN ENGLAND

In this section we examine the growth of the English regions and explain the role of the key institutions in relation to rural affairs. First we provide a brief overview of the two key regional bodies before looking in more detail at how regionalisation has impacted on the implementation of the major programme for rural development in England. A map of the English regions is provided in Figure 14.1 with our two case studies highlighted.

Figure 14.1 The English regions.

Regional Development Agencies

The creation of regional institutions was designed to provide an enabling framework that would actively promote economic development appropriate to that territory. Established in 1999, the Regional Development Agencies (RDAs) were seen as the primary means of providing this framework. The RDAs had a common mission statement: 'to transform England's regions through sustainable economic development'. They had considerable financial resources at their disposal to achieve this mission. In the financial year 2009–2010 total RDA funding was £2,260 million. Allocations to each RDA differed markedly. The North-west Development Agency received £398 million while the East of England Development Agency budget was less than half this at £136 million (Department for Business, Innovation and Skills 2010). Multiple national government departments contributed to the RDA budgets. These contributions were pooled together to make up a 'single pot' over which the RDAs had considerable autonomy in investment decisions. In addition to their financial power the agencies also produced Regional Economic Strategies, designed to provide a strategic overview of the economic situation of the region and to guide public sector–led regeneration in both urban and rural areas.

Each of the RDAs, with the exception of London, had a rural team from their inception. These groups were initially created through the transfer of regeneration functions and staff from a national rural development agency. The rural remit of the RDAs grew steadily over the 1999–2010 period (Woods 2008). Most significantly, in terms of funding for rural development, RDAs took on key funding streams of the EU's Rural Development Regulation 2007–2013, enacted in England as the Rural Development Programme for England (RDPE). RDAs were given responsibility for the economic and social measures in the programme including the LEADER approach (see also Bryden and Warner, this volume). The national RDPE budget for the RDAs was set at £536 million. Individual RDAs were then allocated total RDPE budgets ranging from £48 million in the north-east region to £102m in the south-west region (DEFRA 2008c).

The scale of investment made by the RDAs, accompanied by their relative autonomy in decision-making, meant that RDAs were always politically contentious institutions. The Conservative Party persistently criticized them on the basis of value for money and the lack of direct democratic accountability. With the election of a new Conservative/Liberal Democrat coalition government in May 2010, the abolition of RDAs was quickly announced. Many functions were taken back into national government. For example, the administration of European rural development funds was assigned directly to DEFRA. Other functions, such as the requirement for a regional economic strategy, simply disappeared. Instead, it was announced that partnerships between businesses and local government could bid for national regeneration funds. Partnerships were expected to be formed for 'natural economic regions' thus rejecting the standardised administrative regions.

Government Offices

In contrast to the economic development focus of the RDAs, an agenda around coordinated government drove the initial creation of Government Offices in each of the regions (Winter 2006). First established in 1995, the Government Offices grew rapidly in terms of personnel and areas of responsibility in the 2000s. The Government Offices enabled the UK state to implement policies and programmes from a wide range of government departments in ways which, depending on perspective, allowed for tailoring to regional circumstance or the more effective extension of central government control. The Government Offices rapidly evolved to create a conduit through which the central state gathered information on the social, economic and environmental condition of the regions. The Government Office network also formed a convenient way to deliver major European programmes to fit with a wider European regional structure.

The Government Offices in the regions hosted various forums and partnerships focused on understanding what was happening 'on the ground' in order to deliver regional intelligence to central government. This included a forum on rural affairs in each of the regions. 'Regional Rural Sounding Boards' or 'Rural Affairs Forums' were announced in the English Rural White Paper of 2000. The narrative of government at that time was that there was a need to 'listen to the rural voice' (M. Woods 2008). For over a decade these rural forums helped to define the region as the scale at which to identify and tackle 'rural problems'. In addition, they provided some means of monitoring the activities of regional institutions from the perspective of community and business representatives. The Coalition government announced the abolition of Government Offices within weeks of being elected in 2010. This was justified in terms of a desire to devolve certain functions to the local rather than a regional level and to take back other functions into national government.

Regionalisation and the RDPE

Throughout the 1997–2010 period there was a strong interrelationship between evolution of rural policy and the process of regionalisation (Goodwin 2008). Regional institutions were required to establish rural forums, make rural plans and deliver rural funding programmes. The major example of this regionalised approach to rural policy is the RDA role in the RDPE during the 2007–2013 programming period. From 2005 the RDAs began to prepare regional plans showing how they would implement the EU rural development programme, choosing from the menu of 'measures' incorporated in the national plan, setting out how they would select LEADER areas and creating the necessary administrative bureaucracy. DEFRA took a non-interventionist stance, merely coordinating overall activity and undertaking the monitoring and reporting required by the EU.

A divergence in the regional plans could be expected to result from this devolution to the relatively autonomous RDAs. Analysis of each RDA's plan for the RDPE does show significant differences between the English regions. There were significant variations in the funding measures used. For example, with regard to vocational training, the East Midlands devoted 7 per cent of the total budget compared to 40 per cent in the West Midlands and south-west. The percentage share of regional funds allocated to a measure on 'cooperation for the development of new products' ranged from 6 per cent in the East Midlands and south-east to 21 per cent and 24 per cent in the south-west and north-east. There are similar variations in many of the other measures, suggesting that distinctive choices were made in each region.

There were also significant differences between regions in the activities that LEADER local action groups were involved in. The north-west, north-east and south-east regions opted for all or most of the fifteen measures to be available to local groups. In contrast, the other regions chose to focus on a narrower range, with the Yorkshire and the Humber region electing to concentrate on three measures. Differences in the commitment to LEADER as a way of doing rural development was evident in the scale of the total funds allocated to it. The north-east planned to spend about 6 per cent of the funds for improving the economic state of agriculture through LEADER, whereas the north-west planned to spend 20 per cent and the south-east 17 per cent via this approach.

Variations in the plans for each region could indicate that choices were made to reflect the distinctive rural context and development needs of the region as a whole. The differences could be argued to have been 'devolution in action' and there is some evidence which supports this argument. The regional plans included an analysis of regional challenges and in-depth examination of how the RDPE could assist in addressing them. Hence spending priorities were directly linked to analysis of the state of the rural region and its development needs. However, the differences in the percentages allocated to each RDPE measure cannot be accounted for solely in terms of the variability of rural economic and social conditions from region to region. It seems implausible that the differences between adjacent regions were so great that differences in the allocation of funds can be traced back solely to an examination of regional strengths, weaknesses, opportunities and threats.

Documentary analysis, in combination with interview research and observation of regional and national events, leads us to the conclusion that there are two factors which accounted for divergence in addition to regional context. First, the EU and national plans were interpreted very differently in each region. Decisions on how to go about delivering the RDPE relied on the interpretation of a complex European Regulation by small numbers of individuals often with limited prior experience of EU rural development policy. A national discourse of not interfering in regional decision-making enhanced the importance of this interpretation. Second, the prevailing culture within each RDA favours some measures and modes of delivery over others. It could be argued that the RDAs tended to see the RDPE as an opportunity to develop their rural activity according to their own wider regional priorities, rather than a task to be undertaken in order to contribute to the EU's policy objectives or participatory local development. Hence objectives that did not accord with each RDA's priorities were marginalised or excluded. In summary, the RDAs took the decisions on programme design that they were empowered to make (within the constraints of the EU and national frameworks). The agencies made these decisions in the context of wider regional objectives set out in plans such as the Regional Economic Development Strategies.

Regionalisation of the RDPE not only resulted in regional divergence, it also drove homogenisation within regions. For example, analysis of the strategies of each LEADER group within the three northern English regions revealed very limited intraregional differentiation despite the emphasis on local-level planning and objective setting inherent in LEADER philosophy. Similarities within regions are explained by the need to work to a common regional process that ensures local strategies cohere with regional ones. LEADER groups bid to the RDAs for funds on the basis of a plan that addressed the priorities of the regional strategies. The result was consistency in terms of the measures and funding allocations used by LEADER groups. However, as the challenges faced within the areas varied significantly, it could be expected that the bids would reflect this high degree of diversity. The lack of intraregional variation suggests that decentralization did not extend below the regional level. Rather the reverse was the case with local variation tending to succumb to wider imperatives.

PERCEPTIONS OF REGIONALISM: FINDINGS FROM CASE STUDIES IN RURAL ENGLAND

The regionalisation of rural policy transformed the way in which rural policies and programmes were delivered in England from 1997 until 2010. In this section we draw on empirical work for Hewitt's doctoral thesis carried out in 2008–2009 to examine how rural actors reflect upon their engagement with the regional institutions. The empirical work consisted of a series of semi-structured interviews with key local and regional actors in two English regions (the north-west and east of England) supplemented with observation of regional rural meetings and events. The research data was analysed using a Foucauldian discourse analysis. This section reports the findings on 'discourses of response', the ways in which those involved in rural development construct regionalism. Typically from local government, the not-for-profit sector and business organisations, they broadly adopt three positions, though it is important to note that the discourses are ideal types and actors drew on multiple discourses. The 'responses' were evident across the groups, who played a variety of roles in the facilitation of rural development and many of whom were directly involved in the implementation of the RDPE.

The three discourses of response were: (1) 'buying into' regionalism; (2) 'reluctant' regionalism and (3) 'local autonomy'. 'Buying into regionalism' involved accepting that the region should lead and that this was the 'right' scale to act with regard to the regeneration of rural localities. In the second discourse of 'reluctant regionalism', people were motivated to engage in order to influence regional activities and ensure access to funding. There was a sense of 'making the best' of the institutional arrangements. However, this was tempered by a lack of enthusiasm because actors did not fully 'buy into' the regionalism discourse. They guarded their ability to influence decisions and activities but could only do so by engaging with the regional institutions and their networks. In the third discourse of 'local autonomy' regionalism was rejected and the political imperative to devolve decisions to local elected bodies asserted. These people chose not to engage with the region, or did so highly reluctantly whilst voicing their opposition and seeking change to the systems of regional governance.

Buying into Regionalism

'Buying into regionalism' involved the acceptance of the institutional structures and premises of regionalism. Those who bought into regionalism willingly took part in alliances that supported the growth and development of the regional level. There were different groups associated with this response. The first group was from agencies of national government. Regionalisation strengthened joint working between these national agencies and the regional bodies. The national agencies had established regional offices, often co-located with Government Offices. Two, Natural England and the Forestry Commission, together with the RDAs, were all involved in the delivery of different elements of the RDPE. Hence they shared a common objective of making a regionalised system of the delivery of rural policy and programmes work. People in these agencies identified with their region and reinforced its construction as an appropriate political/administrative unit through their articulations of policy issues. In short, the challenges of rural areas often became part of the broader regional development narrative for those working for national government within the region.

The second group of actors who bought into regionalism came from the not-for-profit sector. These people saw a benefit to operating at the regional scale. For example, the Rural Community Councils (RCCs) in the north-west perceived that joint working with the regional bodies in the early years of regionalisation could result in significant gains in terms of access to finance and ability to influence the regional agenda. As one north-west RCC member explained:

> We jointly established a company . . . called North-West Rural Community Councils, to wave that regional structure flag. That enabled us to get the seat on the North-West Rural Strategy Board. We also use the flag in the North-West Rural Affairs Forum and we've used it in our negotiations with the Development Agency.

A close working relationship had positive consequences for all parties in this case. The regional institutions benefitted from being able to engage the rural community sector through working with one corporate body whose boundaries were co-terminus with that of the region. For the RCCs, the regional structure allowed them access to networks and grant money which would have been harder to obtain as individual, county-based organisations.

Reluctant Regionalism

Both of the discourses of 'buying into regionalism' and 'reluctant regionalism' were shaped by perceptions of what could be achieved by working with regional institutions. However, the distinguishing feature of reluctant regionalism was a lack of enthusiasm, unwillingness and frustration that had to be curtailed or managed if the benefits of collaboration were to be reaped. An example from Essex Rural Community Council in the east of England region shows an attitude of frustration although action was taken to align to regional priorities in order to access funding:

> To put it bluntly and simply, when I wanted my £1,000 from the regional forum I had to draw up priorities for funding that linked with the delivery framework.

Similarly, and in contrast to the regional networking of RCCs in the north-west region, Cambridgeshire RCC (also in the east of England) chose to refocus its work on county-based networks and local partners, developing relations with regional institutions only where funding programmes such as the RDPE required it. The experience here was that working with the regional level was often difficult, with good relations only maintained for the sake of access to funding. Reluctance and opposition was rarely articulated in official documents and meetings but was apparent in individual interviewees on the detailed workings of relations with regional bodies.

Rural local authorities may arguably have had more freedom to express reluctance and opposition as they were less directly dependant on grant income from the regional tier. However, in practice there were significant financial and political constraints on how they could conduct their

relationships with regional bodies. Keeping up an appearance of cooperation was a necessity if the local area was not to lose out on regional development funds. There were also party political reasons why the region had
to be lived with. The need to get on with the regional institutions for pragmatic reasons was commonly expressed by local government actors in both
the case study regions.

Those who expressed 'reluctant regionalism' from both local government and the not-for-profit sector emphasized two causes of this reluctance.
The first was the lack of willingness, especially on the part of the RDAs, to
allow local rural stakeholders to fully participate in decisions on rural policies and to play more active roles in running funding programmes. Some got
involved in order to secure participation but often found that this was constrained and conditional. The second cause related to different understandings of what the problems and issues of rural areas were. The interviewees
tended to be interested in particular topics of concern. For example, a local
authority respondent in the east of England spoke of the need to reconcile
the differences in rural economic and social structures across the county he
worked in. An RCC interviewee in the same region was championing the
cause of rural shops. In the north-west region one of the interviewees was
focusing on fuel poverty as the issue of primary concern. When these local
concerns were not incorporated into regional rural policy actors questioned
the depth of understanding of rural affairs at the regional level.

The discourse of reluctant regionalism accepts that 'it is better to
engage, than not to engage'. Actors sought to introduce their understandings of rural issues into debates at the regional scale in order to influence policy and funding allocations. For many, regionalisation created a
necessity to participate in order to maintain the flow of funding. Finally,
another factor that prompted engagement was, in the words of another
east of England interviewee:

> If the region didn't exist you would to some extent have an even worse
> situation where the direction was very much set by the urban centres.

There was a fear that without regionalism the rural could cease to be an
object of policy at all. In those circumstances, for reluctant regionalists,
it was better to retain a regional infrastructure with a rural development
component than no mechanism for rural support outwith the agriculture-
dominated European programmes.

Local Autonomy

Those who articulated the local autonomy discourses fundamentally
opposed regionalism. They disputed the legitimacy of regional leadership
and the existence of regional identities within England. In practice, local
autonomy was expressed by a quiet lack of engagement as well as vocal

opposition. Most of the expressions of local autonomy in the case studies come from local authority interviewees. Respondents from Cumbria (north-west region) and Cambridgeshire (east of England) County Councils provide examples of quiet disengagement, whereas Essex County Council (east of England) was at the forefront of campaigning against regionalism (Hanningfield 2009).

The interviewee from Cambridgeshire County Council expressed significant discontent with the stance and actions of regional decision-makers on the basis that they were not attuned to what was happening within localities. This resonated with the concerns of the reluctant regionalists, but resulted in a different response. Where local autonomy was the prevailing discourse, elected politicians and paid officials were only partially involved with regional institutions and networks. In the case of Cambridgeshire this partial involvement amounted to a limited number of officials working to run regional funding programmes in the county and one elected member sitting on the regional Rural Affairs Forum. This involved occasional attendance at forum meetings to ensure that they were seen to be engaged at a basic level. The dominant response, expressed by the senior officials in the Authority, was to 'carry on with the day job' of fulfilling the statutory purposes of local government and not to engage with the regional players on anything other than an 'ad hoc', pragmatic basis.

In Cumbria, the County Council interviewee was more strident in his criticism of regional governance. However, in formal forums he maintained similar behaviour patterns as the Cambridgeshire actors. This was in order to ensure that the 'funding tap' was not turned off. He considered that his understanding of Cumbria's rural issues and appropriate policy responses was not shared by regional actors, and could see no way of changing regional working in a way which would accommodate his views on rural development in the county. The prevalent regional development model was argued to assume that rural dwellers are reliant on towns and that the towns should be at the centre of development initiatives. The view of the Cumbrian interviewee was that regional actors simply apply these models without reflecting on what it means for localities.

Regional leadership had no legitimacy in the 'local autonomy' discourse but even those who subscribed to this perception of regionalism were forced to work with 'the region' in various ways. A stance of quiet, partial engagement minimized political conflict for the sake of access to funding.

The interviewee from Essex County Council (east of England) voiced a more confident version of local autonomy:

> Who are these people in Cambridge to be telling us to put 143,000 homes in Essex? We'll build where we want, thank you very much.

This stance, also broadly reflected in the public proclamations of other members of the Authority, was driven by a political belief that regional governance should be abolished because it was unaccountable to local people (see also Hanningfield 2009, 39). The leaders of Essex County Council concluded that locally determined policies and local solutions should not be subservient to programmes determined by a tier of unelected agencies. The Essex interviewee also cited the lack of regional identity in support of local autonomy. On this account, if the region is not a cultural entity, policy responses cannot legitimately be conceived for it.

In practice there was engagement between officers of Essex County Council and the regional structures. There were occasions when it was critical for the council to work with the RDA in order to draw down funds. Nevertheless, the dominant discourse on regionalism in this case was that it emasculates the local and was unnecessary. In contrast to the fears of the reluctant regionalists that without the region 'the rural' would struggle to achieve any political and policy attention, proponents of local autonomy viewed the regional level as largely an unnecessary irrelevance. Indeed, one actor said:

> I don't think it would really affect us that much if the region wasn't there.

The three discourses of response to regionalism are characterisations which necessarily gloss over some important nuances. In reality individual actors are more multifaceted and can exemplify more than one of the discourses of response dependent on the specific example they were referring to. What the discourses illuminate, however, are the complex patterns of cooperation and resistance which arose as a result of regionalisation.

CONCLUSIONS

In England, throughout the period of regionalisation, attention focused on transforming institutions and governance structures using a rhetoric of decentralization. There were a series of changes in rural governance as a result, including the incorporation of key elements of rural policy into regional bodies. National institutional frameworks were dismantled or downgraded, split up into regions or explicitly not permitted to 'do delivery'. The integration of rural policy into wider regional policy had the result that, depending on perspective, rural concerns were 'mainstreamed' into regional regeneration initiative or marginalised in the quest to invest in major projects in the urban areas.

Within the regions, policy tended to be formulated on the basis that the 'the rural' consists of a relatively homogenous territory. Policy formulation at a regional scale had the effect of restricting the choices available at the local level in some instances. This represented a change from previous territorial rural programmes, in particular the operation of the LEADER programmes in earlier periods where decisions on priorities were explicitly made in a local context. Prior to regionalisation there was a higher degree of local autonomy in detailed objective setting, albeit within the constraints of national and European frameworks.

The regionalisation of rural policy also impacted on funding for capacity-building and work to facilitate wider participation in rural development, long recognised by researchers as critical aspects of successful rural development initiative (Shucksmith 2000a). The political imperative for RDAs to transform the economic fortunes of their region meant a focus on the economic at the expense of 'the social'. It also resulted in incentives to invest in large projects and to focus on the tangible at the expense of building social and human capital. The depiction of RDAs in the 'discourses of response' section shows that many actors at the local level chose to do their best with the regionalised arrangements, balancing the need to try and access funding with a perception that the needs of rural areas were poorly understood by these institutions. The wider political imperatives driving RDAs were resulting in gaps in meeting the development needs of rural territories even though rural teams within the regional institutions were often working hard to ensure an enhanced degree of understanding of rural needs within the broader region.

Although the Conservative Party had made steps to regionalise government prior to 1997, Labour's regionalism was driven by a much deeper political conviction on the appropriateness of 'the region' as the scale at which to deliver economic development and coordinated government. With the demise of Labour and the formation of a new coalition government in May 2010, the era of English regionalism came to an end. In the early days of the new government there was a strong determination to wipe out all the structures of regionalism amid rhetoric of localism and austerity. Following abolition of the regional institutions there remain questions on how actors across the public, voluntary and private sectors, now used to regional working, will cooperate to enhance understanding of rural affairs and achieve development objectives. It seems possible that variations on the ad hoc, voluntary, bottom-up regionalism associated with the US will develop. Rural development practitioners and rural communities and businesses may well engage with new extra-local forms to achieve specific objectives and enhance the profile of rural affairs at a national level. Perhaps the next few years will see more interest in American approaches to governing regions as local authorities and business interests grapple with how to ensure effective co-ordination and joint working.

The chapter has shown that there is a marked contrast between the US and UK with regard to the impacts of regionalism on rural policy. In the US, the political and academic discourse of regionalism has been played out largely through encouraging voluntary cooperation. The implications for rural America are highly geographically specific as the form and reach of regionalism varies across the country. In England, regionalisation has had major consequences for socio-economic development in the countryside. It can be argued that the effect was to facilitate both an enhanced degree of regional tailoring and integration with broader regional regeneration policy. However, it can also be argued to have undermined both the ability of rural communities to formulate local solutions and the capacity of national government to develop a coherent and consistent rural policy. For those in both the UK and US with an interest in rural development, the English experience of regionalism highlights how the 'level' of government taking responsibility for the formulation and delivery of rural policy is not a mere technicality. The division of responsibility for shaping the future of rural areas has profound implications for the way in which rural community participation is facilitated and the nature of funding for social and economic development available.

15 Rural Governance

Participation, Power and Possibilities for Action

Megan G. Swindal and Ruth McAreavey

NEW LOCAL GOVERNANCE

The proliferation of local partnerships in recent years between public and civil society sectors is indicative of a global policy shift from government to governance (Organisation for Economic Co-operation and Development [OECD] 2001b, 2005). Public sector modernisation and reform in many Western economies have led to a resituated state. Formerly top-down agenda-setting and decision-making processes have been replaced by multilevel partnerships between the state and different interest groups within civil society (Warner 2001). Much of the stimulus for these changes is to lessen the state and achieve greater efficiency and accountability while also ensuring citizen involvement at a local level (Pemberton and Goodwin 2010). The belief is that decentralization and participation makes for better government as it brings government spatially closer to people and increases the availability and quality of information from citizens to government. This enables citizens to more actively participate in structures of governance and so achieve greater social and economic inclusion (Commins 2004). It also 'adds a different and valuable dimension to local decision-making processes' (Stoker 2004, 12) in that it gives individuals opportunities but also requires them to accept obligation (Blair 1994), thus helping to resolve the tension between state, market and community (Adams and Hess 2001, 13–14).

It is important to note that through systems of governance, the state does not merely hand power over to communities, but it assumes an altered position so that 'power and interest are not simply rendered meaningless but are redefined and relocated' (Hajer and Wagenaar 2003, 5). Local government actors become embedded in increasingly complex networks of 'strategic interdependence' (Agranoff and McGuire 1998, 152). Different degrees of participation and inclusion are evident, including participatory democracy and local control or empowerment (M. Taylor 2000; Callanan 2005). The 'mythologising' (Hayward, Simpson and Wood 2004, 95) power of participation is evident throughout; for instance, in the UK, the 1997–2010 Labour government viewed public participation as achieving all of the following: improving the quality and legitimacy of public bodies' decision-making, addressing the democratic deficit and building community capacity and social capital (Barnes et al. 2003). Even with these aspirations, the literature would suggest that the capacity for communities to exercise genuine power within local governance is limited and asymmetric power relations prevail (Cooke and Kothari 2001; Muir 2004; Somerville 2005).

As state authority becomes redefined there is much more room for experimentation and diversity (Rhodes 1997). Outcomes of governance are very much potentials or possibilities, and mindful of Jessop's (1999) warning, success is therefore not necessarily guaranteed. In other words creating these new structures does not ensure innovation or change, but it provides *circumstances* which encourage this very approach. These new conditions thus have particular implications for rural places, which often have different capacities and face different obstacles than urbanised cores. This is in part because national neo-liberalist ideologies have favoured investment in dynamic urban and suburban areas as a more 'efficient' use of resources in the pursuit of regional growth and regeneration (Brenner 2004).

At the end of the day, much of the imperative for participatory governance is to achieve greater efficiency and effectiveness. Mass participation is unlikely to deliver such efficacy; instead strategic participation would be likely to have more relevance. Ultimately rural development actors do not aspire to realising seismic power shifts. At the least, greater reflexivity by policymakers and multilevel partners might help keep the positive rhetoric of participation grounded in the complex reality of its application. The challenge remains for players in this new rural paradigm: how to transcend artificiality and secure meaningful engagement while creating space for the articulation and implementation of a community agenda.

In this chapter we bear this tension in mind while suggesting that, although devolution has provided the circumstances for participatory governance, in rural areas these processes may remain constrained by broader economic structures and imperatives. Using case studies from the US and the UK, we explore public sector reform and new structures of local governance, considering the way in which different actors participate in rural development within different ideological frameworks and paying particular attention to power relations within the process. The following section reviews agendas of participation before presenting the empirical evidence.

THE IMPORTANCE OF PARTICIPATION

Historically the concept of civic participation has been valued within Western societies as they made the transition from agricultural to industrial-based economies and the resultant dangers of non-participation were highlighted (Durkheim [1893] 1984; Tönnies 1955; Park 1952; Marx 1959). In recent years, civic participation has been valued as a means of enhancing local decision-making (Stoker 2004), of addressing the democratic deficit

(Barnes et al. 2003), of fostering social engagement and social capital (Bourdieu 1986; Putnam 1993; Coleman 1990) and of providing a link to economic development (Putnam 1993). Shortall (2004) and others have noted that the last two goals are often seen as mutually constitutive in both theoretical and policy circles: participation is explicitly or implicitly considered a key ingredient in building leadership and other community capacities, which consequently enable greater commitment to and tolerance of collective goals (Putnam 1993). This lucrative connection is appealing to financially constrained policymakers (Portes 1998).

Civic participation is a notoriously complex dynamic that can empower some individuals or groups at the expense of others. Indeed the link to social capital fosters a 'romantic naïve view of rural communities where civic harmony and inclusion triumphs and there is little room for power struggles, exclusionary tactics by privileged groups, or ideological conflicts' (Shortall 2004, 110). In reality, if traditional elites (such as growth coalitions) remain structurally privileged in their ability to create wealth, new governance processes will likely not redistribute much elite power to citizens. Moreover, by linking social and civic development to economic development, participation becomes devalued as an end in itself: 'the end goal is still the generation of wealth' (ibid.). Besides, evidence from rural research in Scotland suggests that participation goals and economic goals may not be easy to blend in practice (Bryden et al. 1997).

In order to consider the extent, and potential limitations, of these evolving mechanisms it is necessary to consider the underlying context and purpose of reform. In each national context, who is driving the process and why is it being done? Since one key parameter of governance is the notion of market rationality, where states 'stay at arms-length from market forces, merely establishing and defending the framework for market institutions' (Jessop 1999, 2), existing inequalities of resources and power between states, markets and communities may be reproduced despite participation goals.

NATIONAL CONTEXTS FOR NEW LOCAL GOVERNANCE

Modernisation and reform of the public sector is increasingly evidenced across the globe (OECD 2005). National governments struggle with a range of issues that have recently come to the fore including managing ever more scarce budgets, reducing the size of the public sector, ensuring a democratic public sector, achieving effective mechanisms for the active engagement and participation of citizens and transforming the ethos of the public sector. Despite similar global and structural pressures, divergent policy and ideological contexts between the EU and US creates distinct opportunities for rural governance and regeneration. Local political, cultural and institutional circumstances affect the way in which reforms are implemented and felt at the local level (Wright 1994). Public sector transformations in the US and Europe are framed by local circumstances and this section introduces some of these differences.

Generally, in the US policy principles are aligned with market logics such as efficiency and autonomy (Alesina and Glaeser 2004). In keeping with the 'smaller state' goals of decentralization in the US, reshaped governance structures generally encourage rather than command citizen participation at the local level (Radin et al. 1996). Doing away with federal mandates and enabling greater choice in social or economic partnerships are seen as key means of decentralizing power (Brown and Warner 1991). The retreat of the US federal government through 'New Public Management' has meant that state and local bodies have become increasingly charged with regeneration and development initiatives (Agranoff and McGuire 1998) and yet are still dependent on funding sources that may be unpredictable or biased toward particular agendas or toward entities that are economically self-sustaining (Hunt 2007). Primary partners in this task are local government agencies and public–private groups like local development corporations, local enterprise agencies or community cooperatives (Bradshaw and Blakely 2009). Such organisations generally apply for direct loans or grants, which state offices award through programmes within the Departments of Agriculture (USDA) or Housing and Urban Development (HUD). They are tasked with identifying and addressing economic and/or community development needs, with emphases on participation that vary according to community context (Radin et al. 1996; G. Green 2003).

Frequently, these governance mechanisms within the US have helped create vibrant growth poles and new economic opportunities that incorporate significant citizen participation in planning through formal mechanisms such as appointed advisory committees, public hearings and elected neighbourhood commissions. The evidence presented here highlights problems with these bright spots, including their uneven distribution across space, emphasis on economic interests, limited participation by non-elite groups and short-term gains displacing local participation (Sullivan 2004; Hunt 2007). Decreased regulation can exacerbate existing imbalances: communities with resource inequalities may opt out of regeneration processes and defer to elites to plan and carry out policies that would bring much needed investment quickly. At the subnational level this typically requires maximizing capital inflow and minimizing redistribution (Peterson 1981; Gunderson et al. 2004). Clearly, without structured mechanisms in place, opportunities for participation that ostensibly may be provided through devolution, may in practice be limited. Perhaps of more gravity, they may even be tacitly discouraged.

Meanwhile in Europe, state and civil society bodies assume responsibility for development and regeneration activities, organising their strategies through partnerships with representatives from the state, businesses and civil society. Partnership composition is often determined by a combination of programme requirements and equality legislation. Thus while much of the stimulus for participatory governance across Europe is to lessen the state and achieve greater efficiency and accountability, there is a *simultaneous* goal of ensuring citizen involvement at a local level (Pemberton and Goodwin 2010). This is evident in current reform of local government that has occurred across the UK, but the principles are also encapsulated in European rural policy. In *The Future of Rural Society*, the European Commission outlined its fundamental approach to rural development, underlining the need for 'planning, dialogue and partnership' (Commission of the European Communities [CEC] 1988, 36). It indicated a new social agenda and outlined a political direction for Europe as it sought to achieve social and economic cohesion. Against this rhetoric, the reality was that the budgetary weight of the Common Agricultural Policy (CAP) had created pressure for economic efficiency. Even so, devolution in the US has had a somewhat different valence than that in Europe. Warner and Shortall (2010) conclude that efficiency goals stand alone in the US whereas EU policies pursue social inclusion alongside market competitiveness.

Even in a European context of equality and inclusion, there is evidence of dominance of elite interests, as the state agenda can permeate regeneration initiatives without paying attention to wider community interests (Cornwall 2004; M. Taylor 2007; McAreavey 2009a, 2009b). The modernisation agenda that arose from the decentralization of responsibilities for policy-making and delivery in the UK was part of a wider programme of devolution and constitutional change introduced by Labour under Tony Blair's leadership in 1997. At a time when European ideals of convergence were being promoted, local government in the UK was perceived as diverging considerably from other European countries. This was due mostly to its scale, a track record of underachievement and financial remoteness from the citizen (Stoker 2006). These factors combined to contrast sharply with other European nations such as France with its array of municipalities, elected mayors and local taxation systems (ibid.). UK public sector reform has thus been gathering pace since the late 1990s. But the economic pitfalls of devolution are great, and evidence suggests regressive effects similar to those found in the US, including the strengthening of rich areas at the expense of poorer ones leading to questions of equity and efficiency (Rodríguez-Pose and Gill 2005). These wider systems of governance form a myriad of structures within which rural actors must engage and so raise ever more questions of power imbalances.

Although US and EU circumstances differ in terms of ideology, history and policy, it appears that some commonalities exist, namely, problems of equity and participation. And so questions remains: In what exactly are the partners of rural governance participating? Who are the partners? How much power are they afforded? To what extent are they able to exercise change within structures of governance? Are some types of participation more appropriate than others? How do the different contexts impact on power relations among rural development actors?

CASE STUDIES

We now move on to analyse the efficacy of new governance structures within two distinct jurisdictions, that of Alabama in the US and Northern Ireland in the UK. Research in Alabama focusing on state and local development policy was carried out by Swindal from 2008 to 2009 and McAreavey has been researching rural development in Northern Ireland since the late 1990s. Both areas have noteworthy histories that provide for certain types of notoriety. Racism and spatial segregation have often tarnished the reputation of the former, while civil unrest from sectarianism and tensions related to the presence of the UK state are frequently associated with Northern Ireland. And yet despite these imperfect and difficult but somewhat dissimilar histories, our chapter shows how in both areas, rural communities and spaces are being transformed. Our analysis illustrates how processes of governance are interpreted differently across space. Regardless of distinct administrative and political understanding of rural regeneration, the research reveals that the opportunities for 'real' community participation, and the spaces that exist for meaningful engagement of 'the community', are limited and indeed threatened by boundaries and elites that curtail possibilities for action. These factors suggest a potentially broad divergence in rural resources and capacities between the two regions, meaning that bottom-up processes of governance may present different participatory opportunities in each.

Alabama: Unravelling Complex and Entrenched Power Relations

The Southern US has a history of spatial inequality and most of the country's persistent poverty counties are located here (Kusmin 2008). The Southern states were some of the strongest advocates for devolution during the Reagan era, with a long history of demand for states' rights and the relaxation of mandates tied to federal aid (Sanders 1999). Political culture tends to be traditionalistic-individualistic, emphasizing traditional authority and protection of private interests (Elazar 1994). Alabama is in many ways an ideal-type state for this region. Its government is particularly small: it consistently ranks in the bottom five US states in terms of per capita taxation. Human capital is also quite low: time and again the state also ranks in the bottom five or so for per-pupil expenditures, median household income and bachelor's degree attainment (US Census 2008).

The state's economic development agenda has long been dominated by a small-government framework focusing on capital subsidy primarily through low tax rates and low labour costs (Rork 2005). With the increasing entrepreneurialism enabled by new governance processes, innovative multilevel partnerships between state government and transnational companies were formed during the 1990s. They helped to generate a number of new urban and suburban jobs particularly through recruitment of foreign auto manufacturers. The AlabamaGermany Partnership, for example, facilitated valuable economic relationships between transnational firms, state officials and local workforces. Other partnerships, such as the Economic Development Partnership of Alabama, provided a space for the major manufacturers, their support businesses (such as shipping and warehousing) and state workforce training programmes to interact.

These new governance structures had dynamic results for many local economies and were key in establishing a level of regeneration within a state that had long grappled with a stagnant industrial profile. However, the changes emerging from these mechanisms were cursory—they created jobs but they did not engender deeper, more structural transformations such as creating conditions for endogenous development through investment in training or other basic infrastructure. While wealthier suburban locales were gaining from new partnerships and investments, other institutional structures with deep historical roots prevented these economic flows from benefitting the state as a whole. In particular, the state constitution (created by landowning elites in the post–Civil War era) codified anti-regulationist principles that made Alabama an attractive location for foreign manufacturing firms, but it also lacked basic mechanisms that would ameliorate the inevitable social contradictions of growth. An extremely regressive system of taxation (weighted heavily on the sales tax), a lack of county home rule and a highly 'earmarked' budget that is largely controlled by the state and special interests are the key elements of this institutional structure (Permaloff and Grafton 2008). The tax arrangement meant that revenues from wealthy areas would not be shared with poor (often rural and black) local schools and governments. The lack of county home rule meant that legislative 'gatekeepers' would determine, from the top, what local policy goals were accomplished. And, the earmarked budget (about 87 per cent of revenue) meant that new social demands would not find support or accommodation. As a result, historically disadvantaged areas continued to slide relatively further backward in terms of publicly funded human development factors such as educational attainment. Local conditions such as poor schools, few amenities and inferior jobs opportunities (especially in the 'Black Belt'—twelve contiguous counties with majority African-American populations) contributed to a persistent cycle of rural underemployment and low endogenous development capacity.

This key aspect of the state's institutional structure has been durable for a number of reasons. It has maintained long-standing power relationships even in times of economic prosperity, when capital influxes should have been converted to more stable economic bases such as human capital investment (Rork 2005). It also reproduces a particular perception of the proper distribution of power between state, market and community: for maximum civic freedom, the state should be tightly bounded and free market processes privileged (a key neo-liberal tenet see Peck and Tickell 2002). As a result, collective ideologies emphasize trust in market elites and mistrust in the political process, which further stymies citizen empowerment and ultimately bottom-up development. Economic elites have also had an instrumental role in maintaining these conditions. It is widely acknowledged that certain groups—particularly powerful rural interests like large agricultural and timber landowners and their lobbies—systematically influence the policy behaviour of local legislators and voters both directly and indirectly. This further contributes to suspicion of politics and politicians among the masses.

Further obstacles to bottom-up development are evident across the Alabama landscape. Although locally led organisations such as development corporations have sprung up to take advantage of new governance structures, interview data and a perusal of the Alabama Development Office's local development organisation (LDO) directory suggest that the majority are somewhat narrowly focused on growth, with community development and empowerment a much lesser consideration. While growth coalition theory (Logan and Molotch 1987; Molotch 1976) would predict that membership of LDOs would be dominated by business and landowner interests (chambers of commerce, etc.) rather than community actors, this exclusion has a particularly racial dimension in rural Alabama. How have community interests become marginalised here when governance and New Public Management was supposed to bring government closer to citizens? It is clear that in some state contexts, social inclusion and broad democratic participation have been achievable goals (Radin 1996). But majority–minority rural communities in the South face an array of spatial, personal and economic 'intensifiers' that block entry to participation for those who most need a voice (Parent and Lewis 2003).

For example, one legacy of the decades of tightly guarded political control by white elites in Alabama is an inflexible budget and low state tax revenues, resulting in low public infrastructural investments into, for example, broadband access and public transportation. These conditions prevent local people from pursuing available education and training opportunities and from establishing or nurturing valuable social and economic networks outside of their immediate communities (personal communication, community planner, 2009). Human capitals are often low due to poor local education opportunities and few skilled in-migrants, meaning a dearth of many of the civic and entrepreneurial capacities important to community development efforts (personal communication, 2009) and individual empowerment. Hunt's (2007) research in rural Arkansas (similarly poor and racially stratified) indicates that without such basic human capital stocks, local communities' participation remains very limited due to intimidating participation spaces or more general time and transportation constraints facing low-income rural people. History, culture and resources thus constitute major barriers to grassroots participation.

During the late 1990s and 2000s the state government became concerned by issues of spatial inequality and the minimal opportunities and capacities available in much of rural Alabama. Economic growth appeared to be threatened by trends such as the overseas exodus of traditional industries and the accelerating competitiveness of workforces in neighbouring states like Florida and Georgia. The state considered a number of modernising reforms including education investments and a moderately progressive reshuffling of the tax code. However, given the conservative partisan and ideological commitments of these leaders, increasing capacities in lagging areas was not regarded as an emancipatory end in itself, but was seen exclusively as a means to achieve growth. A more educated rural workforce would make these areas more appealing to employers and might ideally make them net contributors to, rather than net drains on, state resources. Proposed reforms to existing governance structures aimed to break up some of these entrenched relationships of power and influence because their macroeconomic effects had finally become apparent to state government, which otherwise avoided disrupting market processes. But voter resistance to such reforms endures since local elites are able to paint them as government, and thus inappropriate, expansions.

Even in their ambitiousness, the programmes which the state proposed in an attempt to ameliorate unevenness still adhered to very similar power frameworks. These were 'hard' reforms administered from the state level in a top-down manner; few aspects of these development policy proposals would have actually brought participatory agency down to the level of local communities or enabled endogenous development. Quite specifically, none of the targeted policies that have been identified as key to facilitating endogenous development (Radin et al. 1996)—promoting local government cooperation, allowing jurisdictions to share locally generated tax revenues, promoting local land-use planning, establishing training for civic leaders—were proposed during the period under study. In part, this is again traceable to institutional barriers, but it also appears that the local dependence fostered by Alabama's governance structure and its dominant capital-subsidy paradigm has prevented local governments and citizens from even conceptualizing development as a bottom-up process. The rhetoric of 'job deliverance' has dominated speech from public officials for decades, and the publicity afforded successful industrial recruitments saturates the media. Subsidies for exogenous employers (tax abatements, workforce training, site preparation, etc.)—even small subventions—are not matched by subsidies for home-grown employers. As such, development efforts by local governments and partnerships often mirror these state-level approaches—for example, turning public land parcels into industrial parks that frequently go unused or appealing to external government or business patrons (personal communication, 2009).

Because the logics of development in Alabama are framed in top-down terms and through market rationality themes like 'economies of scale', the ideas of creating jobs through local enterprise or of building community capacities that are not connected to immediate economic benefits are less familiar and possibly seen as inefficient, not only by state and market elites, but also by local communities themselves. Currently, most of the top-down reforms that were proposed to break up stagnant relationships of economic inequality have been defeated in referenda through aggressive campaigns by elite opponents such as the agriculture lobby. In this way the model of participation through encouragement rather than obligation seems to fall short in the face of powerful groups. Without any parallel state attempts to build endogenous development capacities, many rural communities appear to be in much the same place as they were twenty years ago despite the success of partnerships and new governance mechanisms in the capital subsidy sphere of development. The Alabama case is unique with respect to the institutionalised reproduction of spatial inequality, but the broad popularity of market logics is prevalent across the US. Research by Dewees, Lobao and Swanson (2003) in the state of Ohio suggests that its circumstances are part of a broader pattern whereby US counties most disadvantaged by changing macroeconomic conditions tend not to be able to make use of the community-led development opportunities that new governance structures were supposed to facilitate.

Northern Ireland: From Civil Unrest to 'Needless Bureaucracy'

A reality of policy-making is that it is affected by wider political processes (Young et al. 2002, cited in Knox 2009). This is certainly the case in Northern Ireland, a 'public administration backwater' within the UK (Knox 2009, 437) where phrases including *mal-administration, over-administration, inefficiency* and *layers of bureaucracy* have been used to describe its public sector over recent years. A turbulent period of over thirty years of often violent civil unrest from the mid-1960s had been initiated partially by the unfair allocation of, and access to, public services including housing and employment. The Northern Ireland Good Friday Agreement came into force in late 1999, bringing with it a raft of major changes, not least of which was a new constitutional status. This led to the creation of a devolved administration, the Northern Ireland Assembly, which assumed responsibility for direct rule over many policy areas from Westminster. The role of the public sector in Northern Ireland is considerable with just under one third of the Northern Ireland workforce employed therein compared with a UK average of 22 per cent (Knox 2009). An active and engaged community and voluntary sector has in the past contributed to the delivery of public services while also helping to ensure civic confidence (Knox and Carmichael 2006). But even so, the public sector is perceived to be remote from the people with the most democratic forum, local government, having responsibility for only 4 per cent of the public budget (ibid.).

While regional capacity and economic efficiency are driving devolution and reform in England (Pearce, Ayres and Tricker 2005), political and constitutional factors combine with economic efficiency to form the key drivers of public sector reform in Northern Ireland. An element of this is the Review of Public Administration (RPA) that aims to align administrative boundaries so that public services can be delivered more effectively. It seeks to do this by strengthening the role of local government so that 'under the new system councils will have responsibility for a wide range of functions and a strong power to influence a great many more. This will enable them to respond flexibly to local needs and make a real difference to people's lives (. . .) and through community planning the opportunity exists to promote good relations, address poverty and environmental issues, and develop normal civic society' (Northern Ireland Executive 2006, 8). Significantly, one of the proposals is to reduce the number of councils from twenty-six to eleven. Persistent delays due to political posturing could mean that the expected implementation of the new councils during 2011 will not be realised. Whatever the outcome of these setbacks, participatory governance is embedded within the proposed new councils. Part of their enhanced function includes responsibility for rural development, urban and rural regeneration, local public realm aspects of roads and community planning. It is anticipated that eventually they will have responsibility for the delivery of European regeneration programmes, including the rural development programme.

It is of little surprise that, symptomatic of multi-scalar governance, many other rural development partnerships exist within Northern Ireland. Some approaches, such as the European INTERREG programme, which promotes territorial cooperation across border regions, or the European Rural Development Programme, which embodies the LEADER approach, are found across member states. Others are distinctive to Northern Ireland and reflect circumstances particular to that region. For example, under new legislation emerging from the Good Friday Agreement (North/South Co-operation [Implementation Bodies] [Northern Ireland] Order 1999), six cross-border non-departmental public bodies were established 'to implement policies agreed by Ministers in the North/South Ministerial Council and to develop cross-border co-operation on practical matters of mutual concern'. Meanwhile the Special European Union Programme Body was created to administer EU-funded programmes, including the European Programme for Peace and Reconciliation (i.e. the PEACE programme). PEACE funding is typically awarded to larger public bodies who, as intermediary agents, distribute the monies to smaller community and voluntary sector–based organisations. Reflecting Northern Ireland's recent and turbulent past, the programme aims to promote reconciliation through measures that include creating shared public space and developing institutional and community capacity.

Figure 15.1 shows a project managed by Derry City Council and supported by a local LEADER partnership. A play area for all residents, it is part of a wider regeneration strategy that aims to improve availability of, and access to, community facilities. Its funding profile reflects one dimension of the complexities of governance as it receives financial support from the Parks Development Programme, the European Union (PEACE II Programme) and the International Fund for Ireland.

Questions have been raised in relation to the extent of power that the new local councils can ever have. It is claimed that there is little in the way of strong local government where asymmetrical power relations prevail between central and local government and conditions for regional central- ism remain (Knox 2009). Further, from an EU budgetary perspective rural development funding is small at approximately 10 per cent of the CAP budget. It is of little surprise that Knox (2009) claims that in a jurisdiction such as Northern Ireland, without major reform of central government and given the limited range of enhanced local council functions, this can only ever offer limited local governance. Our analysis continues by exploring the potential for participatory engagement through these emerging structures of governance, with particular emphasis on the European Rural Develop- ment Programme.

Figure 15.1 Site launch for a community play facility, Derry, Northern Ireland. Photograph courtesy of Derry City Council.

The Department of Agriculture and Rural Development (DARD) is the central government body that co-ordinates the rural development programme in Northern Ireland with agreement from the European Commission. The implementation of national plans, such as the Northern Ireland Rural Development Programme (NIRDP), is reliant on local action groups that adopt the LEADER approach 'including partnership capacity, implementation of local strategies, cooperation, networking and acquisition of skills' (CEC 2005, 6). These partnerships comprise representatives from the voluntary and community, public and private sectors and they devise area-based strategies from which individual projects are funded. The programme very neatly epitomizes the governance approach that is evident globally within the new rural paradigm (OECD 2006). Top-down and bottom-up structures intermingle, but the power differentials between the different actors becomes clear when we examine the practice of governance.

DARD originally intended that the boundaries of the local action groups would be 'co-terminus' with the new councils, but this has been complicated by delays to the implementation of the RPA; namely the delay in operationalising the new councils. Eventually local government will have responsibility for working with DARD to deliver the rural development programme, but in the transition period groups of councils are working together on this and on other funding streams. The example of the north-east area illustrates the complexity of the interim arrangements for participatory governance. 'At the local level the Programme is strategically delivered by a Joint Committee (JC) representing all five Councils and implemented by a Local Action Group (LAG) comprised of an equal number of locally elected representatives and social partners' (see http://northeastrdp.com/about_us.htm). The local action group has thirty members of which fifteen are from statutory and government bodies and fifteen represent social and community organisations. The council cluster (in this case five: Ballymena, Ballymoney, Coleraine, Larne and Moyle) nominates elected representatives to the local action group and also to the joint committee. Meanwhile individuals applied to the north-east area council cluster for a place as a social partner using application forms (designated by DARD). Following the scoring of each application using criteria devised by the council cluster, with direction from DARD, an open meeting was then held to seek agreement on the fifteen social and community partners. Individuals' suitability was assessed on a number of issues, including skills and experience in financial appraisal, economic development, programme delivery and business planning (DARD 2007). The council clusters were required by DARD to have transparent scoring criteria and to actively promote equality of opportunity for all interest groups (in line with Section 75 of the Northern Ireland Act 1998, a mainstreaming measure designed to ensure public bodies achieve desirable levels of participation from different social groups in all of their activities). DARD subsequently approved a local action group for each area. The local action group is responsible for developing and implementing a local rural development strategy that addresses the measures outlined within Axis Three of the NIRDP 2007–2013. At a local level it makes recommendations to the joint committee that then approves applications. Individual projects enter a financial agreement with DARD. The council cluster is financially and administratively responsible for the funds and for the operation of the local action group, but significantly the contract for local programme implementation and delivery is between DARD and a lead council that has been agreed by the cluster (DARD 2007). Meanwhile funding is paid directly from DARD to the relevant project; the council clusters are not involved.

Broadly then, the local action group's role is to assist with animation of the area, and to cooperate with and make recommendations to the joint committee that represents the council cluster. It has neither legal nor financial responsibilities. Meanwhile a single council is legally responsible for delivering the programme, and it is expected that eventually the eleven new councils will take on this role. As the central government department, DARD assumes an influential role. Firstly, it agrees with the national programme with the EU and from this point it determines how it will be operationalised. The extent to which DARD currently gets involved in the day-to-day running has led some practitioners to comment that in their experience of working in rural development since the early 1990s, the current programme is by far the most challenging and complicated due to what is perceived by rural development actors as 'needless bureaucracy' (personal communication, 2009). For example, at one point an official within DARD failed to provide a definitive position on the type of training courses that are considered eligible for funding, changing the guidelines from one day to the next. Another funding stream within the programme was delayed by nearly two years due to DARD's belated approval of economic audits which arose from ongoing inquiries (personal communication with staff, 2010). Perhaps this is a consequence of risk aversion, but it would also seem that preoccupation with such technicalities, rules and regulations is at the expense of meaningful engagement between the different actors. As the potential for expedient interaction between different layers of governance is curtailed, what hope then of resolving tension between the state and civil society? Important questions remain: In practice what is the potential of these emergent structures to contribute to meaningful participatory rural governance? Given the enduring centralized power structures that are evident within local governance, how much power do local communities have to pursue their own agenda?

FRESH APPROACHES TO GOVERNANCE: NEW POSSIBILITIES FOR ACTION?

An overview of these case studies suggests that institutional frameworks for rural development can hinder community empowerment even where central state authority is tightly bounded and devolved governance mechanisms have taken hold. In both cases, 'state projects and strategies rest on a prior (. . .) identification of suitable objects of intervention and activity' to describe the social, political and cultural characteristics of a created space (Pemberton and Goodwin 2010, 276), that is, the rural development arena. These are not necessarily 'popular spaces' that emerge from within and are defined by the community; they are instead 'invited spaces' that are conceptualized by the state and into which communities are invited (Cornwall 2004). To paraphrase Lagendijk (2007, 1199), as it is the state's imaginaries of rural space that define the subjects and objects of development, the state also shapes the strategies and actions that emerge.

In Northern Ireland, although individuals were able to become involved in the local action group (subject to meeting certain criteria), they were not able to participate in the restricted decision-making realm that existed across the different levels of governance such as within the council cluster. Individuals are therefore not able to alter the *boundaries* of action of the rural development programme, and thereby affect change through this channel. Power is unevenly distributed among regeneration actors, being skewed towards the state in the form of central and local government. The field of what is possible is ultimately determined by central government and by the European Commission, and to a lesser extent by the local council cluster. Decisions were confined to specific, predefined issues; 'real' interests were not necessarily identified. In this sense hidden power was evident as those outside certain boundaries were not only omitted from the political process, but they were denied entry (Lukes 2005).

The same themes are also starkly evident in the US as highlighted by the Alabama case. Although rural development frameworks have become more inclusive of non-state actors, this inclusivity is limited by pre-existing power structures that prevent community actors from claiming their right to boundless participation. In Alabama, the efficiency imperative more overtly shaped rural development agendas and 'processes' appear collectively deemed less important than 'product'. Meanwhile, at a very minimum, the rhetorical value of participation is evident within local governance in Northern Ireland.

Attempts to increase rural development capacities in both programmes were envisioned and imposed in a top-down manner, suggesting that traditionally disadvantaged communities continued to be objects rather than subjects of development. Power operated through social systems so that individual practices and strategies were shaped by culture, society and social group rather than being personally determined (Foucault 1982). In Northern Ireland and in Alabama, elite-defined norms and agendas are continually maintained. The power of DARD, for example, was manifest through the culture and practices of the civil service that were in turn imposed on rural development actors. The framework within which regeneration initiatives actually operate in both the cases would appear to be allied to systems of managerial control or established authority rather than to processes of community empowerment (Raco and Imrie 2000). The programmes exhibit elitism as the power of the ruling class is reinforced through recreation of their structures, norms and process. In other words, there was little debate around *how* rural development programmes are to be delivered. The very means by which interaction occurs is shaped by statutory agencies, oftentimes with other partners of governance oblivious to this manipulation and control. The inherent assumption of organisational superiority is a symptom of the privileged ruling stratum; it is part of the ideology of the elite (Mills 1956; Katz 1975). It follows that this elite shapes the very nature of ensuing action and creates a privileged regeneration community (McAreavey 2009a). If these structures have struggled with citizen engagement in the past, then how can they now hope to achieve participatory governance?

The preceding analysis provides quite a bleak prognosis for community empowerment and participation. A more considered analysis is required to make sense of the dynamics of the privileged space inhabited by regeneration actors. Ayres and Pearce remind us that 'government in most states retains control over the key policy levers' (2008, 540), driving reform and determining the parameters of that change. Consequently rural areas' potential economic contributions may be jeopardized if local governance processes are situated within bigger agendas that are not congruent with local objectives. It is therefore critical that rural governance is aligned to democratic systems and is complemented by broader policy agendas. The invited space of rural governance may represent the best opportunity for the state and civil society to interact. Remaining outside of the privileged regeneration space limits the capacity of local communities to engender change. But entering that space is not trouble free. It indicates an acceptance by participants of the terms of engagement and the accompanying imbalances of power that have been frequently been highlighted within the literature. While debate is likely to continue in relation to such uneven power relations and actors' capacity to participate, we are mindful that asymmetrical power relations are perhaps less of a problem than we might think (Derkzen, Franklin and Bock 2008). Is it appropriate for individuals or groups without professional experience in development work to be granted responsibility for skilled tasks such as financial monitoring and budget prioritizing? Equally, is it appropriate for statutory agencies alone to determine the institutional arrangements for implementing development programmes?

Within both study areas the influencing role of the state was evident: it is in a position to exert considerable influence on creating conditions that may stimulate or indeed dampen endogenous development activities. Though devolution aims to bring government closer to citizens, structures like the state constitution maintain certain distributions of power. Ultimately, the scope for community engagement differed within the privileged space of rural governance in Northern Ireland and the US. Input from the local community, through the joint committee and in a more limited way the local action group, represents a point of departure of the Northern Ireland model of governance from that of the US. In Northern Ireland the active role of civil society is a cultural norm and so the value of participation is recognised. This was demonstrated through the creation of a process that sought to provide mechanisms for individuals to become involved, even though those participants had limited scope to shape the programme design or even the resulting outcomes. These structures of governance are in actual fact uncovering new power relations; they are creating space for new players to exert a degree of power while allowing 'old players' to maintain their position. Local action group members within NIRDP have the capacity to exercise power firstly through the act of participation as this ensures that DARD complies with European programme requirements. There is the prospect for local action group members to exert further power, albeit within the bounds of the rural development framework, as they are responsible for stimulating local development and also for making recommendations to the joint committees. Thus circumstances within Northern Ireland are conducive to actors asserting a degree of agency. After all, they are not entirely impassive recipients of state action; they have particular experiences, interests and beliefs, all of which affect how and where they choose to act (Hay 2002; Bevir and Rhodes 2006).

This potential is much more limited within the US, where the state and many of the development agencies appear to be disbelieving of the valence of 'capacity-building' or creating community (and other) infrastructure and so severely restrain the agency of rural actors. By placing more emphasis on process, the national development discourse might encourage subnational places to expand local power bases, enhancing spheres of influence. This would necessitate a sea change among the local political elite, such as relinquishing certain accoutrements of power. In a state such as Alabama, with such marked racial divisions, such shifts may not be easily achievable, but the rewards would be telling. It would facilitate a more considered form of rural development that takes account of aversion to mandates as well as the necessary role of top-down policies, while creating a space for bottom-up activities and in so doing addressing some of the inequalities that were highlighted earlier in the chapter.

Ultimately the apparatus of the state does not and indeed cannot lose power, but perhaps it is in a stronger position to affect change through a combination of top-down and bottom-up approaches. By creating spaces of governance that actively engage with the local community, the overarching capacity of an area to shape regeneration is enhanced. Power is thus not a zero-sum proposition. In the Northern Ireland case, and mindful of past criticisms of the LEADER methodology,[1] the way in which new governance structures have been designed means that they immediately overcome the problem of legitimacy. By aligning the local action groups and the joint committee with the local councils, the programme is demo-cratically accountable, it has legitimacy and it becomes a more powerful force.[2] This is hopeful for a society that for many years existed within a democratic deficit. Meanwhile in Alabama, greater consideration of institutional design (starting with constitutional structures and spanning through to community infrastructure) would be critical in establishing similar levels of legitimacy, given the high levels of mistrust surrounding government and governance. Sustainability of these governance structures also becomes more viable and this is not without significance given the likelihood of diminishing external funding (from the EU or the US federal government) in the future. It is perhaps this financial aspect of the argument that would appeal to cash-strapped policymakers as local government deals with budgetary cuts.

These critical explorations of the extent to which participation is actually achievable given diverse governance structures are important because local governments in both regions have been tasked with considerable responsibility for regeneration (HM Treasury 2007; Reese 1994; OECD 2006; CEC 2005). If local people and knowledges are to be formally valued as much as higher level economic forces (such as macroeconomic policies coming from the central state) the continued operation of traditional and/or hidden power relationships should be acknowledged. However, because the state 'is merely an institutional ensemble' that 'reflects the prevailing balance of forces' (Jessop 1990, cited in Pemberton and Goodwin 2010, 274), limiting the state does not necessarily change the balance of economic or social forces. Indeed, we would argue that power within rural governance is not limited: creating conditions that enhance the power of local communities to act from below does not automatically mean reduced state power, nor does it necessarily undermine the role of the state. On the contrary, our analysis would suggest that it strengthens the capacity of a community to shape what is possible.

16 Constructing the Rural–Urban Interface

Place Still Matters in a Highly Mobile Society

Mark Shucksmith, David L. Brown and Jo Vergunst

INTRODUCTION

In this book we contend that rural people and communities continue to play important social, economic and environmental roles in post-industrial societies such as the UK and US. This is the case even as localities experience dramatic socio-demographic and economic transformations, and profound changes occur in the governance and economic contexts in which they are embedded. Place of residence remains an important aspect of personal identity, and where one lives and works continues to affect opportunities and life course trajectories. Yet dramatic technological and organisational changes have fundamentally transformed rural and urban communities during recent decades so that society and economy have been reconfigured around 'mobilities' rather than 'stabilities' (Urry 2000, 2007). While many scholars argue that we live in a world of flows rather than of discrete places (Castells 1989), others also recognise the continuing importance of place. The interrelationships among social and economic environments are of paramount interest in contemporary society, yet many chapters in this book establish that local agency has by no means been completely undermined by macro-structural changes. The durable social relationships that characterise many local communities produce endogenous social and economic change and resistance thereby countering, at least to an extent, these large-scale, universalising exogenous forces (Shucksmith 2000a).

The increased interpenetration of urban and rural society is made possible by large-scale macro-structural changes such as neo-liberalism and globalisation, detailed in Shortall and Warner's introduction and in several other chapters of this volume. Migration and other socio-demographic dynamic processes, governance institutions, nature–society relationships and the locus of power in economic and political transactions are all affected by the diminished friction of space and what heretofore was regarded as the 'protection of distance'. It is not that place no longer matters, but rather that the social meanings of place and distance have been reconfigured in our hyper-mobility society.

This chapter thus summarises and extends the key lines of thinking that emerge in the book. By making connections with the academic literature on mobility, we show how key historical, cultural and policy differences between the US and the UK affect rural transformations and rural policies. We begin by evaluating our approach to difference within and between the nations and then make a more detailed appraisal of the 'mobilities turn' in relation to results reported in the book's various chapters. Exogenous and endogenous forces that are shaping current rural social change are discussed next, particularly with a view to identifying the nature of 'agency' in rural development. The final section looks to the future and presents both the potential of new forms of agency through place-based initiatives and the role that academic research could play in engendering such outcomes.

DIVERSITY AND DIFFERENCE

As Shortall and Warner observe in this book's introduction, supposedly similar contexts such as the UK and US turn out to be full of complexity and difference. While this book is not a comparative study of rural society and rural social change in the UK and US in the strict methodological sense, it does place social, economic and environmental changes in the two societies in parallel so that similarities and differences can be identified and examined. Lowe (Chapter 2) points out that this comparative social scientific approach is important for judging 'whether and how knowledge gained in a particular context is applicable elsewhere'. Of course, this brings us back to the theme of 'mobilities' since knowledge also travels, especially in a globalised world where information technology makes instantaneous scholarly communication and collaboration possible.

Hence, while we are hesitant to make overarching statements about similarities and differences between the UK and US, this book's first part clearly delineates a number of diversity dimensions that characterise both countries. To begin with, rural populations in both the UK and US are ageing, and because migrants are moving to rural areas in both nations, rural populations are becoming more culturally and racially diverse. The economic activities of residents of rural communities are also becoming more varied partly because many rural residents work in urban labour markets, and hence are not dependent on a narrow range of employment opportunities where they live. The traditional sources of rural employment, extractive and manufacturing industries have given way to a wide array of service industries. While some rural economies are still dominated by one or a few industrial categories, the rural economy as a whole is much more diverse, containing everything from farming to tourism to high-tech producer services. The narrowing of the rural–urban digital divide suggests that an even broader range of economic pursuits will characterise the rural economy of the future.

Even though rural society in both the UK and US is characterised by high urbanisation, relatively low employment in agriculture, population ageing, immigration, lack of public transport and so on, rural people and communities in the two nations are situated in entirely different institutional frameworks. In particular, the UK and US have differing regulatory regimes, different worlds of welfare capitalism, differing governance and institutions, contrasting geographies of 'the rural' and differing structures and politics of knowledge used to examine the role and status of rural areas in contemporary society. Accordingly, a transatlantic dialogue can contribute to theory and policy development regarding the nature and roles of rurality in post-industrial society.

Bryden and Warner's chapter (Chapter 10) on rural policies draws out many fundamental differences between the UK and US. In Europe generally there has been a stronger sense of social solidarity which, together with a more centralized government, led in the UK to the founding of the welfare state after the Second World War. Moreover, the UK's rural areas are associated not only with food production, but also with cultural images and identities, history, nature and industrial development. The US, by contrast, is a nation of immigrants. The notion of a frontier territory available for the taking to homesteaders and to developers laid the basis for the 'American Dream' as a land of individualistic values, inviolate private property rights and minimal regulation. Federalism in the US means that the centre is weaker and the constituent states are stronger, leading to considerable interstate diversity in policy. Attention to community obligations and social rights is often relatively weak. In light of these differences it is crucial to understand the cultural and political context both historically and with a view to the future.

SOCIAL, DEMOGRAPHIC AND ECONOMIC TRANSFORMATIONS: A MOBILITIES TURN?

A key dynamic in this book has been the relationship between 'agricultural' and 'rural' policy and practice, where 'rural' denotes a concern with non-urban society, economy and environment that is broader than that simply related to farming. 'Rural' also denotes a critique of the weight and resources given to agricultural policy compared to wider rural issues. Many of the authors here concur with this critique, while noting the recent re-emergence of sustainable food systems and food security on national and international agendas. In rural social science, the issue to some extent maps onto debates around 'productivism' and 'post-productivism' under way in Europe in particular since the 1990s (Ilbery 1998; Wilson 2001; Ward et al. 2008). And yet, as we suggested in the introduction to this chapter, other societal trends may have even more relevance in encapsulating the object of research that we are concerned with. While the agriculture/rural debate questions the extent to which the rural community is based in primary production, an even more fundamental rethink might involve renewing attention to relations between the entities usually separated out into rural and urban. Population geographers and rural sociologists have consistently worked in this field, but recent social theory helps to reframe the question in ways that are more consistent with contemporary society.

Urry (2007), for example, has drawn attention to the development of social practices which presuppose huge increases in the speed and distance of travel. He claims that forms of life are now 'mobilised'. Moreover, he contends that these mobility practices diminish the friction of distance to such an extent that rural society is now fully integrated within overall society. Urry (2007) observes that economies and societies have been reconfigured around mobilities, founded upon an emergent 'mobility complex', a new system of economy, society and resources spreading around the globe which together remake consumption, pleasure, work, friendship and family life. Bauman (1998) has argued that as a consequence mobility (the freedom to move perpetually) becomes the most stratifying factor of our late modern or postmodern times. This has implications for place, and for notions of boundedness and community, as well as for stratification. For the richest third of the world's population, at least, lives come to be determined less by site-specific structures, of class, family, age and especially of neighbourhoods. Urry writes: 'Family and friends are more a matter of choice, increasingly spreading themselves around the world', dependent upon 'an extensive array of inter-dependent systems of movement in order to connect with this distributed array of networks (. . .). Paralleling this is the way in which touring the world is how the world is increasingly performed, with many people becoming connoisseurs and collectors of places' in a further amplification of mobility. 'Contemporary capitalism thus presupposes and generates some increasingly expressive bodies or habituses relatively detached from propinquitous family and neighbourhoods; many other people are employed in servicing such habituses through the 'experience economy' (Urry 2010, 10–11).[1]

This 'mobilities turn' raises many questions for rural social science disciplines, and many of the chapters in this book contribute to this new perspective in terms of migration, commuting, retirement, poverty and social exclusion, tourism, global divisions of labour and peak oil and climate change. More fundamentally, the mobilities turn calls into question the notion of 'place' itself, and issues central to this book of social and economic boundedness. Historically, rural sociology, like other spatially oriented social science disciplines, has presupposed a rural–urban binary, a clear division which may have different meaning in UK and US contexts, but also a lineal space at the rural–urban interface that is rich in social and economic interactions. In this book we continue this tradition by exploring how place, neighbourhood and boundedness are affected by increasing mobility and the laxity or absence of governance and regulation that accompany neo-liberalism. What does this mean for ideas of place-based rural communities and for endogenous rural development? Would this support Lowe, Murdoch and Ward's (1995) concept of a network-based neo-endogenous rural development?[2]

While the extent and nature of mobility have increased in contemporary society, and new forms of mobility are restructuring people's social and economic lives, people still solve the challenges of everyday life in geographically bounded communities. Several chapters in this volume demonstrate that community of residence still contributes to one's personal identity, and that 'place' and 'locality' are still important contexts of social life in the UK and US (see Hinrichs and Charles, Chapter 9). Where the mobilities turn has emphasized the digitized 'systems' of mobility in postmodern life, we might also note how distinctive forms of movement have for much longer been associated with rural societies—from village to market, for example, or farm-to-farm circuits of labour. Perhaps the error was in assuming that a genuine or authentic rural community ever involved a stable, bounded and immobile society, instead of a place constituted by the various kinds of mobility happening within and through it (Vergunst 2011). Accordingly, the contributions in this book indicate that contemporary mobilities are restructuring the nature of urban–rural relationships, rather than diminishing the importance of place: for example see Pfeffer, Parra and de Lima (Chapter 5) on immigration to rural communities and Champion and Brown on urban–rural migration (Chapter 3). If there is an 'interface' between rural and urban, it acts to both separate and conjoin rural and urban society. We see it as a space that is constructed and reconstructed by mobile people and workers, information and capital that sometimes flow freely and are sometimes regulated, along with public policies that facilitate some kinds of mobility and constrain others. In this, we have drawn upon Lichter and Brown's (2011) nine domains of interpenetrating activities that integrate urban and rural society in the US. These include: rural as a cultural repository, as a backwater, as an engine of urbanisation, as exurbia, as a place of consumption, as an immigrant destination, as a location of concentrated poverty, as a food basket and as a resource repository and dumping ground. Each of these domains of activity involves the movement of people, workers, materials and information, and while specificities may differ between the UK and US, all nine examples of enhanced levels of urban–rural interaction are shown in the contributions to this book to be present in both countries.

With heightened mobilities and the increased volume of rural–urban transactions comes the potential for increased or diminished rural agency— the ability for rural people to initiate their own activities and relationships. Some chapters do suggest possibilities for increased rural agency, including those on urban–rural migration (Chapter 3), immigration (Chapter 5), local food systems (Chapter 9) and entrepreneurship (Chapter 8), but those on population ageing (Chapter 3) and agricultural policy (Chapter

11) instead suggest a diminution of rural agency. More generally, the chapters in this book support the general notion that enhanced mobility serves to bind urban and rural areas together in new and enhanced ways. People, information and capital flow—though not always freely, as the chapters on immigration and social exclusion demonstrate—within the rural–urban interface, producing a space that is rich in social relationships, interdependencies and mutuality, whether we are discussing counterurbanisation (or reversals therein); commuting and the journey to work; globalisation and the restructuring of rural economies; social exclusion in a wide variety of institutional settings; the emergence of local foods production and marketing in the urban periphery; elderly migration from urban origins to rural destinations; the development of 'working landscapes', including those focusing on tourism and other types of urban consumption; international migration to new rural destinations; in-migrating entrepreneurs in both the economic and social realms; or governance models featuring cooperation between civil society and the state. This new landscape of rural–urban relationships sets the conditions for localities to act and/or be acted upon in the UK, US and most other post-industrial societies. The next section discusses the interplay of endogenous and exogenous forces in the context of this new hyper active rural–urban interface.

EXOGENOUS AND ENDOGENOUS FORCES

A number of chapters in this book examine the relation between exogenous and endogenous forces in rural change and development. Discussions of 'policy', for example, are often predicated on the ability of executive centres (usually global and/or urban) to govern society at a distance. In rural social science, there has been a shift over recent decades from explorations of the ways in which the 'global' is dominant over the 'local' towards more complex theorizations of actor-networks and neo-endogenous rural development, although as Lowe (Chapter 2) points out, these themes have played out differently in research in the US and the UK. Such developments do not always fit into a simple dichotomy of exogenous versus endogenous, but resonate well with the mobilities research described earlier. Bosworth and Glasgow (Chapter 8), for example, describe how rural in-migrants can be entrepreneurial in both social and economic senses, with in-migrant business owners in the UK contributing disproportionately to the local economy and older in-migrants in the US being particularly active in voluntary work and social networks.

To some extent, though, more general questions still remain about the extent to which state or other outside involvement is required to support and facilitate rural development. Certainly, 'state-led delivery mechanisms for rural modernisation were challenged by the rise of neo-liberalism as the dominant political ideology' (Woods 2011, 140), a situation reflected by van der Ploeg et al. (2000, 395) in their observation that 'rural development is on the agenda precisely because the modernisation paradigm has reached its intellectual and practical limits'. A 'New Rural Paradigm' was proclaimed both by practitioners and rural social scientists, based on ideas of endogenous rural development (i.e. development from within). The key elements of this paradigm shift, as described by Bryden and Warner in Chapter 10, were changes in policy emphasis from inward investment to endogenous development; from top-down government to bottom-up, deliberative governance; from sectoral modernisation to territorial place-shaping; and from continuing subsidy to investment and capacity-building. While some researchers have argued that endogenous development should be founded on rediscovering, or even inventing, 'indigenous cultures' to valorise places through their cultural identity (e.g. Ray 2006), others contend that some endogenous approaches risk exacerbating inequality, both between places because of the uneven capacity of place-based communities (Shortall and Shucksmith 1998; Árnason, Shucksmith and Vergunst 2009), and within communities because internal power relations are ignored or obscured (Shucksmith 2000a; Schafft and Brown 2003). These risks could be moderated by the state engaging in capacity-building. Finally, there is debate about the extent to which issues of fundamental structural disadvantage can be addressed solely through endogenous development approaches. The European Commission's Barca Report (2009) raised the question of whether remote rural areas have 'territorial potential' at all, and this remains a crucial empirical question for both research and policy.

Rural sociologists in the UK and US continue to document the impacts of neo-liberalism, transnational corporations and multinational agribusiness in particular, on rural communities and economies, on the agro-food system and on social, economic and environmental policies (e.g. Lawrence 1987; Bonnano et al. 1994; Gereffi 2006; van der Ploeg 2008). While more attention is paid now to endogenous or neo-endogenous actions, particularly in local food initiatives and environmental movements, these tend to be celebrated as spaces of resistance to overwhelming neo-liberal exogenous forces (van der Ploeg 2008; McMichael 2010), without much confidence that these expressions of agency or resistance have broader transformative traction.

Mackenzie (2006a) and Shucksmith and Rønningen (2011) find evidence for post-neo-liberal possibilities in their studies of community-based land reform, and the role of small farms in upland areas, in Scotland and Norway. Evidence presented in this book could be seen as less encouraging. Hinrichs and Charles (Chapter 9) see possibilities for post-neo-liberal alternatives, such as public sector food procurement initiatives which enable schools to offer healthier school meals with locally sourced food. However, this still takes place within the larger context of agricultural policy's fundamental commitment to productionist, export-oriented agriculture. They also point out that a policy emphasis on local food accords with the prevailing neo-liberal reliance on market-based solutions to broader problems facing rural areas. Meanwhile, Swindal and McAreavey (Chapter 15) find that supposedly endogenous initiatives (in Alabama and Northern Ireland) did not emerge from within nor were defined by the local community. Far from being autonomous, participation and engagement take place only in the 'invited spaces' of rural governance defined by the state's imaginaries, 'conceptualized by the state and into which communities are invited'. In Swindal and McAreavey's UK case, 'the field of what is ultimately possible is determined by central government and by the European Commission, and to a lesser extent by the local council cluster', while in the US case the bounds of community actors' participation are similarly limited by pre-existing power structures and special interests that have strong influence on elected government. Meanwhile, in Hewitt and Thompson's UK case (Chapter 14) it is the regional, national and EU strata which together limit the possibilities for local agency. In each of these cases, traditionally disadvantaged groups continued to be objects rather than subjects of development.

The tension between exogenous and endogenous forces affecting rural communities plays out quite differently in the US compared to the UK because the American state is a much weaker actor in local affairs. Hence, while American social scientists clearly recognise the potential for exogenous forces to undermine local agency (McMichael 2003; Bonnano and Constance 2003; Gereffi 2006), this global–local conflict is played out almost entirely between national and transnational economic entities such as transnational corporations and local society. The public sector's role in local and regional development is quite variable across the fifty US states because governments at all levels have significant autonomy in development decision-making. In some instances states and sub-state governments resist articulating holistic policies to shape local and regional futures, while other states and localities are quite active in planning for the future. Similarly, some states take a top-down approach to local and regional development while others are more grassroots in their approaches. For example, the governors of Michigan, New York, Tennessee and Colorado have all proposed bottom-up regional economic development strategies where regions drive development and inter-municipal cooperation is often significant (Brookings Institution 2011). This situation can be contrasted with the 2010 UK coalition government's anti-regional policy in economic development, as described by Hewitt and Thompson (Chapter 14).

In other US states, top-down approaches continue to dominate. Minnesota's JOBZ programme, for example, is essentially an enterprise zone programme, and the Department of Employment & Economic Development's Enterprise Network System tool represents a top-down, targeted industrial policy with an emphasis on selling Minnesota as a low-tax economy and influencing business location decisions with tax subsidies (Morrison 2010). Accordingly, in contrast to the UK where a vision for rural policy-making is articulated by the national government, the US lacks an overriding framework for local and regional development, and offers no clear role for civil society and only a facilitative role for the public sector. However, just because the local and regional role is not dictated from the centre does not necessarily mean that states and localities have no vision or civil society. It simply means that the vision and impetus for development and change is more variable in the US. This can produce more place-specific policies that are responsive to local needs or, alternatively, it can exacerbate spatial inequality if more advantaged places also have more effective local and regional planning capacities.

Globalisation and unrestrained capitalism challenge the relevance of conventional modernisation thinking, and in fact suggest that the idea has reached its intellectual and practical limits. Peck et al. (2010, 112) have argued that, as a result of the banking crisis and the ensuing sovereign debt crisis, neo-liberalism has lost all intellectual and moral authority, yet is so politically and institutionally entrenched that it will survive in a zombie phase, 'in which residual neoliberal impulses are sustained not by intellectual or moral leadership, or even by hegemonic forces, but by underlying macroeconomic and macro-institutional conditions'. This view of potential future macro-structural transformation is highly relevant to rural society and economy in countries such as the UK and US because while such a climate will constrain the transformative potential of progressive post-neo-liberal alternatives, it offers opportunities for 'the (re)mobilisation, recognition and valuation of multiple, *local* forms of development, rooted in local cultures, values and movements'—what Peck et al. have called the 'progressively variegated economy' (ibid., 111). This more positive view is supported by several of this book's contributions, which offer alternatives to neo-liberalism on an intellectual and moral level. Perhaps this opens up new possibilities for place-based rural communities in the UK and US to 'spur the post-neoliberal imagination' (ibid.).

New forms of governance and community empowerment, for example, can build agency while simultaneously placing limits on it. Swindal and McAreavey explain that, notwithstanding that it is imposed and bounded, 'the invited space of rural governance may represent the best opportunity for the state and civil society to interact' since staying aloof from this space 'limits the capacity of local communities to engender change. But entering that space is not trouble free' since it indicates an acceptance of the terms of engagement and of imbalances of power. New forms of environmental governance are also spheres in which these themes are playing out, as the chapters by Potter and Wolf (Chapter 12) and by Vergunst, Geisler and Stedman (Chapter 13) describe. Other alternatives are built on new mobilities and networks (terms which transcend the endogenous–exogenous dichotomy), such as those engendered by entrepreneurial in-migrants, for example. There is potential for government to play an enabling role, however imperfectly, building the capacity of local communities to engage with, resist and subvert broader forces of neo-liberalism. A corollary is that removing state support, as in the UK post-2010, is unlikely to foster empowerment.[3]

TOWARDS THE FUTURE

The past forty years have been characterised by an overarching policy context of neo-liberalism, privatization and deregulation. The period has been bookended by the twin global crises of the 1970s oil shock and the 2008–2011 (and continuing) banking crisis, now transmuted in the UK, US and several other countries into a sovereign debt crisis and fiscal crisis which affects many of the most vulnerable people and places in society as services and social welfare benefits are cut and jobs are lost. Against such a background, this book has documented the changes within rural areas in terms of population change, ageing, migration, immigration and population redistribution, the restructuring of rural economies from extractive and transformative activities to much greater reliance on services and the new forms of governance and institutional restructuring. Many rural areas in the UK have prospered during this period, challenging stereotypical representations of the rural as pastoral or backward, while other rural areas face continuing economic, social or environmental challenges. In the US, except in the 1970s, the overall trend for rural areas has been downward for the majority of areas and regions. Growth has been stagnant or negative as youth continue to move to cities, jobs continue to be moved offshore and the rural poverty rate is comparable to that in urban centres. While most US rural areas are not poor in the conventional sense, rural economies are not typically centres of growth. There are exceptions in both directions. Persistent deep poverty is concentrated in regions such as Appalachia and the Mississippi Delta, while other types of rural areas benefit by being able to dominate particular niches, as in retirement destinations, centres of recreation and tourism, areas experiencing energy-related booms and dormitory communities that are located within commuting range of expanding metropolitan labour markets.[4] Meanwhile, the chapters on rural policy (Bryden and Warner, Chapter 10), agricultural policy (Brasier et al., Chapter 11) and economic transformation (Atterton, Bryden and Johnson, Chapter 7) show that rural policy in both countries has remained fundamentally agricentric, falling some way short of the New Rural Paradigm anticipated by the Organisation for Economic Co-operation and Development (OECD).

Yet all these chapters also point to the possibility of change. The rural policy and economic transformation chapters highlight how the current economic crisis shows up problems with unfettered marketisation, which affects rural areas as much as anywhere. And while the agricultural policy chapter notes the 'in-built conservatism' of agricultural policy in both countries, it lists a wide range of features and forces that are producing change. From the perspective of managing the landscape, the chapters overall find that governance and democracy issues are significant, 'the people' can be involved in food production and relations in place and region are as significant as global or national discourse. These are the kind of transformations that are under way, and could become even more important in the future.

Given this experience of the past forty years in the UK and US, can we say anything in conclusion about rural areas' futures? How well placed are rural communities in the UK and US to face the challenges and opportunities of the twenty-first century? What further rural transformations are likely? And, what role might social science research play in guiding policies aimed at ameliorating rural problems or capitalising on rural opportunities?

A Bright Future for Rural Areas?

As Ward and Ray (2004, 4) have pointed out, referring to the future and rural in the same breath may appear to be something of an oxymoron when rural areas are so often 'cast as inherently traditional and conservative', lying in the domain of the past. 'Overwhelmingly the assumption has been that the source of futures—the drivers of change and innovation—are invariably to be found in the urban context and, more particularly, within large, urban-based corporations and governmental institutions'. In this book we have seen how a view of rural areas as idyllic places of peace, as repositories of national identity and yet also as backward areas in need of modernisation, continues to dominate popular perception and policy in both the US and UK, albeit each within their own discourses identified by Shortall and Warner in Chapter 1. In this way, rurality is seen as a brake on modernity and progress, in the sense that (in a world of flows) 'real places'—where organic communities, stubborn local attachment and continuities with the past survive (Dirlik 2001)—are seen as less malleable and therefore as obstacles to economic development and modernity.

As well as being rooted in the past, rural areas tend to be seen, then, as passive recipients of modernity, 'and at best as moderating 'filters' of exogenous forces for change' (Ward and Ray 2004, 4), despite abundant evidence in this book of the endogenous potential of rural areas and of the agency of rural dwellers. This is apparent in several recent futurology studies, based on the construction of rural scenarios, and in the warnings of well-known scientists of an imminent 'perfect storm' which will wash over everyone like a tsunami. The UK's chief scientific advisor, Professor John Beddington, struck a chord in 2009 when he warned that by 2030 we face a 'perfect storm' of food shortages, scarce water and insufficient energy, which together will unleash public unrest, cross-border conflicts and mass migration as people flee from the worst-affected regions. While public officials in the US seldom articulate subnational development policies, either urban or rural, such views would be broadly shared. A number of formal 'futures studies' have been commissioned in the UK in recent years, some of which focused specifically on the future of rural areas. One was undertaken for the former Ministry of Agriculture by the Henley Centre in 2001, although never published, and it is instructive to note that the 'drivers' of change it identified are all exogenous to rural areas.[5] The curious thing in these scenarios is that people in rural areas appear to have no agency themselves in imagining and pursuing their future, instead being 'acted upon', whether by environmentalists, big business or by the 'perfect storm'.

In contrast, the research presented in this book contributes to a more agentic view of rural people and communities. As discussed in the book's various chapters, we see contemporary rural society as constructed by a broad range of demographic, economic, social and political transformations that result in a highly interactive social space joining rural and urban areas. Rural areas, especially those with competent governance, high levels of civic engagement and well-prepared workers, are capable of negotiating on more even grounds with urban and global actors than in the past. Accordingly, while we are not contending that rural areas now dominate their urban counterparts, we do believe that the potential for more egalitarian urban–rural relationships has been established as urban consumers, businesses and governments increasingly need goods, services, resources and space that are as likely to come from rural places as urban. Of course, the key issue is the locus of power.

Is there any evidence that rural people are taking a more 'active' role in shaping their futures and the future of their places? Is it possible to envisage rural areas as *sources* of the future, as places of innovation and engines of social renewal and economic growth? In the UK recently there have been some suggestions that this might be possible. It has been found, for example, that innovation is greater in rural areas than in urban (Experian 2007; National Endowment for Science, Technology and the Arts 2007), that productivity is growing faster and that around two million people are using broadband to work from home in rural England. Such findings encouraged the Commission for Rural Communities ([CRC] 2008a) to claim the untapped economic potential of rural areas might be worth an extra £347 billion to the national economy.

Place-based rural development initiatives based on community ownership of land and other assets appear to have particular promise for challenging neo-liberalism. Such possibilities are most likely to emerge from 'the (re)mobilisation, recognition and valuation of multiple, *local* forms of development, rooted in local cultures, values and movements' but which 'spur the post-neoliberal imagination' (Peck et al. 2010. 111). For example, Mackenzie (2006a) sees community-centred land reform not only as a movement towards collective ownership with strong historical resonances, but also as the removal of land from circuits of global capital, in turn permitting a revisioning of the political possibilities of place and a commitment to social justice and sustainability. There are examples in this book that show similar dynamics, and although they are arguably less radical in political terms they may represent a more widely accessible model for reshaping rural societies and landscapes. Hinrichs and Charles's work (Chapter 9) on community-supported agriculture, as described earlier, shows how communities can gain a sense of ownership and participation in food production in specific localities. Vergunst, Geisler and Stedman (Chapter 13), meanwhile, trace a shift in the management of state and national parks towards collaborative management and the maintenance of a working landscape rather than wilderness. In a different sphere, Bosworth and Glasgow (Chapter 8), Atterton, Bryden and Johnson (Chapter 7) and Champion and Brown (Chapter 3) emphasize the benefits of in-migrants in linking *between* places and providing valuable kinds of mobility. Whether such models, emerging from place-based but highly networked rural communities, turn out to be alternatives to neo-liberalism or merely exceptions only time will tell.

Nor is the US bereft of examples of endogenous rural development, as is evident from the chapters by Swindal and McAreavey, and Hinrichs and Charles. Flora et al. (1992) found over one hundred examples of self-development projects in a nationwide study of rural economic development in the US. These projects were characterised by a strong role for local organisations and government, investment of local resources and local ownership and control of enterprises. They were contrasted to conventional smoke-stack chasing and/or efforts to lure branch plants of large national or trans-national corporations. The Centre for Rural Entrepreneurship, part of the University of Missouri's Rural Policy Research Institute, with insight and help from leading practitioners across North America, is building a new generation of entrepreneur-focused development frameworks and processes for communities and regions. They report success even in parts of the Great Plains that have experienced continuous population decline and economic stagnation for decades (Centre for Rural Entrepreneurship 2010).

However, while examples of endogenous development in the US can be identified, and while governmental devolution should theoretically shift responsibility to the local level, the overall picture of local agency in rural America is dim. Warner's (2003) studies of devolution and privatization indicate that the even though the US national government has block granted responsibilities down to states and to local areas, insufficient resources typically accompany these block grants to assure success in accomplishing programme goals and objectives. This situation undermines the potential for redistribution and often exacerbates spatial inequality as community well-being is increasingly dependent on local government capacity. Richer communities can invest more, promoting economic development, while poorer rural communities are caught in a vicious cycle of underinvestment and economic decline (Warner and Pratt 2005).

Lichter and Brown's (2011) notion of enhanced rural–urban interpenetration and greater relative rural power across a broad range of social, economic and political domains contrasts with this view, and is more consistent with the view of increased rural agency articulated in many of this book's chapters. Accordingly, we recommend that both scholars and policymakers should focus more attention on the rural–urban interface, the social spaces that are continuously reconstructed by the interplay of urban and rural forces, rather than on either urban or rural environments separately. Viewed from this perspective, and acknowledging the enhanced levels of mobility in almost every institutional sector—mobilities that are restructuring the urban–rural interface itself—rural areas may become less dependent and acted upon than in the recent past. But, we suspect that only rural places with initial advantages will benefit from the enhanced mobility of people, capital and information. In contrast, less-well-endowed[6] regions and places are poorly placed to compete in the globalised, neo-liberal world characterised by highly mobile people, workers, information and capital. Accordingly, there is a possibility that the 'mobilities turn' will result in increased spatial inequality within rural regions themselves as well as between rural–urban areas in the aggregate.

This book's contributions also address the environmental challenges ahead, again suggesting transformative potential emanating from rural agency. Potter and Wolf (Chapter 12) highlight two central issues: (1) the extent to which the spectre of climate change will elicit changes in policy, whether toward biofuel expansion or multifunctional agriculture; and (2) the institutional form of environmental management, whether a continuing agri-politics coalition or a marketised ecosystem services model. In their place-based approach, focusing on two specific parks, Vergunst, Geisler and Stedman (Chapter13) are able to show how these large-scale themes get enacted and made real in specific localities. In each case environmental change and institutional governance forms is very significant, tending towards multifunctionality and deintensification. Each sought a reconnection to a notion of working landscapes that involved a rejection of universalising preservationist and wilderness discourses in favour of governance at a regional scale. (The latter, interestingly, is just what is being jettisoned in England, as Hewitt and Thompson show in Chapter 14.) It is less clear from these cases how the institutional issue will resolve: there has been a concern to involve more voices from diverse sectors in landscape management, but at the same time commodification of the environment and ecosystem services is rolling out through land management contracts and tourism and leisure development. Ahead lie two forks in the road and these choices may be enacted and manifested quite differently in different places.

Research into Policy

In this volume we have presented research-based information on rural transformations in parallel with discussions of new and evolving policy frameworks meant to enhance rural well-being in the UK and US. However, research does not automatically inform policy. The transfer of research into policy development depends on institutional structures and arrangements. Ironically, as Philip Lowe argued in Chapter 2, US rural sociology historically responded to an external demand for social science to inform policy, while no such demand existed in the UK or elsewhere in Europe except in production agricultural economics. Now, the situation appears to have reversed. Whereas rural policy is the focus of numerous UK (and EU) commissions and policy studies, the US resists articulating even the most basic framework for considering public investments in rural regions.

This turnaround in the US may be explained by the ascendency of the market and the decline of the legitimate powers of the state in American life. The degree of legitimate central power in the US has been debated ever since the nation's founding (Wills 1981). Federal authority reached its peak during the New Deal and during and after World War II, as illustrated in Chapter 6 (Shucksmith and Schafft). Similarly, the demand for social scientific research in general and rural sociological analysis of a variety of policy questions in particular reached its zenith at this time (Larson and Zimmerman 2003). Since then, there has been a conservative backlash in American society as the power of the national state has receded and the legitimacy of federal intervention in local affairs has diminished. In fact, the legitimacy of government intervention at all levels has been disputed by the ascendency of the political right. Unsurprisingly, the demand for policy relevant rural research has diminished along with public perception of the legitimate role of government in local affairs.[7] Accordingly, rural social science research, outside of agricultural economics, is now mostly shaped and motivated by disciplinary debates and university reward systems.

Perhaps the prime example of this disconnect between contemporary rural issues, rural research and rural policy is that rural social scientists in American universities amassed an impressive amount of rigorous research on the determinants of rural poverty and the potential effectiveness of alternative anti-poverty schemas in alleviating poverty (Summers 1993) only to see the nation's 1996 welfare reform be structured in ways that had predictable negative effects on the rural poor (Zimmerman and Hirschl 2003). Research highlighted the role of social and economic structures and historical legacies in producing persistent rural poverty while welfare reform emphasized personal responsibility regardless of the availability of jobs, job training, childcare and/or transportation in rural areas needed to assist poor rural people in making the transition from 'welfare to work' (Shucksmith and Schafft, Chapter 6).

In the UK there has been a stronger demand from government for research to inform 'evidence-based policy-making' (M. Woods 2008, 21), even though many academics are sceptical of the extent to which policy really takes note of research, with some suggesting research findings are selectively enlisted to justify policies which are politically and ideologically derived. Notwithstanding this scepticism, policymakers in the UK have shown an interest in rural research. In preparing its Rural White Paper in 2000, the government commissioned a series of research reviews by academics on such issues as social exclusion in rural areas, homelessness, rural economies and governance[8] and a major study of 'Rural Economies' (Performance and Innovation Unit 1999) by a team within the Cabinet Office (see Ward 2008 for an insider's account). The Scottish government also drew on a study of disadvantage in rural Scotland (Shucksmith et al. 1996) in preparing its Rural White Paper, even opening its public consultation meetings with a summary of this research by the authors; and the Crofting Reform Act 2010 built upon a research-based inquiry (Shucksmith and Rønningen 2011). Indeed, it is common for official inquiries to feed evidence into policy formation in the UK, with other notable examples including the Affordable Rural Housing Commission (2006) and the CRC's Uplands Inquiry (CRC 2010a). Meanwhile the Welsh Assembly funds a Wales Rural Observatory within Cardiff University, and Northern Ireland's Rural White Paper in 2011 benefitted from the secondment of Sally Shortall from Queen's University Belfast. In England, the CRC formed a formal institutional link between rural research and policy from 2005 to 2012, given its statutory role as expert advisor to the government on rural issues, with a particular focus on disadvantaged groups and places. The Coalition government has announced the CRC's abolition from 2012. The US has not witnessed this level of attention to rural issues since the last year of the Carter administration when Kenneth Deavers and David Brown were seconded to the White House Domestic Policy Staff to prepare a background paper supporting the Rural Policy Act of 1980 (Deavers and Brown 1980).

Aside from the institutional concerns raised in the preceding, one questions whether current research in the UK or US will elucidate new possibilities and alternatives rather than reproducing conventional approaches to rural development. We are not alone in this concern (Ward and Ray 2004). Accordingly, we conclude this volume with a call for creative new research, grounded in disciplinary legacies and training but not held hostage by them. New problems require new ways of thinking. We are optimistic that tomorrow's scholars will be up to the task of producing policy-relevant research that contributes to innovative new approaches of meeting rural challenges and taking advantage of rural opportunities. The challenge will be to build academic, policy and financial support for such initiatives.[9]

Moreover, research-based information does not travel on its own. Bridges need to be built between scholars and policymakers to ensure that research is responsive to current needs and that research results are brought to bear in the policy development arena. In the US, historically, the land -grant university system was responsible for knowledge production and dissemination in the area of rural development, but interest is broadening to other universities and departments as recognition of the urban–rural interaction grows. It remains to be seen what institutional support will survive for such research in the US.

In the UK, there is a large output of excellent rural research. But despite the greater interest of government in being informed by rural research, the challenge is to achieve 'political purchase of critical ideas beyond the walls of the classroom or the pages of academic journals' (Blomley 1994, 383). This has led both Milbourne (2000) and Cloke (1997) to call for 'critical' geographers to seek out new audiences beyond the walls of the academy, as academic insularity has become a significant obstacle to rural research informing policy in the UK. Nevertheless, a few rural researchers are highly engaged with communicating research findings to government and to practice, and universities in the UK are increasingly supportive of such engagement. One notable instance is the Northern Rural Network, which between 2008 and 2011 involved over six hundred rural development practitioners and researchers in Northern England in a knowledge-exchange, organised through Newcastle University's Centre for Rural Economy. Such engagement with policy and practice is likely to grow now that UK universities' funding will depend partly on evidence that their research is having an impact.

The future of rural areas in the UK and US, then, is likely to be characterised by rapid and uneven change, with growing inequality and diversity amongst rural areas, mediated both by the substantially different cultural and political contexts of the two countries, by the degree to which the state supports and enables rural development and by the endogenous actions of the people living in these rural areas themselves. We hope that research, of which this volume is an instance, will play a role in supporting people to realise their hopes for rural futures.

Annex

The Statistical Measurement of Urban and Rural Residence in the UK and US

Tony Champion and David L. Brown

DEFINING URBAN AND RURAL IN THE UK

The UK uses a variety of approaches to define 'rural'. This is partly because there is variation between the four countries of England, Wales, Scotland and Northern Ireland in how rural areas are officially defined for statistical reporting purposes. It is also because of the use of different approaches for different applications, with this being influenced not just by the purpose of the analysis but also by data availability.

The finest-grained definition uses physical criteria, identifying as 'urban' those separate areas of built-up land that reach a certain minimum threshold of areal extent and population size. In England and Wales these are labelled 'urban areas', while in Scotland the equivalent process produces 'localities'. Some consistency across the UK can be achieved by restricting the description 'urban' to such places that are over a certain population size, with ten thousand and three thousand being the most commonly used by government departments and with the 'rural' being the territory that does not meet the particular threshold selected.

While this approach yields the most accurate measure of the level of urbanisation using data from each of the ten yearly population censuses, it is less suitable for analysing population change over time, partly because these places are redefined for each census but mainly because population counts for years between censuses are not produced for such a refined geography. The only exception is where small-area census data on where people were living twelve months before can be used to measure the effect of one year's worth of residential mobility on each urban area's population.

The principal alternative way of distinguishing rural from urban in the UK is through the use of socio-demographic classification techniques to develop typologies of places. The Office for National Statistics (2004) offers UK-wide place classifications for at least four alternative levels of standard statistical geography: (1) Census Output Area (or Data Zone in Scotland), (2) Lower Level Super Output Area (which are groupings of these), (3) Census Ward and (4) Local Authority (known as Local Authorities and Unitary

Authorities in England, Unitary Authorities in Wales, Council Areas in Scotland and Local Government Districts in Northern Ireland but referred to generically as 'districts'). These classifications normally have three hierarchical levels, the highest being 'families', followed by 'groups' and the most disaggregated version called 'clusters'. On the other hand, these do not provide users with a single rural–urban dichotomy, so decisions have to be made about which of the classes should be deemed 'rural' and which level to choose for this, with the 'cluster' level yielding the most precise results. In Table 3.1 and Figure 3.2 of this book, three clusters of the district-level classification have been used to represent rural Britain, namely, 'urban fringe', 'agricultural' and 'rural extremes'.

There are a variety of other classifications available for one or more of these geographical scales. For rural research, probably the most appropriate one—even though it covers only England—is the sixfold DEFRA district-level typology used in Tables 3.2 and 3.3 of this book. This classification is based on the proportion of the 2001 Census population that was 'rural' (i.e. not living in an urban area with ten thousand or more residents nor in a 'market town' if larger) and/or on the size of the urban area that the district was part of (Rural Evidence Research Centre 2005). For instance, 'Rural-80' denotes districts where the rural population share was at least 80 per cent, while at the other extreme a district is classified as 'Major Urban' if the majority of its population was living in an urban area which was home to 750,000 or more people.

DEFINING URBAN AND RURAL IN THE US

The United States uses two parallel systems to measure urbanisation: urban versus rural and metropolitan versus nonmetropolitan. The US Bureau of the Census differentiates urban places from their rural counterparts by using population size and density thresholds. The second approach, employed by the US Office of Management and Budget (OMB), uses both demographic and economic criteria to identify metropolitan regions. Similar to the urban–rural distinction, nonmetropolitan areas are treated as residuals, i.e. they are defined by what they are not, rather than what they are.

Urban vs. Rural

Urban areas include urban clusters and urbanised areas. *Urban clusters* are defined as central places and adjacent territory with at least twenty-five hundred people and an overall density of one thousand persons per square mile. *Urbanised areas* are a special subset of urban clusters with a population of fifty thousand or greater. The distinction between urban clusters and urbanised areas is important because, as will be shown in the following, metropolitan areas must be organised around an urbanised area.

Metropolitan vs. Nonmetropolitan

Metropolitan areas are urban regions comprised of a central county plus adjacent counties that are highly integrated with the centre. Central counties contain the urbanised area that gives the area its name. Urbanised areas often extend beyond the central county into adjacent areas, but the majority of the urbanised area is contained in the central county (or counties). Outlying counties qualify for inclusion in the metropolitan area if they have a sufficient rate of commuting linkage with the central county's urbanised area. The city–hinterland concept was influential in shaping this statistical practice.

Nonmetropolitan areas are counties that neither have an urbanised area of fifty thousand population nor are integrated by workforce commuting with a metropolitan central county. About two-thirds of US counties (2,151 of 3,141) were classified as nonmetropolitan after the 2000 Census, but these areas contain only 17 per cent of the nation's population (ERS-US Department of Agriculture [USDA] 2007). Scholars have criticized this system not only because the nonmetropolitan population is a residual, but because it is also an undifferentiated residual (Brown and Cromartie 2004). As early as 1975, the USDA observed that the nonmetropolitan sector was extremely diverse and recommended that it be disaggregated by combining the urban–rural classification with the metropolitan vs. nonmetropolitan delineation (Hines, Brown and Zimmer 1975). Following the 2000 Census, the OMB finally responded to this critique by creating a statistical system in which nonmetropolitan counties are grouped into two types of core-based statistical areas. *Micropolitan* areas are organised around an urbanised area of 10,000 to 49,999 persons, while *non-core-based areas* lack even one place with ten thousand population (Brown et al. 2004). For the first time, the US government is now displaying nonmetropolitan data in a way that compares unambiguously rural counties with more highly urbanised micropolitan areas.

COMPARING THE UK AND US APPROACHES TO MEASURING URBAN AND RURAL RESIDENCE

While statistical practices in the UK and US are sufficiently different that precise comparisons of population redistribution cannot be made, official statistical geographies are similar enough to place the two nation's experiences into a comparative framework and thereby examine the fundamental dimensions of rural (and urban) change in the two nations. It should also be noted that while both the UK and US use official classification systems for displaying census data, various government agencies in both countries are free to use other geographic schema for targeting and administering programmes, and to determine programme eligibility (Cromartie and Bucholtz 2008).

Contributors

Jane Atterton is a Policy Researcher in the Rural Policy Centre at Scottish Agricultural College (SAC), UK. Her research focuses on rural and regional development, rural businesses, demographic and social change in rural communities and the rural policy-making process. Prior to working at SAC, Jane was a Lecturer in Rural Development in the Centre for Rural Economy, Newcastle University. Her PhD research focused on the geography of networking relationships maintained by business owners in the Highlands and Islands of Scotland.

Gary Bosworth is a Reader in Enterprise and Rural Economies at the University of Lincoln. Having recently completed his PhD at Newcastle University, he has published several papers on the economic impact of counterurbanisation and is pursuing further research in the fields of commercial counterurbanisation, rural development and small businesses.

Kathryn Brasier is an Assistant Professor of Rural Sociology in the Department of Agricultural Economics and Rural Sociology at the Pennsylvania State University. Her research and extension programmes focus on collective action and networking around agricultural and environment issues. Specific interests include network effects on learning and innovation, particularly among farmers using conservation practices; social impacts of energy development; grassroots community environmental organisations; civic engagement in public policy dialogue and deliberation; value-added and sustainable agricultural production systems; and the effects of space and scale on farm management and environmental decision-making. Dr. Brasier received her PhD in Sociology from the University of Wisconsin-Madison in 2002.

David L. Brown is Professor and Chair of Development Sociology, Co-Director of the Community & Regional Development Institute and Director of Graduate Studies in Demography at Cornell University in Ithaca, New York. Professor Brown's research focuses on migration and population redistribution in the US and Europe with a particular focus on how migration affects and is affected by local community organisation. His work also focuses on the production and reproduction of social and economic inequalities between regions and rural versus urban areas. He has written and edited eight books on rural population and society. His most recent books include: *Rural Communities in the 21ˢᵗ Century: Resilience and Transformation* (2011), *Rural Retirement Migration* (2008, with Nina Glasgow), *Population Change and Rural Society* (2006) and *Challenges for Rural America in the 21ˢᵗ Century* (2003). He is past president of the Rural Sociological Society.

John Bryden is Professor at the Norwegian Agricultural Economics Research Institute in Oslo and Emeritus Professor at the University of Aberdeen where he was Chair of Human Geography from 1995 to 2004, and Co-Director of the Arkleton Institute for Rural Development Research. He formerly worked for the Arkleton Trust, the Highlands and Islands Development Board, the University of East Anglia, and in the UK Government Economic Service. John has been an advisor on rural policy to the OECD, the EU, the World Bank and the Scottish government, as well as Secretary of the Cross Party group on Rural Policy in the Scottish Parliament from 2005 to 2008. He has coordinated six EU-funded transnational research projects on rural development issues. John has been a visiting scholar at the University of Guelph, Canada; the University of Missouri-Columbia; Cornell University; and the Centre for Development Studies in Kerala, India.

Tony Champion is Emeritus Professor of Population Geography at the University of Newcastle upon Tyne. His research interests include change in population distribution and composition, with particular reference to counterurbanisation and population deconcentration in developed countries and the policy implications of changes in local population profiles. He led the IUSSP's Working Group on Urbanization in 1999–2002 and is author or co-author of several books and reports, including *New Forms of Urbanization: Beyond the Urban-Rural Dichotomy* (2004), *The Containment of Urban Britain: Retrospect and Prospect* (2002), *Urban Exodus* (1998), *The Population of Britain in the 1990s* (1996) and *Counterurbanization* (1989).

Liz Charles is in the final stages of completing a PhD at Newcastle University, UK. She chose a participatory action research approach to investigate the development of community-supported agriculture in the north-east region of England. Liz has also worked in the field of rural community development for over fifteen years and is currently employed by Durham Rural Community Council.

Philomena de Lima is the Director of the Centre for Remote and Rural Studies, University of the Highlands and Islands, Scotland. A sociologist, her research interests include social justice and equalities with a particular focus on migration, ethnicity and belonging. She has undertaken a wide range of research and published widely on ethnic minorities and migrants in rural Scotland and the UK. Forthcoming and recent publications include: Migration, race equality and discrimination: A question of social justice, in Mooney and Scott, eds., *Social Justice and Social Welfare in Contemporary Scotland* (forthcoming, Policy Press); Welcoming migrants? Migrant labour in rural Scotland? (*Social Policy and Society* 2009, with Wright); and Migrant workers in rural Scotland: Going to the middle of nowhere? (*International Journal on Multicultural Societies* 2007, with Jentsch and MacDonald).

Jill L. Findeis is Distinguished Professor of Agricultural, Environmental and Regional Economics at Penn State. She is in the Department of Agricultural Economics and Rural Sociology, and is affiliated with the Population Research Institute. In August 2011, she will assume the position of Director, Division of Applied Social Sciences at the University of Missouri. Dr. Findeis is keenly interested in public policy, particularly as related to agriculture in developed and developing country contexts.

Charles Geisler is a Professor in Development Sociology at Cornell University, Ithaca, New York. He has a sustained interest in changing property relations in conditions of exception/emergency/crisis. He specializes in topics of homeland securitization and property rights; the militarization of land-use planning; possession and dispossession as a by-product of the global war on terror; conservation evictions in and around parks and protected areas; development-induced displacement; *terra nullius* narratives in making/breaking development spaces; and drug wars and child soldier recruitment.

Nina Glasgow is Senior Research Associate in the Department of Development Sociology, Cornell University. She conducts research on the sociology of ageing and the life course, especially in rural environments. Glasgow (with David L. Brown) co-authored the research monograph *Rural Retirement Migration*, published by Springer (2008). She has published three books, numerous journal articles and book chapters, as well as several policy and research briefs using evidence from her research to communicate with broader, non-academic audiences.

Sally Hewitt is Rural Policy Manager at Lincolnshire County Council in the UK. Her role focuses on the implications of European and national policy for rural areas, and socio-economic initiatives in rural Lincolnshire. Her PhD research with the Centre for Rural Economy at Newcastle University is on the impact of regionalisation in England on rural development.

Clare Hinrichs is Associate Professor of Rural Sociology at the Pennsylvania State University. Her research and teaching focus on the intersections of social change and development with food, agricultural and environmental systems. She has been an ESRC/SSRC Visiting Fellow with the Rural Economy and Land Use Programme in the UK. Her publications include *Remaking the North American Food System: Strategies for Sustainability*, a book co-edited with the late Thomas Lyson.

Carmen Hubbard is a Research Associate in the Centre for Rural Economy, School of Agriculture, Food and Rural Development, University of Newcastle upon Tyne. She trained as an agricultural economist and has particular expertise in agricultural and rural development policy with a focus on Central and Eastern Europe. Dr. Hubbard has substantial experience in a variety of policy-oriented international projects funded by the European Union. Most recently she has applied her skills in an interdisciplinary context and developed additional areas of expertise in animal welfare and consumer behaviour and, since 2009, has been Research Manager in the CRE.

Lionel Hubbard is a Senior Lecturer in the School of Agriculture, Food and Rural Development in the University of Newcastle upon Tyne, and former Head of Department of Agricultural Economics and Food Marketing. He has experience of working in Central and Eastern Europe (Romania, Hungary, Czech Republic, Latvia and Moldova) and in Australia and New Zealand. His main research interests are in international trade, applied general equilibrium modelling, the Common Agricultural Policy and post-communist economies. Currently, Dr. Hubbard is associate editor of the *Journal of Agricultural Economics* and external editor for *Food Policy*.

Thomas G. Johnson is the Frank Miller Professor of Agricultural and Applied Economics and the Truman School of Public Affairs at the University of Missouri-Columbia. Professor Johnson directs the Analytic and Academic programmes for RUPRI. He has studied the role of policy in rural economic development in North America, Europe and Asia for over thirty-five years.

Philip Lowe is Director of the Rural Economy and Land Use (RELU) Programme of the UK Research Councils. In 1992, he founded the Centre for Rural Economy at the University of Newcastle upon Tyne, where he holds the Duke of Northumberland Chair of Rural Economy. He has played an active role in rural policy development at the national and European levels and in the north of England. For his contribution to the rural economy he was appointed OBE in 2003. Between 2007 and 2009 he was Chair of DEFRA's Vets and Veterinary Services Working Group.

He has also served on DEFRA's Science Advisory Council and the Board of the Countryside Agency.

Ruth McAreavey has held a range of professional positions working for local government and non-governmental organisations. She has skills and experience in research development and management, research funding and community development and regeneration. Ruth has recently completed research for the Nuffield Foundation on the lives of migrants in Northern Ireland. Her research publications reflect this and her other research interests, which include rural development theory, policy and practice; participation, governance and regeneration; regional and economic development; and research methodologies.

Pilar A. Parra is a Research Associate and Senior Lecturer at the Division of Nutritional Sciences and in the Latino Studies Program in Cornell University. Her research examines immigrant integration in rural communities, and the role of immigration, acculturation and poverty in the health status of minority populations.

Max J. Pfeffer is International Professor of Development Sociology and Senior Associate Dean of the Cornell University College of Agriculture and Life Sciences. His interests span several areas including rural labour markets, international migration, land use and environmental planning.

Lorna Philip is Senior Lecturer in Geography at the University of Aberdeen. Her research interests focus upon ageing and social exclusion in rural communities. She has recently completed a project on retirement transition migration into remote rural areas in Scotland, Wales and Northern Ireland and is investigating the potential of new technologies to support independent living amongst the older rural population in Scotland and Wales

Clive Potter is Reader in Environmental Policy at Imperial College London and Visiting Professor in the Centre for Rural Policy Research at the University of Exeter. His research interests include the policy and politics of rural sustainability, land-use change and biosecurity.

Rodrigo Salcedo Du Bois is a PhD Candidate in Agricultural, Environmental and Regional Economics & Demography at the Pennsylvania State University. He has collaborated in several projects in Peru, such as the Assessment of the Land Titling Program and the Analysis of Efficiency of Small Agricultural Producers. Since 2007, he has worked as part of the research team of the Transitional Zone Ecosystem Initiative at the Pennsylvania State University. His current research focuses on the analysis of rural households' socio-economic decisions and their interaction with natural resources and the provision of ecosystem services in areas affected by urbanisation pressure.

Kai Schafft is an Associate Professor of Education at Penn State University. He serves as the Director of the Center on Rural Education and Communities at Penn State, and edits the *Journal of Research in Rural Education*. He is the co-editor of *Rural Education for the Twenty-First Century: Identity, Place, and Community in a Globalizing World*, published in 2010 by Penn State University Press, and the co-author (with David Brown) of *Rural People and Communities in the 21st Century: Resilience & Transformation*, published in 2011 by Polity Press.

Sally Shortall is a Reader in Sociology in Queen's University Belfast. She has published on rural development theory and practice, community and stakeholder engagement in policy processes and the position of women in the farming industry. She recently spent a year in the Department of Agriculture and Rural Development as an ESRC Research Fellow and is currently writing about the social construction of rural policy priorities.

Mark Shucksmith is Professor of Planning at Newcastle University. Mark was First Vice-President of the International Rural Sociological Association for 2004–2008 and was Programme Chair for the XI World Rural Sociology Congress in Norway in 2004. He is the author or co-author of several books, including *Rural Communities to Rural Consumption* (Emerald, 2010); *Comparing Rural Development: Continuity and Change in the Countryside of Western Europe* (Ashgate, 2009); *CAP and the Regions* (CABI, 2005); *Young People in Rural Europe* (Ashgate, 2004); *Housing in the European Countryside* (Routledge, 2003); and *Exclusive Countryside? Social Inclusion and Regeneration in Rural Britain* (JRF, 2000). He is a Commissioner with the Commission for Rural Communities, chaired the Scottish government's Inquiry into Crofting and was awarded the OBE for services to crofting and rural development in 2009.

Richard Stedman is an Associate Professor in the Department of Natural Resources at Cornell University, and Associate Director of the Human Dimensions of Natural Resources Research Unit. His research and teaching focus on the relationship between elements of the environment, sense of place and place-protective behaviour; the well-being of resource dependent communities; and vulnerability/adaptive capacity in the face of rapid social and environmental change.

Aileen Stockdale is a Professor in Environmental Planning at Queen's University Belfast, UK. Her research focuses on rural demography and primarily rural migration trends and processes. Recent studies have focused on the broad question of rural change and have included the role of life course migration and associated socio-economic drivers and consequences. She has recently completed a two-year ESRC-funded project on *The Retirement Transition and the (UK) Celtic Fringe: Mobility Trends and Migrant and Rural Community Consequences* (with Lorna Philip).

Megan G. Swindal is a PhD candidate in Development Sociology at Cornell University. Her research focuses on development and the role of ideology in socio-economic policy-making.

Nicola Thompson is a Researcher at the Centre for Rural Economy at Newcastle University, UK. Her research focuses on rural governance and policy in the UK and EU, including the implications of state rescaling for rural areas.

Jo Vergunst is a Lecturer in the Department of Anthropology at the University of Aberdeen. His research interests are in relations between rural society and landscapes in Scotland and Europe, focusing particularly on environmental governance and outdoor access. Amongst his publications are the books *Comparing Rural Development*, co-edited with Arnar Árnason and Mark Shucksmith, and *Ways of Walking*, co-edited with Tim Ingold.

Mildred E. Warner is a Professor of City and Regional Planning at Cornell University. Her research focuses on local government issues: privatization, devolution, economic development and social welfare. Her work spans the US, Europe and the developing world.

Steven Wolf is Associate Professor in the Department of Natural Resources, Cornell University, Ithaca, New York, and Senior Lecturer in the Centre for Environmental Policy, Imperial College, London. His research and teaching address tensions represented in land use and environmental conservation. He studies the production of socioeconomic and ecological (in)coherence from an institutional perspective with particular emphasis on the distribution of property rights, organisational forms, accountability mechanisms and knowledge creation.

Notes

3 MIGRATION AND URBAN–RURAL POPULATION REDISTRIBUTION IN THE UK AND US

Champion and Brown

1. There is a substantial debate among policymakers regarding the necessity of public interventions to retain population and economic activities in rural areas or whether to simply let the market allocate resources among locations (Brown 2008).
2. Cosby's analysis compares age adjusted all cause mortality rates. Smith et al. (2008) have shown that rural mortality rates are somewhat lower between ages fifty-five and eighty.
3. In addition to their younger age structure, nonmetro Hispanics have slightly higher fertility rates than non-Hispanic whites.
4. Thirty-one per cent of residents of rural communities with high rates of Mexican immigration reported that immigration is an asset while 12 per cent reported it was a burden.

4 DEMOGRAPHIC AGEING IN RURAL AREAS: INSIGHTS FROM THE UK AND US

Philip, Brown and Stockdale

1. The state pension age for men born before 6 April 1959 is currently sixty-five and women born on or before 5 April 1950 are eligible for their state pension at age sixty. Between 2010 and 2020 the state pension age for women born on or after 6 April 1950 will increase to sixty-five. Between 2024 and 2046 state pension eligibility age will increase, in three stages, to sixty-eight years for both men and women. For more details, see http://www.direct.gov.uk/en/Pensionsandretirementplanning/StatePension/DG_4017919.
2. Eligibility for Social Security is sixty-two at the present time in the US. Full benefits can be obtained after age sixty-six. However, the age at which people can retire with full Social Security varies depending on when they were born. The upward shift in the age at which people can receive full benefits is being phased in over time, and is sixty-eight for the youngest cohort. These changes in the system were instituted in order to ensure the system's solvency. It should also be noted that Social Security was designed to be an income supplement, not to provide full economic support for retirees. A 'full pension' seldom exceeds $30,000 even for persons who work until age seventy.

3. For an overview of the methodology used to calculate population projections see, for example, Section 5 Methodology and Assumptions in GROS (2010).
4. The rural–urban distinction in this chapter utilizes data disaggregated by metropolitan–nonmetropolitan status. See the Annex for a definition of metropolitan and nonmetropolitan populations in the US.
5. See Chapter 6 in this volume for a discussion of poverty measurement in the US.
6. While this phenomenon is labelled 'retirement migration' Brown and Glasgow (2008) reported that 37 per cent of in-movers to nonmetro retirement destinations were working at least part-time. Hence, the phenomenon should more correctly be labelled 'retirement-age migration'.
7. Immigrants from Eastern Europe have filled some of this labour need (see Chapters 3 and 5 in this volume) but only time will tell if these immigrants remain residents of remote rural communities occupying low-paid jobs in the future and/or whether an inflow of EU A8 migrants will continue in remote rural communities.

5 CONCEPTUALIZING CONTEMPORARY IMMIGRANT INTEGRATION IN THE RURAL UNITED STATES AND UNITED KINGDOM

de Lima, Parra and Pfeffer

1. We use the term 'unauthorized' to refer to persons who enter the US without an officially issued permit. The government issues non-citizens various types of visas upon entry to the US, but there is widespread forgery of these documents, so many persons we refer to as unauthorized may have some type of documents in hand. Others enter without any documents. We use 'unauthorized' to refer to all immigrants without valid documents.
2. de Lima acknowledges the involvement of B. Jensch and R. Whelton in the 2005 study 'Migrant Workers in the Highlands and Islands', and M. Chaudhry, R. Whelton and R. Arshad in the 2007 'Study of Migrant Workers in Grampian'.

6 RURAL POVERTY AND SOCIAL EXCLUSION IN THE UNITED STATES AND THE UNITED KINGDOM

Shucksmith and Schafft

1. The Progressive Era, from the 1890s to the 1920s, was a period in which various reformers argued for a wide range of political, social and economic change, often advocating increased government regulation of business and enhanced social safety protections. Prominent poverty-related social scientific work included that of Jane Addams, W.E.B. DuBois and Chicago School sociologists such as W.I. Thomas, Robert E. Park and Louis Wirth (O'Connor 2004).
2. See, for example, Matt Wray's (2006) fascinating account of the American eugenics movement in the first part of the twentieth century and the attempts to undo the South's cultural 'backwardness' and poverty.
3. The poverty line is set at three times the cost of what is thought to be a minimally adequate diet, a threshold based upon findings from the 1955

Household and Food Consumption Survey by the USDA. This survey indicated that for families of three or more, the average amount spent on food was about one third the total household income after taxes.

4. In March, 2010, the US Census Bureau announced that it was developing a Supplemental Poverty Measure (SPM) as an additional means of gauging economic need. The SPM will incorporate tax payments and work expenses in addition to income measures to estimate family resources. As such, it represents the latest effort by the US federal government to refine how poverty is measured and assessed.

5. Individual-level explanations of poverty also strongly resonate with certain commonly held American values about self-reliance, meritocracy, persistence and self-realization, as well as myths about America as a 'land of opportunity' (Rank 2005; Strauss 2002).

6. 'One of the major puzzles of social history is why a political party (soon to be renamed the Liberal Party) which stood for all that was enlightened and progressive at the time introduced a Poor Law system which has become a byword for inhumanity' (Jones 2000, 7).

7. However, Philip and Shucksmith (2003) have argued that a broader approach is needed since these processes extend far beyond the labour market and indeed are multidimensional.

8. Households in or on the margins of poverty were defined by McLaughlin as those with an income up to 139 per cent of their welfare (supplementary benefit) entitlement at the time.

9. Since identification of this as a research priority by Shucksmith et al. (1997), research in the UK began to be conducted on dynamic processes, and the identification of 'bridges and barriers' to exclusion and integration, through a combination of longitudinal analysis of rural households in the British Household Panel Survey (BHPS), following the same randomly selected 7,164 individuals each year between 1991 and 1996 (Chapman et al. 1998), alongside a suite of nine qualitative, place-based studies conducted by several universities.

7 RURAL ECONOMIC TRANSFORMATIONS IN THE UK AND US

Atterton, Bryden and Johnson

1. The actual number of migrant workers is likely to be much higher as not all will be registered.

2. This is data from the Annual Business Inquiry, which is collected from places of work (i.e. business units) rather than places of residence.

3. These are definitions of rurality used by the UK Department of Environment, Food and Rural Areas (DEFRA). Rural-80 are districts with at least 80 per cent of their population in rural settlements and larger market towns. Rural-50 are districts with at least 50 per cent but less than 80 per cent of their population in rural settlements and larger market towns. Source: http://www. defra.gov.uk/evidence/statistics/rural/rural-definition.htm, see also Annex.

4. This data is based on VAT registration rates which tend to underreport business formation in rural areas. Using records of new business accounts opened in mainstream clearing banks suggests greater entrepreneurial activity in rural than urban areas (CRC 2007, 99).

5. It should be acknowledged, however, that output-based measures such as GVA are problematic when measuring the economic health of rural areas for several

reasons. GVA includes the profits and rents of external owners of rural capital and in cases where there are high levels of external ownership this can be important. It also does not capture unearned household income, which for some rural areas constitutes substantial proportions through pensions, receipts from property and other investments, savings and benefit payments (CRC 2008a, 89). Local area productivity may reflect more on the sector composition of local labour markets than on weaknesses in other drivers of productivity (CRC 2007, 99). Finally, GVA downplays the contribution of areas from which people commute and thus contribute to wealth creation elsewhere (CRC 2006, 68).
6. This definition includes those who work mainly in their own home as well as those who work in different places using home as a base.
7. The 'creative class' has been defined by Richard Florida (2002) as a key driving force for economic development in the US and includes scientists, engineers, arts and design workers (who are creating commercial products and consumer goods) and knowledge-based workers in health care, business and finance and legal professions (who draw on complex knowledge to solve problems).
8. *Rural proofing* is the term used in the UK to refer to the process by which all policies are 'checked', to ensure that they will not have a detrimental impact on rural areas or rural actors (see Atterton 2008 for more information).

8 ENTREPRENEURIAL BEHAVIOUR AMONG RURAL IN-MIGRANTS
Bosworth and Glasgow

1. On the questionnaire, the questions about attitudes towards growth and expansion of the current product range were consecutive so it is reasonable to assume that the respondents made this connection and were not simply saying that they would like to grow without giving thought to how they may achieve it.

9 LOCAL FOOD SYSTEMS AND NETWORKS IN THE US AND THE UK: COMMUNITY DEVELOPMENT CONSIDERATIONS FOR RURAL AREAS
Hinrichs and Charles

1. See Blythman (2006) and Pollan (2006) for recent popular critiques of the state of the food and agricultural system in, respectively, the UK and the US.
2. Examining environmental and ecological impacts is important for assessing the development of local food systems and networks, but remains outside the main focus of this chapter. See Edwards-Jones et al. (2008) and Duram and Oberholtzer (2010) for representative research in this area.
3. However, see Barham, Bingen and Hinrichs (2011) for a discussion of the prospects for initiatives to organise and protect 'American origin products' premised on locality considerations.
4. Details about Earthshare are from an informal interview conducted with the main grower on site, 24 August 2009.
5. Food policy in the UK is devolved so that the remit for the Commission was for England only. This chapter does not discuss in detail food policies and strategies that have been developed in Scotland, Wales and Northern Ireland.

10 POLICY AFFECTING RURAL PEOPLE, ECONOMIES AND COMMUNITIES

Bryden and Warner

1. The main exceptions were in northern Europe—the Highlands and Islands Development Board (HIDB) in Scotland, established in 1965 by the Labour government. Its name was changed to Highlands and Islands Enterprise (HIE) during the Thatcher years of the 1980s. Similarly, the Appalachian Regional Commission and Tennessee Valley Authority in the 1950–1960s US and still today constitute specific rural territorial policy initiatives.
2. An English Countryside Agency Report confirmed that the outbreak affected 40 per cent of businesses in the region of Cumbria in north-west England, and that these were mainly tourist, service, agricultural supply and other land-based firms. The worst hit was the tourist industry, which suffered losses of over £4 billion, compared with the £1 billion paid to farmers in compensation (Bryden and Hart 2004, 300).
3. During the 1990s LEADER was only available in the Cohesion policy priority regions of Objective 1 and 5b. LEADER I was regarded as so successful that the budget and number of local action groups was more than doubled for the second programming period 1994–1999.

11 THE EVOLUTION OF AGRICULTURE AND AGRICULTURAL POLICY IN THE UK AND US

Brasier, Findeis, Hubbard, Hubbard and Salcedo Du Bois

1. Authorship is given alphabetically, and based on contributions by Hubbard and Hubbard for the UK and Findeis, Brasier and Salcedo Du Bois for the US.
2. Refers to all UK food production, including exports, and is calculated as the farm-gate value of raw food divided by the value of raw food for human consumption (DEFRA).
3. Some 8.5 million animals were slaughtered under the Over Thirty Month Scheme between 1996 and 2006 due to BSE (http://www.defra.gov.uk/food-farm/farmanimal/diseases/atoz/bse/statistics/schemes.htm). Another 6.5 million were slaughtered during the FMD outbreak in 2001 (Donaldson et al. 2006).
4. The cost of BSE for 1996 and 1997 is estimated at £641 million for each year (Pretty et al. 2000).
5. However, in 1999, the European Commission did allow the UK to export boneless beef and beef products from animals aged between six and thirty months under the Over Thirty Month Scheme.
6. 1 ESU = €1,200 Standard Gross Margin (SGM).
7. Unlike UK classification schemes that measure farm size by 'amount of land farmed', the US typically measures farm size by annual farm sales. The USDA small family farm definition combines small and medium sales classes, including all farms with less than $250,000 in annual farm sales. Operations with annual sales of $250,000 or more are considered large farms.
8. The documented 'official' increase in US small farms is partly due to the National Agricultural Statistics Service's efforts to locate and count all farms, including some that had not been included in previous censes. This effort was initiated for the 2002 Census.

9. If more than a single third country is involved in producing and processing the beef, the product may be labelled as 'non-EC'.

12 AGRI-ENVIRONMENTAL POLICY, RURAL ENVIRONMENTS AND FORKS IN THE ROAD: A COMPARATIVE ANALYSIS OF THE US AND THE UK

Wolf and Potter

1. Baylis et al. (2007) recognise that agri-environmental payments are entangled with the impulse to transfer income from non-farm to farm segments of the population, but they downplay this feature of the policies in their analysis of the US. Additionally, our analysis differs from theirs in that these authors emphasize sharp differences in US and EU agri-environmental policies while we emphasize important similarities.
2. Later, disputes over the Universal Soil Loss Equation's inability to adequately address wind erosion (a major concern in the Palouse region of Oregon and Washington) led to the Revised Universal Soil Loss Equation (RUSLE). Further evidence of the political, rather than scientific, basis of the technical consensus that emerged around RUSLE is the fact that the standard for cross-compliance was increased from T to 2T—a 100 per cent increase in tolerance for erosion—as part of a pursuant political settlement between productivist and sustainability interests.
3. The USDA's Conservation Effectiveness Assessment Program initiated in 2003 deserves attention as a focus for empirical research on the ambiguous status of rationalization within agri-environmental policy.

13 NATURE CONSERVATION AND ENVIRONMENTAL MANAGEMENT: WORKING LANDSCAPES IN ADIRONDACK PARK, US, AND CAIRNGORMS NATIONAL PARK, UK

Vergunst, Geisler and Stedman

1. In 1869 W.H.H. Murray produced a popular book, *Adventures in the Wilderness, or Camp Life in the Adirondacks*, setting in motion many pilgrimages to the Adirondacks (Rezelman 1998).
2. Banner (2005) argues, however, that the British often purchased Indian lands they desired, notwithstanding the inadequacy of price or the reluctance or naivety of the sellers. "Enclosure" in North America was thus significantly different from its namesake in Britain.
3. Tax-delinquent lands are lands that owners either purposely or inadvertently stop paying property taxes on. After a certain grace period and notifications to get the owner to pay the 'back' taxes, the land is seized or reverts to the taxing authority and may be retained or sold by that authority.
4. See the Laws of New York, 1885, Chapter 283 for the legal mandate of the NYS Forest Preserve.
5. There are additional rules and regulations in the plan that govern shorelines, map amendments, variance procedures, etc., but the density guidelines and permit decisions are the 'big sticks' carried by the agency.

15 RURAL GOVERNANCE: PARTICIPATION, POWER AND POSSIBILITIES FOR ACTION

Swindal and McAreavey

1. Questions have been raised in the past in relation to the legitimacy of local partnerships, representation, economic versus social objectives and power relations (see, for example, D. Storey 1999; Ray 2000; Shortall and Shucksmith 2001).
2. In a similar way, partnerships under the most recent PEACE III programme are also aligned to council clusters and their membership comprises of mostly elected representatives, with approximately one-third representing social partners.

16 CONSTRUCTING THE RURAL–URBAN INTERFACE: PLACE STILL MATTERS IN A HIGHLY MOBILE SOCIETY

Shucksmith, Brown and Vergunst

1. Urry's ideas bear some resemblance to Barry Wellman's (1979) notion of 'liberated communities' although Wellman focuses more narrowly on the role networks play in constructing social relations within metropolitan areas.
2. The concept of neo-endogenous rural development recognises that rural development initiatives are rarely truly endogenous, but depend upon the construction and mobilisation of networks of actors from both within and beyond the locality (Lowe, Murdoch and Ward 1995; Shucksmith 2010).
3. This discussion is somewhat similar to P. Evans's (1995) notion of the entrepreneurial state, as well as his notions about how civil society mediates between state and market.
4. This is true overall, yet nonmetro areas as a category exceed metro counties in poverty rates and the vast majority of persistent poverty rate counties in the US (340 of 386) are nonmetro counties (Jolliffe 2007). See also Schafft and Shucksmith, Chapter 6 in this volume.
5. These included: the growth of 'empowered consumerism'; the search for authenticity and simplicity in consumption practices; residential preferences for rural localities; the spread of broadband and ICT; the rise of e-commerce and genomics; the relative decline of agriculture; rising incomes; increasing inequalities; international economic integration; increasing pressure for action to mitigate climate change; pressure for Common Agricultural Policy (CAP) reform; and the continued dominance of neo-liberalism.
6. We refer here not to 'natural resource' endowments but to institutional capacity, social capital, education and skills, entrepreneurship, governance, etc.
7. The Economic Research Service (ERS) of the USDA is an exception to this rule. The ERS, and its predecessor units, have maintained a strong programme of rural development–related social science research since 1919. While the unit's strength and influence has waxed and waned during this time, rural people and communities have been a continuous, if relatively small, part of the USDA's internal analytical capabilities.
8. See http://www.defra.gov.uk/rural/pdfs/research/social_excl_lit_review.pdf.
9. For example, Cornell's Community and Regional Development Institute conducts applied research and outreach on rural development. Penn State's

322 *Notes*

Center for Rural Education and Communities addresses rural education and community-based issues and the four regional rural development centres at Michigan State University, Utah State University, Mississippi State University and Penn State support region-wide research and educational efforts on rural issues in their various regions.

References

Action for Market Towns. (2002) Market towns and local food. Discussion paper. Accessed 24/11/09 http://p1.countryside.gov.uk/Images/Market Towns and Local Food_tcm2–17314.pdf.

Adams, D., and Hess, M. (2001) Community public policy: Fad or fountain? *Australian Journal of Public Administration* 60(2): 13–23.

Adams, T.K., and Duncan, G. (1992) Long-term poverty in rural areas. Pp. 63–93 in C. Duncan, ed., *Rural Poverty in America*. New York: Auburn House.

Adelaja, S., Hailu, Y., Kuntzsch, R., Lake, M., Fulkerson, M. McKeown, C., Racevskis, L. and Griswold, L. 2007. "Economic Valuation of Natural Resource Amenities: A Hedonic Analysis of Hillsdale and Oakland Counties." Michigan State University: Land Policy Institute, East Lansing, MI.

Agarwal, S., Rahman, S., and Errington, E. (2009) Measuring the determinants of relative economic performance of rural areas. *Journal of Rural Studies* 25(3): 309–321.

Agranoff, R., and McGuire, M. (1998) The intergovernmental context of local economic development. *State and Local Government Review* 30(3): 150–164.

Agricultural Economics Research Institute. (1938) *Agricultural Economics 1913–1938 25th Annual Report*. Oxford: Agricultural Economics Research Institute.

Aitken, A. (2006) Needs assessment of migrant workers. Pp. 24–30 in *National Resource Centre for Ethnic Minority Health Case Studies for Change*. Glasgow: NHS Scotland.

Alba, R., and Nee, V. (2003) *Remaking the American Mainstream: Assimilation and Contemporary Immigration*. Cambridge, MA, and London: Harvard University Press.

Albrecht, D.E., Albrecht, C.M., and Albrecht S.L. (2000) Poverty in nonmetropolitan America: Impacts of industrial, employment, and family structural variables. *Rural Sociology* 65(1): 87–103.

Alesina, A., and Glaeser, E. (2004) *Fighting Poverty in the US and Europe: A World of Differences*. New York: Oxford University Press.

Allen, P. (2004) *Together at the Table: Sustainability and Sustenance in the American Agrifood System*. University Park, PA: Penn State University Press.

Allen, P., and Hinrichs, C. (2007) Buying into 'buy local': Engagements of United States local food initiatives. Pp. 255–272 in D. Maye, L. Holloway and M. Kneafsey, eds., *Constructing 'Alternative' Food Geographies: Representation and Practice*. Oxford: Elsevier.

Ambler-Edwards, S., et al. (2009) *Food Futures: Rethinking UK Strategy*. Chatham House Report.

American Farmland Trust. (2009) Farming on the edge. http://www.farmland.org/resources/fote/default.asp.

Amin, A., and Thrift, N. (1994) *Globalization, Institutions, and Regional Development in Europe.* Oxford: Oxford University Press.

Anderson, D., and Berglund, E. (2003) *Ethnographies of Conservation.* Oxford: Berghahn.

APA. (1980) *A Citizen's Guide to Adirondack Park Agency Land Use Regulations.* Ray Brook, NY: Adirondack Park Agency, State of New York.

Armer, M., and Grimshaw, A.D. (1973) *Comparative Social Research: Methodological Problems and Strategies.* London and New York: John Wiley and Sons.

Arnade, C., Calvin, L., and Kuchler, F. (2010) Consumers' response to the 2006 foodborne illness outbreak linked to spinach. *Amber Waves* 8(1): 34–40.

Árnason, A., Shucksmith, M., and Vergunst, J. (eds.) (2009) *Comparing Rural Development. Continuity and Change in the Countryside of Western Europe.* Aldershot: Ashgate.

Atterton, J. (2011) A vulnerability index of Scottish towns, *Rural Policy Centre Research Briefing (RPC RB 2011/10).* Available online at: http://www.sac.ac.uk/ruralpolicycentre/publs/thrivingcommunitiespublications/vulnerabilityindextowns/.

———. (2008) Rural proofing in England: A formal commitment in need of review. Centre for Rural Economy Discussion Paper Series No. 20. University of Newcastle.

———. (2007) The 'strength of weak ties': Social networking by business owners in the Highlands and Islands of Scotland. *Sociologia Ruralis* 47(3): 228–245.

———. (2005) *Networking in the Highlands and Islands of Scotland: A Case Study of the Embeddedness of Firms in Three Small Towns.* Unpublished PhD thesis. University of Aberdeen.

Atterton, J., and Affleck, A. (2010) *Rural Businesses in the North East of England: Final Survey Results (2009). Centre for Rural Economy Research Report.* University of Newcastle: Centre for Rural Economy Research.

Atterton, J., Annibal, I. and Bates, D. (2011) The vulnerability of Scottish local authorities to public sector spending cuts, *Rural Policy Centre Research Briefing (RPC RB 2011/02).* Available online at: http://www.sac.ac.uk/ruralpolicycentre/publs/thrivingcommunitiespublications/viscottishlocalauthorities/.

Atterton, J., Newbery, R., Bosworth, G., and Affleck, A. (2011) Rural enterprise and neo-endogenous development. In S. Carter, E. Ljunggren and G. Alsos, eds., *The Handbook of Research on Entrepreneurship in Agriculture and Rural Development.* Edward Elgar: Cheltenham, UK.

Ayres, S., and Pearce, G. (2008) Transforming regional governance in Europe. *Policy and Politics* 36(4): 539–544.

Bagdonis, J.M., Hinrichs, C.C., and Schafft, K.A. (2009) The emergence and framing of farm-to-school initiatives: Civic engagement, health and local agriculture. *Agriculture and Human Values* 26(1–2): 107–119.

Bailey, L.H. (1911) *The Country-Life Movement in the United States.* New York: Macmillan Company.

Banner, S. (2005) Why Terra Nullius? Anthropology and property law in early Australia. *Law and History Review* 23(1): 95–131.

Barbier, J-C. (2005) When words matter: Dealing anew with cross-national comparison. Pp. 45–68 in J-C. Barbier and M-T Letablier, eds., *Politiques Sociales: Enjeux Méthodologiques et pistémologiques des Comparaisons Internationals; Social Policies: Epistemological and Methodological Issues in Cross-national Comparison.* Brussels: P.I.E.-Peter Lang.

Barcus, H.R. (2006) New destinations for Hispanic migrants: An analysis of rural Kentucky. Pp. 89–109 in H.A. Smith and O.J. Furuseth, eds., *Latinos in the New South.* Burlington, VT: Ashgate.

Barham, E., Bingen, J., and Hinrichs, C. (2011) Geographical indications in the United States. In B. Sylvander and E. Barham, eds., *Labels of Origin for Food: Local Development, Global Recognition.* CABI.

Barca F (2009) An agenda for a reformed Cohesion Policy: a place-based approach to meeting European Union challenges and expectations. Independent Report prepared at the request of Danuta Hübner, EU Commissioner for Regional Policy.

Barker, A., and Stockdale, A. (2008) Out of the wilderness? Achieving sustainable development within Scottish national parks. *Journal of Environmental Management* 88: 181–193.

Barkley, D., and Henry, M. (1997) Rural industrial development: to cluster or not to cluster. *Review of Agricultural Economics* 19(2): 311–312.

Barnard, C. (2005) *Population Interaction Zones for Agriculture. Amber Waves. June.* Washington, DC: Economic Research Service, US Department of Agriculture.

Barnes, I., and Cox, V. (2007) Migrants as entrepreneurs in Lincolnshire. Paper presented at the 5th Rural Entrepreneurship Conference, University of Lincoln.

Barnes, M., Newman, J., Knops, A., and Sullivan, H. (2003) Constituting 'the public' in public participation. *Public Administration* 81(2): 379–399.

Batie, S. (2003) The multi-function attributes of northeastern agriculture: A research agenda. *Agricultural and Resources Economics Review* 32(1): 1–8.

Bauere, V., Densham, P., Millar, J., and Salt, J. (2007) Migrants from Central and Eastern Europe: Local geographies. *Population Trends* 129: 7–19.

Bauman, Z. (1998) *Globalisation: The Human Consequences.* Polity Press.

Baylis, K., Peplow, S., Rauser, G., and Simon, L. (2008) Agri-environmental policies in the EU and United States: A comparison. *Ecological Economics* 65(4): 753–764.

BBC News. (2010a) Ageing Europe warned of 'unsustainable' pensions, 7 July. http://www.bbc.co.uk/news/10545280.

———. (2010b) Health 'poses a huge challenge', 31 March. http://news.bbc/cuk. uk/go/pr/fr/-/1/hi/uk_politics/election_2010/8535902.stm.

Beale, C. (1975) *The Revival of Population Growth in Non-Metropolitan America. ERS Report 605.* Washington, DC: USDA-ERS.

Beggs, J.J., Haines, V.A., and Hurlbert, J.S. (1996) Revisiting the rural–urban contrast: Personal networks in nonmetropolitan settings. *Rural Sociology* 61(2): 306–325.

Bel, G., Fageda, X., and Warner, M.E. (2010) Is private production of public services cheaper than public production? A meta-regression analysis of solid waste and water services. *Journal of Policy Analysis and Management* 29(3): 553–577.

Bel, G., Hebdon, R., and Warner, M.E. (2007) Local government reform: Privatization and its alternatives. *Local Government Studies* 33(4): 507–515.

Bell, K., Jarman, N., and Lefebvre, T. (2004) *Migrant Workers in Northern Ireland.* Belfast: Institute for Conflict Resolution.

Bell, M. (1994) *Childerley: Nature and Morality in a Country Village.* Chicago: University of Chicago Press.

Benn, H. (2009) *The Future of Farming. Report.* DEFRA.

Bennett, K., and Phillipson, J. (2004) A plague upon their houses: Revelations of the Foot and Mouth Disease epidemic for business households. *Sociologia Ruralis* 44(3): 261–283.

Berghman, J. (1995) Social exclusion in Europe: Policy context and analytical framework. Pp. 10–28 in G. Room, ed., *Beyond the Threshold: The Measurement and Analysis of Social Exclusion.* Bristol: Policy Press.

Berk, M.L., Schur C.L., Chavez, L.R., and Frankel, M. (2000) Health care use among undocumented Latino immigrants. *Health Affairs* 19: 51–65.

Berle, P.A.A. (1990) *Commission on the Adirondacks in the Twenty-First Century*. Albany: Office of the Governor of New York.

Bernat Jr., A. (1999) Industry clusters and rural labor markets. *Southern Rural Sociology* 15: 182–183.

Berry, B. (1976) *Urbanization and Counterurbanization*. Beverly Hills, CA: Sage.

Bevan, M., Cameron, S., Coombes, M., Merridew, T., and Raybould, S. (2001) *Social Housing in Rural Areas*. London: Chartered Institute of Housing for the Joseph Rowntree Foundation.

Beveridge, W. (1942) *The Beveridge Report: Report of the Inter-Departmental Committee on Social Insurance and Allied Services*. London: HMSO.

Bevir, M., and Rhodes, R.A.W. (2006) Defending interpretation. *European Political Science* 5: 69–83.

Birch, K., and Whittam, G. (2008) The third sector and the regional development of social capital. *Regional Studies* 42(3): 437–450.

Blackstock, K., White, V., McCrum, G., Scott, A., and Hunter, C. (2008) Measuring responsibility: An appraisal of a Scottish national park's sustainable tourism indicators. *Journal of Sustainable Tourism* 16(3): 276–297.

Blair, T. (1994) Sharing responsibility for crime. P. 90 in A. Coote, ed., *Families, Children and Crime*. London: IPPR.

Blake, S. (2009) Subnational patterns of population ageing. *Population Trends* 136(Summer).

Blank, R.M. (2005) Poverty, policy, and place: How poverty and policies to alleviate poverty are shaped by local characteristics. *International Regional Science Review* 28(4): 441–464.

Blomley, N. (1994) Activism and the academy. *Environment and Planning D: Society and Space* 12: 383–385.

Bloom, J.D., and Hinrichs, C.C. (2011) Moving local food through conventional food system infrastructure: Value chain framework comparisons and insights. *Renewable Agriculture and Food Systems* 26(1): 13–23.

Blythman, J. (2006) *Bad Food Britain*. London: Fourth Estate.

Boatman, J., Ramwell, C., Parry, H., Jones, N., Bishop, J., Gaskell, P., Short, C., Mills, J., and Dwyer, J. (2008) *A Review of Environmental Benefits Supplied by Agri-Environmental Schemes. Research Report for Land Use Policy Group, London.*

Bogdanor, V. (2009) *The New British Constitution*. Oxford: Hart Publishing.

———. (1999) *Devolution in the United Kingdom*. Oxford: Oxford University Press.

Bollman, R., and Bryden, J. (eds.) (1997) *Rural Employment: An International Perspective*. Wallingford: CAB International.

Bonanno, A., and Constance, D. (2003) The global/local interface. Pp. 241–251 in D. Brown and L. Swanson, eds., *Challenges for Rural America in the Twenty-First Century*. University Park, PA: Penn State University Press.

Bonds, A. (2009) Discipline and devolution: Constructions of poverty, race, and criminality in the politics of rural prison development. *Antipode* 41(3): 416–438.

Bonnano, A., Busch, L., Friedland, W., Gouveia, L., and Mingione, E. (1994) *From Columbus to Conagra: The Globalisation of Agriculture and Food*. Lawrence: University Press of Kansas.

Bonnen, J., Browne, W., and Schweikhardt, D. (1996) Further observations on the changing nature of agricultural policy decision processes. *Agricultural History* 70: 130–152.

Booth, C. (1889–1903) *Life and Labour of the People of London*, 17 vols. London: MacMillan.

BOP and Experian. (2007) Creative countryside: Creative industries driving new rural economies. Multi-client study for One Northeast, Scottish Enterprise,

Highlands and Islands Enterprise, East Riding Council and Lancashire County Council.

Born, B., and Purcell, M. (2006) Avoiding the local trap: Scale and food systems in planning research. *Journal of Planning Education and Research* 26: 195–207.

Borsodi, R. (1929) *This Ugly Civilization*. New York: Simon and Schuster.

Boswell, C. (2003) *European Migration Policies in Flux. Changing Patterns of Inclusion and Exclusion*. London: Royal Institute of International Affairs, Blackwell.

Bosworth, G. (2010) Commercial counterurbanisation: An emerging force in rural economic development. *Environment and Planning A* 42(4), 966–981.

———. (2009) Education, mobility and rural business development. *Journal of Small Business and Enterprise Development* 16(4): 660–677.

———. (2008) Entrepreneurial in-migrants and economic development in rural England. *International Journal of Entrepreneurship and Small Business* 6(3): 355–369.

———. (2006) Counterurbanisation and job creation: entrepreneurial in-migration and rural economic development. Centre for Rural Economy Discussion Paper Series No. 4. University of Newcastle.

Bourdieu, P. (1986) The forms of capital. Pp. 241–258 in J.G. Richardson, ed., *Handbook of Theory and Research for the Sociology of Education*. Westport, CT: Greenwood Press.

Boyne, G.A. (1998) *Public Choice Theory and Local Government: A Comparative Analysis of the UK and the USA*. Houndmills, UK, and New York: Macmillan and St. Martins Press.

Bradley, A. (1986) Poverty and dependency in village England. Pp. 151–178 in P. Lowe, A. Bradley and S. Wright, eds., *Deprivation and Welfare in Rural England*. Norwich: Geo Books.

Bradshaw, T.K., and Blakely, B.J. (1999). What are "third-wave" state economic development efforts? From incentives to indistrial policy, *Economic Development Quarterly* 13(3): 229–244.

Brady, D. (2003) Rethinking the sociological measurement of poverty. *Social Forces* 81(3): 715–752.

Bramley, G., Lancaster, S., and Gordon, D. (2000) Benefit take-up and the geography of poverty in Scotland. *Regional Studies* 34(6): 507–520.

Brasier, K.J., Goetz, S., Smith, L., Ames, M., Green, J., Kelsey, T., Rangarajan, A., and Whitmer, W. (2007) Small farm clusters and pathways to rural community sustainability. *Community Development* 38(3): 8–22.

Brenner, N. (2004) *New State Spaces: Urban Governance and the Rescaling of Statehood*. Oxford and New York: Oxford University Press.

———. (1999) Globalization as reterritorialization: The re-scaling of urban governance in the European Union. *Urban Studies* 36(3): 431–451.

Bridge, J., and Johnson, N. (eds.) (2009) *Feeding Britain. Report*. Smith Institute.

Brighton and Hove Food Partnership. (2006) *Spade to Spoon: Making the Connections. A Food Strategy and Action Plan for Brighton and Hove. Report*. Brighton: Brighton and Hove Food Partnership.

Broadway, M. (2007) Meatpacking and the transformation of rural communities: A comparison of Brooks, Alberta and Garden City, Kansas. *Rural Sociology* 72(4): 560–582.

Brookings Institution. (2011) Michigan Governor Snyder's regional recipe central to fix-it agenda. Accessed 15/12/11 http://www.brookings.edu/opinions/2011/0131_state_restructuring_bradley.aspx.

Broomby, R. (2009) Turnstiles not floodgates for Polish workers. Accessed 7/2/09 http://news.bbc.co.uk/go/pr/fr/-/1/hi/business/8244256.stm.

Brown, D.L. (2008) The future of rural America through a social-demographic lens. Pp. 229–248 in J. Wu, P. Barkley and B. Weber, eds., *Frontiers in Resource and Rural Economics.* Washington, DC: RFF Press.

———. (2002) Migration and community: Social networks in a multilevel world. *Rural Sociology* 67(1): 1–23.

Brown, D.L., Bolender, B., Kulcsar, L.J., Glasgow, N., and Sanders, S. (2010) Inter-county variability in older migration to nonmetropolitan counties as a path dependent process. Paper presented to the Population Association of America, Dallas, 15 April.

Brown, D.L., and Cromartie, J. (2004) The nature of rurality in postindustrial society. Pp. 269–284 in T. Champion and G. Hugo, eds., *New Forms of Urbanization: Beyond the Urban-Rural Dichotomy.* Aldershot: Ashgate.

Brown, D.L., Cromartie, J., and Kulcsar, L. (2004) Micropolitan areas and the measurement of American urbanization. *Population Research and Policy Review* 23: 399–418.

Brown, D.L., Fuguitt, G., Heaton, T., and Waseem, S. (1997) Continuities in size of place preferences in the United States, 1972–1992. *Rural Sociology* 62(4): 408–428.

Brown, D.L., and Glasgow, N. (2008) *Rural Retirement Migration.* Dordrecht, the Netherlands: Springer.

Brown, D.L., and Hirschl, T.A. (1995) Household poverty in rural and metropolitan-core areas of the United States. *Rural Sociology* 60(1): 44–66.

Brown, D., and Schafft, K. (2011) *Rural People and Communities in the 21st Century: Resilience and Transformation.* Cambridge: Polity.

Brown, D., and Swanson, L. (2003) *Challenges for Rural America in the 21st Century.* State College, PA: Penn State Press.

Brown, D., Walker, R., Manson, S., and Seto, K. (2004) Modeling land use and land cover change. Pp. 395–409 in G. Gutman, A. Janetos, C. Justice, E. Moran, J. Mustard, R. Rindfuss, D. Skole and B. Turner, eds., *Land Change Science: Observing, Monitoring, and Understanding Trajectories of Change on the Earth's Surface.* Dordrecht, the Netherlands: Kluwer Academic Publishers.

Brown, D.L., and Wardwell, J. (eds.) (1981) *New Directions in Urban-Rural Migration: The Population Turnaround in Rural America.* New York: Academic Press.

Brown, D., and Warner, M.E. (1991) Persistent low income nonmetropolitan areas in the United States: Some conceptual challenges for policy development. *Policy Studies Journal* 19(2): 22–41.

Brown, S., and Getz, C. (2008) Towards domestic fair trade? Farm labor, food localism and the 'family scale' farm. *GeoJournal* 73: 11–22.

Browne, W., Skees, J., Swanson, L., Thompson, P., and Unnivher, L. (1992) *Sacred Cows and Hot Potatoes: Agrarian Myths in Agricultural Policy.* Boulder, CO: Westview Press.

Brunner, E. deS. (1957) *The Growth of a Science: A Half-Century of Rural Sociological Research in the United States.* New York: Harper and Brothers.

Brunner, E. deS., Sanders, I.T., and Ensminger, D. (eds.) (1945) *Farmers of the World: the Development of Agricultural Extension.* New York: Columbia University Press.

Brunner, E. deS., and Yang, E.H.P. (1949) *Rural America and the Extension Service: A History and Critique of the Cooperative Agricultural and Home Economics Extension Service.* New York: Columbia University.

Bryden, J. (2005a) Horizontal coordination at local and regional levels. Paper presented at the Mexican Ministry of Social Development and OECD International Conference: Designing and Implementing Rural Development Policy, Oaxaca, Mexico, 7–8 April.

————. (2005b) Rural development in the enlarged EU. *Gibson Institute for Land, Food and Environment Research Paper Series* 1(1).

————. (1999) Rural Policies in Predominantly Rural Regions of OECD Countries. A review of recent trends and issues. Commissioned paper for inter-governmental meeting, OECD Paris, October 1999. DT/TDPC/RUR(99)2, OECD Paris.

Bryden, J. with Bell, C., Gilliatt, J., Hawkins, E. and MacKinnon, N. (1993) *Farm Household Adjustment in Western Europe 1987-1991*. The Arkleton Trust (Research) Ltd. Luxembourg: European Commission.

Bryden, J., Efstratoglou, S., Johnson, T.G., Ferenczi, T., Knickel, K., Refsgaard, K., and Thomson, K.J. (eds.) (2010) *Towards Sustainable Development in Rural Europe: Using System Dynamics to Explore the Relations between Farming, Environment, Regional Economies, and Quality of Life*. New York: Routledge.

Bryden, J., and Geisler, C. (2010) Community-based land reform: Lessons from Scotland and reflections on stewardship. In J.E. Davis, ed., *Common Ground: The Community Land Trust Reader*. Cambridge, MA: Lincoln Institute of Land Policy.

————. (2007) Community-based land reform: Lessons from Scotland. *Land Use Policy* 24: 24–34.

Bryden, J., and Hart, J. (2004) *A New Approach to Rural Development: Germany, Greece, Scotland and Sweden*. Lampeter: Edwin Mellen Press.

Bryden, J., and Sproull, A. (1997) New technology and rural development. Paper presented at the European Association of Agricultural Economists Seminar, Dijon, March.

Bryden, J., Watson, R.D., Storey, C., and van Alphen, J. (1997) *Community Involvement and Rural Policy. Report*. Edinburgh: Scottish Office Central Research Unit.

Bullock, H.E., Williams, W.R., and Limbert, W.M. (2003) Predicting support for welfare policies: The impact of attributions and beliefs about inequality. *Journal of Poverty* 7(3): 35–56.

Bulmer, M., and Solomos, J. (1999) *Racism*. Oxford: Oxford University Press.

Bunce, M. (1994) *The Countryside Ideal: Anglo-American Images of Landscape*. London: Routledge.

Burchardt, T., Le Grand, J., and Piachaud, D. (2002) Introduction. Pp. 1–12 in J. Hills, J. Le Grand and D. Piachaud, eds., *Understanding Social Exclusion*. Oxford: Oxford University Press.

Bures, R.M. (1997) Migration and the life course: Is there a retirement transition? *International Journal of Population Geography* 3: 109–119.

Burt, R.S. (2001) Structural holes versus network closure as social capital. Pp. 31–56 in N. Lin, K. Cook and R.S. Burt, eds., *Social Capital: Theory and Research, Sociology and Economics: Controversy and Integration*. New York: Aldine de Gruyter.

Busch, L. (2000) The moral economy of grades and standards. *Journal of Rural Studies* 16: 273–283.

Butler, R. (1989) Dispelling ageism. *Annals of the Academy of Social and Political Science* 503: 138–147.

Buttel, F.H. (2002) Continuities and disjunctures in the transformation of the US agro-food system. Pp. 177–189 in D.L. Brown and L.E. Swanson, eds., *Challenges for Rural America in the 21st Century*. University Park, PA: Penn State University Press.

Byrne, D. (1999) *Social Exclusion*. Milton Keynes: Open University Press.

Cabinet Office. (2008) *Food Matters: Towards a Strategy for the 21st Century. Report*. London: Cabinet Office Strategy Unit.

————. (2000) *Sharing in the Nation's Prosperity. Report*. London: Cabinet Office and HMSO.

Caffyn, A., and Dahlström, M. (2005) Urban–rural interdependencies: Joining up policy in practice. *Regional Studies* 39(3): 283–296.

Cairngorms National Park Authority. (n.d.) Accessed 30/9/10. http://www.cairn-gorms.co.uk/thepark/keyfacts/.

Calhoun, C. (1998) Community without propinquity revisited: Communications, technology and the transformation of the urban public sphere. *Sociological Inquiry* 68(3): 373–397.

Callanan, M. (2005) Institutionalizing participation and governance? New participative structures in local government in Ireland. *Public Administration* 83(4): 909–929.

Cannavò, P.F. (2007) *The Working Landscape: Founding, Preservation, and the Politics of Place*. Cambridge, MA: MIT Press.

Cantillon, R. (1931) *Essays on the General Nature of Commerce*. Edited and translated by H. Higgs. London: Macmillan.

Cardwell, M. (2004) *The European Model of Agriculture*. Oxford: Oxford University Press.

Castells, M. (1989) *The Informational City: Information Technology, Economic Restructuring, and the Urban Regional Process*. Oxford: Blackwell.

Castles, S., Korac, M., Vasta, E., and Vertovec, S. (2002) Integration: Mapping the field. Report of a Project carried out by the University of Oxford Centre for Migration and Policy Research and Refugee Studies Centre, contracted by the Home Office Immigration Research and Statistics Service (IRSS). Home Office Online Report 28/03.

Castles, S., and Miller, M. (1998) *The Age of Migration*. 2nd ed. New York: Guilford Press.

Center for Rural Entrepreneurship. (2010) *Entrepreneur Coaching Update*. Columbia, MO: RUPRI. Accessed on 21/3/11 http://www.rupri.org/entrepreneurship.php.

Cerrutti, M., and Massey, D.S. (2004) Trends in Mexican migration to the United States, 1965–1995. Pp. 17–44 in J. Durand and D.S. Massey, eds., *Crossing the Border: Research from the Mexican Migration Project*. New York: Russell Sage Foundation.

Chadwick, E. ([1842] 1965) *The Sanitary Condition of the Labouring Population of Great Britain*. Edinburgh: Edinburgh University Press.

Chakraboti, N., and Garland, J. (eds.) (2004) *Rural Racism: Contemporary Debates and Perspectives*. Devon: Willan Publishing.

Champion, A. (2005) Migration's role in producing regional and local population ageing in England. Paper presented at the Royal Geographical Society—Institute of British Geographers conference, London.

———. (2003) Testing the differential urbanization model in Great Britain, 1901–91. *Tijdschrift voor Economische en Sociale Geografie* 94(1): 11–22.

———. (1998) *The Determinants of Migration Flows in England; A Review of Existing Data and Evidence. Report Prepared for the Department of the Environment, Transport and the Regions*. London: DETR.

———. (ed.) (1989) *Counterurbanisation: The Changing Pace and Nature of Population Deconcentration*. London: Edward Arnold.

Champion, A., and Shepherd, J. (2006) Demographic change in rural England. Pp. 29–50 in P. Lowe and L. Speakman, eds., *The Ageing Countryside: The Growing Older Population of Rural England*. London: Age Concern.

Champion, T. (2008) *The Changing Nature of Urban and Rural Areas in the UK and Other European Countries. Report of the UN Expert Group Meeting on Urbanization, Population Distribution, Internal Migration and Development*. New York: United Nations.

Champion, T., Atkins, D., Coombes, M., and Fotheringham, S. (1998) *Urban Exodus*. London: Council for the Protection of Rural England.

Champion, T., Coombes, M., and Brown, D.L. (2009) Migration and longer distance commuting in England. *Regional Studies* 43: 1245–1259.

Chapman, P., Phimister, E., Shucksmith, M., Upward, R., and Vera-Toscano, E. (1998) *Poverty and Exclusion in Rural Britain: The Dynamics of Low Income and Employment*. York: York Publishing Services.

Charles, L. (2010) Local food and community development. Paper presented to the QUCAN conference,Newcastle, UK, March.

Chaston, I. (2008) Small creative industry firms: A development dilemma? *Management Decision* 46(6): 819–831.

Chavez, L.R. (1988) Settlers and sojourners: The case of Mexicans in the United States. *Human Organization* 47: 95–108.

Chavez, L.R., Hubbell, A., Mishra, S.I., and Valdez, R.B. (2007) Undocumented Latina immigrants in Orange County, California: A comparative analysis. *International Migration Review* 31(1): 88–107.

Chell, E., and Baines, S. (2000) Networking, entrepreneurship and microbusiness behaviour. *Entrepreneurship and Regional Development* 12: 195–215.

Christopherson, S. (2010) Afterword: Contextualized comparison in local and regional economic development: Are united states perspectives and approaches distinctive? *Regional Studies* 44(2): 229–233.

Cimbaluk, L., and Warner, M. (2008) Devolution and spatial inequality: implications for rural counties. Paper presented to Rural Sociological Society, New Hampshire.

Citizens Advice Bureau. (2005) *Home from Home? Experiences of Migrant Workers in Rural Parts of the UK, and the Impact on Local Service Providers. Report*. London: Citizens Advice Bureau.

Claassen, R. (2007) Emphasis shifts in US conservation policy. *Amber Waves*. Perspectives on Food and Farm Policy 5.

Clancy, K., Hammer, J., and Lippoldt, D. (2007) Food policy councils: Past, present and future. Pp. 121–143 in C.C. Hinrichs and T.A. Lyson, eds., *Remaking the North American Food System: Strategies for Sustainability*. Lincoln: University of Nebraska Press.

Clancy, K., and Ruhf, K. (2010) Is local enough? Some arguments for regional food systems. *Choices* 25(1).

Cloke, P. (1997) Country backwater to virtual village? Rural studies and the 'cultural turn'. *Journal of Rural Studies* 13(14): 367–375.

Cloke, P., Goodwin, M., and Milbourne, P. (1997) *Rural Wales: Community and Marginalisation*. Cardiff: University of Wales Press.

Cloke, P., and Little, J. (eds.) (1997) *Contested Countryside Cultures*. London: Routledge.

Cloke, P., Marsden, T., and Mooney. P. (eds.) (2006) *Handbook of Rural Studies*. London: Sage.

Cloke, P., Milbourne, P., and Thomas, C. (1994) Lifestyles in rural England. Rural Development Commission Rural Research Report 18.

Cochrane, A. (2001) Comparative approaches and social policy. Pp. 1–18 in A. Cochrane, J. Clarke, and S. Gewirtz, eds., *Comparing Welfare States: Britain in International* Context. London: Sage.

Cochrane, W. (2003) *The Curse of American Agricultural Abundance: A Sustainable Solution*. Lincoln: University of Nebraska Press.

Coladarci, T. (2007) Improving the yield of rural education research: An editor's swan song. *Journal of Research in Rural Education* 22(3): 1–9.

Coleman, J.S. (1990) *Foundations of Social Theory*. Cambridge, MA: Belknap Press.

Commins, P. (2004) Poverty and social exclusion in rural areas: Characteristics, processes and research issues. *Sociologica Ruralis* 44(1) 60–75.

Commission for Rural Communities. (2010a) *High Ground, High Potential: A Future for England's Upland Communities. Report.* Cheltenham: CRC.

———. (2010b) *The State of the Countryside 2010. Report.* Cheltenham: CRC.

———. (2008a) *England's Rural Areas: Steps to Release Their Economic Potential, Advice from the Rural Advocate to the Prime Minister. Report.* Cheltenham: CRC.

———. (2008b) *State of the Countryside 2008. Report.* Cheltenham: CRC.

———. (2007a) *A8 Migrant Workers in Rural Areas—A Briefing Paper. Report.* Cheltenham: CRC.

———. (2007b) *Rural Migrant Worker Projects: Boston Citizens Advice Bureau. Report.* Cheltenham: CRC.

———. (2007c) *Rural Migrant Worker Projects: Bridging Arts and West Cornwall Faith Forum. Report.* Cheltenham: CRC.

———. (2007d) *Rural Migrant Worker Projects: Mobile Europeans Taking Action (META) in Thetford. Report.* Cheltenham: CRC.

———. (2007e) *State of the Countryside 2007. Report.* Cheltenham: CRC.

———. (2007f) *State of the Countryside Update: Population and Migration. Report.* Cheltenham: CRC.

———. (2006) *State of the Countryside 2006. Report.* Cheltenham: CRC.

———. (2005) *Under the Radar: Tracking and Supporting Rural Home-Based Businesses. Report.* Cheltenham: CRC and the Live Work Network.

Commission of the European Communities. (2010) *Europeans, Agriculture and the Common Agricultural Policy. Eurobarometer Special Survey. Report Number 336.* Brussels: Commission of the European Communities.

———. (2006) *Fact Sheet: The EU Rural Development Policy 2007–2013.* Brussels: Directorate-General for Agriculture and Rural Development, Commission of the European Communities.

———. (2005) *Council Regulation (EC) 1698/2005 on Support for Rural Development by the European Agricultural Fund for Rural Development (EAFRD) OJ L277.* Brussels: European Commission.

———. (1988) *The Future of Rural Society. Commission Communication Transmitted to the Council and to the European Parliament on 29 July 1988. Com 88 (501).* Brussels: CEC.

Communities and Local Government. (2009) *Local Government Financial Statistics England, 19.* London: Department for Communities and Local Government.

Community Development Foundation. (2007) *The Community Development Challenge.* Wetherby: CLG Publications.

Conlan, T. (1998) *From New Federalism to Devolution: Twenty Five Years of Intergovernmental Reform.* Washington, DC: Brookings Institute Press.

Constandse, A.K., and Hofstee, E.W. (1964) *Rural Sociology in Action.* Rome: Food and Agriculture Organization of the United Nations.

Cooke, B., and Kothari, U. (2001) The case for participation as tyranny. Pp. 1–15 in B. Cooke and U. Kothari, eds., *Participation: The New Tyranny?* London: Zed Books.

Coombes, M., Champion, T., and Raybould, S. (2007) Did the early A8 in-migrants to England go to areas of labour shortage? *Local Economy* 22: 335–348.

Cooper, T., and Arblaster, K. (2008) *Climate Change and the Rural Environment in a European Union Context. Report.* London: Institute for European Environmental Policy.

Cooper, T., Hart, K. and Baldock, D. (2010) *The Provision of Public Goods Through Agriculture in the European Union.* Report prepared for DG Agriculture and Rural Development, London, Institute for European Environmental Policy.

Corbett, M. (2007) *Learning to Leave: The Irony of Schooling in a Coastal Community*. Halifax, Nova Scotia: Fernwood Publishing.

Cornwall, A. (2004) New democratic spaces? The politics and dynamics of institutionalised participation. *IDS Bulletin* 35(2): 1–10.

Cosby, A., Neaves, T., Crossman, R., Crossman, J., James, W., Feierabend, N., Mirvis, D., Jones, C., and Farrigan, T. (2008) Preliminary evidence for an emerging nonmetropolitan mortality penalty in the United States. *American Journal of Public Health* 98(8): 1470–1472.

Cotter, D.A. (2002) Poor people in poor places: Local opportunity structures and household poverty. *Rural Sociology* 67(4): 534–555.

Coulombe, P., Delorme, H., Hervieu, B., Jollivet, M., and Lacombe, P. (1990) *Les Agriculteurs and La Politique*. Paris: Presses de la Fondation Nationale des Sciences Politiques.

Council of Economic Advisors. (2010) *Strengthening the Rural Economy. Report*. Washington, DC: Executive Office of the President, Council of Economic Advisers.

———. (1964) *Economic Report of the President*. Washington, DC: US Government Printing Press.

Countryside Agency. (2004) *State of the Countryside 2004*. Cheltenham: Countryside Agency.

———. (2003a) *Rural Economies: Stepping Stones to Healthier Futures*. Cheltenham: Countryside Agency.

———. (2003b) *State of the Countryside 2003*. Cheltenham: Countryside Agency.

Cox, K. (2010) The problem of metropolitan governance and the politics of scale. *Regional Studies* 44(2): 215–227.

Cox, R., Holloway, L., Venn, L., Dowler, L., Ricketts Hein, J., Kneafsey, M., and Tuomainen, H. (2008) Common ground? Motivations for participation in a community-supported agriculture scheme. *Local Environment* 13(3): 203–218.

Crabtree, J. (1991) National park designation in Scotland. *Land Use Policy* 8(3): 241–252.

Cromartie, J. (2007) *Rural Population and Migration: Trend 4—Natural Decrease on the Rise Briefing Room*. Washington, DC: USDA-ERS.

Cromartie, J., and Bucholtz, S. (2008) Defining rural in rural America. *Amber Waves*. Accessed 10/12/10 http://www.ers.usda.gov/AmberWaves/June08/Features/RuralAmerica.htm.

Cromartie, J., and Nelson, P. (2009) Baby boom migration tilts toward rural America. *Amber Waves* 7(3): 16–22.

Cronon, W. (1995) *Uncommon Ground. Rethinking the Human Place in Nature*. New York: Norton.

Cross, P., Edwards, R.T., Opondo, M., Nyeko, P., and Edwards-Jones, G. (2009) Does farm worker health vary between localised and globalised food supply systems? *Environment International* 35: 1004–1014.

Crowley, M., and Lichter, D.T. (2009) Social disorganization in new Latino destinations? *Rural Sociology* 74(4): 573–604.

Cultivating Communities. (2005) Cultivating communities news. *Soil Association* 4(Spring).

Cushing, B. (1999) Migration and economic restructuring. Pp. 13–36 in K. Pandit and S.D. Withers, eds., *Migration and Restructuring in the United States*. New York: Rowman and Littlefield.

Dales, J. (1968) *Pollution, Property and Prices*. Toronto: University of Toronto Press.

Danbom, D. (1997) Why Americans value rural life. *Rural Development Perspectives* 12(1): 15–18.

Darnhofer, I., and Schneeberger, W. (2007) Impacts of voluntary agri-environmental measures of Austria's agriculture. *International Journal of Agricultural Resources, Governance and Ecology* 6(3): 360–377.

Davis, J.E. (ed.) (2010) *The Community Land Trust Reader: Roots and Branches of the CLT Movement.* Cambridge, MA: Lincoln Institute of Land Policy.

Deavers, K., and Brown, D.L. (1980) *Social and Economic Trends in Rural America. Rural Development Background Paper.* Washington, DC: White House.

DeCarolis, D., Litzky, B., and Eddleston, K. (2009) Why networks enhance the progress of new venture creation: The influence of social capital and cognition. *Entrepreneurship Theory and Practice* 33(2): 522–545.

de Haan, H. (1993) Rural crisis and rural research in the Netherlands. *Sociologia Ruralis* 23(2): 127–136.

DeLeon, L., and Denhardt, R.B. (2000) The political theory of reinvention. *Public Administration Review* 60(2): 89–97.

de Lima, P. (2009) *Building Inclusive Communities. Report. The Rural Action Research Programme Briefing Series. The Carnegie UK Trust.*

———. (2004) John O'Groats to Land's End: Racial equality in rural Britain? Pp. 36–60 in N. Chakraborti and J. Garland, eds., *Rural Racism: Contemporary Debates and Perspectives.* Cullompton: Willan.

———. (2003) Beyond place: Ethnicity/race in the debate on social exclusion/inclusion in Scotland. *Policy Futures in Education* 1(4): 653–667.

———. (2001) *Needs Not Numbers—An Exploration of Minority Ethnic Communities in Scotland. Report.* London: Commission for Racial Equality and Community Development Foundation.

de Lima, P., Chaudhry, M., Whelton, R., and Arshad, R. (2007) *Study of Migrant Workers in Grampian. Report.* Edinburgh: Communities Scotland.

de Lima, P., Jentsch, B., and Whelton, R. (2005) *Migrant Workers in the Highlands and Islands. Report.* Inverness: UHI PolicyWeb and National Centre for Migration Studies.

de Lima, P., and Wright, S. (2009) Welcoming migrants? Migrant labour in rural Scotland. *Social Policy and Society* 8(3): 391–404.

Deller, S.C., Tsung-Hsiu T., Marcouiller, D.W., and English, D.B.K. (2001) The role of amenities and quality of life in rural economic growth. *American Journal of Agricultural Economics* 83(2): 352–365.

Department for Business, Innovation and Skills. (2010) RDA finance and governance. Accessed 05/3/10 http://www.berr.gov.uk/whatwedo/regional/regional-dev-agencies/funding-financial-gov/page20136.html.

Department of Agriculture and Rural Development in Northern Ireland. (2007) *Guidance for Selection of Local Action Groups and Submission of Funding Bids. Report.* Belfast: DARD.

Department of Communities and Local Government. (2008) *Communities in Control: Real People, Real Power. Report.* Wetherby: CLG Publications.

———. (2006) *Strong and Prosperous Communities: The Local Government White Paper. Report.* Wetherby: CLG Publications.

Department of Environmental Conservation. (1977) *The Adirondack Park. Booklet LF-P109 (March).* Albany: New York State Department of Environmental Conservation.

Derkzen, P., Franklin, A., and Bock, B. (2008) Examining power struggles as a signifier of successful partnership working: A case study of partnership dynamics. *Journal of Rural Studies* 24(4): 458–466.

Devine, J. (2006) Hardworking newcomers and generations of poverty: Poverty discourse in Central Washington. *Antipode* 38(5): 953–976.

Dewees, S., Lobao, L., and Swanson, L. (2003) Local economic development in an age of devolution: The question of rural localities. *Rural Sociology* 68(2): 182–206.

Diamond, J. (2005) *Collapse: How Societies Choose to Fail or Succeed.* New York: Penguin.

Diechert, J. (2001) *Components of Population Change, Nebraska Counties, 1990–2000. Nebraska Focus 01–1.* Omaha: University of Nebraska.

Dietz, T. (2007) *A Brain Drain or an Insufficient Brain Gain? Upstate NY at a Glance.* Buffalo: Federal Reserve Bank of New York. Accessed 8/2/10 http://www.newyorkfed.org/research/regional_economy/glance/upstate_glance1_07.html.

Dimitri, C., Effland, A., and Conklin, N. (2005) *The 20th Century Transition of US Agriculture and Farm Policy. Economic Information Bulletin No. 3.* Washington, DC: US Department of Agriculture, Economic Research Service.

Dirlik, A. (2001) Place-based imagination: globalisation and the politics of place. Pp. 15–51 In R. Prazniak and A. Dirlik, eds., *Places and Politics in an Era of Globalosation.* Lanham, MD: Rowman and Littlefield.

Dobson, J., Koser, K., McLaughlan, G., and Salt, J. (2001) *International Migration and the United Kingdom: Recent Patterns and Trends. RDS Occasional Paper 75.* London: Home Office.

Dogan, M. (2004) The quantitative method in comparative research. Pp. 324–38 in P. Kennett, ed., *A Handbook of Comparative Social Policy.* Cheltenham.

Dollahite, J S., Nelson, J.A., Frongillo, E.A., and Griffin, M.R. (2005) Building community capacity through enhanced collaboration in the farmers market nutrition program. *Agriculture and Human Values* 22: 339–354.

Donahue, J.D. (1997) *Disunited States.* New York: Basic Books.

Donaldson, A., Lee, R., Ward, N., and Wilkinson, K. (2006) Foot and Mouth five years on: The legacy of the 2001 Foot and Mouth Disease crisis for farming and the British countryside. Centre for Rural Economy Discussion Paper 6. Newcastle University.

Donato, K.M., Stainback, M., and Bankston III, C.L. (2005) The economic incorporation of Mexican immigrants in Southern Louisiana. Pp. 76–102 in V. Zuniga and R. Hernandez-Leon, eds., *New Destinations: Mexican Immigration in the United States.* New York: Russell Sage Foundation.

Donato, K.M., Tolbert II, C.M., Nucci, A., and Kawano, Y. (2007) Recent immigrant settlement in the nonmetropolitan United States: Evidence from internal census data. *Rural Sociology* 72(4): 537–559.

Donnison, D. (1998) *Policies for a Just Society.* London: MacMillan.

Douglas, D. (2010) *Rural Planning and Development in Canada.* Toronto: Nelson.

Drabenstott, M., Henry, M., and Gibson, L. (1987) The rural economic policy choice. *Economic Review* 72(1): 41–58.

DTZ Pieda. (1998) *The Nature of Demand for Housing in Rural Areas. Report.* London: Department of the Environment, Transport and the Regions.

Duchon, D.A., and Murphy, A.D. (2001) Introduction: From Patrones and Caciques to Good Ole Boys. In A.D. Murphy, C. Blanchard, and J.A. Hill, eds., *Latino Workers in the Contemporary South.* Athens: University of Georgia Press.

Duffy, K. (1995) *Social Exclusion and Human Dignity in Europe.* Council of Europe.

Duncan, C.M. (1999) *Worlds Apart: Why Poverty Persists in Rural America.* New Haven, CT: Yale University Press.

———. (1996) Understanding persistent poverty: Social class context in rural communities. *Rural Sociology* 61(1): 103–124.

———. (ed.) (1992) *Rural Poverty in America.* Westport, CT: Auburn House.

Duncan, C.M., and Sweet, S. (1992) Introduction: poverty in rural America. Pp. xviii–xxvii in C.M. Duncan, ed., *Rural Poverty in America.* Westport, CT: Auburn House.

Dunnell, K. (2008) Ageing and mortality in the UK. National Statisticians' annual article on the population. *Population Trends* 134(Winter).

Duram, L., and Oberholtzer, L. (2010) A geographic approach to place and natural resource use in local food systems. *Renewable Agriculture and Food Systems* 25(2): 99–108.

336   *References*

Durand, J., Massey, D., and Capoferro, C. (2005) The new geography of Mexican migration. Pp. 1–20 in V. Zuniga and R Hernandez-Leon, eds., *New Destinations: Mexican Immigration in the United States.* New York: Russell Sage Foundation.

Durkheim, E. (1895) *Les Règles de la Method Sociologique.* Paris: F. Alcan.

———. ([1893] 1984) *The Division of Labor in Society.* New York: Free Press.

Dwyer, J., Baldock, D., Beaufoy, G., Bennett, H., Lowe, P., and Ward, N. (2002) *Europe's Rural Futures, the Nature of Rural Development II. Comparative Report.* IEEP.

Dwyer, J., and Findeis, J.L. (2008) Human and social capital in rural development—EU and US perspectives. *Eurochoices* 7(1): 38–45.

Eales, J., Keefe, J., and Keating, N. (2008) Age-friendly rural communities. In N. Keating, ed., *Rural Ageing.* Bristol: Policy Press.

Economic Research Service. (2009) Conservation Policy Brief Room. Accessed 4/3/10 http://www.ers.usda.gov/Briefing/ConservationPolicy/background.htm.

———. (2004) Data sets: County typology codes. Accessed 17/2/10 http://www.ers.usda.gov/Briefing/rurality/Typology.

———. (2007) *Nonmetro Population Grows Slower Now than during 1990s. Rural Population and Migration Briefing Room.* Washington, DC: ERS-USDA. Accessed 31/12/09 http://www.ers.usda.gov/Briefing/Population/NonMetro.htm.

Edwards, C. (1981) The bases for regional growth. In L. Martin, ed., *A Survey of Agricultural Economics Literature: Economics of Welfare, Rural Development and Natural Resources in Agriculture 1940s-1970s.* Minneapolis: University of Minnesota Press.

Edwards-Jones, G., Milà i Canals, L., Hounsome, N., Truninger, M., Koerber, G., and Hounsome, B. (2008) Testing the assertion that 'local food is best': The challenges of an evidence based approach. *Trends in Food Science and Technology* 19(5): 265–274.

Egan, T. (2002) Pastoral poverty: The seeds of decline. *New York Times,* 8 December.

Ekos Research Associates. (2004) *Evaluation Study of the Community Access Program (CAP). Final Report for Industry Canada.*

Elazar, D. (1994) *The American Mosaic: The Impact of Space, Time, and Culture on American Politics.* Boulder, CO: Harper and Row.

Elcock, H. (2003) Regionalism and regionalisation in Britain and North America. *British Journal of Politics and International Relations* 5(1): 74–101.

Ellis, A. (2002) *Power and Exclusion in Rural Community Development: The Case of LEADER2 in Wales.* PhD thesis, University of Swansea.

Eliot, T.S. (1944) *Four Quartets.* London: Faber and Faber.

Elster, J. (1978) *Logic and Society: Contradictions and Possible Worlds.* Chichester: Wiley.

Entwistle, T. (2005) Why are local authorities reluctant to externalise (and do they have good reason)? *Environment and Planning C: Government and Policy* 23(2): 191–206.

Entwistle, T., and Martin, S. (2005) From competition to collaboration in public service delivery: A new agenda for research. *Public Administration* 83(1): 233–242.

Environment and Rural Affairs Committee. (2009) *The Potential of England's Rural Economy: Government Response to the Committee's Eleventh Report of Session 2007–08. First Special Report of Session 2008–09.* London: Stationery Office.

———. (2008) *The Potential of England's Rural Economy. Eleventh Report of Session 2007–08.* London: Stationery Office.

Errington, A. (2001) Handing over the reins: A comparative study of intergenerational farm transfers in England, France, Canada and the USA. Paper presented at Agricultural Economics Society Annual Meeting, Aberystwyth, UK, April.

Esping-Andersen, G. (1990) *The Three Worlds of Welfare Capitalism.* Princeton, NJ: Princeton University Press.

European Commission. (1997) *Rural Development.* Brussels: European Commission.

European Society for Rural Sociology. (1960) Draft of constitution/List of members. *Sociologia Ruralis* 1: 77–101.

Evans, D. (1997) *A History of Nature Conservation in Britain.* 2nd ed. London: Routledge.

Evans, P. (1995) *Embedded Autonomy: States and Industrial Transformation.* Princeton, NJ: Princeton University Press.

Evely, A., Fazey, I., Pinard, M., and Lambin, X. (2008) The influence of philosophical perspectives in integrative research: A conservation case study in the Cairngorms National Park. *Ecology and Society* 13(2).

Experian. (2007) Creative countryside: Creative industries driving new rural economies. Multi-client study for One NorthEast, Scottish Enterprise, Highlands and Islands Enterprise, East Riding Council, and Lancashire County Council.

Fagin, M., and Longino, C. (1993) Migrating retirees: A source for economic development. *Economic Development Quarterly* 7(1): 98–106.

Fairweather, J.R., and Gilles, J.L. (1982) A content analysis of 'Rural Sociology' and 'Sociologia Ruralis'. *Sociologia Ruralis* 22: 172–179, 311–313.

Falk, W.M., Schulman, M.D., and Tickamyer, A.R. (eds.) (2003) *Communities of Work: Rural Restructuring in Local and Global Contexts.* Athens: Ohio University Press.

Fargione, J., Hill, J., Tilman, D., Polasky, S., and Hawthorne, P. (2008) Land clearing and the biofuel carbon debt. *Science* 319(5867): 1235–1238.

Farmer, F., and Moon, Z.K. (2009) An empirical examination of characteristics of Mexican migrants to metropolitan and nonmetropolitan areas of the United States. *Rural Sociology* 74(2): 220–240.

Farmer, J., Philip, L.J., King, G., Farrington, J., and MacLeod, M. (2010) Territorial tensions: Misaligned management and community perspectives on health services for older people in remote rural areas. *Health and Place* 16: 275–283.

Favell, A. (2005) Assimilation/integration. In M. Gibney and R. Hansen, eds., *Immigration and Asylum: From 1900 to the Present.* Santa Barbara, CA: Clio.

Feagan, R. (2007). The place of food: Mapping out the 'local' in local food systems. *Progress in Human Geography* 31(1): 23-42.

Feenstra, G.W. (1997) Local food systems and sustainable communities. *American Journal of Alternative Agriculture* 12(1): 28-36.

Feenstra, G.W., Lewis, C., Hinrichs, C.C., Gillespie, G.W., and Hilchey, D.L. (2003) Entrepreneurial outcomes and enterprise size in US retail farmers' markets. *American Journal of Alternative Agriculture* 18: 46–55.

Fennell, R. (1997) *The Common Agricultural Policy: Continuity and Change.* Oxford: Clarendon Press.

Fernandez-Cornejo, J., and Casewell, M. (2006) *The First Decade of Genetically Engineered Crops in the United States. Economic Information Bulletin No. 11. April.* Washington, DC: US Department of Agriculture, Economic Research Service.

Fielding, A. (1982) Counterurbanization in Western Europe. *Progress in Planning* 17: 1–52.

Findeis, J., Brasier, K., and Salcedo Du Bois, R. (2009) Demographic change and land use transitions. In S. Goetz and F. Brouwer, eds., *New Perspectives on Agri-environmental Policies.* London and New York: Routledge.

Findlay, A.M., Stockdale, A., Findlay, A., and Short, D. (2001) Mobility as a driver of change in rural Britain: An analysis of the links between migration, commuting and travel to shop patterns. *International Journal of Population Geography* 7: 1–15.

Findlay, A., Short, D., Stockdale, A., Findlay, A., Li L.N., and Philip, L. (1999) *Study of the Impact of Migration in Rural Scotland. Report.* Edinburgh: Scottish Office Central Research Unit.

Fine, B. (2010) Locating financialization. *Historical Materialism* 18(2): 97–116.

Fiske, A. (1991) *Structures of Social Life.* New York: Free Press.

Fitchen, J.M. (1995) Spatial redistribution of poverty through migration of poor people to depressed rural communities. *Rural Sociology* 60(2): 181–201.

———. (1994) Residential mobility among the rural poor. *Rural Sociology* 59(3): 416–436.

———. (1981) *Poverty in Rural America: A Case Study.* Boulder, CO: Westview.

Fix, M.E., Papademetriou, D.G., Batalova, J., Terrazas, A., Lin, S.Y., and Mittelstadt, M. (2009) *Migration and the Global Recession.* Washington, DC: Migration Policy Institute.

Fix, M.E., and Passel, J.S. (2001) *US Immigration at the Beginning of the 21st Century: Testimony before the Subcommittee on Immigration and Claims Hearing on the US Population and Immigration.* Urban Institute.

Flacke, R.F. (1976) *Comprehensive Report. Adirondack Park Agency Vol. 1 (February).* Ray Brook: Adirondack Park Agency, New York State.

Flora, C.B., Flora, J.L., and Fey, S. (2003) *Rural Communities: Legacy and Change.* 2nd ed. Boulder, CO: Westview Press.

Flora, J., Green, G., Gale, E., Schmidt, F., and Flora, C. (1992) Self-development: A viable rural development option. *Policy Studies Journal* 20(2): 276–288.

Florida, R. (2010) *The Great Re-Set: How New Ways of Living and Working Drive Post-Crash Prosperity.* New York: HarperCollins.

———. (2005) *The Flight of the Creative Class, The New Global Competition for Talent.* New York: HarperCollins.

———. (2002) *The Rise of the Creative Class, And How It's Transforming Work, Leisure and Everyday Life.* New York: Basic Books.

Fluharty, C. (2009) The impact of the crisis on regional actors and on the governance of regional policy. Paper presented at Regional Policy Innovation and Green Growth: The Regional Dimension, OECD Symposium, Paris, 2 December.

———. (2008) Toward a US shift from agriculture to rural development policy: Forces of challenge and change. *EuroChoices* 7(1): 46–51.

Foner, N. (2001) Introduction: New immigrants in a new New York. Pp. 1–32 in N. Foner, ed., *New Immigrants in New York.* New York: Columbia University Press.

Ford, R. (1993) The process of mobility decision-making in later old age: Early findings from an original survey of elderly people in South East England. *Espace, Populations, Societies* 3: 523–532.

Foucault, M. (1982) Afterward: The subject and power. Pp. 208–226 in H.L. Dreyfus and P. Rabinow, eds., *Foucault: Beyond Structuralism and Hermeneutics.* Chicago: University of Chicago Press.

Foulkes, M., and Newbold, B.K. (2008) Poverty catchments: Migration, residential mobility, and population turnover in impoverished rural Illinois communities. *Rural Sociology* 73(3): 440–462.

Foulkes, M., and Schafft, K A. (2010) The impact of migration on poverty concentrations in the United States, 1995–2000. *Rural Sociology* 75(1): 90–110.

Frawley, J., Commins, P., Scott, S., and Trace, F. (2001) *Low Income Farm Households: Incidence, Characteristics and Policies.* Dublin: Oak Tree Press.

Freshwater, D. (1999) Rural America at the turn of the century. TVA Rural Studies Staff Paper 99–12.

Frideres, S. (2003) *The World in a City.* Toronto: University of Toronto Press.

Friedland, W.H. (2010) Who killed rural sociology? A case study in the political economy of knowledge production. *International Journal of Sociology of Agriculture and Food* 17(1): 72–88.

————. (1994) The new globalisation: The case for fresh produce. Pp. 210–231 in A. Bonnano, L. Busch, W. Friedland, L. Gouveia and E. Mingione, eds., *From Columbus to Conagra: The Globalisation of Agriculture and Food*. Lawrence: University Press of Kansas.

Frost, M. (2006) *The Structure of Commuting Flows in Rural England and Wales: An Initial Report*. London: Rural Evidence Research Centre, Birkbeck University of London.

Fuglie, K., and Schimmelpfennig, D. (eds.) (2000) *Public–Private Collaboration in Agricultural Research: New Institutional Arrangements and Economic Implications*. Ames: Iowa State University Press.

Fuguitt, G., Brown, D.L., and Beale C. (1989) Fertility. Pp. 185–227 in G. Fuguitt, D.L. Brown and C. Beale, eds., *Rural and Small Town America*. New York: Russell Sage Foundation.

Fukuyama, F. (2006) Identity, immigration and liberal democracy. *Journal of Democracy* 17(2): 5–20.

Furbey, R. Dinham, A., Farnell, R., Finneron, D., Wilkinson, G., with Howarth, C., Hussain, D., and Palmer, S. (2006) *Faith as Social Capital*. Bristol: Policy Press.

Furey, S., Strugnell, C., and McIlveen, H. (2001) An investigation of the potential existence of 'food deserts' in rural and urban areas of Northern Ireland. *Agriculture and Human Values* 18(4): 447–457.

Furstenberg, F.F. (2009) If Moynihan had only known: Race, class, and family change in the late twentieth century. *Annals of the American Academy of Political and Social Science* 621: 94–118.

Gale, F., and McGranahan, D. (2001) Nonmetro areas fall behind in the 'New Economy'. *Rural America* 16(1): 44–52.

Galeski, B., and Mendras, H. (1981) Foreword. Pp. v–vii in J.-L. Durand-Drouhin and L.-M. Szwengrub, eds., *Rural Community Studies in Europe*. Oxford: Pergamon.

Gallagher, E. (2008) *The Gallagher Review of the Indirect Effects of Biofuels Production. Report for the Renewable Fuels Agency, St. Leonards*.

Galpin, C.J. (1918) *Rural Life*. New York: Century Co.

Galster, G.C., and Killen, S.P. (1995) The geography of metropolitan opportunity: A reconnaissance and conceptual framework. *Housing Policy Debate* 6(1): 7–43.

Gardner, B. (2002) *American Agriculture in the Twentieth Century: How It Flourished and What It Cost*. Boston, MA: Harvard University Press.

————. (1996) Agricultural economics in the policy arena: The 1995 Farm Bill. *Review of Agricultural Economics* 18(2): 155–165.

————. (1992) Changing economic perspectives on the farm problem. *Journal of Economic Literature* 30(1): 62–101.

Garkovich, L.E. (2011) A historical view of community development. Pp. 11–34 in J.W. Robinson and G.P. Green, eds., *Community Development: Theory, Practice and Service Learning*. Thousand Oaks, CA: Sage.

Gartland, M. (2005) Interdisciplinary views of sub-optimal outcomes: Path dependence in the social and management sciences. *Journal of Socio-Economics* 34: 686–702.

Gasson, R., and Errington, A. (1993) *The Farm Family Business*. Wallingford, Oxfordshire: CABI.

Gasteyer, S., Hultine, S.A., Cooperband, L.R., and Curry, M.P. (2008) Produce sections, town squares and farm stands: Comparing local food systems in community context. *Southern Rural Sociology* 23(1): 47–71.

Geisler, C. (2003) A new kind of trouble: Evictions in Eden. *International Social Science Journal* 175(3): 69–78.

Gendell, M. (2008) Older workers: Increasing their labor force participation and hours worked. *Monthly Labor Review* (January): 41–54.

General Register Office for Scotland. (2010) Population projections Scotland (2008–based). Population projections by sex, age and administrative area. http://www.gro-scotland.gov.uk/statistics/publications-and-data/population-estimates/mid-year/mid-2008–pop-est/index.html.

———. (2009a) Mid-2008 population estimates Scotland. http://www.gro-scotland.gov.uk/statistics/publications-and-data/population-estimates/mid-2008–population-estimates-scotland/index.html.

———. (2009b) Migration flows between Council areas, 2001–02 to most recent. http://www.gro-scotland.gov.uk/statistics/migration/migration-within-scotland.html.

———. (2009c) Scotland's Population Census 2008. Accessed 20/2/10 http://www.gro-scotland.gov.uk/statistics/publications-and-data/annual-report-publications/rgs-annual-review-2007/index.html.

Gereffi, G. (2006) *The New Offshoring of Jobs and Global Development. ILO Social Policy Lectures.* Geneva: International Institute for Labor Studies and International Labor Organization.

Getz, A. (1995) Locally based, ecologically sound, and socially innovative development: The contributions of community supported agriculture to the global dialogue. In R. Morse, A. Rahman, and K. L. Johnson, eds., *Grassroots Horizons: Connecting Participatory Development Initiatives East and West.* London: IT Publications.

Getz, D., and Petersen, T. (2005) Growth and profit-oriented entrepreneurship among family business owners in the tourism and hospitality industry. *International Journal of Hospitality Management* 24(2): 219–242.

Gibbs, R.M. (2002) Rural labor markets in an era of welfare reform. Pp. 51–75 in B.A. Weber, G.J. Duncan and L.A. Whitener, eds., *Rural Dimensions of Welfare Reform.* Kalamazoo, MI: W.E. Upjohn Institute for Employment Research.

Gibbs, R.M., and Bernat Jr., A. (1997) Rural industry clusters raise local earnings. *Rural Development Perspectives.* USDA Economic Research Service 12, No. 3.

Gilbert, A., Philip, L., and Shucksmith, M. (2006) Rich and poor in the countryside. Pp. 69–93 in P. Lowe and L. Speakman, eds., *The Ageing Countryside. The Growing Older Population of Rural England.* London: Commission for Rural Communities and Age Concern.

Gilbert, J. (2008) Rural sociology and democratic planning in the third New Deal. *Agricultural History* 82: 422–444.

———. (2001) Agrarian intellectuals in a democratizing state: A collective biography of USDA leaders in the intended New Deal. Pp. 232–244 in C.M. Stock, and R.D. Johnston, eds., *The Countryside in the Age of the Modern State: Political Histories of Rural America.* Ithaca, NY: Cornell University Press.

Gilbert, J., and Howe, C. (1991) Beyond state vs. societies: Theories of the state and New Deal agricultural policies. *American Sociological Review* 56: 204–220.

Gilborn, C. 2009. *Great Camps and Conservation.* Syracuse: Syracuse University Press.

Gilchrist, A. (2004) *The Well-Connected Community.* Bristol: Policy Press.

Gilligan, J. (1987) Visitors, tourists and outsiders in a Cornish town. Pp. 65–82 in M. Bouquet and M. Winter, eds., *Who from Their Labours Rest? Conflict and Practice in Rural Tourism.* Aldershot: Avebury.

Gilpin, N., Henty, M., Lemos, S., Portes, J., and Bullen, C. (2006) The impact of free movement of workers from Central and Eastern Europe on the UK labour market. Department for Work and Pensions Working Paper no. 29, London.

Gimpel, J.G., and Lay, J.C. (2008) Political socialization and reactions to immigration-related diversity in rural America. *Rural Sociology* 73(2): 180–204.

Glasgow, N., and Brown, D.L. (2006) Social integration among older in-migrants in nonmetropolitan retirement destination counties: Establishing new ties. Pp.

177–196 in W. Kandel and D.L. Brown, eds., *Population Change and Rural Society*. Dordrecht, the Netherlands: Springer.

———. (2008) Grey gold: Do older in-migrants benefit rural communities? Policy Brief 10. Carsey Institute, University of New Hampshire.

Glasgow, N., and Reeder, R. (1990) Economic and fiscal implications of non-metropolitan retirement migration. *Journal of Applied Gerontology* 9(4): 433–451.

Glendinning, A., Nuttall, M., Hendry, L., Kloep, M., and Wood, S. (2003) Rural communities and wellbeing: A good place to grow up? *Sociological Review* 51: 129–156.

Global Commission on International Migration. (2005) *Migration in an Interconnected World: New Directions. Report*. GCIM.

Godden, R., and Crawford, M. (eds.) (2006) *Reading Southern Poverty between the Wars, 1918–1939*. Athens: University of Georgia Press.

Goetz, S.J. (2008) Self-employment in rural America: The new economic reality. *Rural Realities* 2(3).

Goetz, S., Han, Y., Findeis, J., and Brasier, K. (2010) US commuting networks and economic growth: Measurement and implications for spatial policy. *Growth and Change* 41(2): 276–302.

Goldman, M. (2005) *Imperial Nature: The World Bank and Struggles for Social Justice in the Age of Globalization*. New Haven, CT, and London: Yale University Press.

Goodwin, M. (2008) Rural governance, devolution and policy delivery. Pp. 45–58 in M. Woods, ed., *New Labour's Countryside: Rural Policy in Britain Since 1997*. Bristol: Policy Press.

Gorton, M., Hubbard, M.C., and Hubbard, L.J. (2009) The folly of EU policy transfer: Why the CAP does not fit Central and Eastern Europe. *Regional Studies* 43: 1305–1317.

Gorton, M., White, J., and Chaston, I. (1998) Counterurbanization, fragmentation and the paradox of the rural idyll. Pp. 215–236 in P. Boyle and K. Halfacree, eds., *Migration into Rural Areas: Theories and Issues*. Chichester: John Wiley.

Gosselin, M. (2010) *Beyond the USDA: How Other Government Agencies Can Support a Healthier, More Sustainable Food System*. Minneapolis, MN: Institute for Agriculture and Trade Policy.

Grabher, G., and Stark, D. (1997) Organizing diversity: Evolutionary theory, network analysis, and post-socialism. Pp. 1–32 in *Restructuring Networks in Post-Socialism*. New York: Oxford University Press.

Graham Jr., F. (1978) *The Adirondack Park: A Political History*. New York: Alfred A. Knopf.

Granovetter, M. (1973) The strength of weak ties. *American Journal of Sociology* 78: 1360–1380.

Green, A. (2006) Employment and the older person in the countryside. Pp. 94–118 in P. Lowe and L. Speakman, eds., *The Ageing Countryside. The Growing Older Population of Rural England*. London: Commission for Rural Communities and Age Concern.

Green, A., De Hoyos, M., Jones, P., and Owen, D. (2009) Rural development and labour supply challenges in the UK: The role of non-UK migrants. *Regional Studies* 43(10): 1261–1274.

Green, A., Owen, D., and Jones, P. (2007) The contribution of migration flows to demographic change in the East Midlands. Accessed 20/2/10 http://www.wmro.org/resources/res.aspx/CmsResource/resourceFilename/1788/Economic-Migrants-Final_V1.0_Report_SM.pdf.

Green, G.P. (2003) Civic involvement, organizational ties, and local economic development. *Journal of the Community Development Society* 34(1): 2–17.

Green, G.P., and Haines, A. (2008) *Asset Building and Community Development*. Thousand Oaks, CA: Sage.

Green, G.P., and Robinson, J.W. (2011) Emerging issues in community development. Pp. 295–302 in J.W. Robinson and G.P. Green, eds., *Community Development: Theory, Practice and Service-Learning*. Thousand Oaks, CA: Sage.

Grey, M., and Woodrick, A. (2005) Latinos have revitalized our community: Mexican migration and Anglo responses in Marshallton Iowa. Pp. 133–154 in V. Zuniga and R. Hernandez-Leon, eds., *New Destinations: Mexican Immigration in the United States*. New York: Russell Sage Foundation.

Grieco, E.M. (2009) *Race and Hispanic Origin of the Foreign-Born Population in the United States: 2007*. Washington, DC: US Census Bureau.

Griffith, D.C. (2005) Rural industry and Mexican immigration and settlement in North Carolina. Pp. 50–75 in V. Zúñiga and R. Hernández-León, eds., *New Destinations: Mexican Immigration in the United States*. New York: Russell Sage Foundation.

Groves, A. (2005) *The Local and Regional Food Opportunity*. IGD.

Gunderson, C., Kuhn, B., Offatt, S., and Morehart, M. (2004) *A Consideration of the Devolution of Federal Agricultural Policy. Agricultural Economic Report No. 836*. Economic Research Service, USDA.

Habermas, J., and Derrida, J. (2003) February 15 or what binds Europeans together: A plea for a Common Foreign Policy, beginning in a core of Europe. *Constellations* 10(3): 291–297.

Haines, M., and Steckel, R. (eds.) (2001) *A Population History of North America*. New York: Cambridge University Press.

Hajer, M.J., and Wagenaar, H. (2003) Introduction. Pp. 1–30 in M.J. Hajer and H. Wagenaar, eds., *Deliberative Policy Analysis. Understanding Governance in the Network Society*. Cambridge: Cambridge University Press.

Hajnal, Z. (2007) Black class exceptionalism: Insights from direct democracy on the race versus class debate. *Public Opinion Quarterly* 71(4): 560–587.

Halfacree, K. (2008) To revitalise counterurbanisation research? Recognising an international and fuller picture. *Population Space and Place* 14(6): 479–495.

———. (2007) Trial by space for a 'radical rural': Introducing alternative localities, representations and lives. *Journal of Rural Studies* 23: 125–141.

———. (1993) Locality and social representation: Space, discourse and alternative definitions of the rural. *Journal of Rural Studies* 9(1): 23–37.

Hall, J.A., and Lindholm, C. (2001) *Is America Breaking Apart?* Princeton, NJ: Princeton University Press.

Hall, P.A., and Soskice, D. (2001) *Varieties of Capitalism: The Institutional Foundations of Comparative Advantage*. Oxford: Oxford University Press.

Hall, P.A., Thomas, R., Gracey, H., and Drewett, R. (1974) *The Containment of Urban England*. Hemel Hempstead: Allen and Unwin.

Hallberg, M. (2001) *Economic Trends in US Agriculture and Food Systems since World War II*. Ames: Iowa State University Press.

Hallberg, M., Findeis, J., and Lass, D. (1991) *Multiple Job-Holding among Farm Families*. Ames: Iowa State University Press.

Hamin, E., and Marcucci, D. (2008) Ad hoc rural regionalism. *Journal of Rural Studies* 24(3): 467–477.

Hamnett, C.R. (1992) House-price differentials, housing wealth and migration. Pp. 55–64 in A.G. Champion and A.J. Fielding, eds., *Migration Processes and Patterns: Volume 1—Research Progress and Prospects*. Belhaven: London.

Hanningfield, L. (2009) Going local. Pp. 39–43 in A. Collinge, ed., *Do Regions Matter?* London: Local Government Information Unit.

Hansen, K., Boertlein, C., and Long, L. (1978) *Geographical Mobility: 1975–1977. Current Population Report. P-20, No. 320*. Washington, DC: US Bureau of Census.

Hantrais, L. (2009) *International Comparative Research: Theory, Methods and Practice.* Basingstoke: Palgrave Macmillan.

Hardesty, S.D. (2010) Do government policies grow local food? *Choices* 25(1).

Harrington, M. (1962) *The Other America: Poverty in the United States.* New York: Penguin.

Harris, J., Sapienza, H., and Bowie, N. (2009) Ethics and entrepreneurship. *Journal of Business Venturing* 24: 407–418.

Hart, J.F. (1995) 'Rural' and 'Farm' no longer mean the same. Pp. 63–76 in E.N. Castle, ed., *The Changing American Countryside.* Lawrence: University of Kansas Press.

Hart, K., Laville, J-L., and Cattani, A.D. (2010) *The Human Economy: A World Citizen's Guide.* Cambridge: Polity.

Hart, K., and Munro, G. (2000) 'The Highland problem': State and community in local development. Arkleton Research Papers 1, University of Aberdeen.

Harvey, D.R. (2010) *The Enigma of Capital: And the Crises of Capitalism.* London: Profile Books.

———. (2008) *The Agricultural Policy Complex in the UK: The Policy Process from Formulation to Evaluation. Report.* Korea Rural Economic Institute.

———. (1995) European Union cereals policy: An evolutionary interpretation. *Australian Journal of Agricultural Economics* 35(3): 193–217.

Hassanein, N. (2008) Locating food democracy: Theoretical and practical ingredients. *Journal of Hunger and Environmental Nutrition* 3(2–3): 286–308.

———. (2003) Practicing food democracy: A pragmatic politics of transformation. *Journal of Rural Studies* 19: 77–86.

Hay, C. (2002) *Political Analysis: A Critical Introduction.* Basingstoke: Palgrave.

Hays, S. (1984) The British conservation scene—a view from the United States. *Ecos* 5(3): 20–27.

Hayward, C., Simpson, L., and Wood, L. (2004) Still left out in the cold: Problematising participatory research and development. *Sociologia Ruralis* 44(1): 95–108.

Hefetz, A., and Warner, M.E. (2007) Beyond the market vs. planning dichotomy: Understanding privatisation and its reverse in US cities. *Local Government Studies* 33(4): 555–572.

Heffernan, W. (2000) Concentration of ownership and control in agriculture. Pp. 61–75 in F. Magdoff, J. Foster and F. Buttel, eds., *Hungry for Profit: The Agribusiness Threat to Farmers, Food and the Environment.* New York: Monthly Review Press.

Heimlich, R., and Anderson, W. (2001) *Development at the Urban Fringe and Beyond: Impacts on Agriculture and Rural Land, Agriculture Economic Report No. 803.* Washington, DC: USDA-ERS.

Hellerstein, D., Nickerson, C., Cooper, J., Feather, P., Gadsby, D., Mullarkey, D., Tegene, A., and Barnard, C. (2002) *Farmland Protection: The Role of Public Preferences for Rural Amenities. Report AER-815.* Washington, DC: US Department of Agriculture, Economic Research Service.

Henderson, J. (2002) Building the rural economy with high-growth entrepreneurs. *Economic Review Third Quarter.*

Henry, M., Barkley, D., and Zhang, Y. (1997) Industry clusters in the TVA region: Do they affect development of rural areas? TVA Rural Studies Contractor Paper December 98–9.

Hepworth, M. (2004) *The Knowledge Economy in Rural England.* London: DEFRA.

Hernandez, R., and Zuniga, V. (2005) Appalachia meets Aztlan: Mexican immigration and intergroup relations in Dalton Georgia. Pp. 244–274 in V. Zuniga and R. Hernandez-Leon, eds., *New Destinations: Mexican Immigration in the United States*. New York: Russell Sage Foundation.

Hewitt, B. (2010) *The Town that Food Saved: How One Community Found Vitality in Local Food*. Emmaus, PA: Rodale.

Highland Council. (2008) Council area population projections 2006–2031. Policy and Information Briefing Note No. 28. Planning and Development Service, The Highland Council, Inverness.

Hills, J. (2002) Does a focus on social exclusion change the policy response? Pp. 226–43 in J. Hills, J. Le Grand and D. Piachaud, eds., *Understanding Social Exclusion*. Oxford: Oxford University Press.

Hines, F., Brown, D.L., and Zimmer, J. (1975) *Social and Economic Characteristics of the Population in Metropolitan and Nonmetropolitan Counties, 1970. Agricultural Economic Report No. 272*. Washington, DC: USDA-ERS.

Hinrichs, C.C. (2003). The practice and politics of food system localization. *Journal of Rural Studies* 19: 33-45.

Hinrichs, C.C., and Kremer, K.S. (2002) Social inclusion in a Midwest local food system project. *Journal of Poverty* 6: 65–90.

Hirsch, D., and Millar, J. (2004) *Labour's Welfare Reform: Progress to Date*. York: Joseph Rowntree Foundation.

HM Government. (2010) *Food 2030. Report*. London: DEFRA.

HM Treasury. (2007) *Sub-National Review of Economic Development and Regeneration. Report*. London: HM Treasury. .

Hodge, I. (2001) Beyond agri-environmental policy: towards an alternative model of rural environmental governance. *Land Use Policy* 18: 99–111.

Hofferth, S.L., and Iceland, J. (1998) Social capital in rural and urban communities. *Rural Sociology* 63(4): 574–598.

Hofstee, E.W. (1963) Rural sociology in Europe. *Rural Sociology* 28: 329–341.

———. (1960) Introduction. *Sociologia Ruralis* 1: 3–6.

Hoggart, K. (1990) Let's do away with rural. *Journal of Rural Studies* 6(3): 245–257.

Hoggart, K., and Paniagua, A. (2001) What rural restructuring? *Journal of Rural Studies* 17(1): 41–62.

Hollander, G. (2004) Agricultural trade liberalisation, multifunctionality and sugar in the south Florida landscape. *Geoforum* 35: 299–312.

Holley, J. (2007) Transforming rural economies through entrepreneurial networks: A case study. Pp. 233–253 in N. Walzer, ed., *Entrepreneurship and Local Economic Development*. Lanham, MD: Lexington.

Hollywood, E., and McQuaid, R.W. (2007) Employers' responses to demographic changes in the rural labour markets: The case of Dumfries and Galloway. *Local Economy* 22(2): 148–162.

Holmwood, J. (2007) Only connect: The challenges of globalization for the social sciences. *21st Century Society* 2: 79–93.

Home Office. (2004a) *Building Civil Renewal. Report*. London: Civil Renewal Unit.

———. (2004b) *Firm Foundations: The Government's Framework for Community Capacity Building. Report*. London: Civil Renewal Unit.

Hoppe, R. (1993) Poverty in rural America: Trends and demographic characteristics. Pp. 20–38 in Rural Sociological Society Task Force on Rural Poverty, ed., *Persistent Poverty in Rural America*. Boulder, CO: Westview.

Hoppe, R., Korb, P., O'Donoghue, E., and Banker, D. (2007) *Structure and Finances of US Farms: Family Farm Report. 2007 Edition. Report EIB-24*. Washington, DC: US Department of Agriculture, Economic Research Service.

House of Commons Environment, Food and Rural Affairs Committee. (2008) *The Potential of England's Rural Economy. Eleventh Report of Session 2007–2008*. London: Stationary Office Limited.

Houston, D., and Lever, W. (2001) *Migration within and from Rural Areas in England*. Cheltenham: Countryside Agency.

Howkins, A. (1992) *Reshaping Rural England: A Social History 1850–1925*. London: Routledge.

Hubacek, K., Erickson, J., and Duchin, F. (2002) Input-output modeling of protected landscapes: The Adirondack Park. *Review of Regional Studies* 32(2): 207–222.

Hubbard, C. (2009) Small farms in the EU: How small is small? Paper presented at Small Farms: Decline or Persistence 111 EAAE-IAAE seminar, Canterbury, UK.

Hubbard, L.J. (2003) United Kingdom: Less resistance to change. In *The Political Economy of Beef Liberalisation*. Canberra: Centre for International Economics.

Hubbard, L.J., and Ritson, C. (1997) Reform of the CAP: From Mansholt to MacSharry. Pp. 81–94 in C. Ritson, and D. Harvey, eds., *The Common Agricultural Policy*. Wallingford: CAB International.

Hubbell, F.A., Waitzkin, H., Mishra, S.I. 1991. "Access to Medical Care for Documented and Undocumented Latinos in a Southern California County." *Western Journal of Medicine* 154:414–417.

Hughes, A., Morris, C., and Seymour, S. (eds.) (2000) *Ethnography and Rural Research*. Cheltenham: Countryside and Community Press.

Hultine, S.A., Cooperband, L.R., Curry, M.P., and Gasteyer, S. (2007) Linking small farms to rural communities: A case study of the local food project in Fairbury, Illinois. *Community Development* 38(3): 61–76.

Hunt, V. (2007) Community development corporations and public participation: Lessons from a case study in the Arkansas Delta. *Journal of Sociology and Social Welfare* 34(3): 9–35.

Hunter, R. (1904) *Poverty*. New York: Macmillan Company.

Hyatt, S.B. (2001) From citizen to volunteer: Neoliberal governance and the erasure of poverty. Pp. 201–235 in J. Goode and J. Maskovsky, eds., *The New Poverty Studies: The Ethnography of Power, Politics, and Impoverished People in the United States*. New York: New York University Press.

IAASTD. (2008) *Agriculture at a Crossroads. Report*. International Assessment of Agricultural Science and Technology for Development.

Ilbery, B. (ed.) (1998) *The Geography of Rural Social Change*. Harlow: Longman.

Ilbery, B., Watts, D., Simpson, S., Gilg, A., and Little, J. (2006) Mapping local foods: Evidence from two English regions. *British Food Journal* 108(3): 213–225.

Ingold, T. (2000) *The Perception of the Environment*. London: Routledge.

Institute of Economic Affairs. (2005) *The New Rural Economy: Change Dynamism and Government Policy*. London: Institute of Economic Affairs.

Intergovernmental Panel on Climate Change. (2007) *Climate Change 2007: Mitigation of Climate Change. Summary for Policymakers. Fourth Report of Intergovernmental Panel on Climate Change*.

Jack, S.L., and Anderson, A.R. (2002) The effects of embeddedness on the entrepreneurial process. *Journal of Business Venturing* 17: 467–487.

Jackson, W., Berry, W., and Colman. B. (eds.) (1984) *Meeting the Expectations of the Land: Essays in Sustainable Agriculture and Stewardship*. San Francisco: North Point Press.

Jackson-Smith, D., and Sharp, J. (2008) Farming in the urban shadow: Supporting agriculture at the rural–urban interface. *Rural Realities* 2(4).

Jacoby, R., and Glauberman, N. (eds.) (1995) *The Bell Curve Debate: History, Documents, Opinions*. New York: Times Books.

Jaffee, D., Kloppenburg, J.R., and Monroy, M.B. (2004) Bringing the 'moral charge' home: Fair trade within the North and within the South. *Rural Sociology* 69(2): 169–196.

Jamieson, L., and Davidson, S. (2007) *CRFR Migration Research Scoping Review—Lived Experience of Migrants in Scotland. Report*. Edinburgh: Edinburgh University Centre for Research on Families and Relationships.

Jamison, A. (2001) *The Making of Green Knowledge: Environmental Politics and Cultural Transformation*. Cambridge: Cambridge University Press.

Jansen, A.J. (1969) Social implications of farm mechanization. *Sociologia Ruralis* 9: 340–407.

Jargowski, P. (1997) *Poverty and Place: Ghettos, Barrios, and the American City*. New York: Russell Sage Foundation.

Jarosz, L. (2008) The city in the country: Growing alternative food networks in metropolitan areas. *Journal of Rural Studies* 24: 231–244.

Jenkins, J., and Keal, A. (2004) *The Adirondack Atlas: A Geographic Portrait of the Adirondack Park*. Bronx, NY: Wildlife Conservation Society.

Jensen, L., Findeis, J.L., Hsu, W., and Schachter, J.P. (1999) Slipping into and out of underemployment: Another disadvantage for nonmetropolitan workers? *Rural Sociology* 64(3): 417–438.

Jensen, L., and McLaughlin, D.K. (1993) Human capital and nonmetropolitan poverty. Pp. 111–138 in L.J. Beaulieu and D. Mulkey, eds., *Investing in People: The Human Capital Needs of Rural America*. Boulder, CO: Westview.

Jensen, L., McLaughlin, D.K., and Slack, T. (2003) Rural poverty: The persisting challenge. Pp. 118–131 in D.L. Brown and L.E. Swanson, eds., *Challenges for Rural America in the Twenty-First Century*. University Park, PA: Penn State University Press.

Jentsch, B., de Lima, P., and MacDonald, B. (2007) Migrant workers in rural Scotland: 'Going to the middle of nowhere'. *International Journal on Multicultural Societies* 9(1): 35–53.

Jessop, B. (2005) The governance of complexity and the complexity of governance, revisited. Paper presented to Complexity, Science and Society conference, Liverpool, UK, 11–14 September.

———. (2003) The spatiotemporal dynamics of capital and its globalization—and how they challenge state power and democracy. In W.E. Scheuerman and H. Rosa, eds., *Social Acceleration: Conceptions, Causes, Consequences*. London: Verso.

———. (1999) The dynamics of partnership and governance failure. In G. Stoker, ed., *The New Politics of Local Governance in Britain*. Oxford: Oxford University Press.

———. (1997) The entrepreneurial city: Re-imaging localities, redesigning economic governance, or restructuring capital? Pp. 28–41 in N. Jewson and S. MacGregor, eds., *Transforming Cities: Contested Governance and New Spatial Divisions*. London: Routledge.

———. (1990) *State Theory: Putting the Capitalist State in Its Place*. Cambridge: Polity Press.

Jobin, B., Beaulieu, J., Grenier, M., Belanger, L., Maisonneuve, C., Bordage, D., and Filion, B. (2003) Landscape changes and ecological studies in agricultural regions. Quebec, Canada. *Landscape Ecology* 18: 575–590.

Johnson, K. (2009) *With Less Migration, Natural Increase Is Now More Important to State Growth. Fact Sheet No. 17*. Durham, NH: Carsey Institute.

———. (2006) *Demographic Trends in Rural and Small Town America*. Durham, NH: Carsey Foundation, University of New Hampshire.

———. (2005) The rising incidence of natural decrease in rural counties. Paper presented to the annual meeting of the Population Association of America, Philadelphia, August.

Johnson, K., and Cromartie, J. (2006) The rural rebound and its aftermath. Pp. 25–49 in W. Kandel and D.L. Brown, eds., *Population Change and Rural Society*. Dordrecht: Springer.

Johnson, K., and Lichter, D. (2007) Demographic components of rural population change: In-migration and natural increase of immigrants. Paper presented to the annual meeting of the Rural Sociological Society. Santa Clara, California, August.

Johnson, K., and Rathge, R. (2006) Agricultural dependence and changing population in the Great Plains. Pp. 197–217 in W. Kandel and D.L. Brown, eds., *Population Change and Rural Society*. Dordrecht, the Netherlands: Springer.

Johnson, K., Voss, P., Hammer, R., Fuguitt, G., and McNiven, S. (2005) Temporal and spatial variation in age-specific net migration. *Demography* 42(4): 791–812.

Johnson, T.G., and Bryden, J.M. (2006) Comparative rural policy in Europe, USA and Canada. Paper presented at International Comparative Rural Policy Studies Post-Graduate Summer School, Brandon, Manitoba.

Jolliffe, D. (2007) *Rural Poverty at a Glance. Rural Development Research Report. No. 100*. Washington, DC: Economic Research Service, US Department of Agriculture.

Jonas, A., and Pincetl, P. (2006) Rescaling regions in the state: The new regionalism in California. *Political Geography* 25: 482–505.

Jonas, A., and Ward, K. (2002) A world of regionalisms? Towards a US–UK urban and regional policy framework comparison. *Journal of Urban Affairs* 24: 377–402.

Jones, C., Kandel, W., and Parker., T. (2007) Population dynamics are changing the profile of rural areas. *Amber Waves* (December). Accessed 9/2/10 http://www.ers.usda.gov/AmberWaves/December09/.

Jones, G., and Jamieson, L. (1997) Young people in rural Scotland: Getting out and staying on. CES Briefing No 13, Edinburgh University.

Jones, K. (2000) *The Making of British Social Policy*. London: Athlone Press.

Jordan, N. (2007) Sustainable development of the agricultural bio-economy. *Science* 316: 1570–1571.

Kalantaridis, C., and Bika, Z. (2006a) In-migrant entrepreneurship in rural England: Beyond local embeddedness. *Entrepreneurship and Regional Development* 18: 109–131.

———. (2006b) Local embeddedness and rural entrepreneurship: Case-study evidence from Cumbria, England. *Environment and Planning A* 38: 1561–1579.

Kandel, W., and Cromartie, J. (2004) *New Patterns of Hispanic Settlement in Rural America. USDA Rural Development Research Report No. 99*. Washington, DC: USDA.

Kandel, W., and Parrado, E. (2006) Rural Hispanic population growth: Public policy impacts in nonmetro counties. Pp. 155–176 in W. Kandel and D.L. Brown, eds., *Population Change and Rural Society*. Dordrecht, the Netherlands: Springer.

Kasinitz, P., Mollenkopf, J.H., Waters, M.C., and Holdaway, J. (2008) *Inheriting the City: The Children of Immigrants Come of Age*. New York: Russell Sage Foundation.

Katz, M. (2001) *The Price of Citizenship: Redefining the American Welfare State*. New York: Metropolitan Books.

———. (1975) *Class, Bureaucracy and Schools: The Illusion of Educational Change in America*. New York: Berger.

Keating, M., and Stevenson, L. (2006) Rural policy in Scotland after devolution. *Regional Studies* 40(3): 397–407.

Keeble, D., and Tyler, P. (1995) Enterprising behaviour and the urban-rural shift. *Urban Studies* 32(6): 975–998.

Keeble, D., Tyler, P., and Lewis, G. (1992) *Business Success in the Countryside: The Performance of Rural Enterprise*. London: HMSO.

Kirkendall, R.S. (1966) *Social Scientists and Farm Politics in the Age of Roosevelt.* Ames: Iowa State University Press.

Kirwan, J. (2006) The interpersonal world of direct marketing: Examining the conventions of quality at UK farmers' markets. *Journal of Rural Studies* 22(3): 301–312.

Kirwan, J., and Foster, C. (2007) Public sector food procurement in the United Kingdom: Examining the creation of an 'alternative' and localized network in Cornwall. Pp. 185–201 in D. Maye, L. Holloway and M. Kneafsey, eds., *Constructing 'Alternative' Food Geographies: Representation and Practice.* Oxford: Elsevier.

Kneafsey, M. (2010) The region in food—important or irrelevant? *Cambridge Journal of Regions, Economy and Society* 3: 177–190.

Knight, F.H. (1921) *Risk, Uncertainty and Profit.* Boston, MA: Houghton-Mifflin.

Knox, C. (2009) The politics of local government reform in Northern Ireland. *Local Government Studies* 35(4): 435–455.

Knox, C., and Carmichael, P. (2006) Bureau shuffling: The reform of public administration in Northern Ireland. *Public Administration* 84(4): 941–65.

Kötter, H. (1967) The situation of rural sociology in Europe. *Sociologia Ruralis* 7: 254–294.

Kritz, M.M., and Gurak, D.T. (2005) Immigration and a changing America. Pp. 259–301 in R. Farley and J. Haaga, eds., *The American People: Census 2000.* New York: Russell Sage Foundation.

———. (2004) *Immigration and a Changing America.* New York: Russell Sage Foundation.

Kuhn, M., and Remøe, S.O. (eds.) (2005) *Building the European Research Area.* New York: Peter Lang.

Kusmin, L. (ed.) (2008) *Rural America at a Glance. Economic Information Bulletin No. EIB-40.* Washington, DC: US Department of Agriculture, Economic Research Service.

———. (2006) *Rural Employment at a Glance. Economic Information Bulletin No. 21.* Washington, DC: US Department of Agriculture, Economic Research Service.

Kwang-Koo, K., Marcouiller, D.W., and Deller, S.C. (2005) Natural amenities and rural development: Understanding spatial and distributional attributes. *Growth and Change* 36(2): 273–297.

Lagendijk, A. (2007) The accident of the region. A strategic relational perspective on the construction of the region's significance. *Regional Studies* 41(9): 1193–1208.

Lallement, M., and Spurk, J. (eds.) (2003) *Stratégies de la Comparaison Internationale.* Paris: CNRS éditions.

Lambert, D., Sullivan, P., Claassen, R., and Foreman, L. (2006) *Conservation-Compatible Practices and Programs: Who Participates? Report ERR-14.* Washington, DC: US Department of Agriculture, Economic Research Service.

Lambert, R. (2001) *Contested Mountains: Nature, Development and Environment in the Cairngorms Region of Scotland, 1880–1980.* Cambridge: White Horse Press.

Lang, T. (2010) Food Standards Agency: What a carve up. *The Guardian*, 21 July. http://www.guardian.co.uk/commentisfree/2010/jul/21/fsa-what-a-carve-up.

———. (1999) Food policy for the 21st century: Can it be both radical and reasonable? Pp. 216–224 in M. Koc, R. MacRae, L.J.A. Mougeot and J. Welsh, eds., *For Hunger-Proof Cities: Sustainable Urban Food Systems.* Ottawa: International Development Research Centre.

Lang, T., Barling, D., and Caraher, M. (2009) *Food Policy: Integrating Health, Environment and Society.* Oxford: Oxford University Press.

Larson, O.F., and Zimmerman, J.N. (2003) *Sociology in Government: The Galpin-Taylor Years in the US Department of Agriculture 1919–1953.* University Park, PA: Penn State University Press.

Law, C.M. (1967) The growth of the urban population of England and Wales, 1801–1911. *Transactions of the Institute of British Geographers* 41: 125–143.

Law, C.M., and Warnes, A.M. (1973) The movement of retired people to seaside resorts. *Town Planning Review* 44(4): 373–390.

Lawrence, G. (1987) *Capitalism in the Countryside.* Pluto Books.

Lawson, V., Jarosz, I.., and Bonds, A. (2010) Articulations of place, poverty, and race: Dumping grounds and unseen grounds in the rural American Northwest. *Annals of the Association of American Geographers* 100(3): 655–677.

———. (2008) Building economies from the bottom up: (Mis)representations of poverty in the rural American Northwest. *Social and Cultural Geography* 9(7): 737–753.

Le Gales, P. (1998) Regulations and governance in European cities. *International Journal of Urban and Regional Research* 47(2): 482–506.

Legge, J., and Hindle, K. (2004) *Entrepreneurship: Context, Vision and Planning.* Basingstoke: Palgrave Macmillan.

Lenihan, M.H., and Brasier, K. (2010) Eco-modernization and the US Farm Bill: The case of the conservation security program. *Journal of Rural Studies* 26(3): 219–227.

Lenihan, M.H, Brasier, K., and Stedman, R. (2009) Perceptions of agriculture's multifunctional role among rural Pennsylvanians. Pp. 127–150 in K. Andersson, E. Eklund, M. Lehtola and P. Salmi, eds., *Beyond the Rural–Urban Divide: Cross-Continental Perspectives on the Differentiated Countryside and its Regulation.* Rural Sociology and Development Series, Volume 14. Bingley, UK: Emerald Group Publishing Limited.

Levitas, R. (1998) *The Inclusive Society? Social Exclusion and New Labour.* London: Macmillan.

Lichter, D.T., and Brown, D.L. (2011) Rural America in an urban society: Changing spatial and social boundaries. *Annual Review of Sociology* 37.

Lichter, D.T., and Jensen, L. (2002) Rural America in transition: Poverty and welfare at the turn of the twenty-first century. Pp. 77–110 in B.A. Weber, G.J. Duncan and L.A. Whitener, eds., *Rural Dimensions of Welfare Reform.* Kalamazoo, MI: W.E. Upjohn Institute for Employment Research.

Lichter, D.T., and Johnson, K.M. (2009) Immigrant gateways and Hispanic migration to new destinations. *International Migration Review* 43: 496–518.

———. (2007) The changing spatial concentration of America's rural poor population. *Rural Sociology* 72(3): 331–258.

———. (2006) Emerging rural settlement patterns and the geographic redistribution of America's new immigrants. *Rural Sociology* 71(1): 109–131.

Lichter, D.T., McLaughlin, D.K., and Cornwell, G. (1995) Migration and the loss of human resources in rural America. Pp. 235–256 in L.J. Beaulieu and D. Mulkey, eds., *Investing in People: The Human Capital Needs of Rural America.* Boulder, CO: Westview.

Lichter, D.T., and Parisi, D. (2008) Concentrated rural poverty and the geography of exclusion. *Rural Realities* (Fall).

Lichter, D.T., Parisi, D., Grice, S.M., and Taquino, M. (2007) Municipal unbounding: Annexation and racial exclusion in small southern towns. *Rural Sociology* 72(1): 47–68.

Light, I. (2006) *Deflecting Immigration: Networks, Markets, and Regulation in Los Angeles.* New York: Russell Sage Foundation.

Lin, N. (2001) *Social Capital: A Theory of Social Structure and Action*. Cambridge: Cambridge University Press.

Lindstrom, D.E. (1944) What extension rural sociologists are doing. *Rural Sociology* 9: 274–276.

Lipset, S.M. (1997) *American Exceptionalism: A Double-Edged Sword*. New York: W.W. Norton and Company.

Lisle, E. (1985) Validation in the social sciences by international comparison. *Cross-National Research Papers* 1(1): 11–28.

Little, J. (2002) *Gender and Rural Geography*. Harlow: Prentice Hall.

Littunen, H. (2000) Entrepreneurship and the characteristics of the entrepreneurial personality. *International Journal of Entrepreneurial Behaviour and Research* 6(6): 295–309.

Lively, C.E. (1943) Rural sociology as applied science. *Rural Sociology* 8: 331–342.

Lobao, L. (1996) A sociology of the periphery versus a peripheral sociology: Rural sociology and the dimension of space. *Rural Sociology* 61(1): 77–102.

———. (1990) *Locality and Inequality*. Albany: State University of New York Press.

Lobao, L., Hooks, G., and Tickamyer, A. R. (eds.) (2007) *The Sociology of Spatial Inequality*. Albany: State University of New York Press.

Lobao, L., and Saenz, R. (2002) Spatial inequality and diversity as an emerging research area. *Rural Sociology* 67(4): 497–511.

Logan, J. (1997) Rural America as a symbol of American values. *Rural Development Perspectives* 12(1): 15–18.

Logan, J.R., and Molotch, H. (1987) *Urban Fortunes: The Political Economy of Place*. Berkeley: University of California Press.

Lohmann, L. (ed.) (2006) Carbon trading: A critical conversation on climate change, privatisation and power. *Development Dialogue* 48.

Loomis, C.P., and Beegle, J.A. (1957) *Rural Sociology: The Strategy of Change*. Englewood Cliffs, NJ: Prentice Hall.

Loretto, W., and White, P. (2006) Population ageing and older workers: Employers' perceptions, attitudes and policies. *Population, Space and Place* 12: 341–352.

Lorimer, H. (2000) Guns, game and the grandee: The cultural politics of deer-stalking in the Scottish Highlands. *Ecumene* 7(4): 431–459.

Lowe, P. (2010) Enacting rural sociology: or what are the creativity claims of the engaged sciences? *Sociologia Ruralis* 50(4): 311–330.

Lowe, P., and Bodiguel, M. (eds.) (1990) *Rural Studies in Britain and France*. London: Belhaven.

Lowe, P., and Brouwer, F. (2000) Agenda 2000: A wasted opportunity? Pp. 321–334 in F. Brouwer and P. Lowe, eds., *CAP Regimes and the European Countryside*. Wallingford: CABI Publishing.

Lowe, P., Buller, H., and Ward, N. (2002) Setting the next agenda? British and French approaches to the second pillar of the Common Agricultural Policy. *Journal of Rural Studies* 18(1): 1–17.

Lowe, P., Murdoch, J., and Ward, N. (1995) Networks in rural development: Beyond exogenous and endogenous models. Pp. 87–105 in J.D. van der Ploeg and G. van Dijk, eds., *Beyond Modernisation: The Impact of Endogenous Rural Development*. Assen: Van Gorcum.

Lowe, P., Ray, C., Ward, N., Wood, D., and Woodward, R. (1998) Participation in rural development: A review of European experience. Centre for Rural Economy, Newcastle University.

Lowe, P., and Speakman, L. (eds.) (2006a) *The Ageing Countryside: The Growing Older Population of Rural England*. London: Commission for Rural Communities and Age Concern.

————. (2006b) The greying countryside. Pp. 9–28 in P. Lowe and L. Speakman, eds., *The Ageing Countryside. The Growing Older Population of Rural England*. London: Commission for Rural Communities and Age Concern.

Lowe, P., and Talbot, H. (2000) Policy for small business support in rural areas: A critical assessment of proposals for the small business service. *Regional Studies* 34: 479–499.

Lowe, P., and Ward, N. (2007a) British rural geography: A disciplinary enterprise in changing times. Pp.1–20 in H. Clout, ed., *Contemporary Rural Geographies—Land Property and Resources in Britain: Essays in Honour of Richard Munton*. London: Routledge.

————. (2007b) Rural futures: A socio-geographical approach to scenarios analysis. http://www.lancs.ac.uk/ias/annualprogramme/regionalism/docs/Lowe_paper.doc.

————. (2007c) Sustainable rural economies—some lessons from the English experience. *Sustainable Development* 15: 307–317.

Lowrance, R., Stinner, B., and House, G. (eds.) (1984) *Agricultural Ecosystems: Unifying Concepts*. New York: John Wiley.

Lubowski, R., Bucholtz, S., Claassen, R., Roberts, M., Cooper, J., Gueorgieva, A., and Johansson, R. (2006a) *Environmental Effects of Agricultural Land-Use Change: The Role of Economics and Policy. Economic Research Report Number 25*. Washington, DC: US Department of Agriculture, Economic Research Service.

Lubowski, R., Vesterby, M., Bucholtz, S., Baez, A., and Roberts, M. (2006b) *Major Uses of Land in the United States, 2002. Report EIB-14*. Washington, DC: US Department of Agriculture, Economic Research Service.

Lucas, C., Jones, A., and Hines, C. (2006) *Fuelling a Food Crisis: The Impact of Peak Oil on Food Security. Report*. The Greens/European Free Alliance in the European Parliament.

Lukes, S. (2005) *Power: A Radical View*. 2nd ed. Basingstoke: Palgrave Macmillan.

Lupri, E. (1969) Theoretical and methodological problems in cross-national research. *Sociologia Ruralis* 9: 99–113.

Lyson, T.A. (2004) *Civic Agriculture: Reconnecting Farm, Food and Community*. Lebanon, NH: Tufts University Press.

Lyson, T.A., Gillespie Jr., G.W., and Hilchey, D. (1995) Farmers' markets and the local community: Bridging the formal and informal economy. *American Journal of Alternative Agriculture* 10: 108–113.

Macaskill, J. (2005) The Scottish foreshore, the crofting community and land reform: An opportunity missed? Paper presented at the conference of the International Rural Sociological Association, Trondheim, Norway, July.

MacDonald, R. (1996) Welfare dependency, the enterprise culture and self-employed survival. *Work, Employment and Society* 10(3): 431–447.

Mackenzie, F. (2006a) 's Leinn Fhein am fearann' (This land is ours): Re-claiming place, re-creating community, North Harris, Outer Hebrides, Scotland. *Environment and Planning D* 24(4): 577–598.

————. (2006b) A working land: Crofting communities, place and the politics of the possible in post–Land Reform Scotland. *Transactions of the Institute of British Geographers NS* 31: 383–398.

————. (1998) 'The Cheviot, The Stag . . . and The White, White Rock?': Community, identity, and environmental threat on the Isle of Harris. *Environment and Planning D* 16(5): 509–532.

MacKinnon, D. (2009) Devolution and regional development in the United Kingdom. *REDES Santa Cruz do Sul* 14: 82–105.

MacLellan, R. (2007) A future model for protected areas and sustainable tourism development: The new national parks in Scotland. Pp. 179–197 in I. Mose, ed.,

Protected Areas and Regional Development in Europe: Towards a New Model for the 21st Century. Aldershot: Ashgate.

Macnaghten, P., and Urry, J. (1998) *Contested Natures*. London: Sage.

Magne, S. (2003) *Multi-Ethnic Devon: A rural handbook. The Report of the Devon and Exeter Racial Equality Council's Rural Outreach Project.* Devon: Devon and Exeter Racial Equality Council.

Mair, J., and Marti, I. (2006) Social entrepreneurship research: A source of explanation, prediction, and delight. *Journal of World Business* 41: 36–44.

Malmsheimer, R.W., "The Legal Structure of the Adirondack Park." 2009. In *Light from an Adirondack Prism:The Great Experiment in Conservation.* W.F. Porter, R.S. Whaley, and J.D. Erickson eds. Syracuse University Press: Syracuse, NY.

Maretzki, A.N., and Tuckermanty E. (2007) Community food projects and food system sustainability. Pp. 332–344 in C.C. Hinrichs and T.A. Lyson, eds., *Remaking the North American Food System: Strategies for Sustainability.* Lincoln and London: University of Nebraska Press.

Marlier, E., Atkinson, A.B., Cantillon, B., and Nolan, B. (2007) *The EU and Social Inclusion: Facing the Challenges.* Bristol: Policy Press.

Marsden, T. (1998a) Economic perspectives. Pp. 13–30 in B. Ilbery, ed., *Geography of Rural Social Change.* Harlow: Longman.

———. (1998b) New rural territories: Regulating the differentiated rural spaces. *Journal of Rural Studies* 14(1): 107–117.

Marsden, T., and Arce, A. (1995) Constructing quality: Emerging food networks in the rural transition. *Environment and Planning A* 27(8): 1261–1279.

Marsden, T., Whatmore, S., Munton, R., and Little, J. (1986) Towards a political economy of capitalist agriculture. *International Journal of Urban and Regional Research* 10(4): 498–521.

———. (1987) Uneven development and the restructuring process in British agriculture. *Journal of Rural Studies* 3(4): 297–308.

Marsh, J. (2001) Agriculture in the UK—its role and challenge. Paper presented at Food Chain and Crops for Industry Panel, September.

Marshall, T.H. (1965) *Social Policy.* London: Hutchinson.

Martinez, S., Hand, M., Da Pra, M., Pollack, S., Ralston, K., Smith, T., Vogel, S., Clark, S., Lohr, L., Low, S., and Newman, C. (2010) *Local Food Systems: Concepts, Impacts, and Issues. ERR-97. May.* Washington, DC: United States Department of Agriculture, Economic Research Service.

Martins, C. (2009) *Farm Structure Survey in the United Kingdom 2007. Agriculture and Fisheries, Statistics in Focus, Eurostat.* Luxembourg: Office for Official Publications of the European Communities.

Marx, K. (1973) *Capital. Volume 1.* New York: International Publishers.

———. (1959) *Economic and Philosophical Manuscripts of 1844.* Moscow: Progress Publishers.

Massey, D.S. (ed.) (2008) *New Faces in New Places: The Changing Geography of American Immigration.* New York: Russell Sage.

———.(2005) *For Space.* London: Sage.

Massey, D.S., and Denton, N. (1993) *American Apartheid: Segregation and the Making of the Underclass.* Cambridge, MA: Harvard University Press.

Massey, D.S., and Sampson, R.J. (2009) Moynihan redux: Legacies and lessons. *Annals of the American Academy of Political and Social Science* 621: 6–27.

Massey, D. S., Alarcón, R., Durand, J. and González, H. 1987. *Return to Aztlan: The Social Process of International Migration from Western Mexico,* Edited by E. A. Hammel, R. E. Lee, and K. W. Wachter. Berkeley: University of California Press.

Massey, D., S., Durand, J. and Malone, N.J. 2002. *Beyond Smoke and Mirrors: Mexican Immigration in an Era of Economic Integration*. New York: Russell Sage Foundation.

Matheson, J. (2009) National Statisticians' annual article on the population: A demographic review. *Population Trends* 138(Winter).

McAreavey, R. (2009a) Community regeneration: An elite or a 'real' community space? *International Planning Studies* 14(3): 311–327.

———. (2009b) *Rural Development Theory and Practice: A Critical Analysis of Rural Development Theory and Practice*. London and New York: Routledge.

McCarthy, J. (2005) Multifunctional rural geographies: Reactionary or radical. *Progress in Human Geography* 6: 1–10.

McCarthy, J., Lloyd, G., and Illsley, B. (2002) National parks in Scotland: Balancing environment and economy. *European Planning Studies* 10(5): 665–670.

McClelland, D.C. (1961) *The Achieving Society*. Princeton, NJ: D. Van Nostrand Co.

McConnell, E.D. (2008) The US destinations of contemporary Mexican immigrants. *International Migration Review* 42: 767–802.

McConnell, E.D., and Miraftab, F. (2009) Sundown town to 'Little Mexico': Old-timers and newcomers in an American small town. *Rural Sociology* 74(4): 605–629.

McGranahan, D.A. (1999) *Natural Amenities Drive Rural Population Change. Agricultural Economic Research Report 781*. Washington, DC: US Department of Agriculture, Economic Research Service.

McGranahan, D.A., and Wojan, T.R. (2007) *The Creative Class: A Key to Rural Growth. Amber Waves*. Washington, DC: US Department of Agriculture, Economic Research Service.

McInerney, J., Turner, M., Barr, D., and MacQueen, G. (2000) Who cares? A study of farmers involvement in managing and maintaining the countryside. *Agricultural Economics Unit*.

McKay, S., and Winkelman-Gleed, A. (2005) *Migrant Workers in the East of England*. London: London Metropolitan University.

McLaughlin, B.P. (1986) The rhetoric and the reality of rural deprivation. *Journal of Rural Studies* 2: 291–307.

McMartin, B.M. (1994) *The Great Forests of the Adirondacks*. Utica, NY: North Country Books.

———. (1992) *Hemlocks and Adirondack History: How the Tanning Industry Influenced the Region's Growth*. Utica, NY: North Country Books.

McMichael, P. (2010) Transitioning the food regime. Paper presented at the ISA World Congress, Gothenburg, Sweden. July.

———. (2001) The impact of globalisation, free trade and technology on food and nutrition in the new millennium. *Proceedings of the Nutrition Society* 60(2): 215–220.

———. (2000) The power of food. *Agriculture and Human Values* 17(1) 21–33.

Mendras, H. (1960) Les études de sociologie rurale en Europe. *Sociologia Ruralis* 1: 15–34.

Mertz, P.E. (1978) *New Deal Policy and Southern Rural Poverty*. Baton Rouge: Louisiana State University Press.

Midgley, J. (2009) *Just Desserts? Securing Global Food Futures. Report*. IPPR.

———. (2008) *Best Before: How the UK Should Respond to Food Policy Challenges. Report*. IPPR.

Midgley, J., Ward, N., and Atterton, J. (2005) *City-Regions and Rural Areas in North East England. Research Report*. Centre for Rural Economy, Newcastle University.

Milbourne, P. (2004) *Rural Poverty: Marginalisation and Exclusion in Britain and the United States*. London: Routledge.

————. (2000) Exporting 'other' rurals: New audiences for qualitative research. Pp.179–197 in A. Hughes, C. Morris and S. Seymour, eds., *Ethnography and Rural Research*. Cheltenham: Countryside and Community Press.

————. (ed.) (1997) *Revealing Rural 'Others': Representation, Power and Identity in the British Countryside*. London: Pinter.

Miller, J. (2009) *The Foresters. The Story of Scotland's Forests*. Edinburgh: Birlinn.

Mills, C.W. (1956) *The Power Elite*. New York: Oxford University Press.

Mishra, A., El-Osta, H., Morehart, M., Johnson, J., and Hopkins, J. (2002) *Income, Wealth, and the Economic Well-Being of Farm Households. Agricultural Economic Report Number 812*. Washington, DC: US Department of Agriculture, Economic Research Service.

Mitchell, C.J.A. (2004) Making sense of counterurbanization. *Journal of Rural Studies* 20(1): 15–34.

Modood, T,,Berthoud,R., Lakey,J., Nazroo, J.,Smith,P., Virdee, S. and Beishon,S. 1997. *Ethnic Minorities in Britain*. London: Policy Studies Institute.

Moffatt S, Glasgow N. (2009). How Useful is the Concept of Social Exclusion When Applied to Rural Older People in the United Kingdom and the United States?. *Regional Studies* 2009,43 10 1291-1303.

Molotch, H. (1976) The city as a growth machine. *American Journal of Sociology* 82: 309–330.

Mordaunt, F. (2009) Farm policy. Pp. 6–7 in F. Mordaunt, ed., *Andersons Outlook 2010*. Andersons the Farm Business Consultants.

Morgan, K., and Sonnino, R. (2008) *The School Food Revolution: Public Food and the Challenge of Sustainable Development*. London: Earthscan.

Morrill, R (2009) When Thanatos meets Eros. Mapping natural population decrease. New Geography. http://www.newgeography.com/content/001070–when-thanatos-beat-erps-mapping-natural-population-decreases.

Morrison, E. (2010) Evaluating Minnesota's JOBZ initiative in rural development. EDPro Weblog. Accessed 15/4/11 http://edpro-weblog.net/news/2010/10/14/evaluating-minnesota-s-jobz-initiative-for-rural-development.

Morton, L.W., and Blanchard, T.C. (2007) Starved for access: Life in rural America's food deserts. *Rural Realities* 1(4).

Muenz, R. (2006) Europe: Population and migration in 2005. Migration Policy Institute. Accessed 9/2/10 http://www.migrationinformation.org/Feature/display.cfm?id=402.

Muir, J. (2004) Public participation in area-based urban regeneration programmes. *Housing Studies* 19(6): 947–966.

Munters, Q.J. (1972) Sociologia Ruralis on the balance. *Sociologia Ruralis* 12: 86–103.

Munton, R. (1992) The uneven development of capitalist agriculture: The repositioning of agriculture within the food system. Pp. 25–48 in K. Hoggart, ed., *Agricultural Change, Environment and Economy*. London: Mansell.

Murdoch, J. (1995) Middle-class territory? Some remarks on the use of class analysis in rural studies. *Environment and Planning A* 27: 1213–1230.

Murdoch, J., Lowe, P., Ward, N., and Marsden, T. (2003) *The Differentiated Countryside*. London: Routledge.

Myrdal, G. (1963) *Challenge to Affluence*. New York: Pantheon Books.

National Academy of Sciences. (1963) *National Academy of Sciences Advisory Committee on Research in the National Parks. Report*. Washington, DC: National Academy of Sciences.

National Advisory Committee on Rural Health Services. (2008) *The 2008 Report to the Secretary: Rural Health and Human Services Issues*. Washington, DC: US Department of Health and Human Services.

National Audit Office. (2002) The 2001 outbreak of Foot and Mouth Disease. HC 939 Session 2001–2002.

National Endowment for Science, Technology and the Arts. (2007) *Rural Innovation. Report.* London: National Endowment for Science, Technology and the Arts.

National Farmers Union. (2006) *Dairy Farming and the Dairy Industry. Report. June.* National Farmers Union.

Nee, V., and Sanders, J. (2001) Understanding the diversity of immigrant incorporation: A forms-of-capital model. *Ethnic and Racial Studies* 24(3): 386–411.

Nelson, E., Mendoza, G., Regetz, J., Polansky, S., et al. 2009. "Modeling multiple ecosystem services, biodiversity conservation, commodity production and trade-offs at landscape scales." Front. Ecol. Environ. 7(1): 4-11.

Nelson, L. (1969) *Rural Sociology: Its Origins and Growth in the United States.* Minneapolis: University of Minnesota Press.

———. (1956) *Land Reform in Italy. NPA Planning Leaflet no. 97.* Washington, DC: National Planning Association.

Newby, H. (1987) *Country Life.* London: Weidenfeld and Nicholson.

———. (1980) *Green and Pleasant Land?* Harmondsworth: Penguin.

———. (1979) Urbanisation and the rural class structure: Reflections on a case study. *British Journal of Sociology* 30(4): 475–498.

Newby, H., Bell, C., Rose, D., and Saunders, P. (1978) *Property, Paternalism and Power: Class and Control in Rural England.* London: Hutchinson.

Newby, H., and Buttel, F. (1980) Toward a critical rural sociology. Pp. 1–33 in F. Buttel and H. Newby, eds., *The Rural Sociology of the Advanced Societies: Critical Perspectives.* New Jersey: Allenheld, Osmun and Co. Publishers.

Newell, P., and Paterson, M. (2010) *Climate Capitalism: Global Warming and the Transformation of the Global Economy.* Cambridge: Cambridge University Press.

Nolan, B., and Whelan, C.T. (1999) *Loading the Dice? A Study of Cumulative Disadvantage.* Dublin: Oak Tree Press.

Nord, M. (1998) Poor people on the move: County to county migration and the spatial concentration of poverty. *Journal of Regional Science* 38: 329–351.

Nord, M., Luloff, A.E., and Jensen, L. (1995) Migration and the spatial concentration of poverty. *Rural Sociology* 60: 399–415.

North, D., and Smallbone, D. (2000) The innovativeness and growth of rural SMEs during the 1990s. *Regional Studies* 34(2): 145–157.

Northern Ireland Executive. (2008) Gildernew confirms RDP council clusters, 21 March 2008. Accessed 4/3/10 http://www.northernireland.gov.uk/news/news-dard-210308-gildernew-confirms-rdp.

———. (2006) *Better Government for Northern Ireland. Report.* Belfast: RPA.

Northern Ireland Statistics and Research Agency. (2005) *Report of the Inter-Departmental Urban-Rural Definition Group: Statistical Classification and Delineation of Settlements. Report.* Belfast: Northern Ireland Statistics and Research Agency.

Notter, M.L., MacTavish, K.A., and Shamah, D. (2008) Pathways toward resilience among women in rural trailer parks. *Family Relations* 57: 613–624.

O'Connor, A. (2004) Poverty research. Pp. 585–591 in G. Mink, ed., *Poverty in the United States: An Encyclopedia of History, Politics and Policy.* Santa Barbara, CA: ABC-CLIO.

———. (2001) *Poverty Knowledge: Social Science, Social Policy, and the Poor in Twentieth Century US History.* Princeton, NJ: Princeton University Press.

ODPM. (2005) *Citizen Engagement and Public Services: Why Neighbourhoods Matter. Report.* London: ODPM.

Odum, H.W. (1951) *American Sociology: The Story of Sociology in the United States through 1950.* New York: Longmans, Green and Co.

Office for National Statistics. (2010) Life expectancy continues to rise. http://www. statistics.gov.uk/cci/nugget.asp?id=168 .

———. (2009) *Migration Statistics Annual Report (2008)*. London: ONS, Home Office, Department of Work and Pensions.

———. (2004) National statistics 2001 area classification. http://www.statistics. gov.uk/about/methodology_by_theme/area_classification/.

Olwig, K. (2002) *Landscape, Nature and the Body Politic*. Madison: University of Wisconsin Press.

———. (1995) Reinventing common nature: Yosemite and Mount Rushmore—a meandering tale of a double nature. Pp. 379–408 in W. Cronon, ed., *Uncommon Ground. Rethinking the Human Place in Nature*. New York: Norton.

One North East. (2006) *Leading the Way. Regional Economic Strategy 2006–2016. Report*. Newcastle: One North East.

Organisation for Economic Co-operation and Development. (2011) *OECD Rural Policy Reviews: England UK. Report*. Paris: OECD.

———. (2008) *OECD Rural Policy Reviews: Scotland UK, Assessment and Recommendations. Report*. Paris: OECD.

———. (2006) *The New Rural Paradigm. Policies and Governance. Report*. Paris: OECD.

———. (2005) *Modernising Government. The Way Forward. Report*. Paris: OECD.

———. (2001a) *Agricultural Policy Reform and Farm Employment. Report*. Paris: OECD.

———. (2001b) *Local Partnerships for Better Governance. Report*. Paris: OECD.

Organisation for European Economic Cooperation. (1954) *Development of the Agricultural Advisory Services in Europe since 1950. Report*. Paris: OEEC.

———. (1950) *Agricultural Advisory Services in European Countries. Report*. Paris: OEEC.

Orszag, P.R., Barnes, M., Carrion, A., and Summers, L. (2009) Memorandum for the Heads of Executive Departments and Agencies, M-09–28. http://www. whitehouse.gov/sites/default/files/omb/assets/memoranda_fy2009/m09–28.pdf.

Osborne, G. (2010) BBC Today programme interview. 17 August 2010. www.guardian.co.uk/politics/2010/aug/17/george-osborne-spending-cuts-progressive-society.

Ostrom, M.R. (2007) Community supported agriculture as an agent of change: Is it working? Pp. 99–120 in C. Hinrichs and T.A. Lyson, eds., *Remaking the American Food System: Strategies for Sustainability*. Lincoln and London: University of Nebraska Press.

———. (2006) Everyday meanings of 'local food': Views from home and field. *Community Development* 37: 65–78.

Oughton, E., Wheelock, J., and Baines, S. (2003) Microbusinesses and social inclusion in rural households: A comparative analysis. *Sociologia Ruralis* 43(4): 331–348.

Pahl, R. (1966) The rural–urban continuum. *Sociologia Ruralis* 6(3–4): 299–329.

Parekh, B. (2000) *Rethinking Multiculturalism*. London: Macmillan.

Parent, F.D., and Lewis, B.L. (2003) The concept of social exclusion and rural development policy. *Southern Rural Sociology* 19(2): 153–175.

Park, R.E. (1952) *Human Communities: The City and Human Ecology*. Glencoe, IL: Free Press.

Parmenter, J. (2010) *The Edge of the Woods; Iroquoia, 1534–1701*. East Lansing: Michigan State University Press.

Parra, P.A., and Pfeffer, M.J. (2006) New immigrants in rural communities: The challenges of integration. *Social Text* 8824(3): 81–98.

———. (2005) *Immigrants and the Community: Farmworkers with Families*. Ithaca, NY: Department of Development Sociology, Cornell University.

Partridge, M.D., and Rickman, D.S. (2006) *The Geography of American Poverty: Is There a Need for Place-Based Policies?* Kalamazoo, MI: W.E. Upjohn Institute for Employment Research.

Passel, J.S., and Cohn, D. (2011) *Unauthorized Immigrant Population: National and State Trends.* Washington, DC: Pew Hispanic Center.

Paul, T., Ikenberry, G., and Hall, J.A. (eds.) (2003) *The Nation-State in Question.* Princeton, NJ: Princeton University Press.

Pearce, G., Ayres, S., and Tricker, M. (2005) Decentralisation and devolution to the English regions: Assessing the implications for rural policy and delivery. *Journal of Rural Studies* 21(5): 197–212.

Peck, J., Theodore, N and Brenner, N. 2010. Postneoliberalism and its Malcontents, *Antipode*, 41(1), 94-116.

Peck, J., and Tickell, A. (2002) Neoliberalizing space. Pp. 33–57 in N. Brenner and N. Theodore, eds., *Spaces of Neoliberalism: Urban Restructuring in North America and Western Europe.* Oxford: Blackwell Publishers.

Peine, E., and McMichael, P. (2005) Globalisation and global governance. Pp. 19–34 in V. Higgins and G. Lawrence, eds., *Agricultural Governance: Globalisation and the New Politics of Regulation.* London: Routledge.

Pemberton, S., and Goodwin, M. (2010) Rethinking the changing structures of rural local government—State power, rural politics and local political strategies? *Journal of Rural Studies* 26(3): 272–283.

Pena, A.A. (2009) Locational choices of the legal and illegal: The case of Mexican agricultural workers in the US. *International Migration Review* 43: 850–880.

Pennix, R. (2004) Integration of migrants: Economic, social, cultural and political dimensions. Background paper for the UNECE conference. Geneva, 12–14 January.

Pennix, R., Spencer, D., and Van Hear, N. (2008) *Migration and Integration in Europe: The State of Research. COMPAS Centre on Migration, Policy and Society Report.* Oxford: University of Oxford.

Performance and Innovation Unit. (1999) *Rural Economies. Report.* London: Cabinet Office.

Permaloff, A., and Grafton, C. (2008) *Political Power in Alabama: The More Things Change . . .* Athens: University of Georgia Press.

Peterson, P.E. (1981) *City Limits.* Chicago: University of Chicago Press.

Pfeffer, M.J. (2008) The underpinnings of immigration and the limits of immigration policy. *Cornell International Law Journal* 41: 83–100.

Pfeffer, M.J., and Parra, P.A. (2009) Strong ties, weak ties, and human capital: Latino immigrant employment outside the enclave. *Rural Sociology* 74: 241–269.

———. (2004) *Immigrants and the Community.* Ithaca, NY: Department of Development Sociology, Cornell University.

Philip, L.J., and Gilbert, A. (2007) Low income amongst the older population in Great Britain. *Regional Studies* 41(6): 735–747.

Philip, L.J., Gilbert, A., Mauthner, N., and Phimister, E. (2003) *Scoping Study of Older People in Rural Scotland. Report.* Edinburgh: Scottish Executive.

Philip, L.J., and Shucksmith, M. (2003) Conceptualising social exclusion. *European Planning Studies* 11(4): 461–480.

Phillip, S., and Macmillan, D. (2006) Car park charging in the Cairngorms National Park. *Scottish Geographical Journal* 122(3): 204–222.

Phillips, M. (1993) Rural gentrification and the process of class colonisation. *Journal of Rural Studies* 9(2): 123–140.

Phillips, S.T. (2007) *This Land, This Nation: Conservation, Rural America, and the New Deal.* New York: Columbia University Press.

Phillipson, J., Bennett, K., Lowe, P., and Raley, M. (2004) Adaptive responses and asset strategies: The experience of rural micro-firms and Foot and Mouth Disease. *Journal of Rural Studies* 20: 227–243.

Philo, C. (1992) Neglected rural geographies: A review. *Journal of Rural Studies* 8: 193–207.

Phimister, E., Theodossiou, I., and Gilbert, A. (2000) The impact of the minimum wage in rural areas. Draft final report to the Low Pay Commission. University of Aberdeen.

Pickering, K., Harvey, M.H., Summers, G.F., and Mushinski, D. (2006) *Welfare Reform in Persistent Rural Poverty: Dreams, Disenchantments and Diversity.* University Park, PA: Penn State University Press.

Pigg, K.E., and. Bradshaw, T.K. (2002) Catalytic community development: A theory of practice for changing rural society. Pp. 385–396 in D.L. Brown and L.E. Swanson, eds., *Challenges for Rural America in the Twenty-First Century.* University Park, PA: Penn State University Press.

Pike, A., and Tomaney, J. (2009) The state and uneven development: The governance of economic development in the post devolution UK. *Cambridge Journal of Regions Economy and Society* 2(1): 13–34.

Pillai, A. (2010) Sustainable rural communities? A legal perspective on the community right to buy. *Land Use Policy* 27: 898–905.

Pillai, R., Kyambi, S., Nowacka, K., and Sriskandarajah, D. (2007) *The Reception and Integration of New Migrant Communities.* Report. London: IPPR.

Piven, F.F. (2001) Welfare reform and the economic and cultural reconstruction of low wage labor markets. Pp. 135–151 in J. Goode and J. Maskovsky, eds., *The New Poverty Studies: The Ethnography of Power, Politics, and Impoverished People in the United States.* New York: New York University Press.

Pohjola, A. (2009) Social networks—help or hindrance to the migrant? *International Migration* 29(3): 435–444.

Policy Commission on the Future of Farming and Food. (2002) *Farming and Food: A Sustainable Future.* Report. Norwich: Stationery Office.

Pollan, M. (2006) *The Omnivore's Dilemma.* New York: Penguin.

Pollard, N., Latorre, M., and Sriskandarajah, D. (2008) Floodgates or turnstiles? Post-EU enlargement migration flows to (and from) the UK. IPPR research paper.

Popple, K. (1995) *Analysing Community Work: Its Theory and Practice.* Birmingham: OUP.

Porter, M.E. (1990) *The Competitive Advantage of Nations.* New York: Free Press.

Porter, M.E., Ketels, C.H.M., Miller, K., and Bryden, R.T. (2004) *Competitiveness in Rural US Regions: Learning and Research Agenda.* Cambridge, MA: Institute for Strategy and Competitiveness, Harvard Business School.

Portes, A. (1998) Social capital: Its origins and applications in modern sociology. *Annual Review of Sociology* 24: 1–24.

Portes, A., and Rumbaut, R.G. (1996) *Immigrant America: A Portrait.* 2nd ed. Berkeley, Los Angeles and London: University of California Press.

Potter, C. (2009) Agricultural stewardship, climate change and the public goods debate. Pp. 247–261 in M. Winter and M. Lobley, eds., *What Is Land For? The Food, Fuel and Climate Change Debate.* London: Earthscan.

———. (1998) *Against the Grain: Agri-Environmental Reform in the United States and the European Union.* Wallingford: CAB International.

Potter, C., and Tilzey, M. (2005) Agricultural policy discourses in the European post-Fordist transition: Neoliberalism, neomercantalism and multifunctionality. *Progress in Human Geography* 29: 581–600.

Powers, E. (1999) *Block Granting Welfare: Fiscal Impact on the States. Occasional Paper 23.* Washington, DC: Urban Institute.

Pretty, J.N. (2001) Some benefits and drawbacks of local food systems. Briefing Note for TVU/Sustain AgriFood Network.

Pretty, J.N., Brett, C., Gee, D., Hine, R.E., Mason, C.F., Morison, J.I.L., Raven, H., Rayment, H.D., and van der Bijl, G. (2000) An assessment of the external costs of UK agriculture. *Agricultural Systems* 65: 113–136.

Putnam, R.D. (2007) Diversity and community in the twenty-first century. *Scandinavian Political Studies* 30: 137–174.

———. (1993) The prosperous community. *American Prospect* 4(13).

Raco, M., and Imrie, R. (2000) Governmentality and rights and responsibilities in urban policy. *Environment and Planning A* 32(12): 2187–2204.

Radin, B. (1996) State Rural Development Councils are creating public–private partnerships. *Rural Development Perspectives* 11(2): 2–9.

Radin, B., Agranoff, R., Bowman, A., Buntz, C.G., Ott, S., Romzek, B., and Wilson, R. (1996) *New Governance for Rural America: Creating Intergovernmental Partnerships.* Lawrence: University Press of Kansas.

Radin, B., and Romzek, B. (1996) *Accountability expectations in an intergovernmental arena: The National Rural Development Partnership.* Publius: The Journal of Federalism 26 (2): 59-81.

Raley, M., and Moxey, A. (2000) *Rural Microbusinesses in North East England: Final Survey Results. Report.* Newcastle: Centre for Rural Economy, University of Newcastle.

Ramesh, M., Araral, E., and Wu, X. (eds.) (2010) *Reasserting the Public in Public Services: New Public Management Reforms.* London: Routledge.

Rank, M.R. (2005) *One Nation, Underprivileged: Why American Poverty Affects Us All.* New York: Oxford University Press.

Rawson, J. 2008. *CRS Report for Congress: Agricultural Research, Extension and Education: Farm Bill Issues.* Congressional Research Service: Washington, DC.

Ray, C. (2006) Neo-endogenous rural development in the EU. In P. Cloke, T. Marsden and P. Mooney, eds., *The Handbook of Rural Studies.* London: Sage.

———. (2001) *Culture Economies. Report.* Newcastle: Centre for Rural Economy Publications.

———. (2000) The EU LEADER Programme: Rural development laboratory. *Sociologia Ruralis* 40(2): 163–172.

Reeder, R. (1998) *Retiree Attraction Policies for Rural America. Agriculture Information Bulletin No. 741.* Washington, DC: USDA-ERS.

Reef, C. (2007) *Poverty in America.* New York: Infobase Publishing.

Reese, L. (1994) The role of counties in local economic development. *Economic Development Quarterly* 8: 28–42.

Reid, J.N. (1999) Community empowerment: A new approach for rural development. *Rural Development Perspectives* 14(1): 9–13.

Reimer, B. (2004) Social exclusion in a comparative context. *Sociologia Ruralis* 44(1): 76–94.

Rennie, A. (2006) The importance of national parks to nation-building: Support for the National Parks Act (2000) in the Scottish Parliament. *Scottish Geographical Journal* 122(3): 223–232.

Rezelman, J.R. (1998) *Forever Wild or Forever Subdivided? An Historical Perspective on the Adirondack Park.* Unpublished doctoral dissertation, Department of Agricultural Economics, Cornell University, Ithaca, NY.

Rhodes, R.A.W. (1997) *Understanding Governance: Policy Networks, Governance, Reflexivity and Accountability.* Buckingham: Open University Press.

———. (1996) New governance: Governing without government. *Political Studies* 44: 652–667.

Richards, C., and Bryden, J. (2000) Information technology and rural development in the Scottish Highlands and Islands: A preliminary review of the issues and evidence. *Geocarrefour: Revue de Geographie de Lyon* 75(1).

Ricketts Hein, J., Ilbery, B., and Kneafsey, M. (2006) Distribution of local food activity in England and Wales: An index of food relocalization. *Regional Studies* 40(3): 289–301.

Rifkin, J. (2004) *The European Dream: How Europe's Vision of the Future Is Quietly Eclipsing the American Dream*. Cambridge: Polity.

Rindfuss, R., Walsh, S., Turner, B., Fox, J., and Mishra, V. (2004) Developing a science of land change: Challenges and methodological issues. *Proceedings of the National Academy of Sciences* 101(39): 13976–13981.

Ritzer, G., Stepnisky, J., and Lemich, J. (2005) The 'magical' world of consumption: Transforming nothing into something. *Berkeley Journal of Sociology* 49: 117–136.

Rizov, M. (2006) Rural development perspectives in enlarging Europe: The implications of CAP reforms and agricultural transition in accession countries. *European Planning Studies* 14(2): 219–238.

Robinson, D., and Reeve, K. (2006) *Neighbourhood Experiences of New Immigration*. York: Joseph Rowntree Foundation.

Rodríguez-Pose, A., and Bwire, A. (2004) The economic (in)efficiency of devolution. *Environment and Planning A* 36(11): 1907–1928.

Rodríguez-Pose, A., and Gill, N. (2005) On the 'economic dividend' of devolution. *Regional Studies* 39(4): 405–420.

Rogaly, B., Crook, C., and Simpson, D (2007) Summary Report of the Workshop on Migrant Workers in UK Agriculture Sussex Centre for Migration Research. University of Sussex, May 2007.

Rogers, E.M. (1962) *Diffusion of Innovations*. New York: Free Press of Glencoe.

Roginsky, S., and Shortall, S. (2009) Civil society as a contested field of meanings. *International Journal of Sociology and Social Policy* 29(9): 473–487.

Rolfe, H., and Metcalf, H. (2009) *Recent Migration into Scotland: The Evidence Base. Report*. Edinburgh: Scottish Government.

Rollett, A., Haines-Young, R., Potskin, M., and Kumar, P. (2008) *Delivering Environmental Services through Agri-Environmental Programmes: A Scoping Study. Report*. London: Land Use Policy Group.

Room, G. (1995a) *Beyond the Threshold—the Measurement and Analysis of Social Exclusion*. Bristol: Policy Press.

———. (1995b) Poverty and social exclusion: The new European agenda for policy and research. Pp. 1–9 in G. Room, ed., *Beyond the Threshold: The Measurement and Analysis of Social Exclusion*. Bristol: Policy Press.

Ropers, R.H. (1991) *Persistent Poverty: The American Dream Turned Nightmare*. New York: Insight Books.

Rork, J.C. (2005) Getting what you pay for: The case of Southern economic development. *Journal of Regional Analysis and Policy* 35(2): 37–53.

Rose Regeneration. (2010) *Rural Vulnerability Index. Report*. Lincoln: Rose Regeneration.

Rosenfeld, S.A., Liston, C.D., Kingslow, M.E., and Forman, E.R. (2000) *Clusters in Rural Areas: Auto Supply Chains in Tennessee and Houseboat Manufacturers in Kentucky*. Carrboro, NC: Regional Technology Strategies.

Rotter, J. (1966) Generalized expectations for internal versus external control of reinforcement. *Psychological Monographs: General and Applied* 80(1): 1–27.

Rowley, T.D. (1996) Value of rural America. *Rural Development Perspectives* 12(1): 2–5.

Rowntree, B.S. (1901) *Poverty: A Study of Town Life*. London: MacMillan.

Royal Commission on the Poor Laws. (1909) *Report of Royal Commission on the Poor Laws and the Relief of Distress. HMSO, Cmnd. 4499 (Majority Report) Break Up the Poor Law and Abolish the Workhouse (Minority Report).* Fabian Society.

Rudiger, A., and Spencer, S. (2003) Social integration of migrants and ethnic minorities: policies to combat discrimination. Paper presented at The Economic and Social Aspects of Migration conference, European Commission and OECD, Brussels.

Rugg, J., and Jones, A. (1999) *Getting a Job, Finding a Home: Rural Youth Transitions.* Bristol: Policy Press.

Ruhl, J., Kraft, S., and Lant, L. (2007) *The Law and Policy of Ecosystem Services.* Washington, DC: Island Press.

Runte, A. (1997/1979) *The American Experience.* Omaha: University of Nebraska Press.

Rural Coalition. (2010) *The Rural Challenge: Achieving Sustainable Rural Communities for the 21st Century. Report.* London: Rural Coalition.

Rural Evidence Research Centre. (2005) *DEFRA Classification of Local Authority Districts and Unitary Authorities in England: An Introductory Guide. Report.* London: Department for Environment, Food and Rural Affairs.

Rural Sociological Society. (1952) *Sociological Research on the Diffusion and Adoption of New Farm Practices: A Review of Previous Research and a Statement of Hypotheses and Needed Research. Report of the Subcommittee on the Diffusion and Adoption of Farm Practices.* Lexington: Kentucky Agricultural Experiment Station, University of Kentucky.

Rural Sociological Society Task Force on Persistent Rural Poverty. (1993) *Persistent Poverty in Rural America.* Boulder, CO: Westview.

Salamon, L. (2002) The new governance and the tools of public action: An introduction. Pp. 1–47 in L. Salamon, ed., *The Tools of Government: A Guide to the New Governance.* Oxford: Oxford University Press.

Salamon, S. (2003) *Newcomers to Old Towns: Suburbanization of the Heartland.* Chicago: University of Chicago Press.

Salant, P., Carley, L.R., and Dillman, D. (1996) *Estimating the Contribution of Lone Eagles to Metro and Nonmetro In-Migration. Technical Report 96–19 of the Social and Economic Science Research Centre.* Pullman: Washington State University.

Sampson, R.J., and Morenoff, J.D. (2006) Durable inequality: Spatial dynamics, social processes, and the persistence of poverty in Chicago neighbourhoods. Pp. 176–203 in S. Bowles, S.N. Durlauf and K. Hoff, eds., *Poverty Traps.* Princeton, NJ: Princeton University Press.

Sanders, E. (1999) *Roots of Reform.* Chicago: University of Chicago Press.

Sanders, S., Brown D.L., and Pfeffer, M. (2010) Regional approaches to retaining youth in New York's southern tier. Paper presented to the annual meeting of the Rural Sociological Society, Atlanta, 13 August.

Sanderson, D. (1917) The teaching of rural sociology: particularly in the Land-Grant Colleges and Universities. *American Journal of Sociology* 22(4): 433–460.

Savage, M. (2002) Social exclusion and class analysis. Pp. in P. Braham and L. Janes, eds., *Social Differences and Divisions.* Oxford: Blackwell, Open University.

Savage, M., Barlow, J., Dickens, P., and Fielding, A. (1992) *Property, Bureaucracy and Culture: Middle Class Formation in Contemporary Britain.* London: Routledge.

Savas, E.S. (2000) *Privatization and Public Private Partnerships.* Chatham, NY: Chatham House.

Schafer, E. (2008) Establishment of the office of ecosystem services and markets. USDA Secretary's memorandum 1056–001. 15 December.

Schafft, K.A. (2006) Poverty, residential mobility and student transiency within a rural New York school district. *Rural Sociology* 71(2): 212–231.

Schafft, K.A., and Brown, D.L. (2003) Social capital, social networks and social power. *Social Epistemology* 17(4): 329–342.

Schafft, K.A., Killeen, K., and Morrissey, J. (2010) The challenges of student transiency for US rural schools and communities in the era of No Child Left Behind. Pp. 95–114 in K. A. Schafft and A. Jackson, eds., *Rural Education for the Twenty-First Century: Identity, Place, and Community in a Globalizing World*. University Park, PA: Penn State University Press (Rural Studies Series).

Schafft, K.A., and Prins, E.S. (2009) Poverty, residential mobility and persistence across urban and rural family literacy programs in Pennsylvania. *Adult Basic Education and Literacy Journal* 3: 3–12.

Schmit, T.M., and Gómez, M.I. (2011) Developing viable farmers markets in rural communities: An investigation of vendor performance using objective and subjective valuations. *Food Policy* 36(2): 119–127.

Sclar, E. (2009) The politicaléconomics of infrastructure finance: The new sub prime. Paper presented at Annual Meeting Association of Collegiate Schools of Planning, Center for Sustainable Urban Development, the Earth Institute, Columbia University.

Scott, J. C., (1999) *Seeing Like a State: How Certain Schemes to Improve the Human Condition Have Failed*. New Haven, Yale University Press.

Scottish Economic Research. (2006) *Tayside Migrant Labour Population Study. Report*. Edinburgh: Communities Scotland.

Scottish Executive. (2002) *City Region Boundaries Study. A Report by Derek Halden Consultancy*. Edinburgh: Scottish Executive Central Research Unit.

———. (2000) *Rural Scotland: A New Approach. Report*. Edinburgh: Scottish Executive.

Scottish Government (2011a) Our Rural Future: The Scottish Government's response to the Speak up for Rural Scotland Consultation, The Scottish Government: Edinburgh. Available online at: http://www.scotland.gov.uk/Publications/2011/03/08135330/0.

———. *Rural Scotland Key Facts 2011*. Edinburgh: A National Statistics Publication for Scotland, Rural and Environmental Research and Analysis Directorate.

———. (2010a) *Rural Scotland Key Facts 2010. Report*. Edinburgh: A National Statistics Publication for Scotland, Rural and Environmental Research and Analysis Directorate.

———. (2010b) *Speak Up for Rural Scotland. Report*. Edinburgh: Scottish Government.

———. (2009) *Rural Scotland Key Facts 2009*. Edinburgh: A National Statistics Publication for Scotland, Rural and Environmental Research and Analysis Directorate.

———. (2008a) *National Parks Strategic Review Report*. Accessed 25/2/10 http://www.scotland.gov.uk/Publications/2008/11/25131614/0.

———. (2008b) *Scottish Government Urban Rural Classification 2007–2008*. http://www.scotland.gov.uk/Publications/2008/07/29152642/3.

———. (2007) *Rural Scotland, Better Still, Naturally. Report*. Edinburgh: Scottish Government.

Sen, A. (2001) Other people. *Proceedings of the British Academy* 111: 319–335.

Serow, W. (2003) The economic consequences of retiree concentrations: A review of North American studies. *Gerontologist* 43(6): 897–903.

Serow, W., and Haas, W. (1992) Measuring the economic impact of retirement migration: The case of western North Carolina. *Journal of Applied Gerontology* 11(2): 200–215.

Siddhathan, K. and Ahearn. M. 1996. "Inpatient Utilization by Undocumented Immigrants Without Insurance." *Journal of Health Care for the Poor and Underserved* 7:355–363.

Shaw, J.M. (1979) *Rural Deprivation*. Norwich: Geo Books.

Shaw, P., and Thompson, D. (2006) *The Nature of the Cairngorms: Diversity in a Changing Environment. Report*. Edinburgh: Stationary Office.

Sherman, J. (2006) (2009) *Those Who Work, Those Who Don't: Poverty, Morality, and Family in Rural America*. Minneapolis: University of Minneapolis Press.

———. Coping with rural poverty: Economic survival and moral capital in rural America. *Social Forces* 85(2): 891–913.

Sherman, M., and Henry, T.K. (1933) *Hollow Folk*. New York: Thomas Y. Crowell Company.

Short, B. (2006) Idyllic ruralities. Pp. 133–148 in P. Cloke, T. Marsden and P. Mooney, eds., *Handbook of Rural Studies*. London: Sage.

Shortall, S. (2008) Are rural development programmes socially inclusive? Social inclusion, civic engagement, participation and social capital: exploring the differences. *Journal of Rural Studies* 24(4): 450–457.

———. (2006) A 'green and pleasant land'? Public attitudes to the countryside in Northern Ireland. Ark Northern Ireland Research Update 47.

———. (2004) Social or economic goals, civic inclusion or exclusion? An analysis of rural development theory and practice. *Sociologia Ruralis* 44(1): 109–123.

Shortall, S., and Shucksmith, M. (2001) Rural development in practice: Issues arising in Scotland and Northern Ireland. *Community Development Journal* 36: 122–133.

———. (1998) *Rural Development in Practice: Issues Arising from the Scottish Experience*. European Planning Studies, 6, 1, 73-88.

Shortall, S., and Warner, M.E. (2010) Social inclusion or market competitiveness? A comparison of EU and US rural development policies. *Social Policy and Administration: An International Journal* 44(5): 575–597.

Shrestha, L. (2006) *CRS Report to Congress: Age Dependency Ratio and Social Security Solvency*. Washington, DC: Congressional Research Service.

Shucksmith, M. (2010) Disintegrated rural development? Neo-endogenous rural development, planning and place-shaping in diffused power contexts. *Sociologia Ruralis* 50(1): 1–14.

. (2009). New Labour's countryside in international perspective. pp.58-79 in *New Labour's Countryside: Rural Policy in Britain since 1997*, ed. by M. Woods. Bristol: Policy Press.

———. (2005) Policy brief: Indicators used for rural and urban poverty in policy processes. Paper. UHI PolicyWeb.

———. (2002) Social exclusion and poverty in rural areas. *Belgeo: The Belgian Journal of Geography* 2001(3): 165–184.

———. (2000a) Endogenous development, social capital and social inclusion: Perspectives from LEADER in the UK. *Sociologia Ruralis* 40(2): 208–219.

———. (2000b) *Exclusive Countryside? Social Inclusion and Regeneration in Rural Areas*. York: Joseph Rowntree Foundation.

———. (1990) *Housebuilding in Britain's Countryside*. London: Routledge.

Shucksmith, M., and Chapman, P. (1998) Rural development and social exclusion. *Sociologia Ruralis* 38(2): 225–242.

Shucksmith, M., Chapman, P., Clark, G., with Black, S., and Conway, E. (1996) *Rural Scotland Today: The Best of Both Worlds?* Aldershot: Avebury.

———. (1994) *Disadvantage in Rural Scotland: A Summary Report*. Perth: Rural Forum.

Shucksmith, M., and Lloyd, G. (1983) Rural planning in Scotland: A critique. Pp. 103–128 in A. Gilg, ed., *Countryside Planning Yearbook*, vol. 4. Norwich: Geo Books.

Shucksmith, M., Roberts, D., Scott, D., Chapman, P., and Conway, E. (1997) *Disadvantage in Rural Areas. Rural Development Commission, Rural Research Report 29*. London: Rural Development Commission.

Shucksmith, M., and Rønningen, K. (2011) The uplands after neoliberalism? The role of the small farm in rural sustainability. *Journal of Rural Studies*.

Shucksmith, M., Shucksmith, J., and Watt, J. (2006) Social inclusion and pre-school education in rural Scotland. *Journal of Social Policy and Administration* 40(6): 678–691.

Shucksmith, M., Thomson, K., and Roberts, D. (2005) *The CAP and the Regions—the Territorial Impact of the Common Agricultural Policy*. Oxfordshire: CABI.

Sim, D., Barclay, A., and Anderson, I. (2007) *Achieving a Better Understanding of 'A8' Migrant Labour Needs in Lanarkshire. Report*. Hamilton: South Lanarkshire Council.

Slack, T. (2007) The contours and correlates of informal work in rural Pennsylvania. *Rural Sociology* 72: 69–89.

Slee, R.W. (2005) From countrysides of production to countrysides of consumption? *Journal of Agricultural Science* 143: 255–265.

Smeeding, T. (2004) Twenty years of research on income inequality, poverty, and redistribution in the developed world: introduction and overview. *Socioeconomic Review* 2: 149–163.

Smith, M., Anderson, R., Bradham, D., and Longino, C. (2008) Rural–urban differences in mortality among Americans 55 and older: An analysis using national longitudinal mortality data. *Journal of Rural Health* 11(4): 274–285.

Smout, T.C. (2000) *Nature Contested: Environmental History in Scotland and Northern England since 1600*. Edinburgh: Edinburgh University Press.

Somers, M.R., and Block, F. (2005) From poverty to perversity: Ideas, markets, and institutions over 200 years of welfare debate. *American Sociological Review* 70: 260–287.

Somerville, P. (2005) Community governance and democracy. *Policy and Politics* 33(1): 117–144.

Somerville, S., Sriskandarajah, D., and Latorre, M. (2009) United Kingdom: A reluctant country of immigration. http://www.migrationinformation.org/feature/display.cfm?ID=736.

Somerville, S., and Sumption, M. (2009) *Immigration in the United Kingdom: The Recession and Beyond*. London: Equalities and Human Rights Commission.

Sorokin, P., and Zimmerman, C. (1929) *Principles of Rural–Urban Sociology*. New York: Holt.

Spence, M.D. 1999. *Dispossessing the Wilderness: Indian Removal and the Making of the National Parks*. New York: Oxford University Press.

Spencer, S., Ruhs, M., Anderson, B., and Rogaly, B. (2007) *Migrants' Lives beyond the Workplace: The Experiences of Central and East Europeans in the UK. Report*. York: Joseph Rowntree Foundation.

Spicker, P. (1993) *Poverty and Social Security*. London: Routledge.

Sproull, A., Bryden, J., and Black J.S. (1997) *Telematics, Rural Economic Development and SMEs: Some Demand Side Evidence*. Bonn: Informationen zur Raumentwicklung.

SQW. (2006) *Next Generation Broadband in Scotland. Report*. Edinburgh: Scottish Executive Social Research.

Sriskandarajah, D., and Drew, C. (2006) *Brits Abroad: Mapping the Scale and Nature of British Emigration. Report*. London: IPPR.

Stack, C. (1974) *All Our Kin: Strategies for Survival in a Black Community*. New York: Harper and Row.

Stallman, J., Deller, S., and Shields, M. (1999) The economic and fiscal impact of aging retirees on a small rural area. *Gerontologist* 39(5): 599–610.

Steedman, P., and Schultz, W. (eds.) (2009) *Future Scenarios for the UK Food System. Report.* Food Ethics Council.

Stillwell, J., and Duke-Williams, O. (2005) Ethnic population distribution, immigration and internal migration in Britain: What evidence of linkage at the district scale? Paper presented at the British Society for Population Studies Annual Conference, University of Kent at Canterbury, 12–14 September.

Stockdale, A. (2006a) Migration: Pre-requisite for rural economic regeneration? *Journal of Rural Studies* 22: 354–366.

———. (2006b) The role of a 'retirement transition' in the repopulation of rural areas *Population, Space and Place* 12: 1–13.

———. (2005) Incomers: Offering economic potential in rural England. *Journal of the Royal Agricultural Society of England* 166.

———. (2004) Rural out-migration: Community consequences and individual migrant experiences. *Sociologia Ruralis* 44(2): 149–176.

———. (2002) Towards a typology of out-migration from peripheral areas: A Scottish case study. *International Journal of Population Geography* 8: 345–364.

Stockdale, A., and Barker, A. (2009) Sustainability and the multifunctional landscape: An assessment of approaches to planning and management in the Cairngorms National Park. *Land Use Policy* 26: 479–492.

Stockdale, A., and Findlay, A.M. (2004) Rural in-migration: A catalyst for economic regeneration. Paper presented at the Global Change and Human Mobility—ICG-UK Conference, Glasgow, August.

Stoecker, R. (2005) *Research Methods for Community Change: A Project-Based Approach.* Thousand Oaks, CA: Sage.

Stoker, G. (2006) Local governance research: Paradigms, theories and implications. Lecture prepared for presentation at Zhejiang University.

———. (2004) *New Localism, Participation and Networked Community Governance. Report.* Manchester: IPEG, University of Manchester.

Storey, A. (2006) The European dream? The European Union's model of economic governance. *Gibson Institute for Land, Food and Environment Research Paper* 2(1).

Storey, D. (1999) Issues of Integration, participation and empowerment in rural development: The case of LEADER in the Republic of Ireland. *Journal of Rural Studies* 15 (3): 307–315.

Strauss, C. (2002) Not-so-rugged individualists: US Americans' conflicting ideas about poverty. Pp. 55–69 in F.F. Piven, J. Acker, M. Hallock and S. Morgen, eds., *Work, Welfare and Politics: Confronting Poverty in the Wake of Welfare Reform.* Eugene: University of Oregon Press.

Stull, D.D., Broadway, M.J., and Griffith, D. (1995) *Any Way You Cut It: Meat Processing and Small Town America.* Lawrence: University Press of Kansas.

Sullivan, D.M. (2004) Citizen participation in nonprofit economic development organizations. *Journal of the Community Development Society* 34(2): 58–72.

Sumberg, J. (2009) *Re-Framing the Great Food Debate: The Case for Sustainable Food.* London: New Economics Foundation.

Summers, G. (1993) *Persistent Poverty in Rural America.* Boulder, CO: Westview Press.

Swain, C.M. (ed.) (1996) *Race Versus Class.* Lanham, MD: University Press of America,

Swidler, A. (1986) Culture in action: Symbols and strategies. *American Sociological Review* 51(2): 273–286.

Swinnen, J.F.M. (2009) The growth of agricultural protection in Europe in the 19th and 20th centuries. *World Economy* 32: 1499–1537.

Swyngedouw, E. (1997) Neither global nor local: 'Glocalization' and the politics of scale. Pp. 137–166 in K. Cox, ed., *Spaces of Globalization*. New York: Guilford Press.

Tangermann, S. (1998) An ex-post review of the 1992 MacSharry reform. Pp. 13–35 in K.A. Ingersent, A.J. Rayner and R.C. Hine, eds., *The Reform of the Common Agricultural Policy*. London: Macmillan.

Tarmann, A. (2003) *Revival of US Rural Areas Signals Heartland No Longer a Hinterland*. Washington, DC: Population Reference Bureau. Accessed 31/12/09 http://www.prb.org/Articles/2003/RevivalofUSRuralAreasSignalsHeartland-NoLongeraHinterland.aspx.

Tate, W.E. (1976) *The English Village Community and the Enclosure Movements*. London: Victor Gollancz.

Taylor, C.C. (1965) The development of rural sociology abroad. *Rural Sociology* 30: 462–473.

Taylor, M. (2008) *Living Working Countryside: The Taylor Review of Rural Economy and Affordable Housing. Report*. London: Department for Communities and Local Government Publications.

———. (2007) Community participation in the real world: Opportunities and pitfalls in new governance spaces. *Urban Studies* 44(2): 297–317.

———. (2003) *Public Policy in the Community*. Basingstoke: Palgrave Macmillan.

———. (2000) Communities in the lead: Power, organisational capacity and social capital. *Urban Studies* 37(5–6): 1019–1035.

Tendler, J. (1997) *Good Government in the Tropics*. Baltimore, MD, and London: The Johns Hopkins University Press.

Terluin, I. (2003) Differences in economic development in rural regions of advanced countries: An overview and critical analysis of theories. *Journal of Rural Studies* 19: 327–344.

Terluin, I., and Post, J. (eds.) (2000) *Employment Dynamics in Rural Europe*. Wallingford: CAB International.

Terrie, P.G. (1997) *Contested Terrain: A New History of Nature and People in the Adirondacks*. Syracuse, NY: Adirondack Museum/Syracuse University Press.

Thompson, N. (2006) The practice of government in a devolved Scotland: The case of the designation of the Cairngorms National Park. *Environment and Planning C: Governance and Policy* 24: 459–472.

Tickamyer, A. (2005) Review of Milbourne (2004) *Rural Poverty: Marginalisation and Exclusion in Britain and the United States. Journal of Rural Studies* 21: 374–375.

Tienda, M., and Mitchell, F. (eds.) (2006) *Multiple Origins, Uncertain Destinies: Hispanics and the American Future*. Washington, DC: National Research Council, the National Academy Press.

Tönnies, F. (1955) *Community and Association (Gemeinschaft und Gesellschaft)*. London: Routledge and K. Paul.

———. (1887) *Gemeinschaft und Gesellschaft*. 2nd ed. Leipzig: Fues's Verlag.

Townsend, P. (1979) *Poverty in the United Kingdom*. Harmondsworth: Penguin.

Townsend, P., and Abel-Smith, C. (1966) *The Poor and the Poorest*. London: Bedford Square Press.

Tracy, M. (1982) *Agriculture in Western Europe: Challenge and Response 1880–1980*. 2nd ed. London: Granada.

Trevor-Roper, H. (1983) The invention of tradition: The Highland tradition of Scotland. Pp. 15–42 in E. Hobsbawm and T. Ranger, eds., *The Invention of Tradition*. Cambridge: Cambridge University Press.

Tromans, N., Natamba, E., Jeffries, J., and Norman, P. (2008) Have national trends in fertility between 1986 and 2006 occurred evenly across England and Wales? *Population Trends* 133(Autumn).

Tweeten, L. (1970) *Foundations of Farm Policy.* Lincoln, NE: University of Nebraska Press.

UK Department for Environment, Food and Rural Affairs. (various) Agriculture in the UK. Various annual issues http://www.defra.gov.uk/evidence/statistics/foodfarm/general/auk/index.htm.

———. (2010a) *Public Sector Food Procurement Initiative. Third Report 1st April 2008 to 31st March 2009.* London: DEFRA Publications.

———. (2010b) http://www.defra.gov.uk/evidence/statistics/foodfarm/browseby-subject/trade.htm.

———. (2010c) http://www.defra.gov.uk/evidence/statistics/foodfarm/farmmanage/diversification/history.htm.

———. (2009) *First Report from the Council of Food Policy Advisors.* London: DEFRA Publications.

———. (2008a) *England Biodiversity Strategy—Towards Adaptation to Climate Change. Report.* London: DEFRA Publications.

———. (2008b) *Ensuring UK's Food Security in a Changing World. DEFRA Discussion Paper.* London: DEFRA Publications.

———. (2008c) RDPE Q and A. http://www.defra.gov.uk/rural/rdpe/qanda.htm.

———. (2006) *Sustainable Farming and Food Strategy: Forward Look. Report.* London: DEFRA Publications.

———. (2005a) *Case Study: Organic Milk Provision at Darlington Hospital. Report.* London: DEFRA Publications.

———. (2005b) *Productivity in Rural England. Report.* London: DEFRA.

———. (2003a) *Local Food—A Snapshot of the Sector. Report.* London: DEFRA Publications.

———. (2003b) *Policy Paper on Local Food. Report.* London: DEFRA Publications.

———. (2002) *The Strategy for Sustainable Farming and Food: Facing the Future. Report.* London: DEFRA Publications.

UN Population Division. (2002) *World Population Ageing, 1950–2050.* New York: United Nations.

United Nations. (2009) *Trends in International Migrant Stock: The 2008 Revision. Report.* New York: United Nations Department of Economic and Social Affairs, Population Division.

United States Bureau of the Census. (2006) *Annual Estimates of the Population for the United States, Regions, States, and for Puerto Rico: April 1, 2000 to July 1, 2006 (NST-EST2006–01).* Washington, DC: USGPO.

United States Census Bureau, Population Division. (n.d.) American FactFinder. Accessed 1/05/10 http://factfinder.census.gov/.

United States Department of Agriculture. (2009a) Census of agriculture 2009. Accessed 10/3/10 http://www.agcensus.usda.gov/index.asp.

———. (2009b) Rural development programs summary. Accessed 2/22/10 http://www.rurdev.usda.gov/al/ProgSummaryGuide.pdf.

———. (2007) Census of agriculture 2007. http://www.agcensus.usda.gov/Publications/2007/index.asp.

United States Environmental Protection Agency. (2002) *National Water Quality Inventory: 2000. Report to Congress.* EPA841-R-02-001. Washington, DC: USEPA, Office of Water.

Uren, Z., and Goldring, S. (2007) Migration trends at older ages in England and Wales. *Population Trends* 130(Winter).

Urry, J. (2010) Consuming the planet to excess. *Theory, Culture and Society* 27(2–3): 1–22.

———. (2007) *Mobilities.* Cambridge: Polity.

———. (2000) *Sociology beyond Society: Mobilities for the 21st Century.* London: Routledge.

USDA Economic Research Service. (2010) Farm household economics and well-being. Accessed 9/3/10 http://www.ers.usda.gov/Briefing/WellBeing.
——. (2005) United States farm and farm-related employment, 2002. Accessed 10/3/10   http://www.ers.usda.gov/Data/FarmandRelatedEmployment/View-Data.asp?GeoAreaPick=STAUS_United+States&YearPick=2002&B1=Submit.
USDA Extension Service and Office of Foreign Agricultural Relations. (1951) *Extension Experiences around the World. Report on Conference, Washington D.C., May 16–20, 1949.* Washington, DC: United States Department of Agriculture.
——. (1945) *The Contribution of Extension Methods and Techniques toward the Rehabilitation of War-Torn Countries. Report on Conference. Washington DC, September 19–22, 1944.* Washington, DC: United States Department of Agriculture.
van der Ploeg, J. (2008) *The New Peasantries: Struggles for Autonomy and Sustainability in an Era of Empire and Globalization.* London: Earthscan.
van der Ploeg, J., and Long, A. (1994) *Born from Within: Practice and Perspectives of Endogenous Rural Development.* Assen: Van Gorcum.
van der Ploeg, J., Renting, H., Brunori, G., Knickel, K., Mannion, J., Marsden, T., de Roest, K., Sevilla Guzman, E., and Ventura, F. (2000) Rural development: From practice and policies to theory. *Sociologia Ruralis* 40: 391–408.
Van Valkenburgh, J.M. 1985. *Land Acquisition for New York State: An Historical Perspective.* Arkville, NY: Catskill Center for Conservation and Development.
Vasta, E. 2004. *Informal Employment and Immigrant Networks: A Review Paper. Centre on Migration, Policy and Society Working Paper no.2.* Oxford: University of Oxford.
Vergunst, J. (2011) Technology and technique in a useful ethnography of movement. *Mobilities* 6(2): 203–219.
Vergunst, J., Árnason, A., Macintyre, R., and Nightingale, A. (2009) Using environmental resources: Networks in food and landscape. Pp. 143–170 in A. Árnason, M. Shucksmith and J. Vergunst, eds., *Comparing Rural Development.* Aldershot: Ashgate.
Vertovec, S. (2006) *The Emergence of Super-Diversity in Britain, Centre on Migration, Policy and Society Working Paper No. 25.* Oxford: University of Oxford.
——. (2002) *Transnational Networks and Skilled Labour Migration. ESRC Transnational Communities Programme Working Paper WPTC 02–02.* Oxford: University of Oxford.
Vihinen, H. (2001) *Recognising Choice: A Study of the Changing Politics of the Common Agricultural Policy.* Helsinki: Agrifood Research Finland (MTT).
Vilsack, T. (2010) Statement before the Subcommittee on Agriculture, Rural Development, Food and Drug Administration, and Related Agencies, Committee on Appropriations. US House of Representatives. 24 February. Accessed 9/3/10 http://appropriations.house.gov/pdf/Vilsack_Opening_Statement-2-24-10.pdf.
von Haaren, C., and Bills, N. (2009) Comparing agri-environmental programs in the United States and the EU. In S. Goetz and F. Brouwer, eds., *New Perspectives on Agri-environmental Policies.* London and New York: Routledge.
Waglé, U.R. (2008) Multidimensional poverty: An alternative measurement approach for the United States? *Social Science Research* 37: 559–580.
Waldinger, R. (1996) From Ellis Island to LAX: Immigrant prospects in the American city. *International Migration Review* 30: 1078–1086.
——. (1994) The making of an immigrant niche. *International Migration Review* 28: 3–30.
Walker, A. and Walker, C. (1997) *Britain Divided: The Growth of Social Exclusion in the 1980s and 1990s.* London: Child Poverty Action Group.

Wallerstein, I. (1996) *Open the Social Sciences. Report of the Gulbenkian Commission on the Restructuring of the Social Sciences.* Stanford, CA: Stanford University Press.

Walsh, K., and O'Shea, E. (2008) Responding to rural social care needs: Older people empowering themselves, others and their community. *Health and Place* 14: 795–805.

Ward, N. (2010) England's rural economies: 20 years on from Faith in the Countryside, Paper presented at Faith and the Future of the Countryside Conference, Derbyshire, UK, November.

———. (2008) Rethinking rural policy under New Labour. Pp. 57–76 in M. Woods, ed., *New Labour's Countryside: Rural Policy in Britain since 1997.* Bristol: Policy Press.

———. (2006) Rural development and the economies of rural areas. Pp. 46–67 in J. Midgley, ed., *A New Rural Agenda.* IPPR North.

———. (2002) *Europe's Rural Futures, the Nature of Rural Development II. The UK National Report.* Leeds: School of Geography, University of Leeds, UK.

Ward, N., Atterton, J., Kim, T-Y., Lowe, P., Phillipson, J., and Thompson, N. (2005) Universities, the knowledge economy and 'neo-endogenous rural development'. Centre for Rural Economy Discussion Paper No. 1, University of Newcastle.

Ward, N., and Brown, D.L. (2009) Placing the rural in regional development: Ruralities, mobilities and diversities. *Regional Studies* 43(10): 1237–1244.

Ward, N., Jackson, P., Russell, P., and Wilkinson, K. (2008) Productivism, post-productivism and European agricultural reform: the case of sugar. *Sociologia Ruralis* 48(2): 118–132.

Ward, N., and Lowe, P. (2001) The 'rural' in the 'region': Towards an inclusive regional policy for the north east. In J. Tomaney and N. Ward, eds., *A Region in Transition.* Aldershot: Ashgate.

Ward, N., Lowe, P., and Bridges, T. (2003) Rural and regional development: The role of the Regional Development Agencies in England. *Regional Studies* 37: 201–214.

Ward, N., and Ray, C. (2004) *Futures Analysis, Public Policy and Rural Studies. Report. CRE WP74.* Newcastle: Newcastle University, Newcastle upon Tyne.

Warner, M.E. (2010) The future of local government: 21st century challenges. *Public Administration Review* 70(SII): 145–147.

———. (2009a) Civic government or market-based governance? The limits of privatization for rural local governments. *Agriculture and Human Values* 26(1): 133–143.

———. (2009b) *Local Government Infrastructure—and the False Promise of Privatization. Century Foundation Report.* New York: Century Foundation.

———. (2008) Reversing privatization, rebalancing government reform: Markets, deliberation and planning. *Policy and Society* 27(2): 163–174.

———. (2006) Market-based governance and the challenge for rural governments: US trends. *Social Policy and Administration* 40(6): 612–631.

———. (2003) Competition, cooperation and local governance. Pp. 262–272 in D.L. Brown and L. Swanson, eds., *Challenges for Rural America in the 21st Century.* University Park, PA: Penn State University Press.

———. (2001) State policy under devolution: Redistribution and centralization. *National Tax Journal* 54(3): 541–556.

Warner, M.E., and Hefetz, A. (2003) Rural–urban differences in privatization: Limits to the competitive state. *Environment and Planning C: Government and Policy* 21(5): 703–718.

———. (2002) The uneven distribution of market solutions for public goods. *Journal of Urban Affairs* 24(4): 445–459.

Warner, M.E., Hinrichs, C.C., Schneyer, J., and Joyce, L. (1999) Organizing communities to sustain rural landscapes: Lessons from New York. *Journal of the Community Development Society* 30: 178–195.

Warner, M.E., and Pratt, J.E. (2005) Spatial diversity in local government revenue effort under decentralization: A neural-network approach. *Environment and Planning C: Government and Policy* 23(5): 657–677.

Warner, M.E., and Shortall, S. (2010) Social inclusion or market competitiveness? A comparison of rural development policies in the European Union and the United States. *Social Policy and Administration* 44(5): 575–597.

———. (2008) Growth coalitions and rural development policy in the EU and the US. *EuroChoices* 7(3): 35–37.

Warnes, A.M. (1992) Temporal and spatial patterns of elderly migration. Pp. 248–270 in J. Stillwell, P. Rees and P. Boden, eds., *Migration Processes and Patterns: Vol. 2: Population Redistribution in the United Kingdom*. London: Belhaven Press.

Warwick, D.P., and Osherson, S. (1973) Comparative analysis in the social sciences. Pp. 3–41 in D.P. Warwick and S. Osherson, eds., *Comparative Research Methods*. Englewood Cliffs, NJ: Prentice Hall.

Watson, C. (2009) *The Great Terrain Robbery*. San Francisco: Sierra Club Books.

Watts, D., Leat, P., and Revoredo-Giha, C. (2010) Local food activity in Scotland: Empirical evidence and research agenda. *Regional Studies*.

Weber, B.A., Duncan, G.J., and Whitener, L.A. (eds.) (2002) *Rural Dimensions of Welfare Reform*. Kalamazoo, MI: W.E. Upjohn Institute for Employment Research.

Weber, B.A., Jensen, L., Miller, K., Mosley, J., and Fisher, M. (2005) A critical review of rural poverty literature: Is there truly a rural effect? *International Regional Science Review* 28(4): 381–414.

Weeks, J. (2005) *Population*. Belmont, CA: Thompson/Wadsworth.

Wellman, B. (1979) The community question: The intimate networks of East Yorkers. *American Journal of Sociology* 85(5): 1201–1231.

Whetham, E. (1981) *Agricultural Economists in Britain 1900–1940*. Oxford: Agricultural Economics Institute.

Wightman, A. (1999) *Who Owns Scotland?* Edinburgh: Canongate.

Williams, M., and Champion T. (1998) Cornwall, poverty and in-migration. *Cornish Studies Second Series* 6: 118–126.

Williams, R. (1973) *The Country and the City*. London: Chatto and Windus.

Wills, G. (1981) *Explaining America: The Federalist*. Garden City, NJ.

Wilson, G. (2007) *Multifunctional Agriculture: A Transition Theory Perspective*. Wallingford: CABI.

———. (2001) From productivism to post-productivism . . . and back again? Exploring the (un)changed natural and mental landscapes of European agriculture. *Transactions of the Institute of British Geographers* NS26: 77–102.

Wilson, W.J. (1987) *The Truly Disadvantaged*. Chicago: University of Chicago Press.

———. (1978) *The Declining Significance of Race: Blacks and Changing American Institutions*. Chicago: University of Chicago Press.

Winson, A. (2010) The demand for healthy eating: Supporting a transformative food 'movement'. *Rural Sociology* 75: 584–600.

Winter, M. (2006) Rescaling rurality: Multi-level governance of the agro-food sector. *Political Geography* 25(3): 735–751.

———. (2003). Embeddedness, the new food economy and defensive localism. *Journal of Rural Studies* 19: 23-32.

Wolf, S. (ed.) (1996) *Privatization of Information and Agricultural Industrialization*. Boca Raton, FL: CRC Press.

Womach, J. (2004) *Average Farm Subsidy Payments, by State, 2002. Congressional Reporting Service Report for Congress.* Washington, DC.

Woods, A. (2009) *Securing Integrated Land Management: Issues for Policy, Research and Rural Communities from the RELU Programme. Report for the Rural Economy and Land Use Programme.* London: ESRC.

Woods, M. (2011) *Rural Geography.* London: Routledge.

———. (ed.) (2008) *New Labour's Countryside: Rural Policy in Britain Since 1997.* Bristol: Policy Press.

———. (2005) *Rural Geography: Processes, Responses and Experiences in Rural Restructuring.* London: Sage.

Worthy, A., and Gouldson, I. (2010) *Regional Trends 42: A Portrait of the North East. Report.* Newport: Office of National Statistics.

Wray, M. (2006) *Not Quite White: White Trash and the Boundaries of Whiteness.* Durham, NC: Duke University Press.

Wright, V. (1994) Reshaping the state: The implications for public administration. *West European Politics* 17(3): 102–137.

Wunderlich, G. (2003) *American Country Life: A Legacy.* Lanham, MD: University Press of America.

Young, L., Weersink, A., Fulton, M., and Deaton, J. (2007) Carbon sequestration in agriculture: EU and US perspectives. *EuroChoices* 6: 32–37.

Yu, L., and Artz, G. (2009) Migration and rural entrepreneurship. Working Paper No. 09017, Iowa State University, Department of Economics.

Zetter R., Griffith, D., and Nando, S. (2006) *Immigration, Social Cohesion and Social Capital.* York: Joseph Rowntree Foundation.

Zimmerman, J., and Hirschl, T. (2003) Welfare reform in rural areas: A voyage through uncharted waters. Pp. 363–374 in D.L. Brown and L. Swanson, eds., *Challenges for Rural America in the Twenty-First Century.* University Park, PA: Penn State University Press.

Index